IMAGINING CRIME

D0143757

IMAGINING CRIME

Textual Outlaws and Criminal Conversations

Alison Young

SAGE Publications
London • Thousand Oaks • New Delhi

Cover illustration: Detail from Home Office Poster,
photograph by Peter Rush

© Alison Young 1996

First published 1996

All rights reserved. No part of this publication may be
reproduced, stored in a retrieval system, transmitted or utilized
in any form or by any means, electronic, mechanical,
photocopying, recording or otherwise, without permission in
writing from the Publishers.

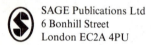

SAGE Publications Ltd
6 Bonhill Street
London EC2A 4PU

SAGE Publications Inc
2455 Teller Road
Thousand Oaks, California 91320

SAGE Publications India Pvt Ltd
32, M-Block Market
Greater Kailash – I
New Delhi 110 048

British Library Cataloguing in Publication data

A catalogue record for this book is
available from the British Library

ISBN 0 8039 8622 X
ISBN 0 8039 8623 8 (pbk)

Library of Congress catalog card number 95–072175

Typeset by M Rules
Printed in Great Britain by Redwood Books,
Trowbridge, Wiltshire

Contents

Acknowledgements

This book was originally planned to be a critical analysis of the discipline of criminology; for many reasons, as I think will be clear from what follows, I am very glad that it turned out differently. Its altered form is partly due to the inordinate length of time it has taken me to write it. In the four and a half years since sending off a book proposal for a project entitled 'Postmodern Criminology', I have not only changed my views on what this book should be about; I have also incurred many debts to friends and colleagues in moving towards the book's new concerns.

Some of the ideas in Chapter 3 began life in other publications: in an article written with Peter Rush ('The law of victimage in urbane realism: thinking through inscriptions of violence', in David Nelken (ed.) *The Futures of Criminology*, London: Sage, 1994; and in '*Caveat sponsa*: violence and the body in law', in Jane Brettle and Sally Rice (eds) *Public Bodies, Private States*, Manchester: Manchester University Press, 1994). I would like to thank all those who invited me to speak (and thus to have an opportunity of presenting my ideas) and who worked with me on those publications. In 1992, I was fortunate to be invited to the Centre for Research and Teaching on Women, at McGill University, Montreal, as a Visiting Scholar. The stimulating intellectual environment of the Centre, and indeed the whole city, encouraged me to think about many of the arguments which appear in Chapter 3. My time in Montreal was funded by grants from the British Academy, the Canadian High Commission and the Leverhulme Trust. I am also grateful to Christine Harrington, of the Institute for Law and Society in the School of Law at New York University, for inviting me as a Visiting Scholar, thus creating the space necessary to finish this project. The British Academy generously funded this visit. *Imagining Crime* has generally been nomadic in its writing, particularly in 1994. I owe much to those who gave me the space to write: Peter Rush in Lancaster; Peter and Margaret Rush in Sydney; Castaways Resort in Mission Beach, Queensland; Christine Harrington in New York.

Many people over the last four years have read versions of this book. My thanks for all their thoughts and comments to: Peter Rush, Ngaire Naffine, Peter Goodrich, Niki Lacey, Les Moran, Ronnie Warrington, Dorothy Nelkin, Piyel Haldar, Julie Wallbank, Colin Hay, Jackie Stacey, Lynne Pearce, Celia Lury and Beverley Skeggs. Gillian Stern at Sage has been a patient editor, never giving up hope that she would receive a book in the end. I also owe intellectual debts, which can probably never be repaid. In the 12 years that have passed since I first experienced the kick of theory, there have been many people who have inspired me to think harder about things taken for granted.

Some of them are obvious: the imprint of the work of Derrida, Foucault, Kristeva and Irigaray is clearly legible upon *Imagining Crime*. Other intellectual spurs have been provided by Jane Gallop's *The Daughter's Seduction* (1982); Barbara Duden's *Disembodying Women* (1993); Peter Goodrich's *Languages of Law* (1990); Peggy Phelan's *Unmarked* (1993).

I have also been fortunate in the supportive and stimulating work atmosphere created and sustained over a number of years by colleagues and graduate students in the Law Department at the University of Lancaster: Peter Rush, Les Moran, Piyel Haldar, Peter Goodrich, Costas Douzinas, Ronnie Warrington, Elena Loizidou, Julie Wallbank and Marinos Diamantidis. I could not have wished for a more congenial work culture. As a teacher and writer, Ronnie Warrington embodied everything an academic might strive for. My friends in the Centre for Women's Studies who gave up their time and energy to maintain a research group amid all the institutional demands made on them helped me work on many of the ideas contained in this book; I also learned an enormous amount from reading their own work. I also owe thanks to the students in various seminars and courses who tolerated my trying ideas out on them: especially, the students in Deviance, Discipline and Social Control 1993/4; in Law and the Body 1994/5; and Gender and the Law 1993/4 and 1994/5. To the unknown student who left behind in my office the xerox of Michael Jack's House of Commons speech, my considerable thanks, as, without it, I might never have written the opening chapter.

Imagining Crime could not have been written without the support, insight and strength of Peter Rush, who lived through its writing and non-writing with great humour. As my closest reader and friend, he kept me working on this project at times when I was tempted to abandon it. He listened patiently as I harangued him with details and arguments from every chapter – especially over lunch in Mission Beach - and he listened critically, always pushing me beyond easy ideas. He is the author as much as I am, for without him this book might never have been written. My very greatest thanks to him.

Since this book was first imagined, several friends and relatives have died. Their ghosts haunt these pages; their absence marks my daily life. I remember: my student and friend, Rachael Todd; my colleague and friend, Ronnie Warrington; my parents, Hugh and Helen Young. This book is dedicated to their memories, and to all that they achieved and gave during their remarkable lives.

1

Textual Outlaws and
Criminal Conversations

It is perhaps one of every academic's anxieties that when a deadline appears on the horizon she will be stricken with writer's block. These anticipated failures of imagination loom ever larger with the increasing demand to publish and the technologized rationality that dominates academic research. On a more circumstantial note, it was exactly such a writer's block that I experienced in contemplating a chapter that would give an introduction to the substantive studies pursued in this book. Instead of sitting gloomily before the computer at home, I went in to my office at work, in order to distract myself by clearing up the detritus of the preceding academic year: xeroxes, administrative memoranda, lecture notes and correspondence were all strewn across desk, table, chairs, bookshelves, cabinets, symptomatic of the breakdown in my filing system. Diverted from the task of tidying up, I began to read old memos, the marginalia on photocopied articles. In the midst of a bundle of miscellany, I came across two xeroxed pages from *Hansard*. They were not mine; I guessed that a student had left them on a chair and forgotten to take them at the end of a seminar. One of the pleasures of teaching is that you never know what ideas a student will suggest during a seminar or what objects they may leave behind accidentally in your office. Looking at the pages, I discovered that they related to a parliamentary debate on crime; the student had written in the margins 'use in essay to refer to attitude of Parliament'. For me, it registered, in a condensed form, many of the concerns of this book. Thus it was that, while attempting to throw things away, to dispose of detritus, I came upon something which enabled me to make a beginning. Thus do the pleasures of the serendipitous enhance the demands of writing.

Crime and the emotional body

In this introductory chapter, I wish to frame the substantive arguments which follow (Chapters 2 to 7) by setting out the major concerns of *Imagining Crime*. The book examines the crisis that has ruptured within what can be called the crimino-legal complex and its effects on the ways in which crime is imagined. Crime's images are structured according to a binary logic of repression. Oppositional terms (man/woman, white/black, rational/irrational, mind/body and so on) are constructed in a system of value which makes one visible and the other invisible. Thus, for example, the victim is currently marked as the essential term of the victim/criminal opposition. Similarly, youth has recently been demonized as the visible and terrifying term of the opposition young/old. The logic of this system of valuation and visualization is considered in each of the subsequent chapters, as it pertains to a variety of substantive issues. It is also elaborated later in this chapter. But before approaching those issues, I wish to explain something of the term 'crimino-legal complex' and my claim that it is suffering a violent crisis.

By 'crimino-legal complex' or 'crimino-legal tradition', I am referring to the collapse and confusion of criminology and criminal law that has been gradually occurring since the 1940s, in which, although the notion of disciplinary boundaries is maintained (and policed), criminal law has increasingly looked like a variant of criminology (with its fascination for the criminal mind and so on) and criminology has come to resemble law (with its technocratic concepts, institutions and procedures).[1] I am thus including as part of the crimino-legal complex the knowledges, discourses and practices that are deemed to fall under the rubric of criminology, criminal justice and criminal law. I am, however, trying to delineate more than simply 'criminology' or 'criminal justice' or 'criminal law'. Rather, I wish to include all of these, together with the popular discourses that are manifested in the media, cinema and advertising, in order to convey the sense that 'crime' has become (been made?) a potent sign which can be exchanged among criminal justice personnel, criminologists, politicians, journalists, film-makers and, importantly, (mythical) ordinary individuals. I am not attempting to claim that 'crime' has never functioned as a sign before, or that the crimino-legal tradition has never before experienced crisis. My aim is simply to elaborate the contemporary forms that this crisis is taking, and to suggest what the consequences of this might be.

It has become a critical commonplace that criminology, criminal justice and law are in crisis. The miscarriages of justice exposed in Britain since the convictions of the Guildford Four were quashed in December 1989 have been the most obvious examples of a schism in the foundations of Western law and justice.[2] As criminology fragments into ever more specialized sub-disciplines and simultaneously cements into dominant paradigms (such as realism or

1. I wish that I had dreamed up a term as rich as 'crimino-legal complex'. Alas, it belongs to Peter Rush who offered it to me as a concept which might enable me to frame more clearly some of my tentative ideas about crime. I am deeply indebted to him for this, as I am for his insightful suggestions throughout this book. For his version of the crimino-legal crisis, see Rush (forthcoming) and his essay and introduction in Rush, McVeigh and Young (eds) (forthcoming).

2. Other miscarriages of justice in Britain include: the imprisonment for 17 years of the Birmingham Six, who were finally freed in March 1991 after forensic and police evidence was discredited; the convictions of the Maguire Seven, quashed in June 1991 after they served between 4 and 14 years in prison; the imprisonment of the Tottenham Three for the murder of PC Blakelock, with dubious police interviewing leading to the convictions being quashed in November 1991; the imprisonment of Judith Ward for 18 years, with unreliable confessions and non-disclosure of material by the prosecution leading to her release in May 1992; police malpractice resulting in July 1992 in the quashed convictions of Paul and Wayne Darvell. Many more prisoners protest their innocence and claim their conviction to be the result of systematic abuse

feminism, for all their own infinite sub-variants), criminal justice pursues a variety of contradictory and incoherent policies. Criminal law, meanwhile, pretends a purity of disciplinary constitution untouched by issues of policy or theory (or, at most, permits them a secondary place outside the rationality of law). In late modernity, the three combine in a complex of competing assumptions, approaches and influences. Foucault comments that '[criminology] is indispensable in enabling judges to judge' (1980: 48), thus adverting to the intersectionality of criminology and criminal law in modernity which should motivate us to think of criminology and criminal law as *crimino-legal*. The aim of this chapter is to investigate the notion that such an incoherent jostling is a symptom of a failure internal to the Western crimino-legal tradition. Such a crisis has arisen out of the inability to solve the conundrum of criminality, to contain its effects and to account for its meanings. While the notion of crisis is now commonplace, it is often presented within a frame of crisis-management, in which the crisis is to be sutured or covered over. My intention is not so much to reknit the crisis as to exacerbate it. This will escape the usual symptomatic reading and relate the apparently dispersed crises to the breach which has taken place in the crimino-legal tradition itself.

As emblematic of the notion that the crimino-legal tradition is in crisis, and in order to display some of the symptomatic responses to that crisis, I will set out here a section from the photocopied pages left in my office. This excerpt is taken from a debate in the House of Commons, on 'Crime':

The Minister of State, Home Office (Mr Michael Jack): In starting this debate, we should reflect for a moment on the word 'crime'. It is a neat word to describe a complex problem. Crime itself is a battle and a battleground. It is like a virus. It is not seen and it is difficult to treat but its effects blight the lives of all too many of our fellow citizens. The language that we use to deal with it is powerful. Words like 'punishment', 'victim', 'murder' and 'arrest', stir deep emotions and powerful feelings in all of us. Crime is frustrating. Crime is frightening. Crime is complicated.

Crime is frustrating to the politician because there is no easy off-the-shelf answer to crime. It is frustrating because there are fashions in both crime and punishment and short-term policies do not always lend themselves to the best long-term solutions. It is frustrating to the public, who rightly want to lead their lives free from fear and in relative security.

Crime is frightening, because it is not easy to predict where and when it will occur. It is frightening for victims because its effects can be both physically painful and mentally traumatic. It is frightening because it represents the fight between good and evil.

Crime is complicated: complicated to fight, because it involves many agencies; complicated because its analysis brings forward as many questions as there are answers. Like the virus, it has a unique ability to keep changing its shape and form. But above all, crime is about its victims.

As a new Home Office Minister, I spent last Easter Monday at Blackpool police station and watched for myself the victims of crime coming in and reporting what

---

of power: for example, T.C. Campbell, imprisoned for murder in Barlinnie Special Unit (which has been closed down; another symptom of crisis). For an account of this crisis as an ethical one, arguing the need for an other justice (an *alter*/altar justice), see Douzinas and Warrington (1994b).

had happened to them: the old lady crying, who had had her purse snatched and lost £270, the man whose car had been broken into. All this made me resolve never to forget that, behind all the statistics of crime, are real people whose lives have been cruelly blighted by crime. (*Hansard*, 5 March 1993, p. 565)

Jack's speech testifies to a faith in the power of language, of representation. 'The language that we use to deal with [crime] is powerful'; it stirs 'deep emotions and powerful feelings in all of us'. The reader responds to the text; the language of crime inspires emotions Jack divides into three types: frustration, fear and bafflement. The speech then devotes a paragraph to each emotion, built upon a threefold structure of address, which oscillates from a universal, generalized audience to a specified, projected individual addressee.

First, Jack states that 'Crime is frustrating'. This frustration is experienced by the politician (because there is no easy answer to crime); by an unspecified universal audience (who might take a short-term view without thinking through long-term implications); by the public who identify crime as the cause of insecurity and fear. Frustration in law describes the doctrine by which a contract is invalidated through the emergence or irruption of a supervening impossibility.[3] Such an impossibility did not exist at the time of making the contract (or it would constitute a simple mistake). Individuals enter the social contract to protect their personal and property interests. They thus desire the sovereign, state or Leviathan to protect these interests. Crime frustrates this social contract, since the prevalence of crime in society means that there exists no perceptible difference between the state of nature and the state of civil society (under the social contract). In Jack's later references to crime as a 'battleground', we see nature *in* culture, the *bellum omnium contra omnes*.[4] Jack refers in his speech to the politician's frustration, because crime is precisely that which has inspired the citizen to enter the social contract (for protection) and that which the politician, as agent of the state, has contracted to prevent. The very existence of crime marks the politician's failure to fulfil that side of the contract. The public experiences frustration because it has given itself up to the power of the state in order to feel secure, to live in trust. The existence of crime, for the public, marks a contract that is continually negating the common purpose or project of the contract. The unspecified audience in the middle section of Jack's evocation of the emotional response of frustration – those who seek short-term gains without thinking through the future – represents the gap in the promise held out by the social contract (protection, freedom, mutual trust, a civic community) and the immediate experience of community as imperfect, burdened by fear and pain, untrusting, full of uncertainty.

Crime, then, signifies a contract which is perpetually being frustrated. In place of the socio-legal contract, crime signifies another bond or obligation of mutual desire. That is, crime is taken to be the place of the meeting of minds that has not come about through the social contract itself. Crime acts as a

3. On the metaphor of frustration in contract, see Frug (1992).
4. I am grateful to Peter Goodrich for clarifying these points.

surrogate for the failed social contract, offering instead the *criminal contract*; the imaginary space where crime is fought and vanquished: Jack's 'battle-ground' where 'all of us' can meet.[5] To reach this location, fear is necessary. The second emotional response to crime that Jack cites is the fear of crime: 'Crime is frightening.'[6] Again, a threefold structure of address can be identified: crime is frightening to an unspecified, general audience; to victims; again to a universal, unspecified audience. The fear of crime has become a commonplace in criminological, governmental and popular discourses on crime. As a commonplace, it requires no explanation, no exact location. Jack's chosen addressees contribute both to the sense of the fear of crime as a commonplace response and to the imagination of a shared community of fear. Membership of the community is bought through the fear of crime; thus, Jack need not specify who is afraid of crime, since the answer is obvious, naturalized, self-evident. Everyone is afraid of crime, whether or not they have experienced it. These generalizable fears can be expressed through crime's unpredictability, through crime's symbolizing of the struggle between good and evil. Those who have experienced crime are victims (Jack's middle and transcendent term). Their fears take the concrete form of physical pain and mental trauma. From the middle, these fears can seep out to the general community which surround the victim: pain and trauma give a name to the imaginary of crime within the community.

Finally, bafflement is cited as an emotional response to crime: 'Crime is complicated.' Complication produces bafflement, with a threefold structure of address that moves from the criminal justice agency, through the unspecified audience to crime itself. Bafflement can result from the multiplication of agencies which respond to crime (each with its own agenda of reform or prevention). It can result from thinking about crime, since the analysis of crime has generated more questions than answers. Within the unspecified audience at this point might reside the criminologists who have never completely answered the questions of criminality. However, this category is meant to incorporate anyone who has reflected on the conundrum of crime: for example, a recent television 'fly-on-the-wall' documentary on the police showed an elderly woman who had been burgled repeatedly asking in great distress 'why do they do it?' as she described the crime.[7] It can also be argued that

5. For an example of the contractual relationship existing within our imagination of crime, see *R* v. *Camplin* [1978] 2 All England Law Reports 168, in which Lord Diplock states: 'the actual violence *offered* by the deceased to the accused remained the badge of provocation' (at p. 171; my emphasis).

6. The fear of crime experienced by individuals has been researched over the last decade by, *inter alia*, Gottfredson (1984); Hindelang et al. (1978); Jones et al. (1986); Shapland and Vagg (1988). The particularly acute differentiation in the amount of fear experienced by women as opposed to men (who are supposed to feature more frequently as victims in crime statistics, although this differential would always be subject to the caveat that many women do not report their victimization) has been investigated by Hanmer and Saunders (1984); Painter (1992); Radford (1987); Stanko (1990b, 1992). On the intersections between fear and risk in modernity, see Beck (1992).

7. This was broadcast in episode one of *The Nick*, 3 October 1994, Channel 4.

bafflement will constitute the dominant response of the citizen, who has given herself and her property up to the social contract and its agents, precisely in order that she should not be the victim of a crime. The criminal justice system promises (albeit in an increasingly jaded and lacklustre manner) to prevent crime. Each criminal occurrence confounds that promise, provoking in its victim the response 'why me?' or 'how did it happen?' Such perplexity is the result of two simultaneously dissonant cognitive experiences: the citizen feels both security and insecurity, which either succeed each other in waves or, occasionally, coincide, with baffling results. Both experiences are 'real'; it is not a question of one being true to the other's falsity. Victimization provokes the sensation of insecurity at the same time as it emphasizes an inability to accept insecurity: 'how could it happen to me?' is a question founded on an inherent belief in invulnerability. Similarly the crime prevention advice which tends to follow on from victimization ironically promises security achieved through unwavering faith in one's insecurity.[8] Crime itself constitutes the third addressee of Jack's comments, in its virus-like ability to mutate and transform itself. The likening of crime to a virus in this respect means that crime is deemed reactive rather than intelligent, an organism which may chemically or instinctively alter its constitution without any rationality. Crime is thus a law unto itself, outside the law, an outlaw. Thus, although crime may be baffling, the puzzlement experienced is implied to be finite. Since crime is reactive and irrational, sooner or later thinking about crime will result in its conquest. All that is outside the law (reactive, non-intelligent) will eventually succumb to the force of law.

The linguistic turn of crime

In setting out these three emotional reactions to crime, Jack's speech is positing a responsive body incorporating variously the state, the community, the individual and the imaginary. I will return to this responsive or emotional body later. The effectivity of crime as cause of the three emotional responses of frustration, fear and bafflement is underlined by Jack's linguistic turns and faith in technological rationality. Jack's speech exemplifies the seductive and material power of language in the representation of crime, through devices such as metaphor, synecdoche, symbol and so on.[9] Jack acknowledges this in his deployment of immensely powerful metaphors: crime is 'like a virus'; it is a 'battle and a battleground'. The metaphor of the 'war' against

8. On this paradox in crime prevention literature, see Stanko (1990b, 1994).

9. In metaphor, certain properties of one thing are carried over or imposed on another object, so that the latter becomes represented *as if* it were the former. Metaphor generally restricts and concentrates meaning, collapsing a multiplicity of connotations into one; whereas metonymy involves one object being placed next to (not *over*) another, resulting in a proliferation of meanings. Synecdoche is the means whereby a part comes to signify the whole; for example, the 'White House' stands for the American government. See generally Derrida (1982) and MacCannell (1986); on metaphor in the press discourse relating to women political protesters, see Young (1990: 89–104).

crime is one of the most notorious in criminology and criminal justice policy: as a militaristic metaphor it effectively eclipses certain areas of discussion and rules out a number of voices. It depends upon the drawing of lines, the establishment of sides and the belief in an ultimate outright winner, no matter that the victory be Pyrrhic. Here, the metaphor of 'battle' adverts to clichés such as losing the battle but winning the war; while all the little battles to be fought are singular components of the overarching (perhaps never-ending) war. Jack's formulation of crime as 'a battle and a battleground' contains something of an equivocation. If crime itself is a battle, then this notion is not straightforwardly captured by the cliché of the war against crime. The notion of 'battleground' speaks more to the war against crime. If crime itself is a battle, who is fighting and against what or whom do they fight? Is crime a battle for the victim (against the criminal, against fear and insecurity)? Is crime a battle for the criminal (against society, against poverty)? The notion of crime as a battle equivocates over the subject of the battle (who is the soldier in this struggle?) and over its object (what end does the battle stand in for?). In the metaphor of the battleground is contained the space of struggle, the ground upon which the struggle takes place. In reducing crime to its spatial dimension, crime becomes merely an activity without subject or object. The metaphor of battle contains the actors, those who fight. In citing a battleground, the speech inadvertently locates the question of responsibility: the battleground is the place where those who fight become implicated in crime itself. As such, battle and battleground seem far less stable metaphors than 'war', which connotes an ability to characterize one side as morally correct in addition to the comforting disavowal of responsibility for the soldiers, who act under superior orders.

In the question of a ground on which battle takes place, the speech betrays an anxiety (also identifiable in the unusual choice of 'battle' as opposed to 'war' as paradigmatic metaphor for crime control). This anxiety locates itself in the question of the grounding of law, order and, indeed, criminology itself. Their common ground is crime. The crimino-legal tradition authorizes itself by reference to crime – a shifting ground if ever there was one. If the ground on which the crimino-legal tradition rests is shifting, self-authorization is fragile and volatile. The result is anxiety. Crime is not fixed (as Jack states, 'it is not easy to predict where and when it will occur'; 'it has a unique ability to keep changing its shape and form'), it is on the move, nomadic. Jack's speech demonstrates anxiety about crime's nomadism (in its choice of battle and battleground as metaphors)[10] and tries to pin it down ('above all, crime is about its victims'). But as the speech moves from battle to virus and to blight, as the metaphors proliferate, crime escapes categorization and moves on. Crime seeps over and through its frame; while the frame bleeds.

10. These concerns have surfaced in the Criminal Justice Bill 1994: see the clauses which relate to 'trespass on land' (clauses 56, 57); 'attendance at a rave' (clauses 58–62); 'aggravated trespass' (clauses 63, 64); 'trespassory assemblies' (clauses 65, 66); 'squatters' (clauses 67–70); 'unauthorized campers' (clauses 72–5).

The shift from metaphorizing crime as a battle to crime as a virus betrays also a faith in technological rationality: crime is a problem of knowledge as *techne*. Militaristic metaphors are often used to represent disease (such as the 'war against disease': Sontag, 1991); here we see crime metaphorized as a 'virus' and thus by implication to be fought and vanquished 'like a disease'. The explicit reference to virus carries a further lamination: since the mid-1980s, the concept-metaphor 'virus' tends to be associated with HIV, the human immunodeficiency virus, which also 'blights lives' as crime does. HIV, at present, seems to lead eventually to AIDS, from which there is no recovery. If the virus of crime is even 'like' HIV, then crime is being constructed as a deadly problem (on HIV and criminal justice, see Chapter 7). 'Blight' is a condition of decay or despair, used of plants, but also, as a metaphor, of urban spaces. It is used here in a way that draws on botanical or horticultural discourses to metaphorize the effect of crime, like a virus, on the lives of those it touches (and that, following on from the argument about Jack's addressees, is the entire community). 'Blight' is a disease carried by insects and affecting plants. The blight of crime is thus carried by criminals (who become like insects) and affecting citizens (who resemble plants in their having 'done' nothing to deserve the blight which 'happens to' them).

The response to blight and to a virus is to enlist technological rationality. Through this, eventually the enigma of criminality will be cracked. Recent British government campaigns have included the slogan: 'Crime: together we'll crack it.' The ambiguity of exactly what is to be cracked is part of the slogan's force: does it refer to crime as a puzzle (the baffling conundrum of Jack's speech) or does it refer to the punitive responses to (certain types of) crime for which the Conservative Party has become infamous? The individuals who make up the agents of the criminal justice system are symbolized as scientists, seeking a vaccine against or cure for the virus that is crime, while crime, as Jack admits, mutates and transforms itself. This draws on popular images of the scientist-as-detective and the detective-as-scientist, cracking the code, finding the source.[11] As such, criminal justice agents are imbued with knowledge, determination, rationality and objectivity. This is a powerful antidote to other, more critical, images of criminal justice personnel such as those emerging in the aftermath of the recent miscarriages of justice.[12] Jack's speech therefore characterizes the agents of criminal justice as, on the one hand, committed and objective scientists, and, on the other, tireless policy makers simply seeking the right reforms and the best practices. In stark contrast, offenders are constructed as the bearers of disease, as evil, as threats to

11. For example, see: the film version of Shilts' book *And the Band Played On*, in which the central character, a scientist working on HIV/AIDS, functions much as a detective pursuing a criminal; the television film of the discovery of the structure of DNA by Watson and Crick; the successful British television series *Cracker*, involving a psychologist working with the police force, thus incorporating in its title both the notion of a code to be cracked (why a crime is committed) and a colloquialism for the insane.

12. See, for example, the media coverage of the release of the Guildford Four, the Birmingham Six and others; also cinematic representations such as *In the Name of the Father*.

the state, the social contract, the community and the individual in an unend-ing battle. Their existence, simply, threatens security. The mere existence of an offender is set up as turning everyone (else) into victims. Thus the lines are rigidly drawn between those who belong to the law (and the community) and those who do not: the outlaws.

Crime, the community and the textual outlaw

Notions of belonging and community have received increasing attention in recent years.[13] Many of these debates have put the concept of 'community' into question, arguing that the community is less a problem to be solved (through such techniques as a 'Citizens' Charter', for example)[14] as a question to be addressed. One of my aims in this book is to question the significance of con-cepts of community for the crimino-legal tradition. To that end, I have made use of the work of Girard (1986) on the scapegoat and inflected it with a ques-tion directed at the Hegelian problematic of community, as to whether Woman might be always already constituted as a surrogate for the originary outlaw of the community.[15] In criminal justice policy, in criminological theory and in the practices of criminal law can be found, first, an imagined community; second, an identifiable subject which represents a threat to the community; third, a desire to inflict violence upon that subject in the name of the community. The 'community' can be represented in various ways: as a particular space, such as a city, or as a group of individuals, that is, the law-abiding. The threat to that community is perceived to come from outside it, although that is a represen-tation that enables the community to turn the violence of all-against-all into the violence of all-against-one. A subject from within the community is there-fore selected and then portrayed as coming from outside. Moreover, that subject is represented as deserving violence in some way, as having brought the community's violence upon it through some fault or flaw of its own. For these purposes, the designation of some individuals as 'criminals' enables them to be viewed as outside the community, and thus outside the law. These outlaws can then be put under surveillance, punished, contained, constrained. The name 'victim' thus marks a doubled movement: it is used to signify 'our' community (we are all victims), while simultaneously expelling the criminal (as surrogate for an originary outlaw). The symbolically sacrificed outlaw is thus the victim of our desire for community (through shared victimization).

13. For exemplary instances see: on the community as a trope and ideality in philosophical and cultural debates, Benhabib (1992), Cornell (1991) and Rorty (1989); on racial belonging and community, Anderson (1983), Ignatieff (1994); on the politics of community, Frazer and Lacey (1993); on embedded notions of community in debates on policing, Loader (1994).

14. This was set up by the British government in March 1991, as part of a series of initiatives (the Parents' Charter, the Patients' Charter and so on) which emphasized the participatory nature of the democratic process and provided a (chimerical) image of free choice available to all individuals. On the Citizens' Charter, see Cooper (1993).

15. For a psychoanalytic reading of Girard's argument, within a discussion of Hollywood cin-ema, see Žižek (1992: 73–4).

This book is concerned to examine, in several discrete instances, the creation of mechanisms which enforce their existence as 'textual outlaws', forever subject to the force of law and criminal justice. Outlaws who commit crime generate a sense of commonality; this can be seen in Jack's speech, where victimization is posited as a communal experience; one which is painful but which leads to citizenship and a shared perspective. When Jack speaks of 'all of us', he is referring to the community of victims; criminals are absent(ed). A community is founded upon victimization and victimization constitutes the necessary entry subscription. The community that results is, of course, a simulacrum of a community; a phantasm that speaks of a nostalgic desire for oneness and unity, while at the same time structuring itself around its dependence upon fear, alienation and separateness for its elements to make sense. Thus modernist criminal justice offers an impoverished, pale version of community, which mimics the recognition of the yearned-for pre-modern community. Recognition is not based upon shared friendship, but upon the awareness of risk and danger. The Conservative government's proposals such as Street Watch and Truancy Watch (see especially Chapter 3) ask the citizen to recognize the dangerous individual (the child who should be in school, the teenage boy standing around on the street corner); that is, the *unfamiliar and strange* instead of the familiar and similar. With the massification of the city, in which individuals cannot know each other, we are told to know the one who stands out, who does not 'belong' or 'fit'. The perspective gained is unequivocally that of one side of the battle: the deviant do not suffer victimization, a criminal cannot be offended against.

Languages of crime, words like 'punishment', 'murder' and 'arrest' according to Jack, 'stir deep emotions and powerful feelings in all of us': those deep emotions and powerful feelings stirred are of a desire to sacrifice. Those that are outlawed by government, by popular culture, by criminology, are being sacrificed in order to maintain a fragile community. The argument that the outlaw is a necessary component of the formation of community differs from the Durkheimian view that in every community, even in his celebrated 'society of saints', someone will be considered deviant (Durkheim, 1964). That view proposes that, whatever the rules, someone will break at least one of them. As Durkheim puts it:

> Imagine a society of saints, a perfect cloister of exemplary individuals. Crimes, properly so called will there be unknown; but faults which appear venial to the layman will create there the same scandal that the ordinary offense does in ordinary consciousness. If, then, this society has the power to judge and punish, it will define these acts as criminal and will treat them as such. (1964: 68–9)

As such, it is an argument based on the notion of the inevitability of rule-breaking within any system of rules, rather than a consideration of why rule-breakers are considered vital to found a community. Durkheim's argument suggests that rule-breakers allow law-abiders to feel bonded together, secure in the *conscience collective*. He writes:

> Crime is, then, necessary; it is bound up with the fundamental conditions of all

social life, and by that very fact is useful, because these conditions of which it is a part are themselves indispensable to the normal evolution of morality and law. . . . The criminal *no longer* seems a *totally unsociable being*, a sort of *parasitic element*, a *strange and unassimilable body* introduced into the midst of society. On the contrary, he plays a definite role in social life. (1964: 70–1; my emphasis)

Durkheim sees rule-breakers and law-abiders as *part of the same community*, a community that was founded as law-abiding and then is subject to deviations from the law. The rule-breaker is necessarily identified as a rule-breaker and awarded a functional role in the establishment of 'morality and law'; she appears 'strange' but has a familiar function (that of bonding the collective unconscious). Due to her rule-breaking, she is to be treated as the scandalous phenomenon that a rule-breaker is. The argument in this book differs, in that for me the rule-breaker is necessarily *expelled* from the community. Such an outlaw can never belong to the community, in that the community's very existence is founded upon her prior and continuing symbolic expulsion from it. The substantive readings within this book seek to identify and interrogate the repetition of such a sacrifice. The textual outlaws who have emerged in the recent crisis of the crimino-legal tradition are the surrogates of a remembered and unresisted desire for the violence that lies beneath all communities.

The figure of the outlaw has been subject to considerable cultural analysis.[16] In a consideration of the psychoanalytic distinctions between the mass murderer and the serial killer, Salecl argues that the mass murderer kills in order to provoke the law into acting, to demand a response: 'What [the mass murderer] really demands is to be subjected to the law. . . . By committing the murder, the criminal demands an agent which would recognize him as a subject. He wants the Other, the symbolic order, to respond to his crime by giving him an identity he did not have before' (1993: 11–12). Thus 'the mass murderer kills in order to provoke the law into . . . "showing its face" by catching the subject and punishing him – but, in contrast, the serial killer, who is just as interested in law's existence, nevertheless ignores or is indifferent to the social law because through his act he *becomes* a *law* unto *him-self*' (1993: 15–16; emphasis in original). Salecl asserts that the serial killer, then, is the genuine outlaw, 'making it in his own image', '*beyond* the law' (1993: 16; emphasis in original). Such an argument makes it clear that law comes into being at the moment of reception of and by the subject. The serial killer acts according to the law made in his own image, a law unto himself. The mass murderer desires the social law (whether for itself or as a surrogate for the Law of the Father). Both instances reveal that law cannot be known without its reception into the subject.[17]

The subject's response to law takes one of two forms. The first, exemplified by the mass murderer, consists in a demand that law recognize and punish:

16. On the lesbian outlaw, see Robson (1992); on the transsexual as gender outlaw, see Bornstein (1994); on racial difference as the mark of the outlaw, see hooks (1995); on the serial killer as outlaw, see Salecl (1993).

17. Salecl (1993: 20) goes on to suggest that the current interest in serial killers is actually a fascination with the indifference to the legal order embodied by the serial killer.

subjectivity can only be achieved through the law. The second, personified by
the serial killer, is the indifference to social law manifested by a subject who
has made himself into his own law. Without necessarily taking on board the
precision of Salecl's arguments with regard to two specific forms of criminal
behaviour, her analysis inspires a questioning of the ways in which the criminal subject is deemed to relate to law. To that extent, Salecl rewrites the
proposition of Rousseau, that an outlaw is the one who breaks a legal or
social rule and who thus *invites* expulsion from the community. Through committing a crime, the outlaw has outlawed herself. Rousseau would have the
outlaw's expulsion as a necessary consequence of her criminality; the community has no choice but to expel her. It is only through such expulsion that the
outlaw can ever be requalified as a future member of the community. The
community, for Rousseau, has no desire for such violent expulsion; it is, rather,
an unavoidable aspect of the social contract. In this book, I seek to question
the self-evidence of such a view, which after all is one that persists in many discourses on crime, not merely in Jack's speech. By focusing on the axis of
expulsion, I wish to question the cultural tendency to read the expulsion of the
criminal as self-expulsion. My argument throughout the substantive analyses
which follow is that expulsion is rather contingent and arbitrary; while paradoxically being founded upon a continuing desire for sacrifice.

The construction of a community founded upon the expulsion of textual
outlaws as surrogates for that originary violent sacrifice requires the establishment of borders and boundaries. *Beyond* the boundary can be identified
the outlaw, within the boundary exist the members of the community,
attempting to 'lead their lives free from fear and in relative security', as Jack
puts it, while struggling with the resonances of the surrogate phantasms who
evoke the annihilated scapegoat.[18] However, there is a problem in that law is
required, as noted above, to be nomadic: 'it is not easy to predict where and
when [crime] will occur'.[19] The localism of crime necessitates the nomadism of
law's response. Thus, it is difficult to maintain a border in one, easy-to-police
location. Criminals can spring up all over, new forms of criminality can be
developed. Prediction becomes a major bulwark of the community's fight
against crime; for prediction can suggest future locations of the boundary.
The family had recently been rediscovered as a potential site for criminogenesis; the result has been an increased policing of the maternal role (see
Chapter 6). Locating crime, pinning it down, becomes a major preoccupation
of the crimino-legal complex. Where crime is located, the border can be
strengthened. As crime is deemed continually to take new forms, new borders
come into crisis, requiring reinforcement and vigilance. Such a crisis will usually take a displaced form: tensions surrounding the aestheticization of
everyday life – the necessity of living as an image – forced a breach in the
cultural order when a 2-year-old child, James Bulger, was filmed being

18. On the significance of the 'beyond' in contemporary legal studies, see Young and Sarat
(1994); in contemporary culture and cultural studies, see Bhabha (1994).
19. On nomadism, see Braidotti (1994).

abducted by two 10-year-old boys, who later killed him (see Chapter 5). In addition to the intense fears and concerns voiced about this case, much of the resulting events derived their force from a confrontation with the trauma of life lived on video and the breakdown of a comforting boundary between image and reality.

Some borders are easily identified: immigration law establishes the nation as a discrete community which is vulnerable to flooding by individuals from other countries. The recent development of a specific form of policing, with its peculiar devices of restraint, testifies to the increasing investment in and anxiety about the (in)vulnerability of the nation. Recent years have seen the intersection of criminal law, immigration policy and the criminal justice system in dealing with immigrants through detention and deportation, brought into sharp critical relief by the death of a woman as she was being deported from Britain (see Chapter 3). The fabled boundary between the public and private spheres exists in late modernity as a paradox: each sphere is comprehensible only by means of reference to the other; each is not the other, nor is each the separate realm it pretends. In the case of conjugal violence, we can see the law's reluctance to intervene in matrimonial (and hence civil) matters; in conjugal homicide, we see the law of marriage laid bare in its stark division between husband and wife.[20]

Within the discipline of criminology, Woman is secreted behind the borders of a discursive closet; feminism constitutes an insistent testimony to the discipline's wilful obscuring of the feminine (see Chapter 2). Realist criminology, as the discipline's contemporary paradigmatic perspective, operates its own fearful boundaries; in its desire for community within the city and for the transparency of civility in place of the opaque borders of the dark city streets (see Chapter 3). Another border lies between crime as experience (the victimization that is essential for membership of the community of late modernity) and crime as phantasm, between the fear of crime and the pleasure of crime. Whether fear or pleasure is experienced, the sensation exists – paradoxically, given the intensely visceral sensations inspired by both – in a vicarious relation to the subject. Crime is experienced through an Other. The commission of a crime affords the vicarious pleasure of becoming a legal subject. Similarly, the pleasure of detective fiction is vicarious in the voyeuristic pleasure it offers its readers (see Chapter 4). Detective fiction's mass readership suggests some perverse attachment to criminality; perverse in the sense that the reader turns away from crime's other representation as dread nightmare towards its textual *frisson*.

Imagining crime: on language, the body and aesthetics

My aim is to provide a reading of the cultural weight of crime as imagination. The book constitutes an archaeology of this weight, retracing its themes and

---

20. For a detailed analysis of two cases of conjugal homicide, see Young (forthcoming). On marriage as a site of sacrifice (of Woman), see Chapter 3 and Young (1994).

motifs and commonplaces. It devolves upon that which in representation ruins representation.[21] For the crimino-legal tradition, crime is that which ruins representation. As such, the readings in this book retell the stories of crimino-legal justice and are concerned not just with the literal truth of those discourses but also with their allegorical truth; that is, a truth that speaks otherwise. The following chapters constitute a series of conversations within the crimino-legal tradition: Chapters 2 and 3 deal with paradigms in criminological theory (feminism and realism); Chapters 3, 4, 5, 6 and 7 with contemporary events which elaborate the allegorical and literal truths of crime's images (conjugal homicide; death during deportation; detective fiction; the abduction and murder of a child by two children; government policy on the family as a site of criminogenesis; the spectacle of HIV/AIDS in criminal justice). I use the term 'conversation' in order to convey a sense of the dialogue aimed at in the book; a dialogue which takes an interdisciplinary form. The remainder of this chapter will attempt to situate these concerns within the conceptual frame which shapes this project. Criminology has long represented itself as *interdisciplinary*, sheltering a wide range of disciplines. Indeed, on my first day as a student on a criminology course I recall being informed that criminology was an 'umbrella' subject. Unfortunately, criminology, unlike Nietzsche, has never been able to forget its umbrella;[22] that is, that it *includes* subjects without insisting on their *interrelation*. It permits its wide range of contributing disciplines merely to co-exist. As such, criminology is multidisciplinary. The boundaries of its member disciplines remain intact and disparate, sometimes distant and hostile. Without the hubris of believing that any single text could influence disciplinary directions, I would wish to enter a plea for a greater willingness in criminology to explore beyond its rigid terms of reference, to open itself to the adventure of other insights.

Borders construct bodies; there can be no body of criminology without a disciplinary self-authorization which remarks its limits. There can be no sense of victimization without a sensuous body, its proprieties and property. Whether that body be social, intellectual, physical, makes no difference. As Jack's speech made clear at the beginning of this chapter, responses to crime are emotional and reside within a responsive body, named as intellectual (the 'analysis of crime'); individual (the 'old lady crying'); or as community ('all of us'). As argued above, the limits of that responsive body are shifting and

---

21. Montrelay (1978) argues that femininity is the ruin of representation. See also Irigaray (1985a).

22. See Derrida's reading of Nietzsche's umbrella in *Spurs* (1979); for an extended analysis of the metaphor of the umbrella in critical legal studies, see Goodrich (1993: 399–402), in which he proposes the umbrella as an icon of respectability, of transient refuge while simultaneously – through its ability to *shield* – duplicitous: 'a place within the hierarchy for the radical and the marginal, and also . . . for the naive and the incompetent, the tired, the masculine, the white and the obscure' (1993: 400). Phelan writes: 'And now . . . the umbrella seems like so much more than an umbrella. Derrida's *Eperons*, spurs towards Nietzsche's styles. The "bottlecap" on the end of Star Wars. The proliferation of condoms: from her head to his. Acid rain. "Drink It Dry". The dangers of wetness everywhere proclaimed. The end of the cold war. Casting away defensive shields. And adding others' (1993: 113).

subject to crisis and change. They are shored up by strategies of policing. The readings which follow in this book seek to address the processes by which borders are created, maintained, thrown into crisis and breached. They examine the construction of individuals and groups as outlaws and trace the consequences of that construction as it seeks to cast out and control. To this end, the book is concerned to ask several questions. These relate to the questions of crime as image; of the violence implicated in the formation of community, identity and law; of the consequences for the crimino-legal tradition of the aestheticization of everyday life.

A question of imagination

I have called this book *Imagining Crime* in order to make explicit its concerns with visibility and invisibility, image and reality. Imagination, the process by which we make images of crime, recalls the drive of spectatorship; the desire to see which in turn touches the desire to be seen. Seeing the Other is a form of self-reproduction. In looking at or for the other (the criminal), we represent ourselves to ourselves. The continual repetition and regeneration of crime's images displays the failure of our imagination of crime to live up to our demands of it (that our imagination of crime should always *be* crime). Thus imagination is distinct from the Imaginary, in which, as Lacan proposed, there is no distinction between what one sees and who one is. With the loss of the specular I/eye of the Imaginary (through which no boundaries are identified), the subject is split. With the pre-eminence of the gaze as founding the economy of exchange through speech, the social I/eye of the Symbolic Order marks the split between the self and other subjects.[23] Since the eye refuses to look inwards and will only look outwards, the subject can only see herself through looking at an other (who is continually looking at herself through her). Through this exchange of gaze – which, as Phelan notes, continually repeats and disguises 'the entry into the Symbolic' (1993: 23) – a never-ending series of images is generated. None of these images is adequate to its task, which is to offer self-representation in its plenitude and exactitude. The self is never in the image that we see; 'you never look at me from the place I see you' (Lacan, 1978: 91).[24] Instead, we find memories of the original moment of entry into the Symbolic. With this book, my concern is to trace contemporary manifestations of memories of the original moment when the outlaw (the Other) was sacrificed to establish the community (as the One, the Self). Within the Symbolic Order of culture, the subject looks for herself among the other subjects that she encounters. Instead of the self, all that is discovered is an endless series of images which replicate the split between subjects, between community and outlaw. Marking such a split we find outlaws emblematic of the violence that splits the community *as* community.

My concern is thus less with the discourse on crime than with how crime

---

23. For more detail, see Lacan (1977a); Phelan (1993: 21–4) provides a useful gloss.

24. Lacan also writes: 'I am unable to see myself from the place where the Other is looking at me' (1973: 120).

is imagined. By 'imagined', I include the written and the pictorial: the linguistic turns and tricks, the framing and editing devices in and through which crime becomes a topic, obtains and retains a place in discourse. Within this place, its topicality as a seat of argument is its commonplace nature, its 'taken-for-grantedness'. From this it follows that crime's images should be imagined as a *response*; that is, part of a dialogue that is always already taking place, a conversation or exchange with others. Moreover, that responsive imagination repeats the crime of which it speaks. As Derrida's (1981: 91) reading of Plato informs us, the scene of representation is the scene of a crime. While re-presenting the crime, a responsive imagination also constructs the event of crime. That is, it constitutes or *legislates* the event of crime. As an event, crime is thus always already *textual*, as are the outlaws symbolically excluded from the community. Crime is mediated as text; the text can therefore be read *as* crime. The text provides the scene of the crime. Crime's images are thus the *seen* of the crime. It is not only the event of crime that is legislated in the discursive imagination; in addition, there is a legislation of what is to count as a legislative discourse on crime. In other words, in the context of criminology, criminology is not only a description of crime, it also prescribes itself, prescribes how it is to speak *as* criminological. It is this self-prescription that constitutes a conversation on crime as textual, for its textual order is the order of self-reference. Its descriptions of crime are also always textual: references to that which falls outside the text are always made within the text.[25]

The crime embedded in representations of crime is always one of *sacrifice*. This concept has been briefly discussed above, and will be elaborated in the substantive readings which follow this chapter. Girard wrote that the human species originated in the aleatory selection of a victim whose elimination put an end to the chaos of random violence (the violence of all against all is translated into the violence of all against one, with one member of the community arbitrarily singled out for destruction). Upon this act of violence is founded the social contract. Girard writes: 'The victim is held responsible for the renewed calm in the community and for the disorder that preceded this return. It is even believed to have brought about its own death' (1987: 26). The victim represents the violence of community and, as displacement of this violence, becomes both revered and reviled. In thus sacralizing the victim, the community turns its violence away from itself. Thus the victim is sacralized for representing the origin of both the community and the unanimous violence that ended with the victim's destruction. The notion of the sacred is thus based upon a mistake that represents the effect of violence for its cause.

Girard gives the victim no identity, no essential attributes of identification that distinguish it from other members of the community. I would suggest that the victim is always predetermined along lines of gender, sexuality, race or age. The case studies which follow investigate the structures of sacrifice

---

25. On the inescapability of textual representation, see Derrida (1973). See also Atkinson (1990).

that adhere to these lines of division and identification. As such, the victim is always already pre-identified. The first sacrifice, indeed, is the attribution of an identity, as sexed, aged, raced. Its *subsequent* representation (as that which is to be sacrificed) is necessary for the foundation of the community's economy of representation, its structures of self-authorization. Modern culture repeats the dynamic of sacrifice over and over through the generation of surrogate outlaws who replay the community's expulsion of the scapegoat: in representations of 'illegal immigrants' as embodying a threat to national security and to national culture; in representations of children as *either* innocent *or* evil; in representations of the maternal relation as potentially criminogenetic; in representations of the marriage contract as based on the subjugation of woman to man; in representations of homosexuality as linked to the transmission of disease. These issues delineate the concerns of the case studies which elaborate the sacrificial structure of representations of crime. Whatever the substantive identity attributed to the outlaw – young, black, homosexual and so on – the violent duality of Man/Woman provokes a feminizing of all textual outlaws in the cultural unconscious. For example, the opposition drawn between 'white' and 'non-white' originates from a focus upon skin as the visible marker of race. As Phelan comments, this is 'a form of feminising those races which are not white. Reading the body as the sign of identity is the way men regulate the bodies of women' (1993: 10). Similarly, youth can be feminized: two boys who murdered another child were described as truanting troublemakers (often signifiers of masculine youth) but the investigation and colonization of their psyches, home backgrounds, bodily drives and so on treated them *as if* they were feminine. In the moment of the *as if*, the hierarchy of sexual difference is reaffirmed and the violence of sacrifice symbolically repeated.

A question of the body

In imagining crime, the body is continually being constituted, brought into crisis, and reconstituted. This body, as stated earlier, may be the body of criminology, the community, the victim, the criminal. The letter of the law excises the body in a *coupure* (cut) which displaces and realizes all the anxieties surrounding the body.[26] The body is thus constituted at a remove from the Symbolic Order, accessible now only through the mediation of the law of desire; that is, through language. Language never simply describes the body, but rather structures, marginalizes and divides the body into organs, into head and heart, into meaningful and meaningless parts.[27] One of the concerns of this book, then, is to seek the unmarked emotional body of and in the crimino-legal tradition; the body that suffers under the weight of imagination as a spectacle to be consumed, disciplined, repressed. As such, the moments

---

26. The term *coupure* is borrowed from Lacan (1977b).

27. I am here indebted to the ideas of Bill MacNeil, especially his paper 'Enjoy your rights! Fantasy, symptom and identification in the discourse of rights' (1994) and its interpretations of Žižek's reading of Lacan.

seized for analysis implicate the body *in extremis*: moments in which the body is in pain, in pleasure, is dying or dead. At this point, however, I should emphasize that 'the body' discussed here is not a 'real' body to be counterposed to a discursive, representational or imaginary body. The body is both real *and* a sign. These are not two separable conditions but rather they demonstrate the corporeality of the sign and the significatory powers of the body. As Grosz states: 'representations and cultural inscriptions quite literally constitute bodies and help to produce them as such' (1994: x). The inescapably cultural dimensions of the body are quintessential to its nature. Thus, this book is concerned with the responsive, emotional body *as textual*, as a thing that can be read, and therefore a thing that is never complete in itself, always open to (re)interpretation.

As stated above, the textual outlaws that are analysed in this book are produced in and through bodies of victims, disciplines, criminals and communities. Chapter 3 examines the central location that has been awarded to the body of the victim in recent criminological thought and criminal justice policy. Its purported structures of suffering are considered as blind spots of a fascination with, variously, the city, the domestic and the nation. Pleasure in danger is the concern of Chapter 4: it examines the *plaisirs* of the text in detective fiction and argues that feminist detective fiction has created a space in which the body of the reader may be transformed into an ethically responsive one. Chapter 5 interrogates the limits of the visible in the body of crime, in relation to the murder of a child by two other children; a case in which the textual scene of the crime was mediated through the media to occupy another scene entirely. The maternal relation (also a concern of Chapter 5) is interrogated in Chapter 6, as a site/sight of governmental regulation of reproduction. Finally, Chapter 7 analyses how the border between life and death in the body of crime was made a spectacle within the various strategies of advertising, activism and criminal justice policy on HIV/AIDS. In the crimino-legal tradition's representations of the body of crime are also found the representations of the body of the crimino-legal tradition itself. I stated above that representations of crime legislate how those representations may speak as self-authorized representations within the crimino-legal tradition. Chapter 2 thus follows the struggles of feminism to speak within the hegemonic masculinity of conventional criminological knowledge. A further point may be made that representations of crime within the crimino-legal tradition legislate the self-constitution of that tradition as crimino-legal. That is, its representations of a body of crime (incorporated as the victim, as the criminal, as the community) prescribe also its representations of a body of criminology and law. There is thus brought into existence a body of crime and a body of criminology; a law of the body and a body of law. One of the concerns of this book is therefore with the interrelations between representations of crime and representations of the crimino-legal tradition; that is, with how the complex of law, criminology and criminal justice *incorporates* itself as a body of knowledge, as a discursive formation, as a tradition.

To that extent, crime is a sign, speaking of that which is most reverenced (as essential for the founding of the community and its criminal contract) and most reviled (signifying the flesh, the impulses, blood, disease). Thus crime as a sign is itself a signifier of violence. As Derrida writes: 'The thing itself is a sign' (1976: 49). Crime is the first and most longed-for sign (as the essential precondition of community); at the same time, it is that which cannot be signified, excess, the unpresentable (Lyotard, 1984: 369). The body of crime is continually being reconfigured as feminine, black, young, homosexual, maternal and on and on. Such a process does not and cannot end. The aim of this book is to provide readings of several contemporary manifestations of crisis in the crimino-legal tradition's representations of crime. Those manifestations always take bodily form; they incorporate crime and make legible and legislatable its limits and desires. Since these manifestations are always displacements of an original crisis (described above, as the founding moment of community), the crimino-legal tradition's representations of crime can only ever approximate a logic of crime, can only ever approach the pale criminal as a chiasmus of fear and desire.[28]

A question of everyday life

As stated above, crime's topicality resides in its commonplace nature. It is constituted as an aspect of everyday life.[29] In its everyday nature, crime takes place as an axiomatic expression of one of the features of ultramodernity: the aestheticization of the everyday, through which life is lived as an image or simulation of life. With life as an image, the subject lives as persona, or mask. As such, subjectivity is a consequence of and dependent on subjectification to and of the image (*assujetissement*). Crime as event and as response may thus be read as *emblematic* of contemporary modes of subjectification and identification. Identification is a necessary aspect of the process of subjectification, since subjectivity through the image is not experienced simply as trauma, but rather as a traumatic form of pleasure. We may be masks but, we would (and will) die for our mask (*pro persona mori*: see Goodrich, 1990).[30] The trauma of identification through subjectification in the image can be read as a series of symptoms which always displace the pleasure in pain onto something else. The issues which are commonly taken as contemporary crises for the crimino-legal complex function as symptoms of the anxiety that lies at the heart of the economy of representation of crime.

This anxiety can be characterized in three ways: first, as a response to the

28. I am borrowing the phrase 'the pale criminal' from Nietzsche (although my deployment of it varies considerably from his). See also Kerr's (1993b) detective story of the same name. I intend the pallor of the criminal to suggest the ways in which, in contemporary manifestations of criminological thought, the criminal is bloodless, insubstantial, a pale, unmarked reflection in the victim's eye of fear, able to re-present whatever the fear seeks to displace: the city, racial difference, sexual difference.

29. On crime and the everyday, see Jones et al. (1986); Stanko (1990a). For a philosophy of the everyday, see de Certeau (1984).

30. Salecl (1993) writes that law shows its face *as* a mask; we are asked to die in and for the mask of law.

realization that 'we' live in and through the technology of the image.[31] The notion of a 'we' is as much a mask as any form of 'I', as shown by my comments above on the 'we' of the community. Founded on the illusion of a social contract, its inclusionary 'we', expressed in Jack's speech as 'all of us', turns out to be exclusionary. The 'we' can only exist through the expulsion of the Others. Second, this leads to a realization that, just as the technologies of the image have their blind spots and dark spots, so does the life led through and of the image. In short, if there is a limit to vision (and the notion of the horizon confirms the limit of vision), there also is found the finitude of the human. Anxiety stemming from the realization that we live through and as images is accompanied by the anxiety that outside or beyond the image there is only death, darkness and the inhuman (as the limit of humanity). This second fear gives rise to a reiteration of life as lived through the image: terrified of darkness and death, of the horizon and the limit of the visible, we turn to the image as bearer of light, we seek to destroy the horizon, we ask the image for consolation. Thus technology can overcome geographical limits (through the immediacy of the telephone, the television, the Internet).[32] It can photograph the invisible and the unknowable (through the endoscope, ultrasound, the infra-red camera).[33] Through this renewed insistence on living through and as images, the original anxiety arises once more. The result is a confusion of the distinction between semblance and substance, image and reality.

As part of this process, the everyday has been aestheticized; the real world has become a myth (Nietzsche).[34] As Barthes writes,

> classical rhetoric had . . . institutionalized the fantasmatic as a specific figure, *hypotyposis*, whose function was to 'put things before the bearer's eyes', not in a neutral, constative manner, but by imparting to representation all the luster of desire . . .; declaratively renouncing the constraints of the rhetorical code, realism must seek a new reason to describe. (1986: 145–6)

He adds:

> The truth of [the referential illusion] is this: eliminated from the realist speech-act as a signified of denotation, the 'real' returns to it as a signified of connotation; for just when these details are reputed to *denote* the real directly, all that they do – without saying so – is *signify*. (1986: 148; emphasis in original)

Again, here I should emphasize that this is not to counterpose a 'real' world to a 'representational' world, or an image to a reality. My point is that nothing can remain of the dichotomy; appearance and reality are abolished to the extent that reality is an appearance and appearance is our reality. Such a

31. See Baudrillard (1987) on the technology of the image.

32. See Duden (1993) on the ravages of the horizon in late modernity; also Ronell (1990) on the telephone; Sparks (1992) on television; Taylor (1994) on the Internet and virtual media communication generally.

33. See Young (1993a) on the production of the foetus as universal subject through technology's invention of its identity.

34. See also Blondel (1985).

collapse provokes extremes of discomfort in the subject, who looks (at an image) to find her self (not an image). On the distinction between the real and the Real, Phelan writes:

> Within the radical contingency of [the] psychic and material Real, subjectivity is performed. This subjectivity is always already gendered. And always already more insecure for and about women. Representation functions to make gender, and sexual difference more generally, secure and securely singular – which is to say, masculine. (She ghosts him.) Representation tries to overlook the discontinuity between subjectivity and the gendered, sexual body, and attempts to suture the gap between subjectivity and the Real. The common desire to look to representation to confirm one's reality is never satisfied; for representation cannot reproduce the Real. This keeps us looking – and keeps us hoping. (1993: 172)

The discovery only of images is an experience of horror the subject continually rejects and rediscovers. This is a necessary corollary of the representational nature of crime. In terms of criminological study, for a discourse to be criminological its knowledge must correspond to the realities of crime and crime control. Such is the demand for a criminological guarantee. And thus criminology understands itself to be a system of knowledge (or discursive formation).

Criminology is not a system of knowledge, despite its faith in the image of its self and despite its creation of symbols for the actions and passions that occur in crime, victimization and criminal justice. Rather, its task is the invention of concepts (to which, if this book can offer itself as one summarized concern, my contribution would wish to be a theory of the ways in which repeated symbolic sacrifice creates cultural outlaws who delimit the boundaries of community). In its *image* of its self as a system of knowledge, criminology resembles a representational structure of reflections, correspondences and contemplation. It insists on a strict division between two orders of being: that of semblance and that of substance. When criminology turns to the event of crime, it suffers anxiety, through a confusion of semblance and substance. Its anxiety is present both in the superficial discourse on any singular event and buried deep in the criminological archive which writes all criminological texts. In the latter, confusion results from responses to crime which have faith in criminology as a representational structure which holds the reality of crime. But criminology exists in its own image, as an image, and therefore is an institution of simulation. This, then, is the way in which criminology is addressed in following chapters.

In the case of the discourses generated in response to any singular event of crime, 'event' must be understood *as* violation, since the event brings to the fore the uncertain anxieties that reside in our living life as an image. With everyday life taking place at the level of simulation, with the distance inserted by the image between reality and its appearance, the event of crime seems to be real but can only ever achieve a semblance of the real. This notion is explored through several of the readings which follow; notably, Chapter 5 on the technology of the image that was crucial to the Bulger case. The event of crime draws attention to the confusion of semblance and substance and the

tremendous trauma that results. Faced with such confusion, the subject
becomes abject. Kristeva writes:

> Any crime, because it draws attention to the fragility of the law, is abject.
> . . . Abjection is immoral, sinister, scheming and shady: a terror that dissembles, a
> hatred that smiles, a passion that uses the body for barter instead of inflaming it, a
> debtor who sells you up, a friend who stabs you. (1982: 4)

In continually rediscovering the representational nature of reality – and in
being unable to break free of the endless dialectic between its rejection and its
rediscovery – the subject experiences the event of crime as a wound; a wound
that must be touched, picked at, shuddered over. The wound makes visible the
boundary between the inside and the outside (of the body, of skin, of culture);
the wound acts as a reminder of the necessity and impossibility of the border
between the real and the Real (see Žižek, 1989). Such a wound must be covered over, sutured together (and that is part of the work of the imagination of
crime). But the suture will never hold the wound together; and the subject will
never leave the wound alone.

In short, whether registered in the event of crime or in the archives of
criminology, the confusion of semblance and substance marks the experience of criminality in ultramodernity. As such, it is the aestheticization of
everyday life – and the place of crime in it – that needs to be addressed.
Address as response is crucial, rather than denunciation or affirmation (two
of the responses which have characterized much of the defensive anxiety aris-
ing from this confusion).[35] 'Simulation' is the name given a concept that
attempts to think the aesthetic differently, otherwise, to provide an allegory of
the confusion between image and reality (allegory: a law of the Other). In
thinking the aesthetic of crime otherwise, as simulation, what may be
redeemed is the body. The body of crime, of the community, of marriage, of
the nation, of health: these plural and discontinuous bodies are, within this
book, told and retold, otherwise. And the name given to the body of these
fragments is the emotional or sensuous body.

The crimino-legal aesthetic of the sensuous body, as proposed here,
revolves around two concepts: first, an aesthetic which must be understood as
representation or simulation; second, an aesthetic which has implications for
the body. As such, the body is always double(d): it is both the body of criminology and the criminology of the body; the self-image of criminology as
knowledge and the criminological representation of knowledge of others. As
with all such doublings, at its heart is a crisis. The crimino-legal tradition has
been constituted through and as a response to crisis. Criminology itself
emerged as a response to a crisis in classical theory. It provided a concept of
the 'criminal' and then noted that classical theory could not 'understand' or

---

35. A paradigmatic example would be the fierce debate between Baudrillard and Norris. On
the Gulf War, Baudrillard writes: 'By making transparent the non-event of the war [as simula-
tion], you give it a force in the image' (1994: 64). As a non-event, the Gulf War took place only
'as a substitute for a Third World War which did not take place' (1994: 62). See also his *La Guerre
du Golfe n'a pas eu lieu* (1991, translated 1995) and Norris's response (1992).

'explain' the criminal. Criminology therefore invented itself as a response to a crisis named as a gap in knowledge's representation of reality. The crisis which structures the crimino-legal tradition, diagnosed and investigated in this book, is a crisis in representation (by which appearances are desired as reality while their representational status is perpetuated). My response to this crisis is to tell stories; other stories and otherwise, to write allegories of the imagination of crime.

Textual outlaws and criminal conversations

In reading the imaginary of crime, this book attempts a resistance to the dominant narratives of the crimino-legal tradition. The stories concern events within the crimino-legal tradition; events which, in recent years, have been taken to represent something essential about crime. The narratives which are elaborated in each chapter thus concern the symptoms of crisis in the crimino-legal tradition and the attempts made to efface that crisis. Chapter 2 examines criminology's confrontation with feminism. Feminist interventions in criminology have taken a variety of forms but fall into three main groups, which are discussed in detail. The aim of the chapter is to diagnose the reasons for criminology's intense and unrelenting resistance to the insistent questions of feminism. It is my argument that criminology has always constructed Woman as an enigma, which can be investigated by criminology and *made to mean* within the metaphorization of sexual difference. The questions of feminism can then be reduced to politics, critique or bias, and thus tolerated within a ghetto, or dismissed outright.

Feminist interventions in criminology have presaged some genuine innovations within that deadlocked discipline. The other dominant paradigmatic programme that emerged in criminology in the 1980s was realism. In contrast to feminism, realism constitutes less an innovation than a restaging of criminology's traditional concerns. Realism, however, has become established as the primary vocabulary within criminology. Chapter 3 examines some of the underpinnings of the realist programme. This is carried out within a general examination of the fascination in the crimino-legal complex with the position of the victim. My argument is that the victim has come to displace the criminal in the victim/criminal opposition to the extent that the identity of the criminal signifies only to shore up the identity of the victim. The chapter ignores the simple vanguardism that has accompanied such interest in victimization and goes beyond the limits of realist vocabulary to consider instead three instances in which the two terms of the victim/criminal opposition cannot be marked as separable. First, I consider realist criminology's construction of the city as the space of social (in)justice. Marking this latter word with parentheses incorporates the ambiguity of the city's status within realist texts. On the one hand, it is the site where crime and victimization flourish; on the other, it is to be the location for reformist programmes that will solve the problem of crime and salve the pain of victimization. The city, of course, is neither one nor the other; its ambiguous meaning provides the chapter's first narrative.

The mythic boundary between the public and the private occasions the next narrative in which the victim/criminal opposition is rendered problematic. That is, in a case of conjugal homicide – where a battered woman kills her abusive husband – we see a woman embodying both victimhood (she is a battered woman) and criminality (she commits homicide). Her dual value within the crimino-legal complex inspires a moment of crisis in which we see the system wrestle with the question of her 'true' status. The third narrative follows a similar course. A black woman dies while being deported from Britain; an investigation is demanded into the cause of her death. If she is an illegal immigrant being treated properly by the deportation squad, she can be categorized as criminal. If she is deemed to have been treated with excessive force by the squad, she becomes a genuine victim, irrespective of her immigration status. The case provoked a fascination with the body of the dead woman and the violence inflicted on it by the deportation officers, within a frame which took for granted the propriety of the border between Britain and 'other' nations. Chapter 3 uses these three narratives to locate the body in crime as an emotional body that is subject to interpretation (is she a victim or a criminal?) and as a source which can cause ruptures in the smooth surface of the crimino-legal tradition.

That tradition incorporates an industry of entertainment as well as a bureaucracy of policing and punishment. I have selected detective fiction, one of the most popular genres of fiction, as the subject of Chapter 4. As a counterpoint to the much-heralded fear of crime that is said to dominate life in ultramodernity, the consumption of detective fiction seems to offer an experience of the pleasures of crime. Here, the scene of the crime can be examined, literally at leisure by the reader, within the genre's narrative desire for the successful detection of the criminal. My particular interest here is to consider whether feminist detective fiction has subverted the conservatism of the genre to the extent whereby it might have created a space in which a feminist ethics can be participated in by the reader. From pleasure to horror: Chapter 5 concerns the trauma produced by the abduction and murder of a 2-year-old child by two other children. This event received global and national news attention and inspired intense scrutiny of the supposed nature of boyhood. This scrutiny included, at the suggestion of the trial judge, examination of the family backgrounds of the two convicted children. This was interpreted, in the main, as concerning the relationship between the boys and their mothers. The significance of the maternal relation became a metaphor in the case for societal vulnerability, for the burdens of familial responsibility and for the duties of the state to intervene in 'dysfunctional' families. The child's abduction was filmed on security cameras and witnessed by three dozen bystanders. Taken together, this produced a technology of the image that was crucial in the construction of the event as traumatic. The chapter argues that the case revealed the limit of representation and the abyss beyond it as an integral part of the crisis in the crimino-legal complex.

Beyond the particular aspects of this case, 1992 saw a governmental campaign in Britain 'against' single mothers. That is, the single mother was singled out as the primary cause of delinquency in children (the connecting of this to the death of James Bulger meant that single motherhood was metonymically linked to murder). The Conservative government generated a series of restrictive interventions against single mothers, cutting welfare benefits, housing access and so on. Chapter 6 links these tactics with the criminological work that was done on juvenile delinquency by Donald West (recently enjoying a minor renaissance). My aim is to show their sharing of a perspective which erases difference and creates a model of sameness, based on the heterosexual couple. The single mother confounds the apparent self-evidence of this prescriptive model and as such constitutes an imaginary threat: imaginary in that her image is one that the government seeks to erase. Image as spectacle is the concern of Chapter 7, with specific reference to the criminal justice system's approach to HIV/AIDS. I have compared the appearance of HIV as spectacle within the discourses and images of an activist photographic campaign, a Benetton advertisement and the policies of criminal justice. In the tensions between appearance and disappearance – life and death – made manifest in these imaginations, we can begin to discern crime's shape as emotional body, as repressed and hidden identity. Where the Bulger case made visible the limit of representation (and drew back from the abyss), the issue of HIV/AIDS demands a marking of the *beyond* located out of our sight.

As these summaries attempt to make clear, the book is written in resistance to the dominant narratives of the crimino-legal complex. However, in addition, *the book itself* operates through an interested indifference to the criminological law of crime. Telling other stories is always outside, beyond, the criminological law of crime. To that extent, this book may be seen as an outlaw text, by virtue of its relation to criminology. Here, I mean to suggest that its arguments may be rejected by the discursive field of criminology; ejected and exiled from the insides of the discipline to the outside. The book, however, has been imagined, written and offered as a border text; that is, it seeks to occupy a border territory between genres and disciplines. It represents the hybridity of my personal and intellectual histories: having trained as a lawyer, studied as a criminologist, taught in law and women's studies and criminology; inspired by feminist theory, by philosophy and cultural studies, by film and advertising as much as by case reports or criminological texts. The book exists in a kind of 'no man's land', which may be a nice place for a woman to write. The border has its productive aspects (unlike the 'outside', even though that place has only an imaginary force from within the 'inside'). From the border, attention can be drawn to the forces of inclusion and exclusion in the establishment of disciplines and of crimes. To write on the border of what is 'criminology' and what is 'not' acknowledges the possibilities of rejection, of eyes that will not 'see'. As an outlaw text, this book seeks to inhabit the space of the beyond, or border, where the crimino-legal complex falls into the real. The moment of falling into the real is paradoxically the moment of hallucination; where infidelity is necessary for faith to be promised. Criminology promises faith to itself, sealing the possibility of infidelity, of stories within and beyond its borders.

My name for this paradox is the 'criminal conversation'. Criminal conversation was a juridical category that emerged at the historical moment when criminal law and family law, civil and criminal law, public and private spheres were being registered as distinct categories of existence. It was a charge used against adulterers and represents to me the uneasy line between the past and the present, the inside and the outside, faith and infidelity. This book, then, offers a series of readings as 'criminal conversations'; dialogues – with that which is *beyond* – undertaken from *this* side of the divide. As an outlaw text, the book also engages in a criminal conversation with criminology itself: offering an outlaw's dialogue with the discourse that imagines law, crime and criminology. The criminal conversation is thus emblematic of two concerns in this book. First: to inhabit the space of the border(lines) is to remain open to the Other; second: in remaining open to the Other, the conversation must be undertaken from *this* side of the border. In disciplinary terms, conversation originates from within the crimino-legal tradition. Thus, there is no need to demand the abolition or abandonment of criminology;[36] rather, the alternative, the Other, is always already *within* criminology. As such, the retelling of other stories – the hope of this book – leaves the subject open to the Other within and beyond criminology. The criminal conversation is thus a tribute to the infidelity necessary for a reading of crime's imagination.

36. To this extent, my argument differs from that of Smart (1990), who has been taken as suggesting that criminology should be abandoned by feminists: see Chapter 2 for further elaboration of the relationship between feminism and criminology.

2

Criminology and the Question of Feminism

Woman as the enigma of criminology

The question of femininity has, in many ways, been criminology's best-kept secret. Its mark has always been (one of) masculinity. That is, in the unmarked surface of the offending body is found the masculinity of criminology. Gender is only re-marked when femininity is in question. Femininity has been secret(ed) in criminology as a result of its construction and metaphorization of sexual difference. The value created for femininity by criminology's metaphorization of sexual difference is that of a phantasm, an inverted negation haunting the twists and turns of masculine desire in the crimino-legal complex. Its status as phantasm is recorded as a secret within the disciplinary complex of law and criminology. By this I do not mean that femininity has some hidden, or arcane, content, but rather that it is performed as a discursive act within a hierarchical ideology that systematically constructs and reconstructs *as* a secret. Its secretion therefore means that, on the one hand, it exists as ghost; while on the other, it oozes from the cracks in the smooth surface of discursive masculinity and manifests itself. Phelan writes: 'within the realm of the visible, that is both the realm of the signifier and the image, women are always seen as Other; thus, *The Woman* cannot be seen. Yet, like a ubiquitous ghost, she continues to haunt the images we believe in, the ones we remember seeing and loving' (1993: 6). Femininity is thus both known and unknown for criminology. It is unknown in that it can only ever register in criminology's symbolic order as the inverted negation of masculinity. It is known in that it is continually measured, recorded, examined and inspected for evidence of its necessary deviance, its waywardness. To that extent, criminology has participated in what Hart has called the 'discursive/material violence of [the] system's effort to secrete (set apart, sift, distinguish)' (1994: ix).

The history of criminology's representation of Woman has been a history of secretion; in which femininity has been closeted and obscured, while simultaneously slipping through its strictures. The notion of femininity as obscurity can be discerned in the construction of women as objects to be decoded. Embedded within this is the attribution of a primary blame or guilt: the woman is to bear responsibility for the fact that she has to be decoded (by the analyst/criminologist/detective). For example, women have been represented as analytic opacity: their nature is not open to be read by the

criminologist, who is thus unable to know them. Women have also been represented as hysterical, thus rendering their real natures hidden to themselves as
well as to the analysing criminologist who is forced to interpret behaviours as
symptoms and symptoms as traits. Finally, women have been conceptualized
as withholding their natures from analysis, exercising an innate ability to dis-
semble and dissimulate (making their nature one of deception). Woman is
thus simultaneously impenetrable enigma, displacement and dissimulation.[1]
From these configurations derive commonplace ideas: that women are more
emotional than men (and more emotionally labile than men); that women
share characteristics (which may resist initial inspection); that women are
inherently deceitful. Despite or no doubt because of the claim that femininity
is obscure(d), women have been subjected to intense scrutiny in the name of
femininity. Woman can then be made to mean something for criminology.
Theories have thus been proffered which have claimed that, for example, since
women share similar characteristics and are thus basically alike, it is difficult
to know (that is, to predict) who is (likely to be) deviant. From this process of
making femininity mean something, there emerges an identity that eludes
detection, confounds discovery and is dangerously slippery and fluid. In
Chapter 1, I referred to criminology's 'umbrella' structure: an umbrella functions most obviously to keep dry the area or person beneath it. Criminology,
sheltering below its umbrella, seeks to keep at bay the fluidity of Woman.
Wetness and fluidity are associated with femininity, with bodily fluids. Goodrich
writes: 'fluid . . . are the allegory of femininity, for fluid dissolves and escapes,
it is inconsistent, disequilibriated, and changing' (1993: 401). Stiff and dry, the
umbrella shields criminology from the slippery wetness of Woman.[2]

Femininity is awarded a place in the classification system of sexual difference, which, like all taxonomies, is structured on the principle of negation.
Femininity is thus both prohibited and at the same time essential. In its function of negating and inverting masculinity, femininity is constructed as a
paradox, or perhaps an aporia. Strategies of representation mean that femininity as impossibility can be discussed as possibility, despite its lack of
purchase on the 'real' of the Symbolic Order. Thus the negated identity is
processed as impossible, while permitting its conditions of possibility (as
impossibility) to be investigated. As impossibility, as inversion, femininity has
always already existed as deviant: deviant from the symbolic order of masculinity, while necessary to it for its structuring of sexual difference.
Criminology, then, has proceeded to investigate the condition of femininity,
secure in the verification of its own foundations that are afforded by the spectacle of femininity as deviance. This process is conventionally taken to have
begun with Lombroso. In *The Female Offender*, an archetype is assumed. She

1. Pollak is the most obvious criminological exponent of versions of these notions: see Pollak
(1960); Pollak and Friedman (1969). For a critical reading of Woman as hysteric, see Cixous and
Clément (1986). For other versions of these feminine fantasies, see Dijkstra (1986); Ellis (1904);
Maclean (1980).
2. See also Cornell (1991: 15–17); Grosz (1994: 202–10); Irigaray (1985a: 237), in which she
states: 'Fluid has to remain that secret remainder'; and (1985b) on the 'mechanics' of fluids.

is the good, or non-criminal, woman, unarticulated in Lombroso's work, but present as a source of fear. Jones writes that Lombroso was 'haunted by the fear that an apparently good woman might, at any unexpected moment, turn out to be bad' (1980: 6). Lombroso's approach is structured around the conceptualizations of Woman discussed above: that the nature of Woman is obscure(d); that an apparently minor symptom might reveal dreadful deviance; that a woman might shield her true nature from others. As Hart describes, Lombroso therefore embarked on a mission requiring 'the excruciating, painstaking calculation of his subjects' physical attributes; the obsessive measuring of their crania, anklebones, middle fingers; the scrutinizing of their handwriting; the registering of their voices; the counting of gray hairs, wrinkles, tattoos – all part of the project to render the female offender visible, and thus containable' (1994: 12).

The physical manifestations of Woman – her hair, her voice, her ankle – are measured, compared, assessed. No pattern, however, reveals itself. Lombroso confessed: 'these accumulated figures do not amount to much, but this result is only natural' (Lombroso and Ferrero, 1895: 74). Lombroso had imagined women as falling into three categories: the normal woman, the occasional offender and the born criminal. His research did not yield results which appeared to support this, leading him to argue that criminal women and law-abiding women appear substantially the same. His conclusions support his starting-point: that it is the nature of Woman to be obscure(d), even when that nature may be criminal. The nature of the law-abiding woman cannot be taken for granted, since it may only appear law-abiding (being instead criminal) or it may be a mask assumed by the criminal woman. In the end, Woman's deviance can be confirmed by her comparison with the masculine. Lombroso writes: 'female offenders seem almost normal when compared to the male criminal, with his wealth of anomalous features' (1895: 107). Crucially, the female offender is described as 'seem[ing] almost' normal. Normality is a simulation, for a female offender can only ever achieve the appearance of it (her 'real' nature underlies and belies her normality). And while a male offender has a 'wealth' of anomalies, the female offender is his inversion. A series of negations is created: normality resides in the law-abiding male; the male offender inverts the normal male's relation to the law but still shares in the normality of masculinity. The female offender inverts the normal subject's relation to the law and the nature of the criminal male. She is thus the inversion of an inversion.

Lombroso constructs another series of inversions with his concept of the born criminal. Woman, for Lombroso, should manifest an absence of sexual desire, a love of children and a dutiful acceptance of maternal obligations, piety, quietude and filial subordination. In the absence of any of these, it was to be suspected that a 'born criminal' was present. Then, Lombroso wrote, 'the innocuous semi-criminal present in the normal woman must be transformed into a born criminal more terrible than any man' (Lombroso and Ferrero, 1895: 151). The normal woman is an inversion of the order of sexual difference in her relation to the law-abiding man; the female born criminal is an inversion of the normal woman, more dreadful than any male offender, belonging 'more to the male than the female sex' (1895: 153). Lombroso's inverted Woman predicts Ellis' congenital invert, with her predilection for violence. Ellis' Woman is a criminal against society rather than against her nature (by seducing members of her own sex or by committing violent acts she *conforms* to her [inverted] nature rather than resists it).[3] The configurations of Woman that structure Lombroso's and Ellis' writings are developed in Freud's image of the hysteric. Kofman has argued that Freud's discourse on hysteria is itself a hysterical reaction to the possibility of the criminality of women. The enigma of Woman as hysteric reverses the knowledge that women are 'great criminals'.[4] Within the writings of Freud, Ellis and Lombroso are buried metaphorizations of sexual difference, with their evaluations of Woman. For Freud, the Woman may be a hysteric, with her visible symptoms masking her true nature. For Ellis, the Woman may be an inversion of femininity, thus deceiving by her appearance of femininity (while it is actually inverted in her). For Lombroso, the Woman may take shape as a normal, good, non-violent figure while easily falling into criminality, since her nature is labile and unstable.

Lombroso's manifestations of Woman are liminal figures that mark out borders between typologies. Much of the anxiety that drives *The Female Offender* derives from the uncertainty of predicting which individual woman might fall into which category. 'Occasional offenders' were often hysteric-like figures, differing only slightly from 'normal' women. Lombroso viewed these occasional offenders as having been seduced into criminality – by their excessive mother-love, by their devotion to a criminal man. The occasional offender may practise monogamous chastity and maternal devotion, but, for Lombroso, 'all the criminality of the hysterical subject has reference to sexual functions' (Lombroso and Ferrero, 1895: 224). The *appearance* of sexual and maternal normality masks a disturbed depth that has led her into criminality. In prison, according to Lombroso, the occasional offender develops attachments to her male gaolers, has faith in her lawyer and may appear fond of her executioner (1895: 195). The 'born criminal', for Lombroso, demonstrates 'insatiable egotism', exercising acts of tyranny and violence 'more often found in the love of a man than of a woman' (1895: 159, 161). Freud saw the hysteric as filled with a desire to confess her secret and be thus restored to the masculine order. Lombroso would concur: in prison, the occasional offender's obsessive relations with men act out her confession of a desire to be understood only through the Symbolic Order. The 'born criminal', however, is regarded as resistant to analysis and to law. She knows she is/has a secret. Her existence is many times more threatening than that of the hysteric/occasional offender, since she represents the abyss into which both the 'normal' woman and the 'occasional offender' might degenerate.

Criminology shares with psychoanalysis a reluctance to solve its riddles. As

---

3. For an analysis of inversion theories as applied to lesbians, see Hart (1994: Chapter 1).
4. See Kofman (1985: 65–6), writing on Freud's 'On narcissism'.

Foucault (1980: 48) pointed out, criminology's repetitions fulfil a need to classify and categorize, rather than to answer its questions. Solution, however, is not its discursive purpose. On the contrary, the reproduction of Woman as criminological enigma (absent, or shadowy, or disturbing) solves the anxiety that haunts the metaphors of sexual difference. Woman can only ever constitute a symptom of that difference. Hence, she is *unknowable*. Criminology's inevitable refiguring of that status is to call her the *unknown*. In Lombroso, Ellis and Freud lies a conviction that the unknowable can be known, the enigmatic can be solved. That conviction is all that is necessary to drive the machines of criminology, sexology and psychoanalysis. And part of that conviction, crucially, resides in the suspicion that women are known to themselves, enigmatic only across the divide of sexual difference. In the self-knowledge of women, there is narcissism. For Freud, women could complete object-love only through having a child. Some exceptions, however, experienced object-love through self-desire. These women are of masculine type; before puberty, they feel boyish and masculine. After puberty, 'they still retain the capacity of longing for a masculine ideal – an ideal which is in fact a survival of the boyish nature they themselves once possessed' (1914: 90).

In art and popular culture since the nineteenth century, narcissism had been linked to deviance in women. Dijkstra shows how the woman who ceases to be the self-sacrificing altruist is renamed as destructive of the masculine ego. The selfish woman, the narcissist, is the one whose 'kiss in the glass' is an 'emblem of her enmity toward man, the iconic sign of her obstructive perversity' (1986: 136). Narcissism is still the mark of the deviant woman, the woman who has self-knowledge (which is obscured from men). In 1989, Sara Thornton stabbed her abusive husband to death and was convicted of murder. Earlier that evening, she had written a message to her husband in lipstick upon the bedroom mirror: 'Bastard Thornton. I hate you.'[5] (She has since been released from prison.) The message on the mirror inverts the norms of femininity: Sara Thornton used the lipstick not to rouge her mouth (in the gestures of conventional femininity), but to inscribe a message of violence to her husband. Instead of seduction, her mouth speaks violence. She writes the message on the mirror, converting its function as reflector of an image of femininity into the text through which she can communicate her hatred. When her husband looked into the mirror, he would see not himself but rather his wife, mouthing obscenities. Here Sara Thornton is portrayed by law as a woman who does not reflect man's image of her but rather reflects her own violent desires. Her mirror lacks the tain (the silvered backing that allows the glass to reflect; see also Gasche, 1986) that would give her femininity. In its place is a depthless aggression. As the agent of the message, she reveals her nature through the mirror: she is (seen as) a violent woman. The medium (the lipsticked mirror) has become the message (narcissism as mask for murderousness).[6]

5. Quoted in *R* v. *Thornton* [1992] 1 All England Reports 306 at p. 310.
6. I take the expression 'the medium has become the message' from Mackey (1991: 341).

The message on the mirror simultaneously reveals Sara Thornton as narcissistic and as deviant. Further, it is viewed within criminal law as evidence of a violent mental state. Thornton is represented as deviant not only because of this violent state of mind but also because her narcissism means that she knows herself to be violent, knows herself as a criminal. The criminal law and criminal justice system, in convicting her of murder and sentencing her to life imprisonment, represent themselves as merely responding to her nature. They react to their knowledge of her, which arrives after she had already demonstrated her own self-knowledge. The self-knowledge of the 'born criminal' and the hysterical delusion of the 'occasional offender' are crucial for the crimino-legal complex because they construct the nature of Woman as prior to any construction that criminology or law has made of her. To this extent, the machinations of the contemporary crimino-legal complex follow the same contours of an enigmatic femininity as did the criminology practised by Lombroso. Femininity is still criminology's secret, obscure and absent; yet, like all enigmas, it represents a desire: that criminology remain masculine, that femininity remain the domain of narcissism.

Criminology has, over the last two or three decades, been criticized for its baffling reluctance to relinquish its enigmas. The perpetual gender dimorphism of the crimino-legal complex has been subjected to a process of reappraisal, rewriting and, on occasion, rejection. The remainder of this chapter will examine the forms taken by this process of critique, as criminology has been brought to account by the questions of feminism. My interest is in what can be achieved for this process by an analysis which is interested in the secretion of the feminine body within the crimino-legal complex. That is, the concerns detailed in Chapter 1 – questions of imagination, of the body and of the aesthetics of everyday life – will be considered within the specific demands of the enterprise of feminist criminology. The aim is not to solve the enigma of criminology's secret(ion) of femininity, for that is an impossibility, but rather to elucidate how criminology's conception of sexual difference is structured by the vicissitudes of the secretion of femininity as enigma.

The questions of feminism

In recent years, there has been a number of stock-taking exercises which have measured the impact of feminism's advent upon various disciplines.[7] The event of taking stock acts as a reminder that feminism, like any practice or knowledge, is tied to its reception, to the response it receives. To this extent, the event of feminism is an advent, always yet-to-come. Unlike the declamations of a post-feminism, as if feminism had been and gone, feminism is a

---

7. These have included: in linguistics, Cameron (1985); in literary criticism, Pearce (1991); in philosophy, Battersby (1989) and Gatens (1991); in sociology, Game (1991); in law, Brown (1991) and Smart (1989); in criminology, Brown (1985); Gelsthorpe and Morris (1990); Naffine (1987) and Smart (1976).

practice which marks the difference between the thought of sexual difference and its realization in the world, between the event of sexual difference and its recognition. In more sociological terms, feminism has always insisted on the continuing traces of 'patriarchy' or 'phallocentrism' as that which disturbs the closure and self-satisfaction of the liberal present. Similarly, the utopia of sexual difference (as manifested in, for example, Irigaray) is one that marks within feminism the difference between the event of difference and its recognition as difference. In other words, the recognition of the difference feminism makes is always still-to-come, always yet to be instituted.

In many ways, it is thus still too soon to write a history or offer up definitions of feminism and feminist thought. As event, as advent(ure), feminism represents the means chosen by certain women to redesign their feminine condition as enigma or secret. Within this heterogeneous complex of practices and struggles, the link between theory and practice has been problematized and reconceptualized, so that feminist thought stands as an open question, from which plans for action can be drawn, without prescribing any definitive methodology. Deeply rooted in contemporary Western culture is the antinomy between 'thought' and 'the feminine' which has led to women's subjectivity still being a matter of political debate (for example, see Irigaray, 1985a). Women have traditionally been defined as suspended between matter (the body, nature, animality) and reason; rationality has been represented as an attribute which is sovereign in origin and inherited in men.[8] The belief in the natural origins of the inferiority of Woman is one of the columns which supports the masculine economy of signification.[9] It has led to the devaluation of women's intellectual faculties, creativity, imagination and thought; to the repression of their civil and political rights; to their exclusion from the places of the production and transmission of knowledge. This is not to overlook the existence of women writers, thinkers or teachers; rather, it is to argue that the canon is made masculine. By tradition, it can include no women. It legislates itself by including no women. A problem for feminists in criminology – as for any feminist approaching any canon – is how to institute women without reiterating a canonical hierarchy; that is, how to institute women *as* difference.

The constantly re-enacted incompatibility of Woman and Reason obstructs the elaboration of a feminist tradition within criminology. Every attempt will come up against a discursive mistrust within the established discipline. This is not to accuse individuals or to ignore the spaces created for feminist work. It is, however, to state, simply but insistently, that in the criminological canon, as in all such disciplines, the very idea of feminist theory seems a contradiction in terms: how could Woman elaborate a theory? Moreover, a theory which would have to be rigorous, systematic and linear? Woman, as prior to criminology and law, is the precondition (the secret) of criminology. She is not intended as a point of discursive beginning *within*

---

8. See, for example, Lloyd (1984) and Naffine (1990).
9. See further on this, Braidotti (1991) and (1994: Chapter 9); Olivier (1990).

theory. Woman, the eternal dark continent of Western culture, is the blind spot of criminological theory.[10] The criminological complex seems content to keep women in the place of beggars at the banquet, feasting on crumbs. A women's tradition seems endlessly fragmented, scattered, divided within itself – and always already devalued. And yet: feminists continue to struggle to speak and to be heard, to keep the *question* of the Other alive. Indeed, feminism, it could be argued, has not simply kept its questions alive against the disciplinary insouciance of criminology. It has rejuvenated the discipline and prevented its degeneration into a moribund exercise of technocracy and pedagogy. To take a simple example from the production of British student-oriented texts: from the first edition in 1982 to the second in 1988, Downes and Rock added a new chapter on feminism to their textbook *Understanding Deviance*. Feminist criminology is indeed a genuine innovation in the criminological complex.[11] Its addition to textbooks should be greeted with caution, however (since it bespeaks incorporation: for example, see the Oxford Handbook's chapter on 'Women': Maguire et al., 1994), but it can and should also be read productively as an emblem of feminism's great impact on criminology itself.

Within the category of 'feminism' in criminology can be found a heterogeneous collection of approaches, standpoints and perspectives. A vast amount of information has been generated about women's experiences in prison, in court, in relation to offending and so on. However, there is uncertainty as to the purposes and implications of feminist research within criminology. This is not to imply that feminists are engaged in acrimonious dispute; rather, it is to note that the increasing number of areas and types of research have produced pluralism and diversity on a grand scale. But the underlying questions of feminist intervention have not been strongly set out and the purpose of feminist research is often unclear: do feminists seek the abandonment of criminology, its reshaping or its incompleteness made complete? The next section of the chapter examines in some detail the predominant forms taken by feminism's questioning of criminology, without attempting to answer the conundrum of what feminists *desire* of criminology. Feminism's questions have generally fallen into three formations: first, the critique of the biologism that has dominated criminology's metaphorization of sexual difference; second, the allegation of gender bias or discrimination within criminology and criminal justice practice; third, the purported conformity of women in comparison with the criminality of men.

10. I use the expression 'dark continent' in order to highlight the imperialist dimension to all such blind spots. On the conjoining of sexual and racial repression, see Braidotti (1994: Chapter 1); Minh-ha (1989); Spivak (1987); Williams (1991).

11. Despite Downes and Rock's begrudging – or even patronizing? – comment as to why they included the new chapter: 'we have added a new chapter on feminist criminology and the deviance of women. Feminist sociology is beginning to make a mark and no introductory book can ignore it' (1988: viii).

Questioning biology

The critique of biologism has been crucial to the feminist intervention in all disciplines. Feminists in criminology have sought to reject biologism's determination of the feminine condition.[12] Heidensohn writes:

> What distinguishes writers on female crime is not only that they represent a particular criminological tradition, but that they seek to rationalize and to make acceptable a series of propositions about women and their consequences for criminal behaviour. Women, in this view, are determined by their biology and their physiology. Their hormones, their reproductive role, inexorably determine their emotionality, unreliability, childishness, deviousness, etc. These factors lead to female crime. (1985: 112)

This passage summarizes the main concerns of feminism with regard to biology. First, there is a tradition within criminology which deploys the notion of biology as exercising a causative influence over individuals. Second, that tradition has deleterious consequences for criminology's representation of women, since women are understood as being determined by biology in ways which make them inferior to men (making them over-emotional, unreliable, childish, devious). Its status *as* tradition means that such propositions have authority and meaning, forcing feminists to *rebut* an existing conceptualization. Third, this tradition systematizes sexual difference: its analysis of women who offend is generalized into an understanding of all women as determined by biology. Finally, its meaning comes from reference to bodily parts, organs and attributes: the male physiology is taken as the unmarked and unremarkable norm, from which the female physiology (of oestrogen, uterus, child-bearing, menopause and so on) differs radically. Within this tradition and within the feminist critique of the tradition, there resides an image of criminology as potentially open to seduction by such notions. This possibility drives both the perpetuation of biologism as an approach to the study of criminality and the continuing critical impulse in feminist research.

Feminist criticism has often directed itself against the fourth of these issues (how biologism derives its force from systematic reference to women's physiology as governing identity). However, I would argue that addressing the first and second of biologism's features should take priority in feminist criticism. It is in the shift from the first to the second that biologism exerts the greatest influence – from the proposition that biology wields power over individual actions or thought processes, to the proposition that biological sexual differences can be understood through a hierarchy of value: in this slippage lies the heart of biologism's threat to the feminist revindication of femininity. Biologism is sometimes taken as arguing that women *alone* are controlled by biological influences. However, the crimino-legal complex is inflected by an interest in biology as it pertains to both sexes. Indeed, assumptions about masculine biology, it could be said, have produced the entire system of criminal law, with its concepts of *mens rea* and the relationship between thought

12. For example, see Brown (1990); Heidensohn (1985); Klein and Kress (1976); Mukherjee and Scutt (1981); Rodwell (1981); Simpson (1989); Smart (1976).

and deed, of what it means to lose self-control, or to become insane. The problem is not that masculinity is not conceptualized by reference to biology. Rather, the problem is that masculinity's biology is not marked as masculine, but rather as the neuter, the norm (and thus its masculinity is unremarked).[13] The biology of femininity stands out in sharp relief against such a background.

Masculine biology can be identified in many of the crimino-legal complex's representations of the individual. For example, there is a commonplace assumption that men are subject to irresistible impulses and sexual drives which cause them to commit acts of violence against women.[14] These assumptions often operate to mitigate guilt or exculpate a male offender. The doctrine of provocation in criminal law, for example, has encoded a notion that men, if confronted with their wives' infidelity, will frequently act violently. If a husband kills his wife when she has committed adultery, provocation is often pleaded: for example, in *R* v. *Camplin*, Lord Diplock uses this as a paradigmatic example of a provocative situation for a man, legitimizing a lethal act as reasonable response to a woman's sexual waywardness.[15] The criminal law enshrines within it as a principle the notion of masculine anger provoked by the behaviour of women. The lack of proportionality (itself a thoroughly masculine concept) between an act of adultery and an act of homicide is not made problematic for the law, since its imbalance is based upon an evaluation of masculine reactions to feminine behaviour. Related to this is the representation of masculine (hetero)sexual desire in criminal law. Estrich describes a female potential job applicant being shown around the worksite by her potential employer. On reaching his office, he had said that he was looking for someone to have sexual intercourse with; the woman responded that she would not do so. He forced her to have intercourse with him and was later charged with rape (Estrich, 1987: 90–1). The admission in court of the defendant's stated desire to have sexual intercourse with a woman tacitly accepts the notion of the male as governed by sexual urges. Thus the law of rape – in its very rules and categories – presumes the intentionality (and naturalness) of male desire.

It is possible to imagine a different kind of criminal justice process (and feminist critiques of such events are inspired by exactly such an imagination) but a distinguishing feature of the feminist response to the biologism of the crimino-legal complex is its denunciation of criminology as biologism *tout court*. That is, criminology, within the feminist interventions which question its biological fascinations, *is* biologism, nothing more or less. Thus feminism imagines itself in relation to criminology as culture is counterposed to nature. Given this starting-point, it is easy to see why the critique of biologism tends

13. Naffine comments: 'The men who have been selected for examination . . . have ceased to be interesting as men.' Also: 'Because women are extinguished, criminology's men have no conspicuous sex at all' (forthcoming: ms pp. 13, 14).

14. For a discussion of some of these assumptions in relation to rape, see Estrich (1987); on sexual murder, see Caputi (1987), Cameron and Frazer (1987).

15. See *R* v. *Camplin* [1978] 2 All England Law Reports 168 at p. 171.

to lead feminism into wholesale denunciations of the discipline, into advocating its abandonment or its total rewriting. Concentrating on the fourth
feature of biologism – the construction of the difference represented by female
bodily parts – leads to the tracing of a trajectory from Lombroso's original
claims about his female offenders to the criminal justice system's contemporary characterizations of women in court. The feminist rejection of Lombroso
and Ferrero's research was inaugurated by Smart's discussion in *Women,
Crime and Criminology* (1976) of the early criminologists (Lombroso and
Ferrero, Pollak, Thomas).[16] She writes:

> Th[e] common stance, which unites these classical theorists even though their
> accounts of female criminality vary widely, is based upon a particular (mis)con-
> ception of the innate character and nature of women, which is in turn founded upon
> a biological determinist position. This emphasis on the determined nature of
> human behaviour is not peculiar to the discipline of criminology, nor to the study
> of women, but it is particularly pertinent to the study of female criminality because
> of the widely-held and popular belief in the non-cognitive, physiological basis of
> criminal actions by women. (1976: 27)

This version of the 'problem' attributes a mistake to the classical criminologists in their representation of women: their conception of Woman is a
'(mis)conception'; as such, all their representations of femininity are misrep-
resentations. It therefore does not matter what might be the variations in
their arguments about Woman and femininity. They are united by their common mistaking of the nature of femininity. Feminism's function is thus the
correction of this mistake, the pointing out of error. Misrepresentation, in the
law of contract, invalidates any contract that has been signed. The denunciation of classical theorists as misrepresenting Woman operates to invalidate the
contract that criminology may have made with itself over the last century.
Implicit within this move is an image of criminology as a discursive community founded upon the textual exchange of women among men. An image of
Woman – albeit a mistaken one – unifies the community of criminology.

What does it mean to assert a mistaken femininity within criminology? As
a discursive formation, criminology structures itself around a serial system of
propositions which are divided into true and false. The Lombroso-esque version of femininity told a particular story of Woman and crime; feminist
criticism has aimed at rebutting its presumptions, rejecting its premises and
rewriting a new story of femininity.[17] Unfortunately, this role requires

16. Their significant texts are: Lombroso and Ferrero (1895); Pollak (1960); Pollak and
Friedman (1969); Thomas (1967).
17. Smart's famous comment on Lombroso and Ferrero's view of female offenders is that such
women are 'doubly damned for not only are they legally sanctioned for their offences, they are
socially condemned for being biologically or sexually abnormal' (1976: 34). Brown notes that
Lombroso has often been misrepresented by feminist critics as describing all women as biologically determined: his typology of three kinds of woman, discussed by me above, interrelate
varying conceptions of femininity. Lombroso's notorious description of (born) female criminals
as monstrous ('as a double exception, the criminal woman is consequently a monster' [1895: 152])
expresses, as Brown (1990) demonstrates, the consequences of constructing Woman as ideally
non-criminal. The born female criminal deviates from the occasional female offender and again

feminism always to follow in the footsteps of Lombroso-esque criminology, protesting its authority all the time, but none the less repeatedly reciting its claims (in order to refute them). Thus, Lombroso-esque criminology lives on in its *reception* into contemporary feminist criticism as *mistake*. Feminism has thus inverted the relationship between biologism and femininity. Where femininity lived in biologism as a (mistaken) story told by classical criminologists and rehearsed in contemporary criminal justice and law, now classical biologism lives on in feminism as a (mistaken) tale of femininity.

Questioning discrimination

This strategy of feminist critical intervention in the crimino-legal complex in many ways acts as a logical extension of the critique of biologism.[18] That is, where criminological theory was denounced for its mistaken characterization of female offenders (and femininity in general), criminal justice practice is here appraised for its inequitable treatment of female offenders (often based upon conceptions of femininity deriving from classical criminology). While the feminist strategy as regards biologism has been to assert mistake, and thus inadvertently to reiterate its claims, here the critical move is to note bias. As with any such anti-discrimination programme, the problem is an unclear *telos*: does feminism seek parity of treatment for female offenders with men? Or, does it seek a reconsideration of the relationship between masculinity and femininity within criminal justice practice?

Various strategies are deployed in the diagnosis of discrimination. First, there is the assertion that criminology has by tradition omitted the experiences, needs, desires and behaviours of women, in comparison with its fascination with the masculine counterparts. The claim about omission can only be made *relative* to criminology's treatment of men. If the assertion of omission were taken literally, this would mean that there is no mention of femininity or female offenders in, for example, Lombrosian criminology. Omission here means instead that the amount of space devoted to femininity is comparatively small. Femininity is not a lack or absence in criminology; it is rather relatively under-represented. Thus Millman writes: 'Since there haven't been many sociologists who take note of women as deviants, women have largely been ignored in the literature or else abandoned to a few deviant

from the ideal law-abiding woman. Her doubled criminality was necessary to give meaning to the two other typologies in Lombroso's schema: the law-abiding woman and her near counterpart, the occasional offender.

18. Many of the criticisms levelled at Lombroso-esque criminology fall into the anti-discrimination category: Lombrosian theory and its derivations were often regarded as biased in their persistent association of Woman with biology as compared to the unmarked nature of masculine biology. Heidensohn implies as much: 'Far from being swamped by the modern tides which have long washed away biological determinism these ideas have flourished in their intellectual rockpools, amazing examples of survival. Neo-Lombrosian studies of girl-delinquents were still being carried out in the 1970s, prostitution was still seen often as evidence of individual psychopathology rather than as a rational economic choice for women in the 1980s . . .' (1985: 113). The implication is clear: men are not treated *in the same way*.

categories (mental illness, prostitution, shoplifting) hard to glamorize (with the potential exception of prostitution) the way male deviant occupations are glamorized' (1975: 258). The relativity of omission is in the consignment of women to 'a few deviant categories' or in the literature's 'largely' ignoring them. The implication of this argument moves for completeness: criminology must discover all the categories that *could* apply to women (which may or may not be all the categories that exist); the deviant occupations of women and men must receive full attribution of glamour (or not at all); women's absence must be corrected so that they are fully present in the literature.

The second major critical strategy is the depiction of discrimination through bias; that is, even when women are present in the crimino-legal complex, their categorization is made dependent on a series of discriminatory practices. These practices are different from those applied to male offenders. Smart, for example, links bias in criminal justice to bias in law: 'Where the law can be seen to discriminate against women it is an inevitable consequence that the administration and enforcement of the law will reflect this lack of impartiality' (1976: 128). Bias is the quintessential lack of impartiality. Its definition as partial implies not only its slanted attributions of value to one group or individual as opposed to another, but also its incompleteness (thus creating the space for criticisms about bias as omission and omission as bias). Smart also comments on 'the influence of the traditional double standard of morality' and the 'commonly held belief that deviancy by a female is a sign of a much greater pathology than deviancy by a male' (1976: 132, 133). Discrimination arguments depend on notions such as the doubling of standards and their consequent separation for deployment against different individuals or groups. Discrimination can also be a matter of degree: criminal justice is being criticized for seeing women offenders as *more* pathological than male offenders, instead of positing an equivalence of deviation for all individuals who break the law.

Feminist critics have analysed every aspect of criminal justice practice in order to discover the nature and scope of potential and actual discrimination against women. Much research has been carried out on the sentencing of offenders, perhaps because the moment of sentencing tangibly suspends the entire process of criminal justice for inspection.[19] Farrington and Morris carried out a study in the United Kingdom which examined the sentences for theft in almost 400 cases (in which 108 involved female offenders). They argued that any lighter sentences received by women (in comparison with men) were the result of their differing circumstances, as interpreted by the judge. They stated that women seemed to benefit from lenient treatment 'only because they had committed less serious offences and were less likely to have been convicted previously' (1983: 245). However, they also asserted that unmarried women (single, divorced, separated women) received relatively severe sentences, implying that the judiciary deployed these more severe sen-

19. See, for example, Eaton (1986, 1987); Farrington and Morris (1983); Green (1961); Knuttschnitt (1982); Nagel and Weitzman (1972); Pope (1975); Rottman and Simon (1975).

tences as symbols of their disapproval for whatever role the women played in
the breakdown, failure or absence of a marital relationship. Eaton's research
on a London court supported and extended this view. She states:

> Throughout the process of summary justice a model of the family is employed
> when dealing with both men and women defendants. This model, with a male
> breadwinner and a dependent woman, is used in pleas of mitigation and social
> inquiry reports. . . . Of course the courts do not question the gender roles of women
> within the family – these are accepted as normal and natural. (1987: 106–7)

Carlen's (1987) research on women's imprisonment also asserted that women
were being imprisoned more as punishment for the type of woman they were
than for the particular crimes they had committed, with single mothers, prostitutes and poor women receiving harsh sentences. These studies refuted the
simplistic view of biased sentencing which, in the 1970s, tended to accept the
notion of judicial chivalry towards female defendants.[20]

In studies of women's imprisonment, bias and omission are depicted as discrimination's dominant manifestations.[21] Dobash et al. comment:
'Revisionists' accounts such as those of Foucault, Ignatieff and Rothman
seldom if ever consider the possibility that patriarchal and gender-based
assumptions might have played a role in the development of modern prisons'
(1986: 9). Thus women are said to be omitted from the history of the prison.
Within prisons, women prisoners received treatment that was inspired by discriminatory theories about the nature of their criminality. Dobash et al. write:

> Until recently, contemporary British research on women in prison was dominated
> by bio-psychological perspectives about women and girls. They are more likely
> than male prisoners to be seen as low in intelligence, maladjusted, emotionally dis-
> turbed and in need of psychological and psychiatric intervention. . . . [T]his
> approach is not some vestige of an earlier era predating contemporary feminist and
> critical analysis. It is still very much apparent. (1986: 6)

As correctives to endemic discrimination through bias and omission in criminal justice treatment, two main approaches are advocated. The first is that of
painstaking historicism (manifested in, for example, Dobash et al., 1986 and
Zedner, 1991) whereby the *reality* of women's experiences can be drawn out
from the archive and made present in criminology. The second is that of phe-
nomenological ethnography, in which life stories, autobiography and personal
reminiscence are given heuristic force in the explanation of discrimination in
the criminal justice system. Carlen et al. write: 'about four criminal *women*,
whose stories are important primarily because they deny the existence of the
criminal *woman*' (1985: 10; emphasis in original). In a later essay, Carlen
gives voice to 'twenty-two young working-class women': 'what follows is a
theoretical commentary on the women's own vivid accounts of how they had

---

20. See, for example, Nagel and Weitzman, who write: 'There exists a paternalistic protec-
tiveness, at least towards white women, that assumes they need sheltering from manly experiences
such as jail and from subjection to the unfriendliness of overly formal proceedings' (1972: 180).

21. As described in: Rafter (1985); Carlen (1983); Carlen et al. (1985); Dobash et al. (1986);
Haft (1980); O'Dwyer et al. (1987); Zedner (1991).

set about making their own lives in conditions that had certainly not been of their own choosing' (1987: 131).

Such a strategy seems double-edged. Its productive force is in the assertion of story-telling as radical resistance to the discursive story-telling of the discipline of criminology. The individual life story, as told by the individual woman, is presented as the antidote to the governmental and all-encompassing generalizations of criminology's stories *about* women. Further, the stories are narratives in denial of the truth-claiming narratives of criminology. As such, they act as profoundly anti-essentialist devices in the elaboration of a feminist analysis of femininity and crime. However, there is a great deal of violence in such a strategy, particularly in its deployment of each woman's tale as part of a theoretical project. Their life stories take on meaning only as a theoretical end and only as tactics in the anti-essentialist enterprise. They become reduced to instances, open to interpretation. The problem for feminist intervention lies in the slippage between the stories as allegories of events and the stories as epistemologies of femininity. In the desire to resist the tall tales of criminology's femininity, feminism can lapse into its own grand narrative of the individual woman, the life history, the femininity that lies (always) elsewhere.

The defining trope of the anti-discrimination move in feminist criticism is the tension between the concept of equality (which presupposes sameness) and the concept of sex (which presupposes difference). Sex equality – which, at base, is what is impliedly desired by many of the critiques – is thus a contradiction in terms, an oxymoron. This problematic is often not addressed, as studies return again and again to the disquieting discriminations in the treatment of male and female offenders. The impasse might be resolved by relinquishing the notion of *sex* discrimination and replacing it with an analysis of *gender* discrimination. Gender is made meaningful by reference to models, forms and roles; categories that describe the shapes of sexual difference and the relationships between masculine and feminine. These forms and models are employed by the criminal justice system to make sense of the shifting categories it identifies in the individuals who pass through it. Eaton (1986), for example, emphasizes the 'model' of the family employed by summary justice; Farrington and Morris (1983) note the consequences of failing at marital roles. The models identified by criminal justice are imposed upon the individuals within the system. In short, 'gender' is used as a mode of epistemological determinism. That is, there is a continuity between the abstract epistemological categories and the concrete practices of criminal justice. What is crucial is their *imposition* on the subjects of criminal justice: a match between individual and 'gender' is made by force. Discrimination is thus as axiomatic for criminal justice as it is for any system of representation, in which individuals are made to own an image of themselves. Images of identity can take shape through gender, race, age, health, nation and so on (and subsequent chapters will elaborate some instances of how this takes place). Feminist critiques of discrimination in criminology tend to locate the gap crucial to their arguments between male and female, when it lies between identity and subjectivity instead.

Questioning conformity

The crimino-legal tradition, particularly as manifested in criminology and the sociology of deviance, is all about 'social order', or conformity to social norms. That is, criminology as a normative discourse is a discourse on conformity. Within feminist debates on women and crime, the 'conformity' that is the object of discussion is not just conformity to the rules of the social order but also to the rules of gender. Thus two forms of conformity are intertwined, since obeying the dictates of gender identity also follows the rules of the social order. To break the rules of the social order can involve a departure from the norms of gender identity. Conformity is the antithesis of criminology's object of study, crime. Conformity has figured within criminological debate as the phenomenon which by virtue of its oppositional status can inform about the nature of crime. Criminology has been fascinated with the distinction that the discipline enforces between law-abiders and law-breakers. The notion of conformity demands attention for its possessing a group of individuals (those who obey the law) who are impliedly excluded from criminological concern. Their function is to reflect the nature and shape of the criminal. They also constitute the body of the victim of crime (as mentioned in Chapter 1; see also the analysis in Chapter 3).

Since conformity represents one of the teleological aims of criminology, it invites consideration: criminology seeks to discover what it is that conformity represents to those who do not break the law. Toby (1957: 516), for example, studied the extent to which different individuals have a 'stake in conformity', arguing that an upper-class, white, Anglo-Saxon Protestant schoolchild is heavily predisposed to have a high stake in conformity. In parallel fashion, 'those who are reared in a milieu indifferent to education are not likely to acquire a high evaluation of it' (Hagan, 1987: 172). Such an individual's stake in conformity is thought likely to be diminished and their chances of criminality more pronounced. Versions of arguments such as these have recently resurfaced in governmental debates on family background and criminality in children, with single mothers being singled out for criticism as criminogenic (see Chapter 6). Feminist criticism in this area has centred upon the persistent tendency in criminology to associate femininity with conformity. Masculinity remains unmarked to the extent that conformity to the law can appear a natural aspect of masculinity; whereas forms of law-breaking have become such a naturalized feature of representations of masculinity that no gender interpretation is required. For example, the violent responses of some men to the suspicion or discovery of their female partner's infidelity have become increasingly viewed as the normal behaviour of a 'betrayed' man.[22] Within the

22. See, for example, the recent English case of Alan Hunt, who strangled his wife during an argument in their car. She had been attempting to get out of the car; he said he tried to 'restrain' her. He was convicted of manslaughter and given a suspended sentence (unreported, see press coverage in November 1994). In another English case, Roy Greech (who stabbed, strangled and beat his wife to death when he overheard her speaking on the telephone to her lover) was found guilty of manslaughter by reason of provocation (unreported; see press coverage in March 1994).

notion of conformity, there is inscribed a system of gender differentiation which enables defendants to be judged for their identity as much as for or instead of the crime that they may have committed. To that extent, the question must be asked whether defendants are found guilty of the crime charged or of the betrayal of their gender.[23]

The notion of female conformity to legal rules is taken as a given starting-point in much of criminology. For example, Hagan states:

> When it comes to criminal forms of deviance, men clearly exceed women. . . . This does not mean that the relationship between gender and criminality is a simple one: the disparity between the sexes varies with the class of crime, time and social setting. . . . Nonetheless, we can begin secure in the assumption that today men in North America are significantly more likely to be involved in the more serious forms of crime. (1987: 267)

Smart comments that 'official statistics consistently provide us with the information that not only are female offenders fewer than male offenders but also that female offenders are, in almost all cases, a tiny minority' (1976: 2). Those writing in the name of feminism often begin from the same proposition. Thus, Heidensohn writes: 'In fact, some women can and do commit offences of the same kind as men, save where legal and technical barriers exist, but they do so in very much smaller numbers, at less serious levels and far less often' (1985: 12).[24] To the extent that this has been regarded as a symptom of conformity, it has been explained by reference, first, to the power of sex-role prescription and, second, to the power of social control.

That most women do adopt their ascribed sex roles has been accepted (albeit for a range of reasons). Heidensohn (1985: 106) notes that the overwhelming majority of women marry and most become mothers. This type of argument appears to take statistics (such as those relating to the decisions of women to marry or to have children) as unquestioned evidence of the realization of sexual differentiation in the world. That is, statistics such as these are held to prove that sex roles are realized in the social world in a manner which proves its division along lines of gender. Such use of statistical evidence accompanies the type of epistemological determinism discussed above in relation to arguments on discrimination, in which gender identities are imputed to and imposed upon individuals. In those debates, the gap between identity as ascribed identity and identity as experienced is not questioned. Here, there is no investigation of the gap between, for example, marriage as an act and marriage as a role or belief.[25]

The popularity of sex role as an explanation of conformity has extended

23. This is my argument in 'Femininity as marginalia: conjugal homicide and the judgement of sexual difference' (forthcoming), which analyses the cases of Sara Thornton and Kiranjit Ahluwalia through their gender(ed) identities.

24. Self-report studies, whether carried out as an alternative or supplement to the official statistics, frequently seemed to confirm these figures: for example, see Smith and Visher (1980).

25. Oakley (1974, 1980) argues that stereotypes of feminine behaviour are extremely powerful, compelling identification with them by most women, even while they might resent aspects of them.

into accounts of women's criminality, so that crimes deemed 'unusual' for a woman (hence, unfeminine) may be rationalized by reference to sex role in, for example, the choice of weapon employed.[26] In recent cases of murder by women (a crime conventionally and statistically associated with men rather than women), the weapons used and the locations of the homicides were suitably 'domestic' (and thus sex-role specific). Kiranjit Ahluwalia threw petrol from a small bucket to set her husband alight as he slept in their bed; Sara Thornton used a kitchen knife to stab her husband on the sofa; Amelia Rossiter stabbed her husband with a steak knife, following an argument as they washed and dried dishes together.[27] For women who kill, committing homicide within the home is taken as confirming a general paradox about femininity: women are less likely to kill because they are more likely to spend their time fulfilling their sex role by cooking, cleaning and shopping for their partners; however, since when they do kill it is done within the same sex-role context, their sex role cannot be taken as a thoroughly benign one (for it brings them into everyday contact with the places and means for committing domestic homicide). To claim that the feminine sex role is understood as one of conformity does not convey the complexity of its representation, which incorporates benevolence and dangerousness into one ambiguous figure: the wife-and-mother.

Debates on social control have provided the occasion for interrogating conformity as an epistemological category as well as a sociological variable. In respect of the latter, Simpson argued that deterrence, as a mechanism of social control, needs to be studied in the light of female conformity, thus raising the question whether women conform to legal and social codes as a result of successful deterrence or as the result of some innate obedience (or, alternatively, whether deterrence is more successful with women due to some innate or essential receptiveness to suggestion) (Simpson, 1989).[28] Hagan regards feminine conformity as a consequence of the gendered division of social pleasure:

> Crime and delinquency can be fun . . . – and perhaps even more important, a type of fun that is infrequently allowed to women. One reason why delinquency is fun is that it anticipates a range of activities, some having to do with criminal and others having to do with conventional occupations, that are more open to males than females. (1987: 271)

From this starting-point, he offers a series of propositions: that risk-taking is seen less positively by women than by men; that crime and delinquency are viewed less positively by women than by men; women are therefore less likely than men to be involved in criminal behaviour than men. Naffine demon-

---

26. Smart (1976: 67) states that women often murder in a sex-specific way: for example, by using a knife rather than a gun, by killing in the home rather than in the street.

27. See *R* v. *Ahluwalia* [1992] 4 All England Reports 789; *R* v. *Thornton* [1992] 2 All England Reports 306; *R* v. *Rossiter* [1994] 2 All England Reports 752.

28. On conformity configured, either explicitly or implicitly, as an inherent aspect of femininity, see Hagan et al. (1979); LaGrange and Ferraro (1989).

strates the circular nature of much criminological theorizing about women, crime and conformity: '"Masculinity theory" asserts that women are less likely to engage in criminal activity because they are not men' (1987: 43).

In Carlen's study of property crimes by women, she discovered offences being committed for reasons which ranged from poverty to excitement in the kick offered by illicit activities (Carlen, 1988). Hagan's starting-point ('Crime and delinquency can be fun . . . ') may be less an analysis of the gendered division of pleasure than the gendered construction of types of pleasure as masculine or feminine. Women are not supposed to derive pleasure from illegal activity, which conforms more, in its supposed sensations, to the masculine thrills of adrenaline and risk-taking. Vicarious pleasure is permitted, however: Chapter 4 of this book examines the consumption of detective fiction, a genre marketed as much to women, through the development of feisty female detectives, as to men. Hagan's supposition also operates as a criminological version of Gilligan's arguments about women's particular forms of morality, with their configurations of a 'generalized and concrete Other' which always take the shape of Woman.[29] Thus, in reviews of a film which portrayed two women operating together outside the masculine symbolic order represented by law and family – *Thelma and Louise* – the protagonists were criticized for being masculine versions of women (that is, *not-women*). Reviewers commented that Thelma and Louise were 'free to behave, well, like men' (*Time*, 24 June 1991); or that 'the good ol' boys are gals' who are 'parodies of men' (*America*, 29 June 1991). The flight that structures the film is a flight not only from the law and from the family, but also from conventional representations of femininity, signified in the characters' gradual divestment of their cosmetics, their jewellery and their 'pretty' clothes.[30] The spectacle of women engaged in the reinvention of their identities and in the commission of various criminal activities (from which, excepting the murder which occasions their flight, they derive great satisfaction and pleasure) was interpreted as women acting like men. Arguments such as Hagan's, which assume that pleasure in the illicit cannot be experienced by women in the same way as men, reinforce criminology's construction of Woman as exception to the masculine law.

The study of conformity presents what can be summed up as one major danger for feminist intervention in criminological configurations of femininity. That is, conformity is coming to be viewed as the location of femininity in the crimino-legal complex.[31] Heidensohn writes: 'We needed to explain female conformity as much, *if not more than*, female deviance in looking at female criminality. Criminologists have, in general, looked too little at conformity,

29. See Gilligan (1982); also Benhabib (1987).

30. Hart (1994: 67–80) provides an illuminating analysis of the film and the reviewers' reactions to it. On the implications of the film for a feminist analysis of law, see Spelman and Minow (1992).

31. Naffine notes this in criminology: 'women have become the aberrant group, even when compared with an aberrant group (and found to display non-aberrant behaviour)' (forthcoming: ms p. 10).

but this neglect is striking with regard to women' (1985: 174; my emphasis). This statement may well be based on a desire to invert the emphasis, taken as conventional since Lombroso's time, on Woman's inherent deviance. However, to call for a feminist investigation of women's conformity colludes with the criminological canon's acceptance of feminine conformity as natural and self-evident. Ironically, the feminist demand for an investigation of conformity overlooks criminology's readiness to accept women as more conformist than men. In criminological terms, such conformity demonstrates Woman's inherent deviance: her repeated and irrevocable difference from the masculine. Naffine writes: 'Even law-abiding women are deficient men' (forthcoming: ms p. 11). Deviance is a relational concept; one can only deviate *from* something. Feminine conformity may demonstrate adherence to the law, but it also proves deviance from the masculine. Associating the feminine with conformity locates Woman as Other, underlines her waywardness and reconstitutes her (again) as enigma.

Sexual difference as the question of feminism

Feminist intervention in criminology has tended to follow one or more of the three forms of questioning that I have outlined above. That is, criminology is criticized for its biologism, for its discriminatory practices and for its lack of attention to the issue of conformity. It is my suggestion in this chapter that the question of feminism exceeds all of these three forms of critique. Further, what is problematic in criminology's representation of femininity exceeds those criticisms that have been made of it. The problem with criminology is never simply its representations of Woman as biologically determined, or as unequal to men, or as innately law-abiding (and therefore uninteresting). Rather, the problem of criminology is one of sexual difference, in that Woman is required to function as the abyss against which masculinity can be comprehended. In the remainder of this chapter, I will offer a reading of sexual difference in criminology, drawing on the notion, proposed at the beginning of the chapter, that Woman is constituted as the enigma of criminology.

Femininity, for criminology, is both known and unknown, as a consequence of its being produced as a symptom of the metaphorization of sexual difference. Sexual difference is metaphorized within and through a series of binary oppositions. Cixous writes: 'The (political) economy of the masculine and the feminine is organized by different requirements and constraints, which, when socialized and metaphorized, produce signs, relationships of power, relationships of production and reproduction, an entire immense system of cultural inscription readable as masculine and feminine.' Some of these metaphorized signs and relationships of power include 'Activity/Passivity, Sun/Moon, Culture/Nature, Father/Mother, Logos/Pathos, Intelligible/Sensible, Head/Emotions' (in Cixous and Clément, 1986: 63). Criminology responds to these metaphors by reading them as evaluations of the difference between masculinity and femininity. Thus, when addressing itself to the question of sexual difference (that is, when addressing itself to the enigma of femininity, since masculinity is not viewed as part of sexual difference), criminology reads Woman within such a system of metaphors and associations. Its studies of femininity can be read as contributions to the metaphorization of femininity as Other. As a symptom of sexual difference, femininity is unknowable, but criminology has reconfigured this to mean 'unknown'. The history of criminology takes place through a struggle to know the unknowable. The impossibility of this project (masculinity is the only knowable term of the couplet of sexual difference) means all that can be achieved is the underwriting of femininity's condition as unknown. Criminological knowledge of Woman exists only to deny her knowability.

As symptom and enigma, Woman must be criminology's secret. Since secrets can be volatile and unstable, Woman must be located somewhere that is easily controlled. Criminology's secretion of Woman locates her in a closet. Thus, Woman can be found in criminology's ghettos, its textbook chapters on 'gender' or 'women', its acknowledgement of feminist theory as an approach (rather than a comment on its foundational authority, system of organization and structures of knowledge).[32] The closet in which Woman has been secreted allows criminology to control any impact that feminism might have upon the self-authorization of the discipline. I use the term 'closet' deliberately, to connote the fabled location of the homosexual in the heterosexual cultural unconscious. The closet can function as a place of refuge from the violence of heterosexuality, but can more often act as the place into which the homosexual is forced in order to survive. Sedgwick (1990: 80) has described the cultural potency of the homosexual's 'coming out' of the closet as a moment of revelation that surpasses all others, being founded upon the disruption of the interlocutor's fantasy that the gay or lesbian individual is heterosexual. For Woman, criminology's closet may hold its attractions (feminists are permitted to write articles about women, to give papers at conferences, to teach 'women and crime' courses). However, its repressive effects should outweigh any of its limited pleasures.

The paradox of the closet is that whatever has been secreted within it will manifest itself beyond the closet's boundaries. Criminology exists in a constant state of struggle with Woman, continually returning her to the closet from where traces of her repression trickle out, demanding attention. Woman is constantly 'coming out' through feminist interventions in the discipline, which, in turn, is compelled to return Woman to its closet. Cupboards and closets are places where secrets are hidden and where their traces are found. The skeleton in the cupboard is the guilty secret that can bring downfall, the trace of a prior violence, the evidence of a crime. Woman acts as a constant reminder to criminology of a discursive violence that is expressed through sexual difference, and in which criminology is complicit. To erase femininity utterly might be criminology's secret desire, but it cannot afford such an act

32. For example, see Downes and Rock (1988), who add 'feminist criminology' in one chapter towards the end of the book; see also the strategy of Maguire et al. in the *Oxford Handbook of Criminology* (1994), which is to include a chapter on 'Women' close to the end of the book.

of total violence (not through any compassion for Woman, but rather since she is essential to the meaning of masculinity). Instead, it moves towards her erasure, while simultaneously permitting her continuation, closeted and enigmatic. Femininity's complex and contradictory status is to be simultaneously prohibited and essential. In this condition, femininity gives meaning to masculinity (which is represented in criminology through the mark of neutrality or sexlessness).

My argument is therefore that the enigma of Woman in criminology can only be understood through her configuration as a *category*. That is, sexual difference in criminology is a question of the symbolic. Criminology, as a modernist discourse, is marked at the level of its self-representation as a symbolic structure.[33] Its symbolism proceeds most often through notions of science, calculation, technique. Garland writes that criminology is about 'everything that might scientifically be said about crime and criminals' (1994: 37); while Rock considers criminology as 'marked by a drift towards normal science' (1988: 198).[34] What is ignored in the scientistic technocracy of criminology is the symbolic structuring of the discipline. The purpose of this chapter (and others in this book) is to explore how, at the level of criminology's symbolic structure (its claim to knowledge), the question of sexual difference is converted into Woman as enigma or secret. Whether given presence in the form of Lombroso's phrenological discourse, or ignored in typologies or theories, the enigmatic secretion of Woman means that criminology is filled with myriad signs and traces of femininity. The most marked of these is criminology's entire self-constitution as (gender-)neutral.

To the extent that I have argued for a feminist analysis of criminology's symbolic structure, I am drawing on and developing the concerns posed in Chapter 1. I argued there that our understanding of crime is a consequence of our imagination of crime; that the body of criminology is in crisis; and that crime and criminology as an aspect of everyday life is experienced through their images. In concluding my reading of criminology's secretion of Woman, I would argue that her condition as enigma results from criminology's imagining of itself as a science within and through a system of cultural inscription whose images mark out the boundary between the real and the 'reality effect' (see also Chapter 1). On the 'reality effect', Barthes writes: 'the very absence of the signified, to the advantage of the referent alone, becomes the very signifier of realism: the *reality effect* is produced, the basis of that unavowed verisimilitude which forms the aesthetic of all the standard works of modernity' (1986: 148; emphasis in original). Within those 'standard works' can be found the discipline of criminology. It therefore becomes less important for feminism to point out that criminology's images of Woman are not 'real' than to investigate their influence and impact as 'realistic'. It is in the received

---

33. On the modernism of criminology, see Henry and Milovanovic (1993, 1994); Morrison (1994).

34. I am grateful to Ngaire Naffine's most recent work (forthcoming) for drawing my attention to these statements.

plausibility and persuasiveness of the image of Woman that power resides. The reality effect of femininity in criminology (made comprehensible through delimitations such as 'statistically insignificant', 'more law-abiding', 'physiologically different') draws upon commonplaces which have been given currency in everyday life. Manifestations of sexual difference, their metaphors and evaluations, are masks with which we are immensely comfortable. Their status as images is made less apparent through the conflation of the real with that which seems real. Thus, criminology does not need to trouble itself with questioning sexual difference, since its masks of femininity seem legible and sensible. The demands and questions of feminism take place within a hierarchy of truths, and are viewed as arguments, as politics, or simply as bias. Feminism is thus always on the defensive against imputations of such bias, such perspectivism, while criminology's generalizations proceed unmarked by sexual difference or by the hierarchy of narratives.

With an investigation of the image of sexual difference in criminology, comes, following Benjamin, a return to the senses, to the body as that which is repressed, buried, lost. Within the realm of bodily senses there occurs the constitution of the body as sexed. The sexed body is always double, split by the regime of sexual difference. The feminine body is always that which interrupts, which breaks through the smooth surface of the neutral mask of the masculine. Kristeva (1984) would describe the feminine as the *chora*, the space within the domain of the symbolic structure in which the repressed semiotic sense is heard. As I have put it in this chapter, the feminine is the enigmatic, to be repressed and decoded simultaneously. The body of criminology – apparent in its images of the offender (the 'kick' of criminality), in its theories of criminality (the masculine bonding of teenage subcultural studies), in its hermetic self-congratulation (evidenced in its most recent 'handbook')[35] – represents only the impoverished imagination of the masculine-made-neutral. To describe the body of criminology thus is not to denigrate the masculine; rather, my purpose is to criticize the discursive violence that results when the masculine version of the sexed and doubled body is made One, made singular and sufficient, made neutral.

There is no doubt that this chapter could be read as a call to abandon the criminological field, given its unremitting 'sexism' and closeted categorization of Woman. I would like, however, to end by suggesting a more productive reading of my argument. The 'object' of this analysis is criminological thought. I have not, though, offered a criminological reading of criminology. Reading criminology non-criminologically is a strategy that might be named 'postmodernist' and 'feminist'. Such a strategy of reading has benefits. First, rather than achieving the extension of criminology (in imperialist fashion, criminology wants to explain – to own – everything, even itself), criminology is instead rendered finite and limited. It is made responsible – that is, subject to others. Second, by rendering criminology limited, the question of feminism (that is, of sexual difference) becomes *heard otherwise*. Feminism and sexual

---

35. See Maguire et al. (1994).

difference are no longer reduced to the inscriptions of their criminological masks. They are no longer reduced to the level of a problem to be solved (or an enigma to be decoded). Third, the question of feminism as sexual difference can then be advanced. It becomes possible, at last, as that which is yet-to-come. The advent(ure) of feminism asks: *what are we becoming, otherwise?*

3

The Universal Victim and the Body in Crisis

The crisis within the crimino-legal tradition has been underpinned by the loss of limits, horizons and certainties occasioned by ultramodernity. In such a situation, attention has been turned toward the figure of the *victim*, who offers us a kind of certainty against such loss of limits. The victim asssures us that there is an end to the loss of faith, that there is a point beyond which nihilism will not go. The victim offers up the finality of reality, the term that secures and determines the value of the real. In this chapter, I will investigate some of the recent popular criminological interest in the victim, notably that displayed by realist criminology. My aim is to offer a nuanced reading of the crimino-legal crisis and to consider then how the concept of the victim, and the concomitant notion of *sacrifice*, might help us to understand three manifestations of crisis: first, the representation of crime as an *urban* problem; second, the question of the home as emotional space and the representation of crime as the responsibility of the *gendered* body; third, the representation of the nation as victim and representations of the threat of the *racial* body. What each of these has in common with the other is their critical status; that is, their problematization as bodily *limits*. Such manifestations of crisis are linked by their attaching to the body as a site of contestation and by the notion of boundaries and borders within space. The result might be a crimino-legal aesthetic of the body and its emotions.

The universal victim

In the early hours of 30 August 1974, local residents in Station Road, Gloucester, called the police to make a complaint about noise in the street. They set off a chain of events which led to Henson George Venna's conviction, three months later, of threatening behaviour contrary to s. 5 of the Public Order Act 1936 and of assault occasioning actual bodily harm. Venna appealed against conviction and the judgement of the Criminal Division of the Court of Appeal was read by Lord Justice James: Venna and four other men were 'creating a disturbance in the public street by shouting and singing and dancing. At one stage there was a banging of dustbin lids.'[1] After 'at least

---

1. [1975] All England Reports 788 at p. 790. All subsequent page references to this report will be in the main text. This case, and some of the later arguments of this chapter, featured in an earlier article written with Peter Rush: see Young and Rush (1994). As ever, I am indebted to Peter Rush for his insightful views on this argument.

one complaint' was made by the local residents to the police, an officer named Leach was sent to investigate the disturbance. The court said that 'Leach patiently and tactfully tried to persuade the four youths to be quiet and to go home.' The result is tersely described as 'a remark by Robinson [one of Venna's companions]: "Fuck off."' The singing and dancing continued. Leach informed them of the complaint about noise, whereupon Robinson stopped singing and dancing and stood apart quietly. Leach warned Venna and the others that arrest was imminent if they did not quieten down. One, Allison, sat down 'in defiance' on the pavement. Leach placed his hand on Allison's shoulder and announced that all five men were thereupon under arrest.

Allison began struggling to free himself, while Venna and the others tried to pull him from Leach's grip. Leach, meanwhile, called for help on his radio. A scuffling fight began. According to the judgement, the scene was such that watching taxi drivers were about to intervene. One passer-by, referred to as 'the fat man', did intervene on Leach's behalf. Other officers arrived and assisted Leach in overpowering Venna and his companions. Venna 'fought so violently that four officers were required to restrain him'. While two police officers held his arms, he kicked another officer; Venna is described by the court as 'lashing out wildly with his legs', causing 'a fracture of a bone' in the hand of the officer. This kick and its injury constituted the assault with which he was charged and convicted. His appeal failed, with Lord Justice James stating: 'The whole incident leading to the charges was, unfortunately, a very ordinary and all too common one. On any view, the appellant and his friends were behaving in an unruly and disgraceful anti-social manner, but it was not a very grave or serious incident' (p.790). In this 'all too common' event, Venna becomes a surrogate for the punishment of all the others who participate in rowdiness. The victims of this common form of criminality are those in whose name Venna is made responsible: first, the police officer who suffers a broken bone; second, the local residents whom the judgement describes as being 'disturbed' (p. 790) (in short, a community). The strategies used by law, criminal justice and criminology to demarcate those who are victimized – here, the injured police officer, the local residents, the 'fat man', the assisting police officers – are important for their role in the delineation of boundaries. The possession of status as a victim means that one cannot be a criminal. Interest in victimization has been so intense that the position of the criminal has become occluded. The criminal is neccessarily sacrificed in order to give the victim such a prominent significance. Such a sacrifice is symptomatic of the contemporary crisis in the crimino-legal tradition. The following sections of this chapter elucidate, first, the parameters of the recent criminological interest in victimization; and second, three critical manifestations of crisis in law, criminal justice and criminology.

Victimization has become an increasingly prominent theme in contemporary criminological writing.[2] One of the most notable exponents of this recent

---

2. For example, as the focus of reflective debate in Elias (1990, 1993); Maguire and Pointing (1989); Walklate (1989).

interest in victimization has been the (left) realist genre of criminology.[3] For realist criminology, the central object to be investigated is 'crime' – an object which takes the realist not so much to the figure of the criminal but to a portrait of the victim. The first section of this chapter follows the contours of the victim as assembled in realist criminological writings. I will then argue that the apparent universalism of the victim is a response to a crisis in late modernity – that of social responsibility – and that realist criminology creates the figure of the universal victim against a backdrop of social justice in the city. The chapter will then proceed to examine two other manifestations of social crisis – those of domestic responsibility and national responsibility. It will be my suggestion that these three representations of crisis should be understood through a notion of sacrifice, a sacrifice that attaches to the physical body.

Visualizing the victim in realist criminology

Realism promises to criminology the capture of the criminal process in its totality (investigation, arrest and trial, judgement). Jones et al. write: 'Criminology must embrace the totality of the criminal process: it must be true to its *reality*' (1986: 3; emphasis in original).[4] What is crucial here is not so much the investment in the real, but the desire to constitute the real as a total, continuous and homogeneous system. In short, it is not the real of the criminal process which is at issue, but its real*ism*. Such a displacement of the real by realism is done for good reason. It makes possible an isomorphic relation between the criminal process and criminology (such an isomorphism is of course impossible, but its envisioning is none the less extremely seductive). This is entirely consonant with the structuralism which underpins realist criminology. As Young notes, realism constructs a 'square of crime' which formally 'consists of two dyads, a *victim* and an *offender*, and of *actions* and *reactions*: of crime and its control. This deconstruction gives us four definitional elements of crime: a victim, an offender, formal control and informal control' (1992: 27; emphasis in original).[5] These four elements constitute the systematized reality of the criminal process which is then subdivided into two sets of opposing couples: the couplet of crime (offender and victim) and the couplet of control (state and informal social control). This, then, is all there is and all that can be said. The criminologist *must not* say more because the criminologist *cannot* say more. It is this doubled prohibition which accounts for the now-familiar claustrophobia of structuralism. Within this

3. As representative, see Crawford et al. (1990); Jones et al. (1986); Kinsey et al. (1986); Lea and Young (1984); Painter (1989); Painter et al. (1989); Young (1987); Young and Matthews (1992).

4. Note how a shaky grammar finesses the isomorphism of 'criminology' and 'criminal process': the lack of a specified referent for 'its' reality allows realism to map the one onto the other *as if* they were congruent.

5. The 'square of crime' should be compared here to the 'semantic rectangle' of the structuralist semiotician, as to which, see Greimas (1970). Greimas's analysis is intrinsically more interesting than the realists', however, since it, in the concept of the *rectangle*, acknowledges inequality (of sides). Geometric metaphors abound in realist criminology: see also the concept of 'pyramidal' relations in Young (1992: 29).

claustrophobia, however, there is always an excess to structuralism; in realist criminology it arrives with the injunction to remember the victim.

The crime couplet involves an opposition between the offender and the victim. Against traditional criminology's over-riding emphasis on the criminal, the realist programme grants a privilege to the victim. Thus 'we must never forget, however, the other half of the dyad of crime: the victim' (Young, 1992: 47). Married to the criminal (its 'other half'), the victim – and not the criminal – is the sign through which the couplet of crime is to be read. Such a reversal does not displace the hierarchical structure referred to by Young as a developing system: 'our approach then views crime as a developing system, from its initial causes to the impact on the victim' (1992: 47). Such a system works as a hall of mirrors in which the identities of offender and victim are significant only as the reflection of each in the other. Within this, realism discovers a supplement which it employs to ground the privilege and importance of the victim: that supplement is the experiences recounted by victims. For all its emphasis on the totality of the criminal process, the reader of realist criminology is insistently reminded that to be true to the reality of crime, it is necessary to posit the experiences of victims as the *a priori* of the criminological enterprise. In short, a claustrophobic structuralism which posits the systematicity of the criminal process has as its necessary supplement an unbounded subjectivism of the victim.

The identity of the victim is fragmented into a proliferation of archetypal categories, which constitute subspecies or *types* of victim. Those favoured most include: ethnic groups subject to racist harassment; residents troubled by burglars; the working class exploited by corrupt employers and corrupt police officers; inner-city dwellers confronted by drug dealers; women victimized by violent men.[6] The exemplary event, however, is street assault, which the realist understands as the minimal unit for the offender–victim dyad. In Venna's situation, discussed above, the local residents are victims of late-night rowdiness while the police officer whose hand is crushed is the victim of an assault. In fact, *Venna* would be exemplary for the realist in as much as assault in a public place operates as the archetypal instance of the offender–victim dyad (see Figure 2.2 in Young, 1992: 29). The proliferation of types does not result in the loss of identity. Rather, all the types are unified as instantiations of the universal category of Victim; the realist proliferation of types becomes a reiteration of identities across the totalized criminal process. In short, then, victimization is the name by which realism systematically references the real. In so doing, realism also provides a portrait of the victim.[7]

6. These are examples taken from Lea and Young (1984: 262) and Young (1992: 50).

7. Note the peculiar position of the so-called 'victimless' crime within an enterprise devoted wholly to the victim. Young's discussion of drug use is illustrative. At all levels of drug use, the interpersonal interactions – between importer and dealer, between dealer and user – are held to be consensual. The only point at which a victim appears is at the level of dealer/user (Young, 1992: 29). The problem here is not the consent between dealer and user, but the fact that the dealing takes place on the street. As such, a third character – the public – is introduced as an index of victimization. It is the consent of the public to the dealing that is lacking. The victim is thus

For the purpose of this chapter, two features frame the victim: first, criminal victimization as analogous to citizenship – and hence a mechanism which asserts *belonging*; second, crime as other and elsewhere – and hence a device which establishes *boundaries*.

Victimization as citizenship

Crime, for realism, is a great leveller. It provides a sense of community: 'crime [is] a unifier' (Young, 1992: 58). But our belonging comes not from the fact that we are all criminals, but rather from the shared fact of victimization. It is through our victimage that we come to belong to the social body. To be a victim is to be a citizen.[8] Young states: 'crime, like illness, is a universal problem' and as such 'rates very highly in people's assessment of problems of their area' (1992: 53). In positing problems as being *of* their area, a community of problems exists parallel to the community of individuals affected by the problems. In recognizing the existence of problems, a victim has self-understanding that speaks to him of his victimage. Moreover, crime 'affects all classes, ages, races; men and women' (1992: 53). Crime does not discriminate: the victim is unmarked, neutral. Secondary characteristics such as race or gender pertain only insofar as they arise from differing distributions of crime across the community.

Realist criminology claims a metaphorical relationship between crime and illness in order to underpin its notion of victimization as citizenship. I will elaborate the details of this analogy. Crime is said to resemble illness in several respects. As Young has stated above, both crime and illness are universal problems. Illness is also unevenly distributed across the community and in its effects on the individual. Young writes: 'Ill-health is a universal human problem, but ill-health focuses more on certain sectors of the population than it does on others.' The object of social control is 'to reduce crime in general. In this [crime policy] is like a community health project.' Crime control must 'target our resources . . . to those in greatest need', just as the health system deals with scarce resources in health management (1992: 53). In asserting resemblances between disparate things, analogies displace the invisible with the visible. Crime is put to one side, and in its place we find the concept-metaphor of illness.[9] Reasoning by analogy is unsurprising – it is, after all, the favoured mode of legal reasoning – but what has to be noted is the productive force that inheres in metaphor (MacCannell, 1986: 98, 103, 105). Through this, the category of crime is laminated with new meanings. Every time realist criminology uses the word 'crime', it is substituted by 'victimization'. The distinctiveness of this substitution becomes clear when we consider the conventional medicalizing comparison in which crime is likened to disease,

the local resident or the passer-by, both of whom, it is implied, do not consent to dealing on the streets (1992: 30). In short, there are only victims when an event takes place in public and there is no consent. According to this logic, if, as Young (1992: 30) states, domestic violence is a private affair, then it is also consensual and there is no victim.

8. For a recent rereading of the demands of citizenship, see Barron (1993).

9. A particular manifestation of illness as metaphor – HIV/AIDS – is discussed in Chapter 7.

evoking the 'sick' criminal. In realism, however, the gaze is turned squarely toward the victim. As such, the criminal becomes a shadowy figure, little more than a blurred reflection in the eyes of the victim.

In terms of crime control, the analogy between crime and illness has other consequences. Crime control becomes a matter of minimizing the risk of victimization and the taking of remedial steps once victimization has occurred. Just as the person who becomes ill is encouraged to respond by soliciting the help of the health care system and by following their advice as to treatment, so the victim of crime is enjoined to call on the criminal justice system to respond with a cure, a panacea or placebo. Passivity, for the victim, is initially unavoidable in that crime, like illness, happens to the individual, with all the force and randomness of circumstance. Agency can be regained, however, if the individual rejects such passivity and takes up a role in the prevention of crime. In this way, citizenship is acquired. As an active social agent, the citizen will fit locks and bolts to doors and windows, avoid dark streets and purchase alarm systems. If everyone is a victim, then everyone has a part to play in the struggle against crime. More strongly, everyone has a *duty*: it is part of the offices of the citizen to minimize the risk of becoming a victim. Just as we are incited to look after the health of our bodies and avoid illness, by eating the right foods, doing the right exercise, cultivating the right mental state, so too, the citizen must participate in his de-victimization. As well as having a part to play, the citizen is now explicitly a *partner* in the British government's recent anti-crime initiative. In September 1994, the 'partnership against crime' initiative was launched, involving an expansion of the 130,000 existing Neighbourhood Watch schemes, under the name 'Street Watch'.[10] In these, the citizen acts in partnership with the police (including an expanded force of neighbourhood constables). Local residents would regularly walk a specified route with the agreement of the police. These were initially envisaged as actively patrolling at all hours of the day or night. Intense criticism from members of Neighbourhood Watch schemes and from the President of the Association of Chief Police Officers forced Michael Howard (the Home Secretary) to scale down the number of Street Watch schemes introduced (to only 25 in the first year) and to abandon the notion of 'patrolling' and night-time activity. Howard stated that he was not advocating patrolling, but rather 'walking with a purpose' (quoted in *The Guardian*, 29 September 1994). Police officers gave out this advice to civic-minded individuals:

Don't :

> Jeopardize personal safety.
> Warn off undesirables.
> Intervene in suspicious circumstances.

---

10. This initiative to expand Neighbourhood Watch seems to ignore the conclusions drawn by many researchers: that Neighbourhood Watch members report higher levels of fear of crime (Mayhew et al., 1989); that they are confused as to what participation membership requires (McConville and Shepherd, 1991); that the schemes do not appear to reduce crime levels in an area (Bennett, T., 1990); see also Stanko (1994).

Enter premises without permission.
Apprehend suspects.
Carry weapons or implements for self-defence.

Do:

'Actively observe' events and report suspicions.
Keep an eye on properties whose owners are on holiday.
Keep an eye on scheme members' cars.[11]

Realism's emphasis on risk leads to a mode of self-government, through an act of self-assertion, an act of will (aided and abetted by police and Neighbourhood Watch schemes). Through such self-assertion, ironically, a sense of community is fostered and a mode of belonging endorsed as natural and conventional. As the uncertain reception of Howard's Street Watch scheme demonstrates, the exhortation to the citizen to strive for the minimization of the risk of victimization necessarily entails an increased risk of victimization which then requires the further issuing of advice on the minimization of risk. Belonging to a community can never be problem-free; all modes of belonging risk and require victimization.

Criminality as Other

In realism's dyad of crime, the victim is the criminal's 'other half' (Young, 1992: 47). Similar marital metaphorics can be found in realism's portrait of the criminologist, as a corollary to its visualization of the victim. Young writes:

Theory is divorced from practice: theoreticians are divorced not just from practitioners, but also from those who are the objects of their study. This is particularly true in criminology; criminologists live in different areas than criminals, they work in an academic milieu: the world of street crime, or corporate crime for that matter, is socially distant from them. (1992: 60)

Crime is elsewhere. But, just as the victim is a unitary category subdivided into subcategories, so the city is a unitary space divided into discrete institutional spaces, each of which is occupied by a different subjectivity: the academy by the theorist, the Home Office by the practitioner, the street by Venna and his friends and so on. Locked in an institutional space, no direct knowledge of crime can be gleaned by the criminologist. However, like anyone, the criminologist can be a victim. Crime may be elsewhere, but it becomes immediate in the experience of victimization. The criminologist may not live near a burglar, but may well have been the victim of burglary.[12] Such an analysis has no place for the feminist criminologist. As feminist studies of victimization, risk and fear have shown, women are assailed and insulted in their everyday lives: by images that line the streets, by comments made in the street, by harassment from colleagues, by sexual violence in the cinema and

11. In *The Guardian*, 29 September 1994.
12. Lea and Young, in the foreword to *What Is To Be Done About Law and Order?*, describe how one of the manuscript's chapters was stolen, on two separate occasions, from a parked car (1984: 7).

on television, by violence in the home.[13] For the woman criminologist who lives with an abusive partner, there is no 'divorce' from the object of study; rather, she is married to it. For other criminologists, and for realism, crime is elsewhere, and criminality is Other. Boundaries are erected between the criminal and the victim; victimization marks the moment of transgression at which the criminal dares to cross the boundary. The community of victims that asserts their belonging through their common victimage is attempting to create a unity out of fragments, to knit together a wound that has irrupted in late modern culture, a wound that marks a crisis in the Western crimino-legal tradition (as discussed in Chapter 1). Three manifestations of this crisis can be identified. The first, and that which is expressed through the crime control policies of realist criminology, is the problem of securing social justice in the modern city.

'The social bricks and mortar of civil society'

The world of realist criminology is one composed of disparate subjectivities defined by disparate spaces. It is here that the crime survey comes into its own, addressed to the specific task of capturing the disparate spaces of the city. A survey is concerned with spatialization; once the spatial dimension is captured, the realist gains access to subjectivities. In short, realism creates a cartography of the modern subject.[14] The self-government prescribed for the subject-as-victim has a spatial quality, taking place at nodal points in the city: for example, the entrance door to one's house must be strengthened and the windows locked; the dark city street must be avoided for the safety of the well-lit pavement; multi-storey car parks must be avoided after dark.[15] Through self-surveillance and self-policing, the victim asserts himself as a citizen of the city. In mapping these actions, realism provides a portrait of urban life, the main terms of which are civility, decency and tolerance, which, moreover, are necessary to promote the cohesion of community against criminogenesis.[16] Thus, crime is 'lack of respect for humanity and for fundamental human decency' (Lea and Young, 1984: 55). Criminal justice policy must determine the 'changes in what is tolerable behaviour and what could be done to achieve a more civilized society' (Young, 1992: 25). Young asks: 'What could be more

13. See Cameron and Frazer (1987); Caputi (1987); and, more generally, the feminist concern with the 'everyday' as a site of oppression and insult.

14. Note the prevalence of cartographic maps in realist texts: for example, see Jones et al. (1986).

15. On one of the nodal points of city living (the window), see Matthews (1992); on the minimization of risk of victimization in general, see Smith (1986: Chapter 8); on risk, see Beck (1992).

16. Note Goldberg's (1993) argument that 'tolerance' legitimates racism, in its positing of difference as something to be *permitted* rather than accepted. On contemporary British multicultural (in)tolerance: the American Jewish Society found that 12 per cent of Britons would prefer not to have Jewish neighbours and 25 per cent objected to non-white neighbours (reported in *The Independent*, 26 October 1993). Meanwhile, 'racial attacks' reported to the police in 1992 rose to 7,800: the actual number of attacks is of course far higher.

central to the quality of life than the ability to walk down the street at night without fear, to feel safe in one's home, to be free of harassment and incivilities in the day-to-day experience of urban life?' (1992: 49–50). Realism seeks, within the spaces of the modern city, the 'social bricks and mortar of civil society' (1992: 45).

Within the geographical area covered by a city, the realist has not found a real *community*, but rather, a highly populated area in which crime thrives. Crime is

> the run-down council estate where music blares out of windows early in the morning; it is the graffiti on the walls; it is aggression in the shops; it is bins that are never emptied; oil stains across the streets; it is kids that show no respect; it is large trucks racing through your roads; it is streets you do not dare walk down at night; it is always being careful; it is a symbol of a world falling apart. (Lea and Young, 1984: 55)

Such an apocalyptic vision recalls Rousseau, who found that the city – a concentration of individuals in a limited space – far from enhancing the social bond, destroys it. Rousseau writes: 'It is [in the city] that men commit, in the midst of their kind, what no other species does among itself: they turn against themselves; they devour one another' (1959: 114). After Kant, and with Rousseau, a central problem of modernity was the question of the subject and how it might escape its tutelage to the Other. As such, the subject continually emerges and re-emerges as the negation of the jurisdiction of the Other. The Other is metaphorized as urban disorder, the interruptions of sound, waste, darkness. As negation, the Other as urban is the logical precondition of the subject. The city, then, represents the continued dominance of the Other and the destruction of the subject, preventing the formation of the subject as citizen, reducing us to denizens. The aim of law and crime control, for Rousseau and for realism, is to subjugate the urban Other by 'enhancing' city life through the promotion of safety (from being 'devoured') and civic-mindedness (through local crime prevention schemes). Individuals would then become full citizens of the city with respect and compassion for each other, transcending the reality of urban crowding and excess in the modern age.

As such, the realist vision of urban space is based on a dichotomous polarization of two conceptions of the city.[17] One of these is *urbs*, the stones of the city, its layout, its provision of shelter, places for warfare and commerce; that is, its planning. The other is *civitas*, the emotions, rituals and convictions that take shape within a city; that is, its community. The *urbs* is simply a pattern of stones, asphalt, wood, concrete, street names, buildings, opaque boundaries. *Civitas*, on the other hand, connotes a neighbourhood, a collective, a shared enterprise of living, a community of homes with common values, a grouping of workplaces organized around mutual goals, lucidity and transparency.[18] *Urbs* could be said to represent law; while *civitas* stands for

---

17. See Sennett (1990:11) on the studies of St Isidore, who wrote of the two separate traditions of the city.

faith, the ethical. The crime survey collapses these two notions of the city into one, replaces *civitas* with *urbs*, thinks civility in terms of bricks and mortar. The crime surveys provide a map of behaviour derided as anti-social and analysed against the topography of individuals' hopes, desires and fears. That is, the emotions and anxieties of *civitas* are being examined as if they were immediately comparable to the layout of the *urbs*. The modern urban space is always already constituted as the space of excess, of criminality; the place where civic ideals fail, where individual morality is lost. So the realists view the city as a place of excess and loss: excess of individualism, loss of civic spirit. Their response is to survey the urban space, searching for communities in the stones of city streets. In this way, crime prevention advice is made to resonate with the demands of planning. In short, the passion of civility is sacrificed to the urban planning of realism.

The notion of sacrifice (as introduced in Chapter 1) will be elaborated and developed in the next section, dealing with the second manifestation of crisis in the crimino-legal tradition. The domestic sphere has been marked out as a region in which responsibilities and identities have been ruptured. Confronted by such a rupture, criminology and law converge in their efforts to suture the resulting wound and efface the revealing scar. In the next section, I will examine the crisis in domestic responsibility through a case study: that of a case of conjugal homicide. Although leaving the streets for the supposed haven that is the home, the situation represented by the case of *Venna* – street assault – acts as a mirror for the responses of criminal law and criminology to violence within the domestic sphere. With street assault constituting the paradigmatic crime of modernity (whether for Rousseau, for realist criminology or for Michael Howard's Street Watch units), it will become clear that crime within the shuttered realm of the home is treated as a pale substitute for the 'real thing'. Within the following section, the notion of sacrifice will be developed and posited as an alternative conception to the realist confusion of civility and urbanity in their response to the crisis of social justice in the city.

'Her sense of duty as a wife'

The complex position of the abused woman who kills her partner forestalls the simplistic vanguardism that has driven contemporary criminological accounts. It has been argued above that realist criminology is unable to offer a satisfactory representation of so-called 'domestic violence': for example, in Young's comments that the criminologist knows nothing of the world of crime we find the assumption that the criminologist cannot be an abused woman living with a violent man. In realism's typologies and taxonomies of victimhood, we find distinctions made between 'assault' and 'domestic violence', on the basis that assault is 'a purely coercive act' which may occur

---

18. In common with Rousseau, who longed for transparency and lucidity, the realists offer lighting, in a pedestrian effort to challenge the dark opacity of the city streets. See especially Painter (1989).

'in the street, in a public house, or in some other public venue' (Young, 1992: 29, 30). Such a decriminalizing impetus leaves conjugal violence in a border zone between criminality and civility, between coercion and consent. Conjugal violence does indeed concern borders and boundaries, but in an entirely different manner which I will detail, by means of one case: *R.* v. *Ahluwalia*, taken as proffering hope for the gloomy prospects of legal reform.[19] On 9 May 1989, Kiranjit Ahluwalia threw petrol over her husband and set it alight. He died six days later, from burn injuries. Seven months later, Ahluwalia was convicted of murder and sentenced to life imprisonment. In July 1992, her appeal against conviction was heard by the Court of Appeal. The conviction for murder was quashed and she was granted a new trial. In September 1992, at the retrial, she was convicted of manslaughter by reason of diminished responsibility.

In this case, as in all legal problematizations, it is not simply a matter of *telling* the truth. Just as victims cannot be victims for criminology until they tell their experiences to criminologists, so legal events cannot be legal events unless the truth is not only told but *displayed* in and for law. The consequence is that 'truth' or 'facts' are displaced and become a trope – albeit a powerful one – of representational practices. In the process of becoming a trope, there occurs a moment of sacrifice. To reach that moment, I will start, as judgements do, with biography. The case report states that Kiranjit Ahluwalia was middle class. Both she and her husband had jobs. They had two sons together. At the time of the appeal, she was 36. Kiranjit Ahluwalia was an Asian woman who entered, at her parents' insistence, into an arranged marriage with a man she had never met. She had moved from India to Canada, having completed an arts degree and begun a law degree. She gave up her legal studies and moved to England to marry Deepak Ahluwalia. They had no shared romance before the marriage, she knew nothing of him nor he of her. The judgement establishes Kiranjit Ahluwalia as a dutiful daughter who abandons her education to marry. Filial duty is emphasized over romantic love. She is bound in filial obligation and ethnic submission; she conforms to the demands of her parents and her culture. In marrying a man she did not know and in moving to a country she did not know, Kiranjit Ahluwalia was made doubly foreign.

She experienced severe violence over 10 years. A variety of her husband's

19. The case report is at [1992] 4 All England Law Reports 889. All page references will be included in the text. In the last few years, national campaigns were organized by Justice For Women and Southall Black Sisters to demand legal reform and to support imprisoned women who had killed their abusers. Ahluwalia was one of the women whose case received national media attention thanks to these campaigns. Sara Thornton's appeal against conviction for murder had failed and her subsequent hunger strike increased media interest in conjugal violence. A number of men who killed their wives received comparatively lenient sentences: see especially Joseph McGrail, who received a suspended sentence for manslaughter, and Roy Greech, convicted of manslaughter by reason of diminished responsibility (after stabbing his wife many times when he discovered her to be having an affair). The implications of Ahluwalia's case for legal reform are considered in Young (forthcoming).

assaults are described in the case report. These include hitting her several times over the head with a telephone; throwing hot tea over her; threatening her with a knife while gripping her throat. Twice she obtained injunctions against him; twice she attempted suicide. From January 1989, we are told, his violence intensified. In the four months leading up to his death in May 1989, Deepak Ahluwalia inflicted a battery of injuries on his wife. She sustained bruising to the cheek, temple and arm, broken teeth, swollen lips. She was knocked unconscious. Around this time, she discovered that he was having an affair. He is said to have taunted her with this relationship. He left her for three days in April 1989 and Ahluwalia wrote to him, begging him to return. The letter is quoted in the judgement:

> Deepak, if you come back, I promise you – I won't touch black coffee again, I won't go town every week, I won't eat green chilli, I ready to leave Chandikah and all my friends, I won't go near Der Goodie Mohan's house again, Even I am not going to attend Bully's wedding, I eat too much or all the time so I can get fat, I won't laugh if you don't like, I won't dye my hair even, I don't go to my neighbour's house, I won't ask you for any help. (p. 892)

Lord Chief Justice Taylor describes this letter as containing 'self-denying promises of the most abject kind' and as evidencing the 'state of humiliation and loss of self-esteem' to which her husband's behaviour had reduced her. Her wish to remain with this violent man is attributed by Lord Taylor to 'her sense of duty as a wife' and 'for the sake of the children' (p. 892). The letter also cements signifiers of foreignness ('chilli', 'Chandikah') and completes law's image of utter victimization. The letter is used to *display* Kiranjit Ahluwalia's loss of autonomy, her subject position as *abject*.

From Kiranjit Ahluwalia's *biography*, the case report switches to a *thanatography*, a narrative of death. On 8 May 1989, Kiranjit Ahluwalia visited her mother-in-law. She was also looking after one of her sons, who was sick. Again, the report weaves a web of familial responsibility around her. In contrast, we are told that Deepak Ahluwalia had promised his girlfriend that he would leave his wife that night; thus, he is constructed as poised to destroy the family unit. Ahluwalia cooked dinner for her husband and put their son to bed. She attempted to talk to him about their marriage; he said it was over. He threatened to beat her in the morning if she did not give him money to pay a telephone bill. He began ironing clothes and threatened to burn her face with the hot iron if she did not leave him alone. The scene, in all its violence, is thoroughly domestic: ironing, cooking, bills.

When they went to bed, Kiranjit Ahluwalia was unable to sleep. She is described as 'brooding' on her husband's refusal to speak to her and his threat to beat her in the morning. After two and a half hours, she got up and fetched the caustic soda and petrol she had bought some days earlier, purchased 'with a view to using them on the deceased'. Her subsequent actions are described as follows: downstairs, 'she poured about two pints of the petrol into a bucket (to make it easier to throw), lit a candle on the gas cooker and carried these things upstairs. She also took an oven glove for self-protection and a stick' (p. 893). Once more, the scene is domestic in its evocation of commonplace items from the kitchen (bucket, candle, cooker, oven glove). Further, the neutral, technical description finesses the question of her intention to kill; presenting the event, in the calm measured tones of law, as a narrative with little causal responsibility attached to the actors. She went into her husband's room, threw in the petrol and the candle. Her husband, on fire, tried to immerse himself in the bath, and then ran outside, screaming 'I'll kill you.' Neighbours rushed out of their houses to help him. Kiranjit Ahluwalia had gone to dress her son and now stood at the window, clutching the child. Domestic responsiveness still structures her narrative role, as her immediate reaction is said to be the fetching and dressing of her sick child. Other neighbours raced to the house, but the door had been locked. She was described as standing at the window, 'just staring and looking calm' and 'with a glazed expression'. When exhorted to leave the burning house, she is said to have replied, 'I am waiting for my husband'. Later, she wrote to her mother-in-law from prison that her husband had committed so many sins 'so I gave him a fire bath to wash away his sins' (p. 893).[20] After neighbours further remonstrated with her, she was persuaded to leave the house. Deepak Ahluwalia died six days later and his wife was charged with murder.

Ahluwalia appealed against conviction, first of all, by arguing that the trial judge had misrepresented the doctrine of provocation to the jury. Previous cases of battered women killing their abusers had failed where very short lapses of time had occurred, between the last provocative act and the lethal response (for example, in a previous case, a lapse of time of five minutes was deemed to be too long to display a sudden a temporary loss of self-control).[21] While not allowing this ground to succeed, the Appeal Court here stated that a lapse of time did not in itself mean that provocation must fail. This does not mean that legal *rules* are manipulable or indeterminate; rather, it demonstrates that the re-presentation of *facts* as *factual* (and thus not the facts themselves) problematizes an event as a crime. Her second ground of appeal was that 10 years of battering were sufficient to count as a legal characteristic of her identity. The court rejected this, stating that there was nothing to distinguish her from the 'ordinary woman' of the community.[22] In Venna's case, the ordinariness of the event ('a very ordinary and all too common event') relates to the court's desire to convict Venna as a surrogate for all the others who have been rowdy or aggressive in the streets. Ahluwalia's ordinariness makes her a surrogate for every wife. The only characteristics permitted for her legal identity were that she was 'an Asian woman, married, incidentally, to an Asian man, the deceased living in this country. You [the jury] may think she is an educated woman, she has a university degree' (p. 897). Ahluwalia's legal identity is that she is immigrant, married, educated, a *woman*. With these fragments, we see the limits of the legal imaginary;

20. The event, and the legal response, must here be articulated with the tradition of suttee/sati. On suttee see Sunder Rajan (1993: Chapters 1 and 2).

21. See *R* v. *Thornton* [1992] 1 All England Law Reports 306.

22. On the 'ordinariness' of women in law, see Young (1993b).

other possible re-presentations of her story (such as her being battered) are foreclosed. Her condition is one that is available to the ordinary run of women and it is through recourse to this ordinary femininity that her conviction is finally quashed.

The final ground of appeal related to medical evidence that had not been made available to the court at trial: a doctor's report stated that she was suffering a 'major endogenous depression' (p. 900). The court interprets this as 'battered woman's syndrome' and finds it to support a conviction for manslaughter on grounds of diminished responsibility. All her domestic behaviour (the way she carried out the crime, her actions in fetching her son, her remaining in the house) are reinterpreted as 'strange'. From being 'ordinary', she is now 'strange'. In her ordinariness is enfolded the strange, her familiarity (as the ordinary woman of the community) contains the kernel of the unfamiliar (the mentally abnormal). At the outset of her legal biography, Kiranjit Ahluwalia is made familiar to us. She is wrapped up in familial obligations, duties and relationships. When she acts homicidally, the law looks into her familiarity and finds enfolded an uncanny strangeness it calls diminished responsibility.[23] Yet this does not mean that Kiranjit Ahluwalia represents a duality between the familiar and the strange: she is no divided unity; rather, she has woven together the familiar and the strange. Dogmatically, the law asserts that Deepak Ahluwalia's violence caused his wife's strangeness. Without it, she would have continued for years as a 'good wife and mother'. Her enfolded abnormality is thus the abnormality of the normal in the ideality of Woman as relational, familial and self-sacrificial. Kiranjit Ahluwalia mistook the object of sacrifice: according to the desires of the law, she should have sacrificed herself (to her husband, to the institution of marriage). Her mistake, in killing her abuser, can be overlooked, incorporated safely into the body of the law as the strange normality of a woman whose mental disorder led her to destroy the one thing that the law tells us she wanted to preserve: her marriage. For, as the report states: 'despite all this [her husband's violence], she wished to hold the marriage together, partly because of her sense of duty as a wife and partly for the sake of the children' (p. 892).

For the sake of her marriage and her children she forsakes her *self*. This sacrifice is what the law desires and it is her will to sacrifice herself that the law takes for granted.[24] It is at this moment that the law underwrites its sacrifice of Kiranjit Ahluwalia's self with an image of racial otherness. Its emphasis on the strangeness of her behaviour after the act of homicide seems based on a reading of Asian ethnicity. It does not matter whether Ahluwalia followed a religion which practises suttee (the self-immolation of a widow on her dead husband's funeral pyre). What matters is the readiness of the law to

23. On the architectural uncanny, which locates the *unheimlich* (literally, 'unhomely') in the home, see Vidler (1992) and Weisman (1992). On the psychoanalytic uncanny, see Freud, who states that the *unheimlich* is 'the name for everything that ought to have remained . . . secret and hidden but has come to light' (1928: 225).

24. For a comparative analysis of *Ahluwalia* and another case (*R* v. *Thornton*) in which such self-sacrifice is not taken for granted – indeed, is disbelieved – see Young (forthcoming).

allow such an associative metaphor to structure its representation of the facts. Whatever Kiranjit Ahluwalia meant when she said 'I am waiting for my husband' or when she wrote of a 'fire bath', the white mythologies of English law read a history of colonialism into her act and allow it to displace other meanings, stories of autonomy and will.

As the flames illuminated the violent home of Deepak and Kiranjit Ahluwalia, so the law can cast light on lost medical evidence and the location of responsibility for the homicide in the violence of her husband and her abnormal mental state. Standing by the blazing window – poised between the violent act of homicide and the law's coming violence towards her – she seems to hesitate between two orders of community (one represented by the domestic sphere and the other represented by the local community of neighbours). But the image of the woman holding her child within a blazing window captures the moment of sacrifice. Wherever she turns, Ahluwalia will be lost to us: consumed by flames, or by law, imprisoned as rational and murderous or acquitted as mentally abnormal. These are not alternatives, however. In the court of law, and in the case report, the flames still burn: they allow the law to call her Other, foreign, strange. In her acquittal, she is still imprisoned, sacrificed in the law's representation of feminine subjectivity.

Such a sacrifice is required not only by the criminal law that relates to homicide, but also by the civil law that concerns the institution of marriage. Thus is the domestic sphere revealed more clearly to manifest an aspect of the crisis of social responsibility that has ruptured the smooth surface of criminolegal relations. Marriage, as Cicero would have it, is nature's essential human union.[25] More than this, it stands as a synecdoche for society itself. In cases such as *Ahluwalia*, the legal model of marriage acts as an archetype for all heterosexual relationships. As such, the status of marriage itself is at stake.[26] Marriage is like a religion in that the laws of marriage demand faith, commitment, vows, reverence and worship. However, this resemblance goes deeper. When two people marry, they become joined in wedlock, locked together, bound. 'Spouse' has a Latin root in *conjugalis*, from *conjungere* (to join) and gives rise to the terms 'couple' and 'yoke'. 'Couple' has of course two senses (from Latin, *copula*), in that it connotes 'two people' and 'bind' or 'tie'. 'Yoke' exists at literal and figurative levels, in its meanings of coupling animals together and subjection, suppression and subjugation. 'Wedlock' contains, in addition to its action of locking people together, a further bonding element: 'wed' is related to the Latin term *vas*, *vad*, meaning 'surety'. Marriage is thus linguistically arranged as an institution of dominance and subservience, labour and bondage, ties that bind.[27] The word 'spouse', a person who is married, derives from the Latin *sponsus*, *sponsa*, meaning bridegroom or bride (from *spondere*, to promise solemnly). However, it is

25. Cited in Goodrich (1990: 286).

26. Some of these ideas were first elaborated in Young (1994: 150–3).

27. For a socio-legal account of the 'ties that bind', see Smart (1984). On the dualism between the sacred and the secular in marriage, see O'Donovan (1993: Chapter 3).

also linked to the Latin *sponsor*, one who gives a guarantee or surety. The one who is married is therefore also one who must underwrite the promise to marry and the vows of marriage with a bond or deposit or fealty. In its recalling of 're-sponse', spouse demonstrates that marriage is conceived as the archetype of social responsibility.

'Marry' has a meaning beyond its obvious one (to enter wedlock). 'Marry' is also the corrupt form of 'Mary', for the Virgin Mary, the Mother of God, and used in the sixteenth century in oaths (a form of promise, bonding, obligation). 'Marriage' is thus a bonding between two people and inscribed with the swearing of a duty to the Virgin Mother. This union of bondage is one that is written by contract. As Goodrich writes: 'To contract is both to include and to repress (to bury) that which cannot be included as part of the system. The contract, in establishing the genre of law, acts as an antidote to other discourses' (1990: 174). The marriage contract effectively blinds us to other ways of seeing, telling, thinking. The contract denotes obligation, that which makes us indebted, which binds and constrains. The marriage contract joins the parties with chains (an early form of divorce was called *ab vinculo*, from the chain, literalizing the captivating and enthralling nature of marriage).

Spouses are divided into 'husband' and 'wife'. Whereas 'wife', from Old English *wif*, means simultaneously 'woman' and 'married woman' (that is, the fact of marriage is irrelevant; all women can be classified the same), 'husband' – in Old English *husbonda* – is 'he who is joined to a woman in marriage'. It further connotes 'he who manages affairs' and 'he who is master of a house(hold)'. A hierarchy is inscribed in the semantics of the institution. The obligations of the husband relate to his mastery of the household; those of the wife relate to her being joined to the man. 'Obligation', the concept which founds the institution of marriage in its contractual nature, is owed beyond the immediate roles which attach to the spouses. As befits a word (marry) which signifies the Virgin Mother as well as a contract to wed, 'obligation' derives from the Latin *religio*, which also gives us 'religion', and which means oath, vow, bond between man and God, scrupulousness, reverence. Here is located the semantics of the law, the order that compels fealty and obeisance to a god, a legislation, a husband. Just as law is exalted and sacralized as that which must be obeyed, so is the obligation (religion) of marriage. Marriage is made holy, or sacred, by our cultural order; that is, by the bonds between man and woman. And the subjugation of Woman consecrates marriage, religion, law. Woman is constituted as victim (from Latin, *victima*, one who suffers death or severe treatment; related to the Gothic *weihan*, to consecrate). Her suffering makes marriage sacred. Her suffering makes marriage holy: Woman is sacrificed (the Latin *sacer facere*, to make holy) and thus becomes a sacrament herself (*sacramentum* in Latin, also caution money, a guarantee, deposit or bond). Marriage, for Woman, is therefore a contract in which her sacrifice is demanded in exchange for a spurious alteration in status (as shown above, wife and woman are the same; the difference between them is chimerical). A woman asks for a change in status when she marries; she seeks citizenship. What is given is secondariness. She remains woman/wife; she gains only subjectivity in subjection to the mastery of the law and her husband. The law of marriage acts as a projectile; it projects Woman into subjection, into a series of masks – sexual partner, mother, domestic servant, unwaged labourer, lover, carer – for which she is required to die, literally, through conjugal abuse, or symbolically, through the foundational subjection of marriage.[28]

What I have endeavoured to demonstrate, by means of this case study in domestic responsibility, is that crisis is best understood through the notion of sacrifice, and that at the heart of sacrifice there exists a paradox: in this example the paradox has been the efforts of law to legislate love. Law sets out its conditions for legal love, but of course its devices of guarantee are elusive and illusory. Where it demands conjugal affection, there is always already the possibility of conjugal violence. Where it seeks the familiar, enfolded within it we find the strange. Within the home, there is only the unhomely, the uncanny. Just as realism seeks to ensure civility through urbanity, and thus ensures only the failure of any such utopian community, so the crimino-legal tradition which legislates the domestic order can see only divorce, broken homes, child abuse, conjugal homicide. In attempting to stitch together its own crisis and in attempting to mask the scar of its original wound, the crimino-legal tradition draws attention to the breach in its unity, the fragments that shore up its ruins. In the third manifestation of this crisis, the gendered body that is represented by Ahluwalia will be replaced by the racial body. Although the racial body features in *Ahluwalia*, as shown above, rather than return to this case for an elucidation of the racial dimensions of crisis I shall move to an event in which race is configured explicitly: the attempted deportation and resulting death of Joy Gardner. Where the gendered body is located in the institution of marriage as a figure for society, so the racial body is located in the city space, as a figure for the nation. This final section will thus elaborate the racial dimension of the crisis in the Western crimino-legal tradition.

'A dead ringer for deportation'

Joy Burke was born in Long Bay, Jamaica, in 1953. She came to Britain in July 1987, leaving an adult daughter behind her in Jamaica. She was given a six-month entry visa as a non-European Community tourist. When she was seven, her mother had moved to London, leaving Joy with her grandmother. This was a common occurrence in the 1950s and 1960s. Bhabha (1990) writes of this movement as a return of the repressed, by which the marginal comes to occupy the centre as the colonized nations migrated to their colonizers (inspiring a crisis of violent (in)tolerance in the imperialist nation).[29] To that extent, Joy Gardner was always already an *emblem* of the relationship

---

28. *Pro persona mori*: to die for one's mask; see Goodrich (1990: 297, 323). See also the comments in Chapter 1 on living (and dying) for one's mask.

29. The *Daily Mail* describes Joy Burke's mother's journey to Britain as part of 'the massive flight of Carribean people to Britain in the 1950s' (27 April 1994).

between colony and imperialist. Her mother remarried, had more children, worked in various jobs. When Joy Burke's visa expired, she did not leave the country, and somehow slipped through the Home Office nets. In September 1990, she married Joseph Gardner and took his name. He wrote to the Home Office announcing that he had married Joy and asking that she be awarded rights of permanent residence in Britain. A month later, before any decision had been taken on Joy Gardner's case, he wrote again, withdrawing the request and stating that they were now separated. Soon afterwards, he took out two injunctions against her – to stop her coming to his house – and later said that this was because she had been violent towards him.[30]

According to the Home Office, they were now dealing with a straightforward case of illegal immigration; in their view, the marriage was a sham, designed to obtain permanent residence rights. Although Joy Gardner's mother was now a British citizen, changes to immigration regulations in 1981 meant that Joy had no right to permanent residence through her mother. They cited in support of this view the fact that Joy Gardner had been four months pregnant when she entered Britain in 1987, a fact that she had not disclosed to the immigration officers (although one might ask why a tourist needs to disclose such a fact). This was suspected to be part of a plan to claim that her son was born in Britain and thus able to claim British citizenship. The foetus is thus viewed as a potential citizen, with its own legitimate or illegitimate rights of residence. Interviews with her husband were also said to support the Home Office's view. From December 1990 until April 1992, the Immigration Department of the Home Office went through the inevitable procedures. It informed Joy Gardner that it intended to deport her. She tried to challenge this in the High Court, but the judges rejected her case. She appealed to the Home Office's Immigration Appeals Tribunal, without success, and a deportation order was served on her. A flight to Jamaica was booked for her by the Home Office in the summer of 1992, but she did not show up at the airport. She argued that she had not received the letter informing her about the flight. A second flight was booked in October 1992. At that point, she 'disappeared'; that is, the Home Office lost track of her. According to one Home Office official, she was now considered a 'dead ringer for deportation'.[31] The phrase turned out to have an awful accuracy.

At this point, her solicitor, Djemal Dervish, wrote to the Home Office asking permission for her to stay on compassionate grounds, pointing out the large family available to her in Britain and the absence of supportive relatives in Jamaica. He emphasized that she was studying for a degree and had a 5-year-old child who had only known London as his home. The request failed. On 28 July 1993, Dervish received two letters, in the same postal delivery,

30. These details, and many more, were given in the newspaper coverage of the event, in August 1993 and after: for example, see the lengthy article 'Why did Joy Gardner die?', *Independent on Sunday*, 8 August 1993. On Joy Burke's marriage to Joseph Gardner, see the article 'The strange 7-day marriage of Joy Gardner; duped husband tells of nightmare life with dead deportee', in the *Mail on Sunday*, 8 August 1993.

31. Quoted in the *Independent on Sunday*, 8 August 1993.

from the Home Office, both emanating from Room 801. The first, dated 26
July, stated that arrangements would 'shortly' be made to deport Joy Gardner
and her child. The second, dated 27 July, stated that arrangements would
'now' be made for expulsion. Dervish decided to contact Gardner about the
possibility of a court challenge. He did not know that at the time he was reading the letters Joy Gardner was dying.

The events of the morning of 28 July at the house of Myrna Simpson, Joy
Gardner's mother, are disputed almost in their entirety and have been the subject of an inquiry by the Police Complaints Authority. For example, Mrs
Simpson states that the raid occurred at about 6.30 a.m. The officers involved
claim that they went into the house between 7 and 8 a.m. The timing is crucial because Joy Gardner was not brought to the nearby hospital until 8.45
a.m. The timing of the raid, whichever time is deemed to be correct, is particularly strange given that the Home Office had booked Joy Gardner on a
flight to Jamaica at 3 p.m. The irresistible inference is that this was a true
'dawn raid', considered appropriate for an incorrigible illegal immigrant
prone, as her husband alleged, to violence. The raid was carried out by five
police officers (three from Scotland Yard's SO1(3) unit specializing in deportations and known as the 'extradition squad',[32] two from the local Hornsey
police station) and an immigration official who carried the deportation order.
All six presented themselves at the door of Mrs Simpson's house. What happened next is as yet unknown. According to Chief Inspector Mark Sanger of
Edmonton police, '[Mrs Gardner] became hysterical and violent and bit one
of the police officers and had to be restrained. She suffered a heart attack and
mouth-to-mouth resuscitation was given.'[33] The press made much of her
alleged violence, both prior to and during the deportation attempt.[34] *The
Sunday Times* blamed her for turning 'what should have been a routine arrest'
into a 'violent' event. Joy Gardner is alleged in this report to have

> struck out, ripping a telephone from its socket, throwing it at the officers. Then,
> after smashing a vase, she grabbed a shard of broken china and raised her arm as
> if to stab them. One police officer grabbed her right arm and a second grabbed her
> left, but Gardner thrashed out again, sinking her teeth deep into his shoulder. (8
> August 1993)

Mrs Simpson offers a rather different account. She stated that Joy Gardner
agreed to let the officers enter the house, but before she could remove the
security chain, the officers cut through it. 'They felled her to the ground and
put handcuffs on her' (quoted in *The Guardian*, 3 August 1993). She also

32. *The Sunday Times* represented the squad's work as both problematic ('doing the Home
Secretary's dirty work') and sought after (officers who accompany the deportees on 'long haul
flights to countries such as Jamaica, Ghana or Nigeria . . . have got the best stocked duty-free
cabinets in the [Metropolitan police]') (8 August 1993).

33. Quoted in *The Guardian*, 3 August 1993, as part of a taped conversation with Bernie
Grant MP.

34. She was described as having tried to kill her husband, Joseph Gardner, in the *Mail on
Sunday*, 8 August 1993. *The Sunday Times* describes her as having 'a violent history' (8 August
1993).

stated that they put tape on her mouth and her feet. 'They sat on her stomach and damaged her kidneys and her brain' (quoted in the *Independent on Sunday*, 8 August 1993). When Joy Gardner was brought to hospital at 8.45 a.m., she had bruises on her wrists, arms and neck and was experiencing great difficulty in breathing. As paramedics had spent 45 minutes attempting to revive her, she was probably not breathing at all: her family claim that she was dead before being taken to hospital. She was placed on a ventilator but never regained consciousness and was later pronounced brain dead. Before the hospital could contact the family, to ask permission to switch off the ventilator, Joy Gardner went into cardiac arrest and died.

In the aftermath of this event, the officers of the SO1(3) squad were suspended, awaiting the results of the Police Complaints Authority inquiry. Essex police were said to be considering whether criminal charges would be brought against three of them. The initial post-mortem found that Joy Gardner died from 'hypoxic brain damage', that is, lack of oxygen. Her family claim that this was as a direct result of being gagged with some kind of adhesive tape or bandage; the police announced that they wished to investigate whether or not Mrs Gardner had had some cardiac condition that had caused her heart to fail during the struggle to deport her. Subsequently, seven different pathologists have failed to agree on the cause of death, making it unlikely that charges could successfully be brought against any of the officers (although a manslaughter charge was brought against three officers in April 1994; in June 1995 all three were acquitted). Charles Wardle, the Home Office Minister then responsible for immigration confirmed to the media that the letters announcing Joy Gardner's deportation were deliberately sent to arrive so that any further judicial appeals were impossible and so that she could not be alerted about a possible raid (reported in *The Guardian*, 14 August 1993). This practice was then criticized by some MPs for its undermining of the rights of immigrants to seek recourse to judicial review or take any other course of resistance. Other MPs appeared less sympathetic to Joy Gardner's situation: Teresa Gorman, a Conservative MP, commented: 'This woman had been fighting extradition because she was an illegal immigrant for five years. She has cost the British taxpayer an enormous amount. If she had gone quietly, none of this would have happened' (quoted in *The Guardian*, 9 August 1993). The *Daily Express* also stated: 'Mrs Gardner not only lived in this country illegally for five years, she lived free, care of the taxpayer' (10 August 1993). Joy Gardner was thus being held, by some, to account not only for the costs incurred by the procedures deemed necessary by the British government but also for her own death. Taxation is, of course, the price an individual pays for belonging to the nation. Joy Gardner could not pay tax, until given rights to reside in Britain. In place of the tax she could not pay, the state exacts her death as the price for attempting membership of a community in which she has been labelled an outsider.

Most attention focused on the devices that were taken by the police officers to Mrs Simpson's house in order to facilitate Joy Gardner's deportation. These were handcuffs, adhesive tape and a body belt made of leather, reinforced with metal, with manacles on long chains. When the Home Office and the Metropolitan Police announced a joint review of deportation procedures, the use of these devices was to constitute a central part of it. The Home Office were later to announce that body belts had been used in 37 cases (out of 139 deportations) in 1993. It admitted that 'leg restraints' (in the form of 'plain leather belts') were also sometimes used and almost all the deportees were flown out of the country *in handcuffs* (*The Guardian*, 13 January 1994). Handcuffs are revealed not merely as the technical instruments of security (which should be satisfied once the deportee is on board the plane). Requiring a deportee to travel in handcuffs confirms that it is the body which is at stake here, the unruly body identified as the illegal immigrant.

Paul Condon, Metropolitan Police Commissioner, had stated that he was 'appalled' by the existence of such an 'apparatus' as the body belt and 'abhorred its use'. While the Home Office appeared to insist that the use of such belts was an 'operational' matter for the police, it also emphasized 'cases which are thought to be difficult, such as if there was a history of violence or absconding' (quoted in *The Guardian*, 9 August 1993). Joy Gardner is thus implied to be a 'difficult' case, her attempts to gain permission to reside categorized as 'absconding' and her husband's complaints as to her 'violence' accepted as true. Other family members claimed that Joy Gardner was herself the victim of conjugal violence and had in fact been housed for some time in a refuge for battered women (*Independent on Sunday*, 8 August 1993). While deflecting responsibility for the use of the body belt onto the police (an 'operational matter and . . . the responsibility of chief constables'), the Home Office simultaneously retains the concept of the 'difficult case' to legitimate the use (past and future) of the belt (*The Guardian*, 9 August 1993).

An intense fascination prevailed with the belt. Some articles featured photographs of the belts being worn, others detailed their composition and manufacture.[35] It was discovered that every prison in England and Wales has at least one body belt and that, until five years ago, they were manufactured in prison workshops. Since then, the Prison Service had been 'making do' with existing stocks, but, as supplies were being depleted, a replenishment of stocks was being sought, even as the Gardner inquiry and the deportation review were underway. The Prison Service defended its use of the belts for 'difficult and violent prisoners', in language exactly echoing the Home Office's justifications for its use in deportation cases. No exact figures could be found for the use of the body belt alone, but figures for the use of all restraints (belts, straps, handcuffs and straitjackets) in a 12-month period, showed 194 different occasions. Five prisons (Brixton, Pentonville, Wormwood Scrubs, Feltham and Full Sutton) were responsible for more than half of this figure (*Independent on Sunday*, 8 August 1993). This information on the belts' deployment by the Prison Service tended to undermine claims that the body belt was a 'special' belt, designed by and used only by the

35. For example, see D. Campbell (1993), which featured a photograph of a body belt apparently being worn by a prisoner.

SO1(3) squad in 'difficult' extraditions.

The outrage expressed about the use of the body belt draws on what Foucault has named and criticized as the 'repressive hypothesis', through which practices become viewed as the inverted limit of a monarchic system. 'Monarchic' here refers to Foucault's (1977) conception of a sovereign mode of power based on the visible degradation of the body. Thus, the Prison Reform Trust call the belt 'medieval', *The Sunday Times* describes it as 'primitive' and Paul Condon is said to be 'appalled' that such devices are 'still in use'. The belt is constructed as a relic, a leftover trace of a less humane system, a punitive, barbaric implement whose function must be to inflict pain as punishment. Responses such as these, however, miss the point of a device such as a body belt, just as the repressive hypothesis misses the purpose of such strategies: training. I use this term to connote a programme through which the body is 'worked retail', in Foucault's terms, to produce docile subjects. The body belt used on Joy Gardner is part of a programme to train the individual body, the social body and the nation. The training undergone is a moral training, inspired by a technocratic rationality that works not only or not even as restraint, but as a productive force. The earlier example, of handcuffs being worn even on the plane as the deportee is flown out of the country, demonstrates the lack of relationship to security as central concern. Instead, as the events surrounding the death of Joy Gardner show, this moral training is part of a more generalized education of the social body whereby the physical body is (re)positioned and (re)worked as a site of risk, of threat and of potential.

To this end, the belt operates as the limit of the physical body. It represents an exoskeleton of submission, turns resistance into compliance. The body is held rigid in an attitude of docility and servility, arms fixed at the sides. Just as Charcot documented the postural attitudes assumed by his hysterics in the Salpêtrière, attitudes made fixed and rigorous by trauma, so the institutions of the nation-state seek to create malleable subjects who can be bundled into vans and onto planes. Where, until recently, prisoners manufactured these belts in prison workshops, they were participating in a process of subjectification: by making the belts, they were being allowed to operate as economic actors (albeit within prison) (see Melossi and Pavarini, 1981) and they were simultaneously being made complicit in the process of their own subjectification to the law that allows them to be 'restrained' if 'difficult'. Just as the woman who marries achieves subjectivity only through her subjectification to the law and to her husband's mastery over her, prisoners are accorded subjectivity only insofar as they are willing to act as docile bodies, subjectified by the law of the prison. In Joy Gardner's situation, she would have been permitted to say farewell to her mother, to pack her belongings only within the rigid limits of the deportation squad's notion of 'difficult' behaviour, limits as rigid as the body belt they produced at the first sign of dissent or resistance. There is also a symmetry between the body belt and the marking of Joy Gardner as racially Other (non-white). The racial labelling and the belt are both brands, stamps, markers. In place of the stamp in her passport that would represent a visa, Joy Gardner was branded an illegal immigrant and bodily marked with gag and handcuffs. Both the racial label 'illegal immigrant' and the body belt bespeak the body within. The biologically generated notion of racial otherness and the culturally manufactured devices of restraint engage in a technical hermeneutics of taming unruly flesh.

In addition to strapping on the body belt, the deportation squad gagged Joy Gardner with what some allege to have been adhesive tape, others to have been an adhesive bandage holding a ball of bandage over her mouth. Police officers claimed that such gags prevent them from being bitten by a deportee suspected of having hepatitis or AIDS.[36] The mouth is a wound which speaks; the cries of the deportee are the voice of the Other, speaking its pain. The bandage seeks to cover the painful wound (the imperialist past and its modern crises) while the gag which binds it to the wound perpetuates the wounding which provokes the Other's cries of pain. Although the Home Office announced new guidelines on deportation in January 1994 which banned the use of gags on deportees, Joy Gardner's is not the only deportation case in which such tactics have been used (and the use of 'arm and leg restraints' would continue, where a deportee 'behaved violently or disruptively'). Alternatives to the gagging of deportees were suggested by Mike Bennett, chair of the Metropolitan Branch of the Police Federation, including spraying deportees with gas pellets the size of squash balls, which 'disorientate for five minutes without doing permanent harm' (*The Guardian*, 18 February 1994). Six other deportees had been gagged in such a way over the last two years (the Home Office called these gags 'mouth restraints'). The case of Dorothy Nwokedi attracted a great deal of attention in the aftermath of Joy Gardner's death, involving as it did a black woman resident in the same area of London (Hornsey and Wood Green). On this occasion, the deportation was carried out by Airline Security Consultants, a private firm employed by the Home Office (which was not a signatory to a self-regulation scheme operated by the government in the hope that such firms would then police themselves).[37]

Dorothy Nwokedi was arrested by local police at her home on 9 July 1993. She was then 31 years old and had lived in Britain for 11 years. She and her 4-year-old daughter were to be deported back to Nigeria. They were taken to Gatwick airport and handed over by the police to the security firm. She started crying; at that point, she alleged that the security men forcibly 'hauled' her out of the van: 'One of the men, the big one, sat on my legs, another one sat on my legs while they tied my legs with broad Sellotape [an adhesive tape]. They sealed my mouth with Sellotape. In the struggle my thumbs were

36. Quoted in *The Sunday Times*, 8 August 1993. See Chapter 7 for a reading of criminal justice's treatment of the (suspected) HIV positive person or person with AIDS. Studies of transmission of HIV in cases of biting conclude that HIV is probably almost impossible to pass on in this way: see, for example, Drummond (1986).

37. Some of the criticism of the case gets its resonance from the recent government initiatives to privatize prisons: Group Four, a private security firm, became (in)famous for its repeatedly 'losing' prisoners as it 'escorted' them outside prison.

broken and I was bruised all over' (quoted in *The Guardian*, 31 August 1993). She was also handcuffed and separated from her child for the duration of the flight to Lagos. The Home Office commented that Mrs Nwokedi was not co-operative in the matter of her deportation, thus requiring an immigration officer, three police officers, five security guards and an escort from Group Four, a private security firm, to accompany her to the plane. Charles Wardle stated that Mrs Nwokedi 'refused to leave the van, kicking an escort in the face and biting a police officer's wrist. . . . There is no evidence to suggest that the degree of force used to restrain Mrs Nwokedi was unreasonable and went beyond what was necessary given the violence of her resistance' (*The Guardian*, 3 November 1993). The cost of her deportation was £7,700. The Home Office said that the event was so costly because Dorothy Nwokedi's case fell into a tiny minority of difficult cases. Once more, a single woman with a child is deemed so violent as to require several men with handcuffs and tape to control her.

There is a stark contrast in the language used to describe those who deport and those who are deported. The men employed by the security firms are 'escorts' (suggesting a friend or companion; indeed, one with sexual over-tones); the firms themselves offer 'security' (against the threat represented by the immigrant). The deportee is 'hauled' from the van, suggesting the cargo that is part of a plane's 'haulage' rather than a passenger. One commentator wrote: 'Let's play pass the parcel. Never mind that it contains a body' (*The Guardian*, 12 August 1993). And Charles Wardle admitted that adhesive tape was 'normally used for securing luggage' (quoted in *The Guardian*, 13 November 1993). In the production of docility, what could be more docile than a package, a piece of luggage, with no body, no emotions? 'Difficulty' and 'violence' on the part of the deportee are met by violence and harsh treatment. What this plan of equivalence of stimulus and response effaces is the reversal of cause and effect that has been achieved. The deportee's resis-tance to deportation is substituted by the violence of the law as response to the predicated violence of resistance. The production of docility works by positing the non-docile as existing prior to the response of the law. Original violence is located in the Other, rather than in the practices of law. Further, the dis-embodied parcel has no voice: the use of the gag suggests more than simply a response to alleged bites inflicted by frightened deportees. In gagging the deportee, the security agent (whether private or from the police) is saying, in continuity with well-known seat belt campaigns: belt up, it's the law. To 'belt up' in a car means that a seat belt in a car will shape the body for safety, hold it in a position where least damage, in an emergency, will be done to it. The potentiality of 'accident' is represented as prior to the *potestas* of the law, the police. To 'belt up' is to be silent, to shut up, and, what is more, to do it in the name of the law. Finally, a 'belting' connotes beating, violence. The body belt and the gag both belt up the body: together they hold the body rigid and silent, a supremely docile parcel waiting to be freighted out of the country.

Out of the country: extradition is the name for the technique of expelling undesired individuals. Deportation flies the illegal immigrant out of the country, away from a safe harbour or haven, and out of history (ex-tradition). Underlying the cases of Joy Gardner and Dorothy Nwokedi is a desire to police the borders of the nation, borders that are seen as in crisis owing to a flow of individuals named as illegal immigrants.[38] (Such a flow is in fact a reflux; a retaking of the colonial path, in reverse.) It does not matter who these individuals are: a single woman and child are represented as a threat to the integrity of the nation-state in this frame as if they were Interpol-named suspects.[39] In the postcolonial frame, the immigrant is always already threatening, violent, outside, a reminder of the violent past. To extradite is to return the outsider to its identity, its location: the outside. In the reactions to Joy Gardner's death few questioned the *concept* of deportation itself, reducing debate instead to the *methods* employed to enforce it. Deportation is one of the techniques viewed as a sovereign right of the post-imperialist state; Britain has a lengthy history of faith in deportation, deriving from its fear of invasion and submergence.[40] Deportation as an instrument of 'security' is a violent response to the perceived violent threat to the security of the social body, the individual, the state, the race.[41] Deportation is a technique which attempts to resist the claims of resemblance: deportation opposes itself to

38. The Home Office was criticized for its treatment of 190 Jamaican visitors – more than half a plane-load – who flew into London's Gatwick airport on 21 December 1993, detaining all of them at Campsfield House Detention Centre, most for over 40 hours. Fifty-two of these were to be permitted to enter as visitors, although on condition that they submitted to further questioning. Fifty-six were to be deported as soon as seats became available. Twenty-seven were expelled from Britain on Christmas Day and later complained that they had been 'treated like killers' (*The Guardian*, 27 December 1993). All said they had come to Britain to visit relatives over Christmas.

39. In early December, a mother of four children, Naheem Ejaz, was granted permission to stay in Britain, against the views of the Home Office, who had been seeking to deport her to Pakistan. Her British citizenship had been withdrawn when her husband applied for a passport using a false name. He was deported in 1991. The couple then became estranged. Mrs Ejaz intends to sue the Home Secretary for false imprisonment (*The Guardian*, 4 December 1993). A Sikh independence activist, regarded in Britain as a 'terrorist threat', said that he faced torture and death in India if deported. The Court of Appeal ruled that the Home Secretary was correct to balance the risk of 'ill-treatment' in India to Karamjit Singh Chahal with his threat to British 'national security' (*The Guardian*, 23 October 1993). See Braidotti (1994: Chapter 3) on the inherently threatening nature of the female reproductive body for the dominant (masculine) culture.

40. See Bhabha (1990); J. Bhabha (1993); Gilroy (1987); Layton-Henry (1992) on the repressive violence of immigration laws and practices; see Goodrich (1992) on the inherent racist fears in the notion of 'Englishness'.

41. These fears extend even to the treatment of asylum seekers: news reports in 1994 revealed that 26 asylum seekers were then on hunger strike in protest over conditions at Campsfield House Detention Centre, where they were being held prior to a decision on their cases. In 1993, two Kurdish asylum seekers threatened to commit suicide in Hull Prison, where they had spent six months as illegal immigrants: their applications for asylum in Britain were rejected as they had spent 90 minutes in Holland waiting for a ferry. Under the Asylum and Immigration Appeals Act 1993, a refugee may be denied asylum in Britain if she has previously entered a 'safe' country (*The Guardian*, 23 October 1993).

transportation, the literal meaning of *metaphor* (*meta pherein*: to carry over).
Just as extradition counters the weight of tradition (the colonial past), so
deportation rejects the carrying over of a claim to resemble a British subject.
Joy Gardner asserted resemblance to a citizen of the British state; her claim
of resemblance is held to be merely a poor copy, to be rejected (expelled) as an
imitation.

It is no coincidence that a deportation squad arrived early in the morning
to seize Joy Gardner. Their purpose was not merely to take her by surprise,
prevent her making an escape. A 'dawn raid' is, for Plato, the hour when
enlightenment ensues: one talks 'till dawn' when knowledge is gained and
community re-established. Dawn brings the light and banishes darkness.
Dawn raids to deport the immigrant similarly reassert the light of a longed-
for national purity against the darkness of the foreign. Since modernity is
associated with the values and spirit of the Enlightenment, it could be said
that the dawn raid is emblematic of modernity's racism. The dawn raid was
deemed necessary because of the Home Office's representation of Joy
Gardner as a violent and persistent 'absconder'. An absconder departs
secretly and hides, so as to evade retribution. No pejorative connotation is
built into the term (it comes from the Latin *condere*, to store up or conceal).
Denigratory lamination has been culturally applied to the term so that the
retribution to be evaded has come to be synonymous with justice, rather than
the pure force of law. Its opposite term is 'abduct'. The Home Office, in seeking to deport Joy Gardner through a sudden dawn raid, desired her abduction
from life in Britain, her home, and her propulsion towards Jamaica, the foreign. Abduction means to carry off, especially a woman or child, by force or
in secret. It is linked to kidnap. From the medical discourse of anatomy, it has
also come to denote the positioning of limbs parallel to the central axis of the
body (in the manner achieved by the body belt). It connotes a purpose to the
carrying off of women: for intercourse or marriage. Having demonstrated
above the sacrificial structure of marriage, it would appear that the deportation of women by means of abduction in the name of national security follows
a similar sacrificial dynamic. The deportation squad silenced Joy Gardner,
trussed her up like a parcel, and certainly contributed to her death (as
evidenced by the outcome of the formal inquiry and the deliberations of the
courts: theirs is the language of the juridical, of equivalence, discrimination
and amoral responsibility which will avoid any questioning of the traditions
of extradition). More than this, they stole her subjectivity: representing her as
a 'dead ringer for deportation', the Home Office rejected her claim to resemble a British subject and saw her instead as a threatening effigy, a simulacrum
of invasion, an excessive image of what is to be feared. They sacrificed her self
to a notion of the white boundary, the national limit.

Conclusion: Locating the body of crime

In this chapter, my aim has been to display the crisis in the Western crimino-
legal tradition. In reiterating the locations of that crisis, my argument has

been that it is best understood through the concept of sacrifice. Realist criminology's attempt to respond to this crisis, in its manifestation of crime as an
urban problem, has failed owing to its confusion of categories and its repetition of sacrifice. Community is not the same as city: to conflate them leads to
a hierarchy in which the only reformist programme that can be undertaken is
coterminous with urban planning. While realist criminology could make
good sense of the type of incident represented by Venna's case – street assault
and rowdiness – it would be unable to nuance the discourses surrounding
Ahluwalia's killing of her husband and Gardner's death. In the former, realism's over-determination of street crime as the paradigmatic form of
criminality means that the wall between household and street becomes an
opaque boundary, sheltering the conjugally violent from observation. In the
latter, a fascination with the mortification of the body produced by devices
such as body belts means that the underlying violence of deportation itself
cannot be addressed. I would argue that the stories of Ahluwalia and
Gardner are *events* which exemplify that which exceeds contemporary for-
mulations of the crimino-legal tradition. They are that very excess, the break
in the frame which must always bleed. Conceptualized in this way, the crimino-legal tradition is the heir to the sacrifice of this excess as the logical
precondition of the community, tradition, the home, the nation. This chapter,
then, has responded not so much to the stories of Ahluwalia and Gardner as
to the failure of the crimino-legal tradition in its very self-representation, its
autogenesis. When the subject of law asserts that it is not subject to law (as did
Ahluwalia in killing her husband, and Gardner in illegally remaining in
Britain), the response of the law is violent. It extradites, deports, convicts,
labels as mentally abnormal, *excommunicates* the subject.

In both events, something is sacrificed. In Ahluwalia's situation, the
woman is required to sacrifice herself to the law of marriage, to make her
body available for her husband to beat, or for sexual intercourse, or for
domestic labour. Her citizenship is a secondary one, of little value compared
to the determining force of law. In Gardner's case, the immigrant is required
to sacrifice herself to the law of nation, to the dominance of the state's agents
and deputies. Her citizenship cannot even achieve secondary status, deemed
instead to be illegal, legitimating the will to (r)eject her across the nation's
border. In both cases, an *unruly body* has been discovered. That is, a body
which displays itself as non-juridical, outside the realm of legal rules. In
Ahluwalia's case, a woman dares to use lethal force against her husband; it is
explicable only through the legal conundrum that a woman can be familiar
and strange at the same time. In Gardner's case, fear and pain, when
expressed through the body as resisting deportation, allow that body to be
re(s)trained. In both instances, docility is desired and achieved: Ahluwalia is
deemed to have been suffering from a mental disorder; Gardner dies. Both
cases deal also with the *location* of crime.[42] In *Ahluwalia*, the court underwrites the domestic sphere as having a different value, a different
responsibility, as the foundational unit of society; Gardner's death highlights
the peculiarly atopic nature of deportation, moving with a police that is not

the police from the vulnerable walls of the home, through the international zone of the airport to the runway, to international space and the countries beyond. What this chapter has provided is an account of these manifestations of crimino-legal crisis that is sensitive to the issues of space or location, of the body and its pains, of the hidden emotional ruptures in juridical discourses on crime.

42. See Bhabha (1994), and Probyn, who writes: 'Location insists on a taxonomy of experience. . . . The classification of experience, moreover, indivisible from what came before and which knowledges stand as previously sanctioned. Location, then, also depends on a constructed chronology' (1990: 184).

4

The Scene of the Crime:
Reading the Justice of Detective Fiction

In the light of the lantern I read, with a thrill of horror, 'The sign of the four'.
(Doyle, 1890: 49)

The problem is that so often the law seems pale in its remedies, leaving us restless
and unfulfilled in our craving for satisfaction. (Grafton, 1994: 285)

Crisis is an occasion for storytelling, for the generation of narratives which
describe, respond to, or displace a critical rupture in the cultural order.
Chapter 2 examined the criminological narrative which secretes Woman as an
enigma to be contemplated and explained. Such a narrative is impelled by a
crisis in sexual difference. Chapter 3 described the crisis of the body as manifested in discourses of the city, the home and the nation. The stories told by
the crimino-legal complex are an integral part of the crisis to which it
responds. This chapter takes the question of storytelling literally, examining
those produced for entertainment, in the form of detective fiction. Detective
fiction has received a considerable amount of critical attention.[1] Here, I wish
to examine its ability to stage aspects of the crimino-legal crisis in a form that
engages with our fears and pleasures in criminality. The chapter will deal with
crime as an aesthetic form that combines the body as a repository of clues
and signs with the trauma of witnessing the event of victimization. The
genre's laws of representation will also be considered: its codes of naming, its
location of crime in the city and in sexual difference, its heroic detectives and
its foundation upon a primal moment of betrayal. My argument concerns the
dialectic between appearance and disappearance, law and ethics, masculinity
and femininity. And finally, in a genre that has often been dismissed for its
inherent conservatism, I seek to discover a place for ethical feminism.

While Chapter 3 dealt with a series of substitutions that moved from the
body in pain to the victim and then to the criminologist (as potential victim),
this chapter describes a series of substitutions which begins with the body in
pleasure. The pleasure is that derived from reading detective stories; the body
in pleasure is thus the reader or consumer of such fiction. Her pleasure consists in the self-administration of fear and suspense. Readers of detective
stories quickly work out which authors provide an acceptable dosage of fear;
too much may sicken, too little will not satisfy. The reader is comforted by the
sense that, whatever happens, the excursion into the fearful world of

---

1. For example, see the analyses of Bloch (1988); Cawelti (1976); Knight (1980); Palmer
(1993); Porter (1981); Sparks (1992); Thompson (1993).

criminality will be followed by a return from fear, as the detective solves the crime and reveals the identity of the criminal.[2] Such guaranteed pleasure is one reason why readers consume detective fiction compulsively, working their way through the alphabet with Grafton, book after book (*A is for Alibi*, *B is for Burglar*, and so on up to, at the time of writing, *K is for Killer*). Many consumers never reread detective stories; knowing the outcome in advance deflates the pleasures of the text. Genres of fiction are formulaic (the romance, for example); however, my interest is in the representations of criminality within these generic formulas and the account that might be made of their significance within a culture that assumes crime is a social problem and a source of unequivocal fear.

My aim is therefore to demonstrate how victimization can operate as a source of horror and pleasure, the one intertwined with the other. On the one hand, the individual is invited to feel fear at the idea of victimization; on the other, the individual may seek out texts that explicitly invite her to experience pleasure in that fearfulness. In most criminological literature, governmental debates and policy documents on crime, it is assumed that individuals approach crime as a source of fear. In Michael Jack's speech on crime in the House of Commons (see Chapter 1), he states: 'Crime is frightening' (*Hansard*, 5 March 1993). Recent writings in realist criminology take as their starting-point the axiom that people are afraid of crime.[3] In contradistinction to this assumed fearfulness, another approach to crime exists: in this, crime is a source of pleasure. Quite apart from the avid interest shown in media coverage of crime (for example, see my discussion of the coverage of James Bulger's murder in Chapter 5), detective fiction constitutes (together with romantic fiction) the most popular literary genre. To that extent, readers approach its representations of crime with something other than the emotions attributed to them in the sphere of 'real' crime. My interest in this chapter is in the disjunction between the fears of crime that pertain in individuals' everyday lives and the considerable pleasures obtained from detective fiction. I also wish to consider what can be learned about crime and law through reading detective stories. In the aesthetic of the senses that structures crime fiction, representations of the police, the body, pain and fear may hold clues as to the hierarchy of values within which crime is approached as a 'real' issue in contemporary culture.

I discovered detective fiction in 1985, when a flatmate lent me *The Chandler Collection*. I had seen movie versions of these and other detective stories, but I had never experienced the compulsion and captivation that came with *reading* such stories. For several years, I was simply a fan, reading my way through novel after novel: all of Chandler, all of James M. Cain. I discovered that

---

2. This is one of the reasons why 'unconventional' detective stories are so disturbing. In Borges' 'Death and the Compass' (1962), the detective solves the crime by following the clues to a man who will kill him: the crime he solves is his own death. For other excellent examples, see the three stories in Auster's *New York Trilogy* (1990).

3. For example, see Jones et al. (1986); Painter (1992).

many academics were also fans, and yet were often embarrassed about their captivation: detective fiction is frequently seen as in poor taste, or as lowbrow literature. In 1988, a friend sent me my first feminist detective novel, to occupy me during a winter cold bug: this was Paretsky's *Killing Orders*. I then read my way through all of Paretsky's novels, following them with as much of the burgeoning feminist detective genre as I could find. In 1990, I wrote a short article on representations of law and disorder in detective fiction, comparing the work of my two first detective loves, Paretsky and Chandler (Young, 1991). This altered my reading experience: previously, I simply ploughed through the book, absorbing plot, characterization and so on as a subordinate aspect of the primary purpose: the revelation that came at the end of all detective stories. Once I began to write about detective stories, I had to read everything twice; once as a pure consumer of suspense (who experienced the visceral sensibilia of the text), and again as a critic (who sought the sense of the text), making pencil notes in the margins and sticking post-its on the pages.

Throughout, I have retained a fascination with the representations contained in the genre of detective fiction. Most texts share a perspective which condemns the infliction of pain or suffering on others; most approve of some kind of retribution (although varying greatly on the nature of that retribution). The texts usually comment on the criminal justice system, upon the legal system and its personnel, upon the very concepts of law, justice, punishment. Their narrative devices are usually prominent and persistent: first, a riddle or enigma is discovered.[4] The distinction between mystery and enigma (also relevant, as Chapter 2 demonstrates, to criminology's categorization of femininity as enigma rather than mystery) is elaborated in Kerr's detective story 'March Violets':

> [She] added: 'I suppose the case has the police baffled.' There was a note of sarcasm in her voice. 'And then you come along, the Great Detective, and find the clue that solves the whole mystery.'
> 'There's no mystery . . .' I said provocatively. It threw her only slightly.
> 'Why, surely the mystery is, who did it?'
> 'A mystery is something that is beyond human knowledge and comprehension, which means that I should be wasting my time in even trying to investigate it. No, this case is nothing more than a puzzle, and I happen to like puzzles.' (1993a: 65)

The text requires a person who is uniquely able to decode the puzzle (through varying means: rationality, forensic science, re-enactment, intuition); a moment of revelation in which the enigma is explained (to the reader, who has ideally been unable to solve the puzzle, and to the other characters in the story); a sense of denouement or adjustment in which the moral order resumes its correct functioning (after the trauma caused by the crime which had to be solved in the story). This narrative structure appears in almost every text within the genre. As such, a detective story follows a blatantly formulaic construction, which at times is almost parodic of narrative in the

---

4. On Woman as enigma in criminology, see Chapter 2.

same way as a folk tale or joke.[5] To that extent, variations in the nature of the crime, the identities of victim, investigator and villain, the geographical and historical location do not affect the generic structure of the narrative. Against that, however, these variations are precisely that which provide the lure by which readers prefer particular stories or authors over others: for example, the reader who enjoys the violent texts of Mickey Spillane will probably not seek out the work of Agatha Christie; whereas the Christie fan may well also read Dorothy L. Sayers.

Similarly, matters such as geographical location can function to lend extremely important narrative value: for example, the city of Chicago is a crucial location for Paretsky's novels, as is Los Angeles in Chandler. High degrees of realization in location and historical period add specificity to the texts (Paretsky is arguing that crime in Chicago takes *this* form, not *that*); yet also contributes to a sense of timelessness, in that crime, its detection and punishment are represented (by the genre) as of unwavering cultural significance. Thus the formula constitutes the general, against which the variations in location or detective constitute the particular to which the reader responds. The crimino-legal convention has always been to impose the general over the particular (thus, law is applied to the facts, or rules to the evidence). What is captivating to the reader of detective fiction, however, is more the particularity of the scene portrayed, than the general depiction of crime as a 'timeless' phenomenon. Thus the reader ensures interpellation into an already imagined scene in which the timelessness of the crime–detection–apprehension scenario can be played out.

Literature on or about crime has been in existence for several hundred years. Among the first examples of detective fiction was the Newgate calendar (1773), which detailed the executions of notorious criminals and the crimes which had led to their demise.[6] However, the genre began to evolve the characteristics which are recognizable from its contemporary, modernist form in the nineteenth century. I use the characterization 'detective story' to describe all those following the efforts of an investigator to solve the puzzle or enigma represented by a crime.[7] Of greater interest here than its historical evolution, however, is the genre's cultural significance. At this point, the difference between the *detective* story and the *crime* story should be emphasized.[8] With the crime story, essential attributes are character, psychology and setting. The enigma or puzzle may be dispensed with altogether.

---

5. On the folk tale, for example, see Propp (1968).

6. On the calendar, see Birkett (1951). The 'true crime' genre in contemporary culture – whether manifested in reconstructions, biographies of criminals or 'unsolved mysteries' – is a very direct descendant of this phenomenon. The calendar can also be seen as the underside of the genre of the law report, which emerged around the same time and which is the staple text of the law student.

7. My definition is wider than that used by some typologists of the genre: for example, see Todorov (1971).

8. On the evolution of the crime novel, see comments in Blake (1990: 54–5); Cawelti (1976); Porter (1981).

That is, the reader may know from the outset who commits the crime; suspense derives from the uncertainty of the criminal's future. The opposite is true for the detective story: the hidden identity of the criminal is the structuring motif of the text. While it is impossible to imagine a detective story without a detective (such a figure is its axiom), a crime story often does not feature one.[9] In the detective story, the presence of the detective guarantees the existence of some kind of moral order and the containment of danger. The reader is encouraged to identify with the detective and to share the detective's worldview. In the crime story, the institutions of law and justice are made problematic; the reader may also be compelled to identify with the criminal or a guilty bystander; and the very existence of a moral order may well be placed in doubt.[10] In this chapter, I will discuss the detective story, as opposed to the crime story, since it combines representations of the fear of crime, the trauma of victimization, the imagined motivations for criminality and the perceived necessity of policing. While the crime story offers the reader a temporary and vicarious guilty mind, the detective story indulges a sociocultural will to hunt, capture and punish the criminal. To that extent, the detective story constitutes a textual exemplification of censure combined with a desire for the pleasure that comes with the voyeurism of witnessing.[11]

An aesthetic of crime

During the nineteenth century, as detective fiction was transformed into its modernist format, the straightforward religious or moral reactions that had held sway over representations of crime were taken over by a more complex combination of censoriousness mingled with aesthetic interest. De Quincey wrote: 'People begin to see that something more goes to the completion of a fine murder than two blockheads to kill and be killed, a knife, a purse and a dark lane. Design, gentlemen, grouping, light and shade, poetry, sentiment, are now deemed indispensable to acts of this nature' (1854: 20). Cawelti (1976: 54–5) has argued that detective fiction's form in the nineteenth century allowed the complete realization of detective fiction as entertainment: the cycles of crime, detection and punishment became the occasion for pleasurable emotional and intellectual stimulation, while the processes of identification locating sympathy with the innocent promoted disapproval of crime and anticipation of the criminal's apprehension and punishment.

9. The distinction between these two genres can be made porous and mobile. Some texts combine the major characteristics of both: for example, by offering a protagonist who is a criminal (and with whom the reader gets to experience the thrill of committing crimes) but who also acts as detective (for example, if she is framed for a crime that she has not committed, she will attempt to discover the true culprit). The 'burglar' novels of Lawrence Block typify this device: for example, see *The Burglar Who Painted Like Mondrian* (1993).

10. Structures of identification in the crime story are set out in Hilfer (1990). Exemplary crime stories include: Cain's *The Postman Always Rings Twice* (1934); Wings' *Divine Victim* (1992).

11. The prefigured response to detective fiction operates through a structure of witnessing. That is, its problem is how to witness that which is culturally unpresentable without translating the unpresentable into representation. Further on this point, see Chapter 5.

Within the aesthetic censure engendered by detective fiction after the nineteenth century, two important strands of representation can be discerned. First, the criminal was romanticized – perhaps due to the influence of Gothic melodrama – as evil beyond redemption or as a rebellious figure. The evil villain features in the work of Sir Arthur Conan Doyle as Moriarty; the rebel was sometimes a social bandit or a reluctant criminal rejecting stultifying social mores. The social bandit often withdrew from urban to rural locations: the folkloric Robin Hood is an excellent and enduring example of this type of offender. The second representational strand relates to a scientization of approaches to crime. As the sciences of phrenology, criminology and physiology expanded in credence and in intellectual standing, criminal acts were increasingly seen not as evil deeds, but as the result of defective conditioning or hereditary pathologies. Criminality, once induced, could still develop within an individual to produce the kind of 'evil monster' deemed not only beyond redemption but also beyond science. From the late nineteenth century onwards, detective stories, such as those by Poe, Doyle, Christie and Sayers, featured detectives who made use of scientific techniques in their processes of detection. Along with their claims to rational thinking, such scientism could be said to be a paradigmatic feature of this period of detective fiction.[12] A further feature is uncertainty as to who might be a criminal and what causes an individual to commit a crime. Despite the claims of sciences such as phrenology, with their implications of a recognizable criminal physique or criminal personality, criminology's major achievement not long after its origins was a failure to produce any clear reason for the commission of crime. With explanations running the gamut from atavism to social conditioning, no truth of criminality, or effective means for its control, could be discovered. Radzinowicz summed up the criminological dilemma as follows:

> On the threshold of the twentieth century there were two opposing opinions to these questions. On the one hand, disappointment that so little had been achieved, combined with a fervent belief that crime can be conquered. On the other, a detached examination of crime as an intrinsic part of social life produced the assertion that it must be accepted as a normal, even useful social fact. (1966: 60)

Criminology oscillated between, on the one hand, a desire to eliminate criminality and, on the other, an acceptance of its inevitability and the concomitant need to manage its consequences. Its opposing desires were for the disappearance (elimination) of criminality and its appearance (inevitability) as a social fact. In both versions, however, criminality is reduced to the observable phenomena of the psyche, the body or the environment. The scientism of the management strategies that won out deployed a positivist rationality which produced, in detective fiction, the detective as positivist: he discovers and interprets the crime according to its observable phenomena. In

---

12. Faith in scientific technique is inherited in many contemporary texts: for example, see the novels of Patricia Cornwell, whose Medical Examiner protagonist makes use of increasingly complicated and obscure procedures to reveal the traces left by a killer in a house, on a body, on a sheet of paper.

phrenology, those phenomena took the form of bodily signs (a large skull, deep-set eyes); in law, they took the form of evidence (Doyle's *The Sign of Four* [1890] is laid out like a legal brief). In criminology, individual and social appearances became the observable details of criminality; the habits and habitats of the criminal. In keeping with the genre's desire for an aesthetic of crime, the reader is invited to observe, to witness, and then – like the criminologist, the police officer or the detective – to *interpret* signs and to deduce the identity of the criminal. The aesthetic of detective fiction therefore conjoined an imperative to read the body as a repository of signs (in physique, psyche, gesture) and to witness the unveiling of a traumatic event (the crime).

Laws of genre

A shifting bundle of structural devices are employed to effect particular types of reading experience, identification and narrative satisfaction.

Reading the city as the scene of the crime

As the scene of the crime, the city is featured as a source of anxiety and fear. For some texts, the city is criminogenic, its crowded streets giving rise to all kinds of criminality: fraud, murder, conspiracy. Chandler's Los Angeles is archetypal: Hollywood is viewed as creating a city in which greed and avarice for celebrity have inspired a lawlessness which takes indiscriminate form, moulded by the general desire for fame and fortune. In other texts, such as Paretsky's novels, Chicago inspires property crimes, ranging from embezzlement through money laundering to blackmail and fraud. Murder usually occurs as a side-effect of the original property crime. Child abuse and domestic violence in one novel (*Tunnel Vision* [1994]) are symptomatic of the perpetrator's corruption by his urban situation. In others, the city is an implicit presence, functioning as a threat to a pastoral location or as a repository of knowledge to which the detective might repair for assistance in the task of solving the crime (Christie and Doyle use versions of these representations).

Together with Poe, Doyle's work inaugurates the city as a legible space; that is, it provides a textual elucidation of the subliminal anxieties associated with urban life. The city becomes the space of signs, commodities, appearances. As such, it requires constant interpretation. The detective is the one who can interpret the signs of crime in the city (and the city as a sign of crime). The city as sign is therefore accompanied by the figure of the detective as semiotician, able to decode the meaning of the city.[13] The client who solicits the detective's help has encountered a gap in the social text, interpreted as a moral unintelligibility. The client is the one who is confronted by the breakdown in meaning; crime is meaninglessness in the heart of meaning. The

13. In Poe's 'The mystery of Marie Rogêt' (1842), Dupin does not need to leave his apartment to solve the crime, learning all he needs to know from the press coverage of the event: crime and the city both function as signs that can be read through the medium of their representation.

detective thus is asked to solve the crime by restoring social meaning. Hence the semiotic nature of detection, as the detective relocates intelligibility and order in the city space. As urban complexity becomes associated with criminal behaviour (with complexity comes the occasion for myriad types of unintelligible events, requiring detection and explanation), the chief source of psychic anxiety is fused with the major symptom and source of physical discomfort: the crowd. Brand writes: 'in this way, the opacity of the urban crowd ceases to be merely confusing. It becomes actively threatening' (1990: 224–5).

As the scene of the crime (the scene of meaninglessness), the city provides the location for detection (making intelligible the unintelligible). The city as legible space allows the illegible crime to be interpreted by the detective for the client (and the reader). As interpreter, the detective can be characterized as an individual, but is better understood as a kind of divided unity: both rational and imaginative (as in Holmes, a positivist who takes drugs). In keeping with such a split subjectivity, the detective is the one who manages the play of meaning and meaninglessness in the text and who occupies a border between the extraordinary and the ordinary, the public and the private. The detective's individuality is always that of the extraordinary hero or genius (at least through her solution of the unintelligibility of the crime) whereas the ordinary individual, such as the client, belongs to the masses, the crowds (through her inability to solve the crime). As an extraordinary individual, the detective is the one who stands out in the crowd; that is, she belongs to humanity, but possesses some additional quality, intelligence, or courage that enables her to succeed where others will fail. She represents a cross-roads between (the pains of) anonymity and (the pleasures of) celebrity. For example, Auguste Dupin's response to his fame is to live like a hermit, never leaving his apartment. Holmes' incandescent brilliance requires drug-taking to assuage its relentless awareness. The detective's partner often functions to keep the detective in touch with the masses: Watson embodies the good heart but slow wits of the ideal ordinary individual.

The detective, then, represents a nodal point connecting the extraordinary with the ordinary, the criminal with the victim (through her interpretation of the puzzle that is the crime). These connections traverse the surface of the city, with the image of the masses as the anonymous backdrop to all events. The detective should thus also be understood as reading the scene of the crime against the city. Hence, the crowd in the city constitutes the source of criminality; it simultaneously contains the promise to obliterate the details of the criminal in the crowd. As the criminal becomes imaginatively knowable to the detective through the traces and clues which accrue to a crime (lipstick, fingerprints, blood, cigarette ash), processes of categorization classify the criminal individual as motivated by some dystopian desire (greed, lust, jealousy and so on). Thus categorized, the criminal's individuality is subordinated to his or her position within a taxonomy of dysfunctions. The revealing clues through which guilt and identity are betrayed define a statistical result (a solved crime) and a criminal type.

Further, detective fiction subjects the hiding-places of the city and its crowds to the controlling gaze of the detective which ultimately allows no secret. The resulting legibility of the city derives from a position of imaginative spectatorial dominance which corresponded to the development of new mechanisms of surveillance producing legibility precisely through the conversion of individuality to a set of knowable traces.[14] Detective fiction watches the detective watching the criminal and thus institutes a panoptic relationship between reader and fictional offender. Initially hidden from view, the offender gradually emerges – through the detective's efforts – as a visible type. The derivation of pleasure from this process implicates the reader in a complicity with the structures of surveillance endorsed by detective fiction. Again, detective fiction came into its contemporary form at a moment which marks a break between cultural regimes. Where the city is represented in detective fiction in ways which calm incipient anxieties about urbanism as a mode of life, so the unavoidable sensations of exposure and vulnerability experienced by the modern subject are converted into the necessary mechanisms for the pleasurable moment of revelation by the detective. The ability to convert the pains of exposure into the pleasures of revelation entail from the schism between the sovereign mode of power and the juridical mode straddled by the detective story.

Crime literature in the *ancien régime* took the form of confessions printed and circulated in broadsheets, dramatizing the apparatus of power and its effects on the body of the condemned. Foucault, as is well known, suggests that in the nineteenth century a shift took place which deployed new forms of surveillance to constitute power in a sort of capillary network, as opposed to the top–down power of the sovereign mode. All domains became visible to the gaze and sight became the dominant metaphor for power (Foucault, 1977).[15] The gaze sought to render any individual available to classification, examination and disposal. The detective fiction of the modernist, oculocentric age adheres to the shift in disciplinary power by providing a detective (whether the 'private eye' of the investigator or the 'public eye' of the police officer) who complements bureaucratic power. The detective realizes imaginatively the oneiric imperative which renders the city totally visible and therefore legible. Holmes and Dupin, for example, act like knowing seers at the centre of the social panopticon. Their deductive techniques make everything apparent; within such a *transparent* society, meaning becomes clear, ambiguity is erased.[16]

In the novels of Patricia Cornwell, Chief Medical Examiner Kay Scarpetta employs a vast range of scientific techniques to render the body of the victim,

14. A similar point is made by Benjamin (1973) in his discussion of detective fiction contingent to his reading of Baudelaire.

15. Freud linked the privileging of the visual to the degradation of smell, relating this to the construction of sexual difference. Montrelay (1978) argues that before sight was so privileged, the menstrual processes affected the male psyche through various olfactory stimuli, threatening because of their tremendous immediacy and nostalgic reference to the mother.

16. See Moretti (1990: 240); Porter (1981: 125); on the transparent society, see Vattimo (1992).

or the crime scene, open to her interpretation.[17] As such, her version of forensic science is a reduction to technical proceduralism, in which technology
has its own bureaucracy. In one novel (*Cruel and Unusual*), the process of
making visible is literalized in an extraordinary scene whereby ancient bloody
stains and fingerprints are painted into visibility and photographed in complete darkness for examination later in a laboratory's special machine. The
apparently normal house lived in by a university academic is then revealed as
still splattered with the blood of a crime that occurred years before (Cornwell,
1993). The proceduralism of the forensic (the technique must be applied
exactly or will not 'work') in making visible the traces of the crime translates
the room into a skeletal image, viewable like an X-ray. What is interpreted is
not so much the room as a *photograph* of the room. The room becomes an
image available for our interpretation. The image is thus a surrogate, standing
in for and displacing the invisibility of the crime in the room's 'normal'
appearance.

That clues are visible to the detective is a companion motif to the detective's ability to interpret those clues. Sometimes clues are revealed as 'false'
('red herrings'), which served only to confuse the reader, narrator and, less
often, the detective. Just as the crowd cannot shelter the criminal in the face
of the panoptic gaze, so the jumble of everyday detritus cannot submerge
those traces the criminal is powerless to avoid leaving behind. The criminal is
betrayed through individuality (the traces left behind are combined by the
detective into an individual identity) and, as such, fits into a recognizable typification of criminality. The items which turn out to be clues are often
apparently inconsequential aspects of character and behaviour, worked
'retail' in the text as obscure or hidden symptoms of identity. It is through
close attention to these that the detective pinpoints the skewed personality
whose crime disrupted the social order. Poe introduced this technique (calling
it 'ratiocination') and Doyle refined it into an essential part of the genre. In
the following exemplary passage, Holmes and Watson have just arrived at the
scene of a crime:

> Beside [the dead man's hand] was a torn sheet of note-paper with some words
> scrawled upon it. Holmes glanced at it, then handed it to me [Watson]. 'You see,' he
> said, with a significant raising of the eyebrows. In the light of the lantern I read,
> with a thrill of horror, 'The sign of the four'.
>
> 'In God's name, what does it all mean?' I asked. 'It means murder,' said he,
> stooping over the dead man. 'Ah! I expected it. Look here!' He pointed to what
> looked like a long, dark thorn stuck in the skin just above the ear.
>
> 'It look like a thorn,' said I.
>
> 'It is a thorn. You may pick it out. But be careful, for it is poisoned.' . . .
>
> 'This is an insoluble mystery to me,' said I. 'It grows darker instead of clearer.'
>
> 'On the contrary,' he answered, 'it clears every instant. I only require a few
> missing links to have an entirely connected case.' (Doyle, 1890: 49–50)

The reader is positioned in alliance with poor, befuddled Watson, party to

---

17. To date, these are: *Post Mortem* (1990); *Body of Evidence* (1991); *All That Remains* (1992);
Cruel and Unusual (1993); *The Body Farm* (1994).

Holmes' reasoning and insight only at second-hand and only when the great detective is ready to explain the clues. Holmes 'sees' immediately that a murder had taken place and how it was achieved. His invitation ('You see?') to Watson (and hence the reader, who shares the narrative 'I'/eye) to experience the same deductions cannot be met: Watson and the reader are still reeling from the strangeness of the scene. As Holmes indicates to Watson where to look ('Look here!'), Watson's lumbering uncertainty is palpable ('It looks like a thorn' . . . 'It is a thorn'). While Watson is still hesitating even as to superficial categorizations, Holmes has already absorbed the details and translated them into immutable clues which form part of the overarching narrative ('It means murder' . . . 'it is poisoned' . . . 'an entirely connected case'). Watson reacts to the scene as meaningless ('what does it all mean?'), to which Holmes has the answer already ('it means murder'). Watson treats even the simplest of signs as tricky ('it looks like a thorn'); Holmes confirms that it is indeed what it seems ('it is a thorn'), but it is also a sign of something that is invisible to all but Holmes ('it is poisoned'). Holmes' deductions make visible that which was invisible and make sense of the senselessness of the scene before them.

The detective method is precisely a *method*; Scarpetta in Cornwell's texts takes the proceduralism of method to its logical extreme. All detectives operate their method as a mode of translation, which converts the random into the connected, the circumstantial into the consequential, the indefinite into the definitive. In short, the detective method translates cause into effect, and signified into signifier. The detective's semiotic logic works retrospectively, assuming the linearity of cause and effect; Holmes works backwards from effect to cause, on the assumption that causation flows naturally from cause to effect. As a semiotician, the detective is invested in the appearance of crime, its culture and evidence. The detective's work therefore is to make the crime come (in)to light. The retrospection of this process requires an interpretation which cannot be guaranteed by the natural order of causality. Detective fiction's loyalty to 'science' or 'rationality' attempts to guarantee a link between naturalism and interpretivism. That this link cannot be guaranteed is one of the contentions of this chapter. In the oscillation between belief in naturalism and dependence on interpretivism, the reader is positioned as having an identity with the detective, interpreting the signs of crime in the city as the detective does. In other words, what is suspended is a distinction between fiction (detective fiction) and reality (detection).

At the same time, the reader is permitted to identify with the unseeing ordinariness of Watson, who offers the common-sense bafflement of the masses when faced with the unintelligibility of the crime. There does not have to be an actual sidekick for the reader to experience this oscillation between powerful knowledge and helpless puzzlement: for example, in the texts of Grafton and Paretsky, the lone female detective's incessant internal dialogue permits the reader to participate in the process of interpretation from both sides (the knowing and the unknowing). In sum, detection functions as a semiotic process which allows the reader to make sense of the senseless event of the crime, located within the threatening anonymity of the masses who make up the life of the city. As such, the scene of the crime in detective fiction is the scene of the interpretation of the hierarchies of social groups (extraordinary versus ordinary, individual versus mass), of the opacities of city life (the meaninglessness of certain events, the randomness of occurrences), and of the relationship between rationality and imagination.

Textual trauma

It has recently been claimed that the pleasures of detective fiction are wholly psychoanalytic in nature, allowing an individual to respond, through textual trauma, to the primal scene. Pederson-Krag (1983) argued that the curiosity aroused by the detective story derives from its association with the primal scene (the child's first, real or imagined, observation of sexual intercourse between its parents). The victim in the detective story represents the parent for whom the reader/child had negative, Oedipal feelings. She writes:

> The clues in the story, disconnected, inexplicable and trifling, represent the child's growing awareness of details it had never understood, such as the family's sleeping arrangements, nocturnal sounds, stains, incomprehensible adult jokes and remarks. The criminal of the detective drama appears hidden until the final page. In real life he was the parent toward whom the child's positive oedipal feelings were directed, the one whom the child wished least of all to imagine participating in a secret crime. (1983: 16)

She concludes that the reading of detective fiction allows the reader/child to enter the parental bed, confront the trauma of what is found there and emerge unscathed. By becoming the detective, through the textual processes of identification, the reader/child may gratify infantile curiosity with impunity, redressing the helpless guilt remembered from childhood. Trauma, however, is always constituted by a delayed action; that is, trauma is the result of retrospective interpretation. The primal scene is not in itself traumatic for the child, but a later event (which sets off a libidinal charge, of pleasure, fear or anxiety) leads to a subsequent libidinal charge being invested onto the primal scene so as to constitute it retrospectively as traumatic. The constitution of trauma thus follows the same retrospective dynamic as the detective's interpretation of the meaning of the crime. As such, the detective's construction of the meaninglessness of crime creates a retrospective trauma to be overlaid upon the ambiguity of the event.[18] To the retrospection of trauma, Hartman adds an insistence on its visual nature:

> Some . . . *heart of darkness* scene, some such *pathos*, is the relentless center or focus of detective fiction . . . I don't mean that we must have the scene of suffering – the actual murder, mutilation, or whatever – exhibited to us . . . (The real violence, in any case, is perpetuated in the psyche.) But to solve a crime in detective stories means to give it an exact location: to pinpoint not merely the murderer and his

---

18. Chapter 5 examines this process in the context of the event of James Bulger's death, as the 38 witnesses, who thought at first that they saw a family scene, later realized that they saw an abduction and suffered trauma as a result.

motives but also the very place, the room, the ingenious or brutal circumstance. We want not only proof but, like Othello, ocular proof. (1983: 212; emphasis in original)

Hartman is arguing that the reader is confronted with the horror of crime; indeed, the reader enters the narrative precisely in order to seek out horror (the 'heart of darkness') in detective fiction. The detailing of a crime (usually murder) provides the reader with a *frisson* of fear.[19] The will to expose one's self to fear and to return from it can be detected in the solitary game of disappearance and return, *fort/da*, played by a very young boy, as recounted by Freud (1935), in which he observed the repetitive movements of the child in throwing away a spindle on a string, exclaiming '*fort !*' ('gone!') as it disappeared, then tugging it back into view, with the exclamation '*da!*' ('there!'). If the game of *fort/da* represents narrative in its simplest form, it is because of the high level of pleasure and fear involved. The mechanism involved in this movement of disappearance and return has an implied third term. As Derrida (1981) has shown, all dialectical moves are predicated upon an absent third term. In the *fort/da* game, the whole structure of the experience of separation and reunion presupposes a union that antedates both: *da/fort/da*. In consuming detective fiction, the reader experiences the fear of crime and its resolution as pleasurable because she predicates it upon an essential state of *crimelessness*, a period or place in which crime is unknown and irrelevant. This takes the form of an invented tradition and expresses itself through a rhetoric of nostalgia for both an imagined Elysian past and a longed-for perfect future.

Hartman's reference to Othello informs us that the trauma may relate to (imagined) female infidelity, as a retrospective projection by the reader/detective. A similar imaginary abandonment is found in Freud's *fort/da* story, since the trauma of that event relates to the child's abandonment by the mother (as played out in the game). Trauma always derives from a source other than the abandonment itself, which turns the abandonment or infidelity into a traumatic event. Thus, for Othello, it was Iago's gossip which interrupted and retrospectively enforced a projection of trauma onto Desdemona as unfaithful. In detective fiction, it is the response of the reader to the scenes of the text that displaces trauma onto the crime and sends the reader, like the detective, on a search for meaning. Just as the detective often insists on a face-to-face confrontation with the criminal, the reader, even if she has solved the enigma, demands ocular proof and reads the text to the end. In short, the trauma of reading projects crime as meaninglessness and the detective as meaning. Such an oscillation between meaninglessness and meaning, between crime and detective, cannot be stopped or fixed. The reader's response reiterates the oscillation, between pleasure and fear, between consumption and criticism. As such, the reader is a split subject, whose response to trauma will always be skewed.

19. Chapter 5 will argue that such representations always contain their own limit. The press coverage of James Bulger's killers frequently employed phrases such as 'the heart of darkness' to describe the crime.

The traumatic fear of exposure in modernist culture, referred to above as producing the transparency of society, also expresses itself through a love of voyeurism. Part of the pleasure of reading detective fiction is its demand that the reader accede to scopophilia. Voyeurism consists, on the one hand, in watching – 'with a clean conscience' as Palmer puts it (1993: 15) – the detective use violence to resolve the violence of crime. On the other hand, the reader must also give herself up to textual gossip, as the detective questions characters as to what they know about other people's lives.[20] More than this, the reader, through the detective's eyes, is permitted to look through other people's belongings. The crime is a gap through which the reader is invited to enter the closed world behind another's door. The detective story gratifies because it legitimates and is dependent upon activities considered reprehensible in its readers' lives. Through the morally validated hero, the detective novel allows its reader to pry and peep, to break into locked houses and to open drawers and cupboards in other people's homes. The detective has a licence to look in and under beds, to read diaries, open private letters and eavesdrop on intimate scenes.[21] The detective gathers up a succession of hints, mysterious stains, fingerprints, torn clothing, weapons, dried blood, letters, photographs. And the reader enjoys without guilt the luxury of watching without being seen. One secret, therefore, of the powerful *frisson* in detective fiction is its trick of making voyeurism a duty. That such a duty is inescapable appears in the representation of the search through other people's detritus as goal-oriented and morally necessary, a sordid means to an admirable end (solving the crime).

The reader oscillates between pleasure and pain, between a fear of exposure and a love of looking. The way detective fiction incites this oscillation is by projecting the pleasure or pain onto others. Thus, the reader takes pleasure in the pain of others. For the reader, then, pleasure and pain cannot be separated; they are enmixed, mutually constitutive. The reader is thus no more and no less than a confusion of pain and pleasure, of being both the subject and the object of the gaze. Such a confusion is logically prior to the Symbolic Order, to the law of subject and object. It is the split subjectivity of the reader. The disavowal of the reader as difference is the price of entering the genre of detective fiction (and its symbolic community of readers and interpreters) as reader. This has implications for the female reader of detective fiction. A feminist response is precluded from the outset by the law of the genre of detective fiction. And this is also why detective fiction's unpresentable crime might be said to be associated with women's infidelity to or abandonment of men. This is little more than a projection of the law of genre: women are precluded from being faithful to their difference as women (to the difference

20. As in *Othello*, gossip can be fatal. See also my comments on Sara Thornton, whose conviction for murder arose partly from the testimony of her friend, who reported conversations she had had with Thornton; gossip can convict. See Young (forthcoming).

21. For example, Millhone listens to a taped conversation in *K is for Killer* (Grafton, 1994); Warshawski eavesdrops on a scene of domestic violence in *Tunnel Vision* (Paretsky, 1994).

within women) and this preclusion is translated into an infidelity to men. The law of genre is also the law of the Symbolic. As noted above, women are precluded from the Symbolic, thanks to their projected infidelity to men within it. The law of the Symbolic is the law of genre, of gender, of law and order. Such a law is also a fiction of law and (dis)order, putting into discourse the oscillations between crime and detective, pleasure and pain, masculine and feminine, reader and detective.

Fictions of law and disorder

In the rest of this chapter, I wish to pursue these concerns in the context of a number of different detective novels. The specific issue to be investigated is how they project into discourse the question of criminal justice as law and (dis)order. I examine hard-boiled fiction, exemplified by the novels of Raymond Chandler and his detective Philip Marlowe; classical detective stories as represented by Sir Arthur Conan Doyle's Sherlock Holmes stories; contemporary feminist detective fiction (embodied in Sara Paretsky's V.I. Warshawski and Sue Grafton's Kinsey Millhone); and contemporary lesbian feminist detective stories (Val McDermid's Lindsay Gordon stories and the novels of Sandra Scoppetone featuring Lauren Laurano). I will discuss four motifs which structure the representations of detective and crime: naming; genres of crime; heroism; and betrayal.

The authority of the name

Naming establishes a discursive frame. The name given to a detective is never simply a denotative device which gives formal identity in a milieu of many other characters. Of all the characters' names in any story, the name given to the detective is most important, since it will ascribe to the individual who bears it features that form liminal aspects of the narrative. Every detective's name provides clues as to the discursive register of the narrative. In Chandler's stories, Marlowe takes pains to establish the spelling of his name ('Marlowe with an *e*'). The last letter displays his alienness and otherness in the philistine world of Southern California. It also has a literary tone, as a corruption of Mallory whose Arthurian epic poem is echoed in the knightly characteristics given to Marlowe and in the mythological references such as *The Lady in the Lake* (1944). Marlowe makes literary allusions throughout the novels, whose titles often refer colloquially to well-known texts: *The Big Sleep* (1939) alludes to Hamlet's 'sleep of death'.[22]

'Sherlock Holmes' was selected by Doyle as a name for his brilliant rationalist, as it signified to him 'the click of an opening lock' as the crime was solved.[23] 'Sherlock' also recalls 'Sherwood' and thus Robin Hood, who represented (in a very English manner) the forces of good struggling, through the guise of a romantic bandit, against those of evil. Holmes is thus made

---

22. On the knightly characteristics of Marlowe, see Durham (1963).
23. Cited in Porter (1981: 60).

romantic by his nostalgic echoing of an earlier folkloric figure. His habits of
drug-taking, disapproved of by Watson, are, by association, made to seem
more like maverick eccentricity than anti-social deviance. 'Holmes' phoneti-
cally recalls 'home', signifying the hearth, the haven, safety and reassurance.
Exoticism merges with homeliness; a deft combination of the known and the
unknown. V.I. Warshawski's naming produces very different resonances. In
her professional existence she goes by her initials: 'Women exist in a world of
first names in business. . . . That's why I use my initials' (Paretsky, 1987c: 83).
For Warshawski, insistence on her initials promotes gender neutrality; thus,
entry to the Symbolic Order (the masculine world of business) requires the
erasure of the sexual difference embedded in her first names. To her friends,
she is 'Vic', not 'Victoria', her given name.

Warshawski's choice of professional name rejects the sexism of the social
structure; her choice of private name refuses the Law of the Father. She
rejects her given name and selects either faceless initials or a masculine abbre-
viation. Only two characters in the stories are allowed to call her by her given
name: one is a police lieutenant – an old friend of her dead police officer
father – who performs the function of paternal supervision and criticism of
her waywardness from traditional feminine conventions. The other is Lotty,
an immigrant woman doctor who is constituted as Warshawski's best friend,
but who performs the role of maternal supervision, advocating caution,
reminding Warshawski of her responsibility towards friends and family.
'Warshawski' emphasizes the detective's own foreignness: her mother was an
Italian immigrant, her father a Polish immigrant. The key to her narrative
destiny is contained in her middle name: Iphigenia. Warshawski discovers in
one novel that her mother, Gabriella, had an affair with her sister's husband,
while staying in their household. The sister refused to divorce her husband
and threw Gabriella out. The husband then committed suicide. Gabriella
married Tony Warshawski, a Polish police officer. Warshawski learns this
from her aunt in the most violent of terms ('daughter of a whore', 'a whore
from the streets', 'that whore, that shameless one' [1987b: 228]). Gabriella
never tells her daughter or husband about the relationship, but makes
Warshawski promise that she will do whatever her aunt asks of her (and it is
such a call from the aunt that begins the narrative). Warshawski interprets
Gabriella's actions as a moment of sacrifice, symbolized in her middle name.
She demands of Lotty: 'Do you know the myth of Iphigenia? How
Agamemnon sacrificed her to get a fair wind to sail for Troy? . . . I can't stop
dreaming about it. Only in my dreams it's Gabriella. She keeps laying me on
the pyre and setting the torch to it and weeping for me . . .' (1987b: 232).
Lotty, as the displaced mother, refuses to accept this interpretation, counter-
ing it with Warshawski's first name, Victoria (victory) and Iphigenia's
alternative connotation as Artemis, the huntress. Warshawski's relation with
her mother therefore combines loss, bereavement, sacrifice and victory, all
channelled into the detection of crime and the maintenance of her relation
with Lotty, as the memorial to her mother.

Grafton's detective runs a business called 'Millhone Investigations' and is often assumed to be a man (for example, in *K is for Killer* [1994], a client, on meeting Kinsey, asks if she is 'Millhone's secretary'). The sexism of the business world constitutes an underlying theme throughout the narratives. However, the detective's given name of 'Kinsey' (her mother's maiden name) has an ambiguous aspect: while recalling feminine names such as 'Kimberley', it also refers to the male author of the infamous report on sexual behaviour. The detective's surname breaks down into two connotative halves: 'mill' suggests labour, the treadmill, the grinding of flour, the burden of a millstone, perhaps the dreary nature of much detective work; 'hone', on the other hand, imagines the sharpening of an object (perhaps the image of the murderer being brought into sharp relief by the detective's labour). McDermid's lesbian detective, Lindsay Gordon, appears at first to have an exceedingly ordinary name; and that initial impression of ordinariness is desired by the texts as an indicator of Gordon's status as an Everywoman, unglamorous, with recognizably mundane problems and concerns. In addition to this, the name achieves other connotations. First, it reads as credibly Scottish, validating Gordon's national origins which constitute an important aspect of the detective's worldview and personality. Second, 'Lindsay' is an androgynous name, capable of belonging to a man as easily as a woman. Since Gordon's lesbianism is a major part of each narrative, the ambiguity of her given name underlines her traversal of sexual gender boundaries.

Each detective has a particular interlocutor as the imaginary Other of the narrative. In the Holmes story, the narrator, Watson, constitutes this Other as himself, projected everywhere as the common or plain man who cannot hope to understand Holmes' deductions. Holmes is therefore further aggrandized as the ordinary man shrinks into mediocrity. Marlowe constitutes his Other as like himself, out of place in California, a man belonging to a more civilized age forced to live as best he can among the fearsome greed of the Hollywood age. His Other is therefore his only true companion, as friends fail him and lovers are proved to be untrustworthy or possessively suffocating. In lesbian detective fiction, as exemplified by the Lindsay Gordon stories, the Other is constituted as a fellow citizen of the lesbian community, privy to the trials of negotiating a homophobic social sphere. For Kinsey Millhone, her interlocutor is quite explicitly acknowledged to be the client, as each text is constructed as a report to be submitted (each novel ends: 'Respectfully submitted, Kinsey Millhone'). Since the client is paying Millhone's fee and inaugurates the investigations through a request for assistance, the client occupies a paternal role, the role of the original law which identifies a wrong and seeks its redress.

Like Millhone, Warshawski allows the reader to share her narrative eye and her worldview. Unlike Millhone, the imaginary interlocutor is not the client – and hence the paternal law – but rather the spectre of her dead mother, whose death haunts the novels as a trauma from which Warshawski cannot recover. In *Killing Orders*, at a point of crisis in the narrative, Warshawski realizes:

> I was carrying on this internal monologue as an argument with Gabriella [her dead mother], who didn't seem pleased with me for bugging out so early. 'Goddamn it,

Gabriella,' I swore silently. 'Why did you make me give that crazy promise? She
hated you. Why do I have to do anything for her?' If my mother were alive she
would shrivel me on the spot for swearing at her. And then turn fierce intelligent
eyes on me: 'So Rosa fired you? Did you go to work only because she hired you?'
(Paretsky 1987b: 46)

Gabriella haunts Warshawski's dreams and creates in her the impulse to seek
the answer to the enigma under investigation: 'Gabriella had come to me [in
a dream], not wasted as in the final days of her illness, but full of life. She
knew I was in danger and wanted to wrap me in a white sheet to save me'
(1987b: 170). In attempting to displace the pain of bereavement, Warshawski's
narrative engages symbolically with the counterpoint provided in each story
by Lotty, the older immigrant woman who offers Warshawski support, affection and ethical advice.[24] Indeed, Lotty performs an idealized maternal role to
which Warshawski responds as a daughter. For example, she says of Lotty:
'She's the one person I never lie to. She's – not my conscience – the person
who helps me see who I really am, I guess' (1988b: 339). And, after a lengthy
disagreement in one novel, traumatic to Warshawski ('Lotty, my refuge,
wouldn't speak to me'), Lotty says to Warshawski: 'You have been the daughter I never had, V.I. As well as one of the best friends a woman could ever
desire' (1987b: 181, 231–2). Warshawski's narratives are significant in permitting a displaced mourning for the maternal relation. As such, they also
create a space in which the ethical can be counterposed to the force of the law:
the outcome of the case is never as important to Warshawski as the restoration of the relationship she has with Lotty as a surrogate for her dead mother.

The law of crime

While some stories are extremely specific as to the types of crime that their
narratives will engender (Paretsky's fondness for property crime has already
been mentioned), others provide a variety, usually centring on a murder. In
the stories of Raymond Chandler, for example, the plot repeatedly revolves
around at least one murder. Other crimes may be committed (such as blackmail, illegal gambling, prostitution, drug use and supply, extortion, theft,
robbery) but the central horror of each story is a brutal homicide. Often, however, the detective is hired on a routine matter which holds no hint of the
horrors ahead: in *The Big Sleep* (1939), Marlowe is hired to investigate a
blackmail attempt; in *The High Window* (1943) he is asked to trace a stolen
coin; in *The Little Sister* (1949) to check on the safety of the client's brother.
Paretsky's V.I. Warshawski increasingly sings the praises of routine work as
the backbone of her job: in *Tunnel Vision* (1994), she frequently refers to the
pay cheque at the end of a job as the only motivation for doing it. Grafton's
Kinsey Millhone also usually begins a case on a seemingly routine matter,
which will lead the detective into a murder investigation; part of the thrill is
the implication that, on any day, the humdrum might become the unusual, as

24. In an interview with me, the author stated that she herself resembles Lotty while
Warshawski was written as her Other (12 April 1990).

the everyday is interrupted by the unfamiliar or uncanny.[25] Grafton makes this explicit in *G is for Gumshoe*:

Three things occurred on or about May 5. . . .

1. The reconstruction of my apartment was completed and I moved back in.
2. I was hired by a Mrs. Clyde Gersh to bring her mother back from the Mojave desert.
3. I made one of the top slots on Tyrone Patty's hit list.

I report these events not necessarily in the order of importance, but in the order most easily explained. (1991: 1)

In Chandler's novels, the acts of murder which lie at the heart of the texts are always born out of fear, greed or innate evil. The victims may have been killed to prevent them from using information against the murderer, or they may be killed as a result of jealousy or anger. However, the motivations which most disturb Marlowe (and hence the reader, sharing his narrative eye) are those which he can only attribute to an innate evil. Murder as a means to an end is found to be more readily explicable than murder as an end in itself. 'Evil' thus functions as a name Marlowe gives to acts which are incomprehensible to the technological rationality of detective fiction. The characters which appear the most deadly (the most prone to committing murder for its own sake) in Chandler's texts are always women: Carmen Sternwood in *The Big Sleep* (1939) is portrayed as utterly amoral, psychologically disturbed, sexually voracious and homicidally violent. She is revealed as the murderer of the missing Regan, through Marlowe's re-enactment of the scene of the crime. Chandler's descriptions of Carmen are unequivocally censorious: her eyes are 'full of some jungle emotion'; she has a 'small corrupt body', 'sharp predatory teeth' and 'thin, too taut lips'. Her teeth are described on several occasions as small and sharp, her face is 'like scraped bone' in the midst of her violent tempers, while she 'makes a hissing sound'. In the final denouement, when she tries to shoot Marlowe, she is described as 'aged, deteriorated, become animal'.

Such misogynist representations are well-known components of other contemporary portrayals of women, such as *film noir*.[26] Chandler adheres to it in all his texts. For Marlowe to appear heroic, a counterpoint is required; an amorality which can be ascribed to femininity. For Marlowe to be the law, a woman must be sacrificed. To that extent, Chandler's detective fiction entextualizes the struggle of sexual difference. Only one honourable female character appears in a Chandler novel (Anne Riordan in *Farewell, My Lovely* [1940]) and Chandler claimed that writing this character gave him enormous problems. The plot requires her to be courageous, friendly, intelligent. She is also one of the few women who does not attract Marlowe sexually. Her position in the text is therefore masculine: she functions as a de-sexed woman who moves the plot along through her interventions but who is not permitted

---

25. On the everyday, see de Certeau (1984).
26. See Hart (1994: 160); Kaplan (1980: 1–5); Modleski (1988); Žižek (1992: 149–64).

to achieve anything in the name of femininity (unlike Marlowe, who is clearly marked as an agent of masculinity at all times). Femininity resides solely in women capable of murder. Marlowe does experience sexual desire for these women. Even his ultimate object of desire, Linda, with whom he falls in love at the end of *Playback* (1958), was a suspect in the narrative. In Chandler's unfinished *Poodle Springs* (completed by Robert B. Parker [1990]), Marlowe is married to Linda. Her great wealth means that he has no need to work. The marriage deteriorates as his identity suffers a crisis of masculine autonomy; he sees himself reduced to the lap dog of the title. The book ends with Marlowe and Linda regretfully agreeing to part; Marlowe is thus enabled to resume his independent, masculine life. Femininity is thus deadly or suffocating and emasculating for Marlowe. Pleasure and danger are inextricably linked and located in the feminine body. While much of the superficial plot deals with the corruption and greed that Chandler saw as afflicting the Los Angeles of the 1940s onwards, each story is merely a variation on that theme, with Woman embodying the evil that will seep out of the text's heart.

It might be thought that women do not feature largely in the stories of Doyle, featuring Sherlock Holmes and Dr Watson. Indeed, the homosociality of these texts predates and predicts the contemporary stereotype of the 'buddy-buddy' narrative. Theirs is a relationship of devotion on the part of Watson and assertive leadership on the part of Holmes. Watson's hesitancy in 'seeing' has been mentioned above; in *The Hound of the Baskervilles* (1902) Holmes' intellectual elevation is made literal. A solitary watcher on top of a hill haunted by the spectral hound of Hell is revealed to be Holmes, hiding out in order to observe the characters in secret. They have their differences (for instance, Watson's dislike of Holmes' drug-taking) but these never threaten their relationship. The steadfastness of the Holmes–Watson friendship serves to emphasize that men can rely on each other, be faithful to each other. After Holmes and Moriarty have disappeared over the Reichenbach Falls, their bodies never to be found, Watson describes Holmes as 'him whom I shall ever regard as the best and the wisest man whom I have ever known' (Doyle, 1894: 255).

The Holmes stories represent crime as a puzzle. Many of the stories do not deal with a criminal offence as such; rather, they examine disorder in the respectable bourgeois family. The threat to established middle-class order, which can be embodied by crime, may also be located in the deterioration or pathological evolution of familial relationships. A major force of destruction is greed, which is often portrayed as capable of overthrowing familial responsibilities and sentiment. In 'The copper beeches', a father interferes with his daughter's marriage prospects in order to keep her money. In 'The man with the twisted lip', money tempts a man away from his respectable life. In 'The Boscombe Valley mystery', the greedy crime lay in the past but returns to haunt an apparently respectable family. (All three stories are from Doyle [1892].) Selfishness – usually for financial gain – is constituted as a major force of destruction. Such a quest for wealth is taken as a manifest cause of an irresponsibility that leads to personal disgrace, criminality and social breakdown.

Greed symbolizes the abyss, the depthless chasm in which all socially cohesive bonds will loosen and where reason, self-control and responsibility wither to nothing. Total self-indulgence and unrestrained individualism are of course the extreme evolutions of the Victorian values of self-help, independence and acquisitiveness. Greed represents the disappearance of Victorian order. All forms of disorder in the Holmes stories – greed, enmity, aggression – should be read as the disappearance of order. To that extent, the Holmes stories represented the dangers of excessive desire. Crime – the result of excessive desire – becomes too visible and must be made to disappear, restoring (the appearance of) order. As such, the disorderly selfishness in the Holmes stories is represented as the dark underside of the demanding individualism fundamental to the economic worldview of the modern city. The textual greed which produced the crime had to be recognizable in a culture which lauded individual and familial economic achievement. It obtained much of its threatening aura, however, from the counterpoint provided by the values of the investigating detective. Holmes stood for rationalism, which was also central to Victorian culture. As greed generated the fears and hopes integral to Victorian society, Holmes represents a textual mediation of the intimate relationship between success and criminality as dominant cultural values.

In addition to the threat of greed, an additional menace can be discerned. As stated above, at first there may appear little place for women in Doyle's texts. Yet that very exclusion is itself a representation of ideological value. That women fail to appear in the Holmes stories is to be read not as a cause but as a symptom of masculinity. When women do appear, they exist only in relation to men: forever wives, daughters of greedy fathers, sisters of dead brothers. Holmes is sufficient unto himself, unmarried, solitary. His friendship with Watson is necessary for the narrative; there is no implication that it is essential for Holmes' happiness. Indeed, their relationship represents the price of detection: the sacrifice of emotion, women, friendship. Thus, when Watson informs Holmes, at the end of *The Sign of Four*, that he has married Miss Morstan, Holmes reacts as follows:

> He gave a most dismal groan. 'I feared as much,' said he. 'I really cannot congratulate you . . .'
> I [Watson] was a little hurt. 'Have you any reason to be dissatisfied with my choice?' I asked.
> 'Not at all. I think she is one of the most charming young ladies I ever met, and might have been useful in such work as we have been doing . . . But love is an emotional thing, and whatever is emotional is opposed to that true cold reason which I place above all things. I should never marry myself, lest I bias my judgement.' (1890: 139–40)

Holmes sees marriage as a loss of 'true cold reason', a loss of control. His will to knowledge, his 'judgement', would be overwhelmed or biased by the power of Woman; his manly skills clouded by feminine demands and whimsy. After their marriage, the Watsons' union appears to be idyllic; however, this is so by default since Watson spends all his time with Holmes, their homosocial bond unaffected by his marriage. After her appearance as a protagonist in *The Sign of Four*, the newly married Mrs Watson never appears again; she exists in shadow, a constant absence whose function is to tend the home that awaits Watson at the end of each adventure with Holmes. The role of Woman is to *be* absent, to be unadventurous. Where Chandler wrote women into his stories as the embodiment of fatality, Doyle's texts exclude women, lest they threaten either the peaceful co-existence of men or the execution of the detective method.

After Doyle's sexual apartheid, Paretsky and Grafton offer considerable pleasures for the feminist reader.[27] Paretsky describes how her detective was conceived as a reaction to Chandler's construction of femininity:

> After reading *Farewell, My Lovely* almost twenty years ago, I found myself wishing for a woman hero. Chandler's women are complex, some venal, some drunk, some sex cats, some gallant, but in most of his books, the seductress, whether Dolores Gonzalez, Velma, or Carmen, is at the root of the trouble. I spent many years working on different ways in which a woman could play a stronger, less sexual role in a mystery and finally, in 1979, came up with V.I. Warshawski. (1988c: 132–3)

The female detectives of Paretsky and Grafton are very different to the seductresses in Chandler's texts: Warshawski and Millhone are independent (financially and emotionally), physically strong, often heroic in action. They move around the urban settings of the narrative, often at night or in threatening locations. They experience fear (and the reader, who shares their narrative eye, experiences it too) but draw on mental and physical resources to overcome any trepidation or actual threat. This, then, is one of the many attractions offered to the contemporary feminist reader: liberating the woman from confinement in her home, circumventing the female fear of attack in the dark urban streets. In a culture where, as Stanko (1990b) writes, 'precaution is normal', Warshawski's and Millhone's circulation around the city space is a seductive spectacle, experienced vicariously by the reader. Critics have commented, however, that the feminist detective's 'successes' in terms of solving crimes often mean a restoring of order to the patriarchal world that oppresses them.[28] Furthermore, when a physical threat is realized and the detective is injured (a frequent occurrence), the price of detection is literalized upon her body. The many injuries suffered by Millhone and Warshawski register the costs of curiosity, of unconfined circulation around the city space.

Paretsky's texts involve urban corruption and greed, corporate subterfuge overlaying individual criminality (in, for example, *Blood Shot* [1988b], the plot superimposes the rape of a young girl by her uncle with the violation of workers' bodies by their employer). Warshawski is hired (in all but the first and latest novels, *Indemnity Only* [1987a] and *Tunnel Vision* [1994]) by a

---

27. For an analysis of the 'recent emergence of the female hard-boiled detective' through a comparison of Paretsky's *Blood Shot* and Grafton's *F is for Fugitive*, see Umphrey and Shuker-Haines (1991).

28. See Blake (1990); Cranny-Francis (1990); Klein (1988).

friend or relative to look into some minor difficulty or irregularity, usually in the corporate world, which inevitably leads her into a murder investigation. The substitution of a friend or relative for the anonymous client enables the reader to enter the private world of the private eye and see it made problematic (especially in *Guardian Angel* [1992] and *Killing Orders* [1987b]).[29] The plots allow much extemporizing on Chicago's social decay, interpersonal violence and declining civilization. The crimes arise out of dominant social institutions, ironic inversions of an institution's apparent social purpose: from union politics comes corruption; from health care budget cuts comes negligent homicide in a hospital; a religious order is used as a front for illegal business deals; housing development corporations are used to launder money. Warshawski is thus permitted to make politically critical points throughout the texts. While many of the characteristics of Warshawski echo those of the hard-boiled loner such as Marlowe (she is as solitary and as cynical as he; she blames the urban decay of Chicago as much as he mourns the decline of Los Angeles), her politics are distinguished by anti-sexism and anti-racism. Similarly, Warshawski's actions and values often cause problems for her friends and lovers: in *Guardian Angel* (1992), her best friend and mother-surrogate Lotty is shot by an assailant who mistakes her for Warshawski; in *Tunnel Vision* (1994), her work leads her into conflict with her lover, who is a (black) police officer, ultimately seeming to destroy the relationship. Paretsky's texts extend the notion of the price of detection: the detective's friends are equally at risk of injury; relationships may be sacrificed in the pursuit of the solution.

Grafton's Millhone exists in a similar condition. She is usually single; occasionally sleeping with lovers who turn out to be problematic (a suspect who turns out to be the murderer; a married police officer; another private investigator with whom she cannot sustain the relationship). She thinks she has no family (and relishes this independence); in later texts, she discovers a group of long-lost relatives whose existence cause her much uneasiness. Her living conditions are a hyper-literalization of the detective's desire for solitariness; yet she continually defines herself in relation to others: her landlord, her two previous marriages, her dead aunt. The plots tend to focus on familial or intimate murder, with a backdrop of corruption or fraud. Perhaps due to the more benign Californian location, her narrative voice is less scabrous than Warshawski's and the plots depend less upon the notion of a precipitous decline in urban civilization. Both, however, embody the pleasures and pains of independent life in a patriarchal society.

Another woman occupying the masculine narrative function of detective is McDermid's Lindsay Gordon (not a private investigator, but an investigative journalist who acts as detective when forced by circumstance to do so). In the first three books, a friend is thought to have committed murder: in *Report for Murder* (1987) a friend is held on remand; in *Common Murder* (1989), another is under suspicion; in *Final Edition* (1991), an ex-colleague is arrested,

---

29. This device was discussed by Paretsky in an interview with me, 12 April 1990.

convicted and sentenced. In the fourth novel, *Union Jack* (1993), Gordon herself is initially under suspicion.[30] Men play subsidiary roles. The texts allow investigation of the criminal justice system's attitudes towards women and the complexities of women's lives. Gordon's help is always enlisted after a murder has been committed, thus establishing from the outset the high stakes being gambled by an unknown player who has everything to lose. Gordon's own life is thus always in danger as a result of her investigations (like Warshawski and Millhone, Gordon is portrayed as ready to pay the ultimate price for detection). The locations vary: a girls' school in rural Derbyshire; a women's peace camp outside an American missile base (a thinly disguised Greenham Common); the reconstructed Glasgow of the 1990s; a Trades Union Congress conference.

McDermid's novels permit Gordon to expound on sexism, racism, class politics, urban renewal and corruption in Glasgow, and homophobia. Gordon's lesbianism is a crucial aspect of each plot, reflected in the community of women that the text investigates and in the political values endorsed by the narratives. Similar underpinnings appear in the novels of Scoppetone.[31] Lauren Laurano's investigations detail not only the unravelling of a mystery but also the day-to-day negotiations of homophobia in New York City: for example, an overheard conversation between a deli owner and another customer involves such homophobic language that Laurano not only challenges the deli owner about it but also decides she can never go to that deli again (Scoppetone, 1993). The urban space is conveyed as a site of complex tensions and conversational hurdles with insults being dealt her by secretaries, neighbours, gay men, parents. The matter of solving the crime is presented as an immediate problem which slots into the overarching issue of the negotiation of everyday life within a sexual identity deemed abnormal or deviant.

The texts of Grafton, Paretsky and McDermid offer a reappraisal of the laws of crime which govern the genre of detective fiction. While Doyle and Chandler were also concerned with the question of legibility and visibility (as the crime appears, order disappears; the detective's task being one of making legible the unintelligibility of the event of crime), the feminist writers extended these notions into various crises of the real and the everyday. Criminality occurs within the same frame as homophobia; sexism co-exists with sexual murder. The embodiment of the detective in Millhone, Warshawski or Gordon is one whose entire existence is criss-crossed with tensions, riven with ambiguities. Romance and sexual involvement are not separate from detection, as even the object of desire is made problematic and open to suspicion. The detective struggles with the police (as the traditional agent of law and order) not just as a result of her profession, but also as a result of her femininity or her sexuality. The feminist critique of traditional detective fiction (as represented by the texts of Doyle and Chandler, for example) seemed at times to desire a feminist version of detective fiction that had

30. Two of the titles play on Gordon's work as a journalist; each one plays on its plot.
31. These are: *Everything You Have Is Mine* (1991); *I'll Always Be Leaving You* (1993).

gone beyond detective fiction. That is, in transcending the strictures of the genre, its feminist rewriting might give birth to a new horizon untrammelled by the limitations of the genre. This echoes the rejection of criminology offered by many feminist critics, who seek a feminist criminology that is not criminology (see Chapter 2). Like criminology, detective fiction is not as monolithic as these critiques suppose; the charm of many feminist re-visions derives from their commitment to capitalize on the tensions and differences within detective fiction, rather than abandon it for some mystical new horizon.[32]

On (extra)ordinary heroism

The naming of the detective and the genres of crime they are required to investigate signify certain structural parameters within the narrative (a foreign origin, a literary disposition, a sexual orientation, a feminist worldview) and simultaneously contribute towards the establishment of the detective as heroic. The detective guides the reader through the world of criminality; as such she must be more than the reader or the client, who was unable to solve the puzzle on her own. This exceptionality is present even when the detective attempts to deny it: despite Warshawski's claims that she feels fear (and is therefore 'ordinary'), her heroism is plain and indeed is crucial to the resolution of each narrative. In *Burn Marks* (1990), for example, she performs acts of great courage as well as physical strength (for example, she rescues her aunt from a burning building, thus preventing the woman's almost certain death); in *Tunnel Vision* (1994), she undertakes a search for homeless children in the flooding sewers beneath a building, risking death by drowning. The effect of these incidents is to engender admiration for the detective, but also to distance her from the reader or client who is deemed incapable of such acts. Unlike the distance felt between the reader and Holmes (or between the reader and the 'elsewhere' of rural village life in Agatha Christie's texts), this is a distance that bespeaks proximity, by locating crime in the everyday.

Chandler admits the heroic nature of the detective: 'down these mean streets a man must go who is not himself mean, who is neither tarnished nor afraid. The detective in this kind of story must be such a man. He is the hero, he is everything' (1964: 198). The world of the reader is congruent with the world of the client, and the criminal, the world which the detective must transcend, the 'Great Wrong Place', in Auden's terms (1962: 151). Chandler describes it thus:

> [A] world in which gangsters can rule nations . . . in which hotels are owned by men who made their money out of brothels, in which a screen star can be the finger man for the mob, and the nice man down the hall is a boss of the numbers racket; a world where a judge with a cellar full of bootleg liquor can send a man to jail for having a pint in his pocket, where the mayor of your town may have condoned murder as an instrument of money-making, where no man can walk down a dark street

---

32. Thus, the attempt to write a 'postmodern' feminist parody of a detective story, which dispensed with conventional devices of plot and structure, left me very bored: see Jiles (1986).

in safety because law and order are things we talk about but refrain from practising; a world where you may witness a hold-up in broad daylight and see who did it, but you will fade quickly back into the crowd rather than tell anyone because the hold-up men may have friends with long guns, or the police may not like your testimony, and in any case the shyster for the defence will vilify you in open court, before a jury of selected morons, without any interference from a political judge. It is not a very fragrant world, but it is the world you live in. (1964: 197–8)

Marlowe's everyday differs from that of the female detective, since, within it, the detective functions as a totalization of the real world ('he is everything').[33] While Marlowe was constructed to appear heroic yet recognizable to his readers, Sherlock Holmes could never be said to represent the heroic ordinary man. Holmes is the 'super-detective, a reassuringly infallible hero' (Blake, 1990: 56). Holmes is in many ways the inverse of Marlowe, yet both function to totalize the Real of their worlds, admitting no differences. Holmes' heroism resides in his powers of intellect. He is multi-talented (musical, literate, highly numerate, cognizant of the latest forensic techniques and criminological theories). He follows Poe's Dupin in his upper class, intellectual eccentricity that distances the reader and prevents identification. This is no distance that bespeaks proximity.

Lindsay Gordon, on the other hand, is represented in the realist mode of recognizable flaws married to courage and bravery: her loyalty to friends and tenaciousness in the face of defeat, her flouting of authority figures from the police to the British government are presented as highly positive characteristics; however, like all the detectives, each admirable trait is mirrored by a flaw which impinges in some way upon the narrative.[34] Gordon's pomposity, temper and independence lead her into difficulties with friends, lovers and the police.[35] Warshawski's bad temper, recklessness and antagonistic attitudes also alienate: *Tunnel Vision* (1994) concludes with a party to celebrate her 40th birthday which she cannot enjoy due to her angry depression which has just broken up a relationship; *Guardian Angel* (1992) has her in a foul temper for the entire narrative. Marlowe is similarly sarcastic, leading him to be beaten up by police and villains alike, while Holmes takes cocaine to alleviate the boredom engendered by his superior intelligence. The existence of a character flaw is crucial to the narratives.[36] The split subjectivity of the detective

33. The modern criminological avatar of Marlowe is the left realist, who also totalizes an experience of the everyday into the Real: see Chapter 3.

34. As noted above, the detective is a split subject or divided unity: thus Holmes' rationalism is married to his imagination; Gordon's tenaciousness combines with a dogmatic pomposity.

35. Scoppetone's Laurano performs in the same way. When asked by her lover not to proceed with an investigation, she pretends to agree, knowing that she will not be able to comply.

36. Lack of an obvious character flaw prevents one contemporary woman detective from functioning as a sympathetic figure: the six foot tall, red-haired, guitar-playing Carlotta Carlyle seems too perfect to be real(istic): see Barnes (1990). On the other hand, Lauren Laurano takes the character flaw to extremes: she seems to have fatally jinxed her former lovers (one is shot while they are kissing in his car; her first lesbian lover and fellow FBI agent is accidentally shot by Laurano herself on an assignment). Her later flaws include an addiction to chocolate and cream cakes at the peril of her high cholesterol count.

allows for identification by the reader to take place with or against the detective: thus, the reader may well feel sympathetic to Warshawski's cussedness yet alienated by Holmes' encyclopaedic knowledge and casual use of cocaine. Identifying against Holmes (as a sympathetic figure) affects neither his narrative function nor his fascination for the reader as powerful, enigmatic and utterly autonomous.

At the same time, all the other detectives discussed are constituted as metaphors for the ordinary person. As heroes, they are populist, in the sense that they resemble the ordinary person. They make virtues out of smallness and anonymity. Marlowe states, in *Farewell, My Lovely*: 'I needed a drink, I needed a lot of life insurance, I needed a vacation, I needed a home in the country. What I had was a coat, a hat and a gun. I put them on and went out of the room' (1940: 207). Warshawski has her extravagances: whisky, expensive shoes, Murano glasses from which to drink good Italian wine (the glasses are her mother's; as the novels progress and Warshawski's apartment suffers arson, burglary and so on, the glasses get smashed one by one, reiterating the trauma of her mother's death).[37] These luxuries are always subordinated to a general attitude of indifference to money-making and a loathing of the suburbanized rich. Gordon drives a sports car but lives hand-to-mouth as a poorly paid reporter; after starting a relationship with a wealthy author she refuses any financial help from her. The detective is small by choice, always succeeding in the end to have the last word against the rich, the powerful and the corrupt. The apparent financial loser is the moral winner, as material poverty stands in for ethical superiority.

Betrayal, or the laws of the Other

Part of Holmes' Ur-heroism is that he does not suffer betrayal at the hands of any other character. His demise comes in a hand-to-hand battle with the arch-villain Moriarty as they plunge together over the Reichenbach Falls.[38] Every other detective suffers loss through a confrontation with the laws, or desires, of the Other. Marlowe is cheated by Terry, a man with whom he had begun a friendship and whom he had helped escape, in *The Long Goodbye* (1953). It should be noted that Marlowe is betrayed by a man; the fact that he experiences this as far more wounding than any small infidelity he experiences at the hands of a woman reveals his fidelity to the heterosexual order of masculinity. Warshawski is betrayed in *Burn Marks* (1990) when a former lover, the presciently named Michael Furey, turns out to be a killer who is willing to kill her. In *A is for Alibi* (Grafton, 1986), Millhone undergoes the shock of discovering that sexual attraction does not guarantee moral steadfastness: her object of desire also turns out to be a murderer and the book ends with

37. Warshawski also loves to sing: 'Along with the red glasses, my voice was my legacy from Gabriella' (1985: 124). When her apartment is set on fire, Warshawski seizes two of her mother's glasses as she escapes: 'I thought of the other five, locked in my bedroom, in the heat and flames. "Oh, Gabriella," I muttered, "I'm so sorry"' (1987b: 129).

38. In 'The final problem' (Doyle, 1894: 236–55).

Millhone shooting him to save her own life. Both of these men are presented in at least an ambiguous manner: Furey is argumentative, Warshawski's attraction to him is ending; Charlie Scorsoni exudes a palpable heat that disturbs Millhone as much as she is unable to resist it. Neither of these matches the devastation that occurs in McDermid's narrative of betrayal, *Final Edition* (1991).

Throughout McDermid's first three novels, a relationship has been charted between Gordon and a wealthy novelist, Cordelia Brown (whose name echoes Lear's daughter and the protagonist of another famous detective story, P.D. James' *An Unsuitable Job for a Woman*). Their affair begins ecstatically in the first story, develops unevenly in the second and has ended before *Final Edition* begins. Brown has taken a new lover and Gordon has to negotiate the fraught space of old love around Brown. The denouement of this narrative, which reveals Brown as the murderer, is genuinely shocking. Gordon is forced to confront the realization that criminality consists in the beloved as well as in the abjured. All belief in trust, in knowing the other through romantic love, is revealed to be a fiction, a construct. McDermid's third novel is the most successful of all of those under discussion for its bringing criminality into the space of loving, of trust and of domesticity.

Final Edition thematizes most explicitly the concern shared by all the feminist writers in the prohibition of woman's desire. Here, that desire is of one woman for another; thus, what is staged or put on display is the prohibition of women's relation with themselves and with other women. In general, the genre of detective fiction projects the trauma of betrayal as women's infidelity towards men. The feminist re-vision of detective fiction makes this ironically explicit, unfaithful to the genre while exploiting it at the same time. To be unfaithful, one must remain within a relationship, while forming (dangerous) liaisons outside it. (To that extent, the feminist infidelities committed against the genre of detective fiction might well mirror the relationship of *Imagining Crime* to criminology: writing a criminal conversation that speaks of belonging and exile, of the familiar and the unfamiliar, at one and the same time.) In feminist detective texts, the object of woman's desire takes its revenge on her: Warshawski, Millhone and Gordon are each betrayed by the one whom they desired. The detective herself becomes the scene of a crime, in that her sexual desire binds her to the one whom she is meant to 'detect' as the criminal. Her desire to interpret, to solve the crime, is then prohibited or impeded by the object of interpretation/desire. This might be read as the revenge of masculinity against a woman who dares to interpret/desire, resulting in the prohibition of self-representation (as a desiring subject) by a woman.

Betrayal derives from the Latin *tradere*, to hand over, deliver, which also gives us 'tradition', handed over to the Other, in betrayal, in trust, confidence, love. Thus, in order to depart from a tradition it is necessary to follow it. Such is the paradox that is brought out in the betrayals experienced by Warshawski, Millhone and Gordon. It is the difference within tradition that makes tradition possible. In the relation with the Other (who betrays), the detective confronts the distance that appeared as proximity, the unfamiliarity that appeared as familiarity. Betrayal thus demands and produces a self, by displaying to the detective (and thus to the reader) that fidelity and infidelity mutually constitute the intersubjective self that can experience betrayal, love, closeness, distance. To be betrayed means to exist in relation to the Other, just as to love and be loved in return invites a relation to the Other. Betrayal is a consequence of all our relationships of trust (as Gordon's experience with Brown shows). Victim and criminal, betrayer and betrayed, are revealed as mutually dependent terms. Meaning exists only relationally.

The criminal (the betrayer) has no meaning without the victim (the betrayed). Criminal law and detective stories together create a taxonomy of relationships, in which a fiction of individualism places the victim above the criminal. The moment when the Other is named as having betrayed the lover is the moment when the criminal law is invoked. Law gives the betrayer the name of criminal (cheat, psychotic, murderer) and sits in judgement. Law gives the betrayed the name of victim and requires mourning at its loss. The victim's judgement of the Other as criminal repeats the moment of original betrayal, by handing the Other over to the force of law, by betraying the Other in the name of the law.[39] Betrayal, therefore, displays the trauma of the distant proximity between criminal and detective, lover and beloved, fidelity and infidelity, tradition and future, text and reader. What is to be affirmed in feminist detective fiction is its staging of the paradox that interrupting tradition is the only way of continuing it. It is this experience of difference which is provoked in the reader of feminist detective fiction. The texts ask to be read against the grain of the tradition while living on within its borderlines. Such a response is the obligation of the reader, the interpreter, the detective. Such is the ethics of reading.

Conclusion: Reading ethics/detecting justice

In their portrayal of crime and punishment, detective stories invariably project the image of a given social order and the implied value system that helps sustain it. These stories confirm that there can be no crime without a community; no individual can transgress without a legal order to condemn. The detective story acts as a mechanism through which the reader censures and abjures certain acts. In so doing, she underwrites a notion which demands a form of policing and a dispensation of criminal justice. What is missing from the narrative formula of the detective genre is recognition that the law itself, with its definitions of crime and its agencies of enforcement and punishment, is problematic. The law itself is not investigated, never put on trial. Occasionally, the detectives make cynical comments about the criminal justice system. In *Farewell, My Lovely*, Marlowe says: 'law is where you buy it in this

39. This reader felt betrayed by McDermid's fourth novel, *Union Jack* (1993), which sees Gordon return to Britain for a Trades Union Congress conference. Having anticipated some acknowledgement of trauma which would be textually worked through, the jokily glib tone of the narrative seemed a betrayal of responsibility towards the weight of what had gone before. As such, it constituted a nice exemplification of the problem of approaching a text with too many expectations.

town' (Chandler, 1940: 164). Warshawski states that she gave up being a public defender ('the muck I'd left behind when I quit being a public defender' [Paretsky, 1988a: 48]) because she was tired of the innocent being convicted and the guilty going free. In McDermid's texts, the police are often presented as bungling or over-hasty in their conclusions, but no indictment is made of the function of the legal system itself. Laurano, in Scoppetone's novels, works with a police officer called Cecchi who, as a decent, honest, reliable police-man, serves to represent the legal system as a benevolent social force.

Grafton's *K is for Killer*, however, stages a momentary revelation of the sep-aration of law and ethics, posing the question of the location of justice for a feminist reader/detective. Millhone has been investigating the death of a young woman, Lorna Kepler, on behalf of Kepler's mother. Throughout the narrative, Millhone has identified more and more with the dead woman, mir-roring her way of life, befriending her friends. She develops a theory as to who killed Kepler, a theory which includes the murderer also having killed at least one other person. The police officer, Cheney, with whom she has been co-operating, pours scorn on her theory and refuses to take further action:

> Cheney cut in, his tone a mixture of impatience and outrage. . . . 'This is not your job. Face it. There's nothing you can do.' . . .
> 'Cheney, I'm sick of the bad guys winning. I'm sick of watching people get away with murder. How come the law protects them and not us?'
> 'I hear you, Kinsey, but that doesn't change the facts. Even if you're right about Roger, you got no way to nail him, so you might as well drop it. Eventually he'll screw up, and we'll get him then.' (1994: 277)

Millhone is frustrated because she can see 'no means of redress'. Upon learn-ing that a friend of the dead woman, whom Millhone has later befriended, has died as a result of being attacked, she experiences 'a mounting fury': 'like some ancient creature hurtling up from the deep, my rage broke the sur-face and I struck'. She telephones a man she knows to be a gangster and the former lover of the dead woman, 'giving absolutely no thought to what I was doing. I was propelled by the hot urge to act, by the blind need to strike back at the man who had dealt me this blow.' She tells the gangster that 'Roger Bonney killed Lorna Kepler' (1994: 278). At this point, she has no proof, only a series of ideas which seem to make sense to her. Suddenly horrified by her vengeful action, she goes to Roger Bonney's place of work, where he assaults her and more or less confesses to murder while indicating that Millhone's own life is now in danger. At that point, he is called away to see a visitor, who turns out to be the gangster, and Bonney is never seen again. Millhone's fury is pre-sented in the text as partially vindicated by her turning out to be right about the murderer's identity. She tells the police exactly what she has done ('to accept the responsibility'); the police decide 'no purpose would be served in pursuing the matter' (1994: 285). At the same time, her vigilante justice has brought retribution upon a man who had killed three people. She has acted through 'fury', 'like some ancient creature hurtling up from the deep', evok-ing the kraken or Eumenides' furies who wreaked retribution upon criminals. Millhone asks the reader:

Homicide calls up in us the primitive desire to strike a like blow, an impulse to inflict a pain commensurate with the pain we've been dealt. For the most part, we depend upon judicial process to settle our grievances. Perhaps we've even created the clumsy strictures of the courts to keep our savageries in check. The problem is that so often the law seems pale in its remedies, leaving us restless and unfulfilled in our craving for satisfaction. And then what? As for me, the question I'm left with is simple and haunting: having strayed into the shadows, can I find my way back? (1994: 285)

This event displays the disjunction between knowledge and action ('giving absolutely no thought to what I was doing', 'propelled by the hot urge to act', 'the blind need to strike back'), between law and ethics. Millhone does not act morally, but obeys an ethical demand. Moral action is equated with legality (represented in the advice of Cheney, the police officer: 'there's nothing you can do', 'eventually . . . we'll get him'). Legality demands pursuit of knowledge: Cheney says 'you got no way to nail him'; that is, Millhone has no proof, no legal knowledge. Instead, Millhone responds first *not* to the rules and principles of detection but to the demand of the dead woman: the (m)other. Her response is therefore not in continuity with law but comes from the body, from 'the deep'. Millhone recognizes that for many the remedies of the law are often adequate; that is, the demands of law are usually satisfied. The ethical imperative, however, remains unsatisfied, as justice and law diverge (and ethics is subsequently devalued in comparison to law).[40] When Millhone has obeyed the momentary principle of justice, she realizes that there must be a return to law ('can I find my way back?') but in making an ethical, feminist response, she has encountered 'the shadows' and will not return unchanged.

Detective fiction allows the detection of crime to be seen as the means to a desirable end: freedom from crime. As mentioned above, this is the third term that structures crime's dialectic. In the move from fear to pleasure that dictates the reading of detective stories, an imagined state of crimelessness pretends to refer to a lost past while pointing towards its possible future. Detection is represented as the conduit which will realize these desires. Detective fiction posits that, as part of the fulfilment of these desires, it is necessary to *know* the criminal, to recognize her and to predict her identity. As a criminal, she is then to be marked, as different, as Other. In its acceptance and validation of the role of the detective, detective fiction is committed to a conservative ethic in which repressive mechanisms are legitimated. In its offer to the reader of pleasure in fear, moreover, it obliges the reader to desire repression and to invite intervention, in the name of the force of law.

And yet: there is something *else*. While the totalizing legality of the genre can be read as a legitimation of a repressive desire to mark the other as Other, to separate and exile the Other as outlaw, detective fiction has also been the scene of a legible feminist ethics. In the texts of Grafton, Paretsky, McDermid and Scoppetone (among others), the detective exists in a continual relation to

---

40. On the separation of law and justice, see the reading of *Antigone* in Douzinas and Warrington (1994b).

the demands of the Other for justice. She sees an ethics which is prior to law, and for which detection (and law) can only ever constitute a surrogate. She sees a moment of difference in which the Other is a friend she has never met, or a mother outwith the law. Warshawski responds to the memory of her dead mother; her endeavours constitute memorials to the maternal relation. Gordon betrays the procedural demands of the law as a response to her betrayal by a lover, discovering the intimacy of crime and justice. Millhone quits the world of legality in a momentary response to an ethical demand from a dead woman whom she had never met, but whose ghost haunted her efforts as a detective. Leaving the law is only ever momentary: Millhone immediately begins the procedure of returning to its imperatives, by telling the police what she has done (and inviting the stern response of the law). She is subject not to prosecution, but to self-doubt. She has seen the realm of ethics which exists prior to law, knowledge and proof; her future actions will be inflected by her accession to justice, in place of the law. Law is thus only ever a return, something that comes after ethics, which attempts to cover up and displace the ethical response. Detective fiction is conventionally understood as a restoration of law after the rupture of the social order by crime. Restoration would thus function as a reunifying of culture (whether termed patriarchy, capitalism or individualism). Above, I have provided a version of this dominant reading of detective fiction. My suspicion, however, is this: detective fiction makes law appear; and makes crime, after a temporary visibility, disappear. Enfolded within this dialectic of appearance and disappearance, law and crime, is a moment of ethics and justice in which we hear the Other's voice, and a response is possible.

5

The Bulger Case and the
Trauma of the Visible

Every day the urge grows stronger to get hold of an object at very close range by
way of its likeness, its reproduction. Unmistakably, reproduction as offered by picture magazines and newsreels differs from the image seen by the unarmed eye.
(Benjamin, 1968: 223)

Many of the witnesses had been shaken to the core when they realized the infant
they had seen was dead. (quoted in *The Guardian*, 20 November 1993)

This chapter deals with representations of crime by and against children, in the
context of the murder of 2-year-old James Bulger by two 10-year-old boys. The
event received massive national and international media coverage and inspired
an enormous amount of public and private debate. Everyone talked about it.
One of the things, however, that was always striking to me was the lack of
vocabulary that was available in talking about the case, whether that be in a
teaching situation (I had tried to use the case to engender a class discussion of
juvenile delinquency, which was not forthcoming since the students seemed
entirely comfortable with the idea that the two boys were 'evil' – a word which
ended all discussions before they began) or in casual conversation (an evening
with friends degenerated into an extremely strained impasse as a result of discussing the case). In writing about the event now, more than two years after
the murder took place, my personal reactions to it are as strong as they ever
were; indeed, in writing this chapter I have had frequent bad dreams and have
felt a deep sense of horror. Trying to determine the nature of the horror that I
felt has led to the shaping of the chapter into the form that it takes. I had been
struck, on reading the press discourse about the case, that two themes dealing
with horror were prominent. The first involved the horror that parents were
said to feel, imagining their child to be at risk of such a terrible death. The second related to a kind of national hand-wringing and guilt, as the event was
held to be indicative of some kind of contemporary malaise. Neither appeared
to respond to the visceral sense of horror that I felt: I have no child of my own,
and I do not feel susceptible to the view that no event as terrible as this had
ever happened before (the case of Mary Bell, who, as an 11-year-old, killed two
small children 26 years before, gives the lie to this view).

Initially, there seemed to be no other available subject-position for responding to the event, but it seems to me that what is appalling about the event has
to do with visibility. This chapter is concerned with the reception of or
response to the event of the killing of James Bulger. Moreover, the chapter
deals with the ways in which the moment of reception or response is tied to a

rhetoric of visibility and invisibility, of images of the seen and the unseen. In the press coverage of the event, as I will show in detail later, there was a fascination with the visibility of the crime, the victim and the criminals, with visual images provided in abundance by the video cameras and eye-witness reports. That an abduction could take place, despite being filmed on security cameras, and witnessed by 38 witnesses, was a critical theme in the press reports. To me, there is no surprise or shock here. Terrible things happen daily, and are overheard by neighbours who do nothing, or are noticed by passers-by who do nothing. Security cameras film encounters constantly, some obviously violent, others simulating 'normality'. This is a condition of modernity; we all watch and listen to others, while feeling detached from the details of what we see and hear. The horror that overwhelms me in this case is located at the point where Robert Thompson and Jon Venables *disappear* from view, climb over the railway embankment in the dusk and go on to the railway line where they carried out the crime in the dark. This brings us up against the limits or finitude of vision, of hearing, of interpretation and imagination. And this is why the case haunted my dreams and left me, at times, close to tears while writing.

The chapter, then, is concerned with the trauma of the event of the killing of James Bulger. It is an event which *demands* interpretation. Its paradox, however, is that something about the event itself *prohibits* its interpretation. As event, then, it both calls for and prohibits interpretation. This is its central paradox and the centre of this chapter. One of the key features of the discourse I am examining – the discourse of the national press – is that it always responds to the call for interpretation but its response is always haunted by its *failure* to interpret (here a necessary condition imposed by the event itself). In this chapter, I wish to ask: what is the nature of the prohibition on interpretation imposed by this event? It is best described as a confusion of two orders of being, which the canons of interpretation have prescribed as orders which should be kept distinct. These are the orders of semblance and substance; the confusion of these results in a misidentification of appearance and reality. Such a confusion is a part of the process of *aestheticization of everyday life* (discussed in Chapter 1) through which we immediately live mediated lives, in love with the image.[1] The confusion between semblance and substance is played out in the press response to the event of James Bulger's death through a series of oppositions (mother/child, father/mother, tradition/generation, child/non-child). In reading these oppositions, my response to the event will *fail*, just as the discourse of the press does, if it aims only to invert the oppositions. Instead, my aim is to maintain the division between appearance and reality, but to speak across that distance. As an attempt to exorcize the phantoms and phantasms of the event, my discussion of it deals with several themes in the press discourse (which revolve around the oppositions mentioned above): the configuration of child and non-child; the maternal relation; the paternal surrogate; the interplay of memory and image; and the writing of

1. See Baudrillard (1987); Benjamin (1968); Goodrich (1990); Lury (forthcoming).

cultural tradition and heritage in discourses on crime by children. To some, these themes may appear irrelevant, remote, academic. No doubt those individuals have other phantasms.

Configurations of child and non-child

On 12 February 1993, Mrs Denise Bulger went to the Strand shopping centre in Bootle, near Liverpool, with her sister-in-law, Nicola Bailey, and her child, 2-year-old James Bulger. They went to several shops, one of them a butcher's, in which both women bought things. Denise Bulger said later that she thought her son was by her side as she was served; however, after she paid for her purchases, she looked around and could not see him. She ran outside the shop but still could not see her son. He was later seen on a video film taken by a security camera in the shopping centre, following two older boys. A search was instigated; two days later, his body was found on a railway line some two miles from the Strand shopping centre. Two 10-year-old boys were charged with his abduction and murder, and with the attempted abduction of another small boy at the same shopping centre that day. They were tried, in Preston Crown Court, in November 1993 and found guilty. Throughout the trial, their names had been withheld. They were sentenced to be detained at Her Majesty's pleasure, the equivalent of a life sentence, making them the youngest prisoners on life sentences in Britain. After the trial, they were named as Robert Thompson and Jon Venables.

The event is filled with absences and blind spots. The mother cannot see her child; security cameras record but cannot 'see'; the names of the two boys are not to be reported (they are called 'Child A' and 'Child B' instead). There seems to be a prohibition on sight, on identity, which confounds the feverish desire to see 'all' (evidenced by the frenzy of reporting which occurred after the boys were named). The 'meaning' of the event was sought in its details: in the video recordings, in the eye-witness accounts, in the litany of injuries, and in the lives of Venables and Thompson. The details of the event are known to a great many people. The event received saturation media coverage (nationally and internationally),[2] both at the time of the murder and eight months later during the trial of the two boys. Moreover, the event inspired a kind of national collective agony, evidenced both within the media and in individuals' conversations. At the end of 1993, in the perennial 'Review of the Year' television programmes and news or magazine articles, the 'Bulger case', as it had become known, was featured as one of the most significant events of 1993, symptomatic of social decay, the decline of morality, the swelling of parents' fears for the children and a spur to government policy relating to juvenile crime.[3]

2. The case was covered in, for example, *France Soir*, which wrote of Venables and Thompson, 'These monsters could have been your children' (25 November 1993); *Süddeutsche Zeitung*, *El País*; the *South China Morning Post*, *La Stampa* and the *Sydney Morning Herald*.

3. See, for example, *Review of the Year*, on BBC1, 30 December 1993, '1993', in *The Times* (31 December 1993) and 'The worst of '93', in *Cosmopolitan*, January 1994.

A consistent theme in the media representations of the case concerned the nature of childhood. James Bulger was represented as the quintessential child: small, affectionate, trusting, dependent, vulnerable, high-spirited. The press coverage emphasized each of these traits. He is frequently called a 'baby' or a 'toddler'; in the descriptions of the two-mile route taken over two hours by Thompson and Venables on the way to the murder site, James Bulger's smallness and lack of physical stamina are prominent in the press reports. In covering the testimony given by individuals who had witnessed the abduction, James Bulger is called variously 'a baby', 'the little boy' and 'the toddler' (*The Guardian*, 5 November 1993); while the *Independent on Sunday* writes of the 'tired, often crying toddler on a more than two mile trek' (13 February 1994). James Bulger's trusting behaviour is returned to repeatedly in press reports, especially the moment, captured on the security video, when he put his hand in the older boy's hand and walked away from the butcher's shop: 'the baby *whose image haunted us* put his hand in the big boy's hand' (*The Guardian*, 26 November 1993; my emphasis); still photographs from the security camera film tended to use the moment in which James is walking hand in hand with one boy, and following after the other one.[4] It is the image which haunts, not the child himself, but his photograph, his appearance. Warner writes: 'the phantom face of James Bulger has become *the most haunting image of present horrors and social failure*' (1994: 36; my emphasis). The horror of James Bulger's death is made to stand in for the horrors of contemporary society; his image speaks of a reality that includes all of us.

An image of child-like enthusiasm is represented in a number of versions of the narrative which focus upon the events leading up to his abduction by the two boys. *The Guardian* writes: '[Denise Bulger, her sister-in-law and James] visited various shops and on several occasions James broke free from his mother and ran off. He seemed to be in high spirits – in one shop a baby suit fell on his head and he started throwing it about. In [a supermarket] he helped himself to some [sweets]' (2 November 1993). Two photographs of James Bulger are used to illustrate articles about the event. One is a head-and-shoulders shot, in which the child is unsmiling and directly facing the camera, wearing a T-shirt or perhaps pyjama top emblazoned with the legend 'Teenage Mutant Ninja Turtles'. His blond hair flops over his forehead and his eyes look large and round. The other photograph is also a head-and-shoulders shot, taken in three-quarters pose. The child smiles out of this photograph, and is wearing a white shirt whose collar lies over a darker top. The hair still flops onto the forehead, the eyes, as in the other shot, directly engage the spectator. The first shot has the look of a candid, unposed snapshot; the second has more the air of an orchestrated pose. In both pictures, the child looks attractive, according to the scales of visible 'cuteness' developed through the

---

4. This image is used in the *Independent on Sunday* (6 February 1994), the *Daily Star* (25 November 1993), and to illustrate an article entitled 'Children who kill' in *Women's Journal* (Tate, 1993).

use of children in advertising.[5] His grandmother is quoted in one article, saying: 'he was a bubbly little boy – he was beautiful' (*Daily Mail*, 16 February 1993). More than this, he looks essentially child-*like*, an ideal child, or an *idea* of a child. Barthes writes, of a photograph of a young man taken in his prison cell as he awaits execution for attempted murder: 'The photograph is handsome, as is the boy. . . . But . . . *he is going to die*. I read at the same time: *This will be* and *this has been*; I observe with horror an anterior future of which death is the stake. . . . I shudder . . . *over a catastrophe which has already occurred*' (1984: 96; emphasis in original). James Bulger's essential child-like-ness is a necessary component both of the ability of the image to *haunt*; and of the comparison which is made by the press with Venables and Thompson.

James Bulger, then, was a 2-year-old who is taken as embodying many of the representative ideals of childhood. In combination, they constitute one of the dominant classical conceptions of childhood; that is, that the child should both be and appear innocent. That James Bulger was regarded as an allegory of the innocence of childhood can be seen, first of all, in headlines which explicitly proclaim this but also through an examination of the representations of the two boys who abducted and killed him. In 'The death of innocence', one of the officers involved in the case is quoted as saying: 'I believe human nature spurts out freaks. . . . These two were freaks who just found each other. You should not compare these two boys with other boys; they were evil.' The journalist agrees with this view, stating: 'They did not look like ordinary boys, even before the murder' (*Independent on Sunday*, 28 November 1993). This is presented as more credible than the views of child psychologists, quoted before the police officer: for example, 'John Pearce, professor of child and adolescent psychiatry at Nottingham University, thinks "there is a much smaller difference between what these children did and what other children do than meets the eye. It would be wrong to assume that these children are evil."' The innocence embodied by James Bulger is given more weight when it is counterposed to the evil held to be personified by Robert Thompson and Jon Venables. They are portrayed as aberrations of children, approximations of what a child might be, or fraudulent impostors. Venables and Thompson *appear* to be children but are not: they are more like evil adults or monsters in disguise. Evil is the lack of correspondence between appearance and being: Thompson and Venables *appear* to be children but *are not*. James Bulger, on the other hand, *appears* child-*like* and *is* the quintessence of childhood. His innocence consists in the absolute correspondence between his image and his substance.

The notion that Thompson and Venables were aberrations is reiterated in the *Daily Express* under the headline 'Freaks of nature' (2 November 1993). The subheading reads: 'The faces of normal boys but they had hearts of evil.'[6] Above both sat a head-and-shoulders photograph of each child. The

---

5. The former, for example, in *The Guardian* (3 November 1993), and the latter in the *Daily Star* (25 November 1993).

6. A similar trope appears in *The Guardian*, 'Journey to the heart of darkness' (12 March 1994), and the *Independent on Sunday*, 'Two hearts in darkness' (28 November 1993).

photographs appear to be school portraits; the one of Thompson is posed in three-quarters shot, school uniform visible, hair neatly combed, eyes gazing a little away from the lens, so that he appears not to engage with the spectator. His lips are slightly parted. Venables, on the other hand, is grinning a full smile in his portrait. He faces the camera, his eyes meet the lens and the viewer. He is also clearly in school uniform and his hair is neat and short. A tooth appears to be missing. Neither child is marked by any signifier so contemporary as the 'Ninja Turtles' T-shirt James Bulger wears in his picture; on the contrary, Thompson and Venables look somehow timeless, ahistorical, an effect produced by the school uniform and their plastered down hair. The school photographs also serve as reminders that the boys should have been in school at the time they abducted James Bulger. The school portrait is also the most formal image available of children, the juvenile equivalent of the police mug shot used to illustrate stories about adult offenders. The disjunction between the normality of these portraits of childhood and the headline ('Freaks of nature') is immense. Other papers employed the same device to create a schism both between the appearance of the two boys and the condemnatory headlines, and between the two boys and James Bulger. The *Daily Star* put photographs of all three on its front page, a smiling James Bulger at the top, Thompson and Venables side-by-side below him, and a headline running across the bottom of the page: 'How do you feel now you little bastards' (25 November 1993).

Descriptions in the press of the behaviour of Venables and Thompson in the Strand shopping centre, prior to the abduction of James Bulger, follow the same lines. Distinctions are drawn between these boys (who only appear to be children) and other imagined 'real' ones. *The Guardian*, summarizing the security video shown to the jury at Thompson and Venables' trial, states: 'some [shots] show them close together, jostling or playfully kicking each other'. A witness, quoted in the same article, described the two boys as 'messing around with a fire hydrant, and thought they should have been at school'. Another witness describes the boys as 'shoving each other' and 'tormenting an old lady'. Yet another saw one boy emerge from a shop with what the witness 'assumed to be a stolen tin of modelling paint' (4 November 1993). Unlike James Bulger, whose antics (throwing a child's suit to the ground in a shop, helping himself to sweets in a supermarket) are represented as child-like high spirits, Thompson and Venables are represented as engaging in behaviour that is menacing (tormenting an old lady), delinquent (stealing paint) and illegitimate (they should have been in school).[7]

7. And yet much of this behaviour mirrors the behaviour lauded in literature and cinema as typical of young boys: skipping school, stealing an item associated with boys' toys, bullying behaviour, mischief (see, for example, the cartoon strip *Dennis the Menace* and movie *Dennis*; the short stories of Ian McEwan). Some attempts were made to characterize Venables and Thompson as 'typical' boys who enacted 'boyish' behaviour in hyperbolic fashion: 'I don't believe my children are more callous than I was (I once plugged a hamster into a fairy-light socket to see what happened. . . . My son . . . was once caught trying to smash the family tortoise on the garden path "to see how it worked"' (*Sydney Morning Herald*, 10 September 1994);

The extent of the distance between the two boys and James Bulger is made explicit in one headline, 'Beyond good and evil' (*The Guardian*, 26 November 1993), where James Bulger stands for the former, and Thompson and Venables the latter. This article focuses on the mixture of child and non-child that it finds in the two boys, homing in on one piece of taped interview between the police and Robert Thompson that was played during the trial. In it, Thompson says that he did not lift James Bulger's body off the railway line because of his fear that the infant's blood would stain his anorak: 'Cos blood stains, doesn't it, and then me mother would have to pay more money and he was pouring with blood so I put him back down.' The article comments: 'This is clearly a child talking, a child who feels responsibility to keep his clothes clean, a child who understands the price of things, a child who doesn't want to burden his mother with cleaning bills. Yet this is the child who killed another child' (*The Guardian*, 26 November 1993).

The maternal relation

Much of the horror which resonates in the event derives from the interpretations that are made of the relationship which exists between mother and child. In the last excerpt above, where Robert Thompson expresses anxiety about the anger his mother would feel about a dirty jacket, the reader is horrified because here a child recognizes maternal authority but has misplaced its proper cause: would his mother not be more angry about his having murdered another child? The discourse surrounding the case resounds with such questions; indeed, one of the ways the event of the killing of James Bulger can be understood is as a crisis in the cultural representation of the maternal relationship. This crisis takes the form of a rupture or breach in the permitted representations of this relationship. Such a rupture causes extreme anxiety, resulting in frantic attempts, within the public discourse of the media, to efface the rupture and restore a sense of order to the maternal and the familial relation. I will recount how this takes place.

The press discourse thoroughly interrogates the relationships between the three children involved – James Bulger, Jonathan Venables and Robert Thompson – and their mothers, Denise Bulger, Susan Venables and Ann Thompson. Just as a schism was established between James Bulger and his two assailants (they are non-children to his essential child-likeness), so an enormous divide is opened up between Denise Bulger and the mothers of the other two children. Denise Bulger was, of course, with her son in the Strand shopping centre at Bootle; in the butcher's shop, 'Mrs Bulger believed James was by her side when she was being served – but when she looked down, he was gone' (*The Guardian*, 2 November 1993). An editorial in *The Guardian*

'something happened when we got together . . . it's not that any of us were evil . . . what started off as a game of rounders would end up as a game of clubbing the neighbour's cat to death . . . if all this sounds uncommonly horrific then I can only say that it did not seem so then' (Andrew O'Hagan in the *London Review of Books*, March 1993).

called her 'the mother who turned away to shop for a second' (27 November
1993). Mrs Bulger's subsequent panicked flight from the shop, as she realized
her son was gone, was recorded on the security cameras and replayed over and
over, on the television news, before and after her son had been found, and then
to the jury at the trial (*The Guardian*, 4 November 1993). What is particularly
significant about the press representations of this moment has to do with the
normality that is imputed to the situation. Mrs Bulger is characterized as a
normal, everyday mother, any mother, out shopping with her 2-year-old child.
Looking away, or allowing him to be outside the shop while she was inside, is
made part of normality, with any possible doubts as to this erased from the
press discourse. An article in the *Daily Mail* admitted that, initially, comments critical of Denise Bulger had been phoned in to a radio show in
Liverpool, but allowed Denise Bulger's mother-in-law, Helen Bulger, to 'set
the record straight. Denise was a very protective mother' (16 February 1993).

The dominant representation of Denise Bulger's role in the event is that a
mother shopping with her child in a shopping centre is an everyday scene. Its
everyday quality, of course, is a result of circumstantial necessity: since the
mother, in most situations, is the one who will be with a young child all day
and who therefore will take the child with her on shopping trips. A woman is
criticized when she does leave a child at home alone (see Chapter 6); the
mother's constant presence with the young child is the result of a prohibition
of her absence from him or her. Since she could not leave her son at home,
Denise Bulger takes him with her. In the shopping centre (designed as a 'safe'
space for women with children), he is 'there' (present) one minute, and 'not
there' (absent) the next. Denise Bulger can be represented as a victim because
she conformed to the maternal convention: being with her child. His absence
from her (walking away from the butcher's shop, as recorded on film) is outside her control. She did not abandon him: thus, the press represent the
moment as involving '*the mother who turned away to shop for a second*'. Her
momentary disregard was unavoidable (she was shopping for food, a familial
necessity) and its consequences, thus, are tragic.

As such, she is a victim. More than this, she is the victim that could be *any
of us*. She is imagined as a member of the community and like every other
member of the community. Such a universalism emerges in articles which
emphasize how readers would be identifying with Mrs Bulger's situation.
Their response to the event is constructed for them as an identification with
Denise Bulger as the maternal archetype. Through this identification, the
mother is regained and the maternal relation reinscribed (although here it
exists between Denise Bulger and the readers rather than between Denise
Bulger and her child). This occurs either through direct statements about
this identification, or through imputation that a parent's child could be victimized in the same way as James Bulger. As an example of the former, one
article claimed 'all parents imagine their own child in little James Bulger's
shoes' (*Independent on Sunday*, 7 November 1993). Parents are said to be anxious that their child could be a James Bulger (that is, a victim) and not a Jon
Venables or a Robert Thompson (a murderer). Implicit identification is

produced through stories relating to children as victims: one reports on the exploding sales of restraining reins on Merseyside and elsewhere after the crime – 'in Bootle mothers started leading their toddlers about on reins, but so they did in Guildford, Penzance and Glasgow' (*The Sunday Times*, 21 February 1993). Another describes the campaigns to educate children about the risks of victimization: for example, the Goldilocks story was being used to warn 'James's peers of the woods', allowing children to 'act out their fears'. It also states that 'parents bought wriststrap leads for their toddlers'. A mother is quoted at length in the article: 'What do you do? You want to protect them, but you wonder how they will turn out if you confine them too much.' A teacher is quoted: 'We used to warn the children about strange men and women. Now we have to warn them about other children' (*The Guardian*, 12 February 1994). A letter to *The Guardian* states: 'Parents are frightened by the Bulger case because they imagine their own children at risk [of such a death]' (29 January 1994). The identification patterns are obvious: it is the experience of Denise Bulger and her son that the individual is to share in, while the situation of the Venables and the Thompsons is to constitute the prohibited and the repellent.[8] Identification is always thus a doubled process: the 'good' are identified *with*; the 'evil' are identified *against*. The universalizing of one experience and the minoritizing of the other produces Mrs Bulger as an archetype of the Mother, and her relation to her son as archetypal of the maternal relation.

Such a maternal archetype is completed when the press begins to report on Denise Bulger's pregnancy and subsequent birth of a son. The *Daily Star* wrote:

> grieving Denise had wanted to attend the whole trial but had been advised not to by other members of her family who wanted to spare her the harrowing ordeal of hearing exactly what had happened to her only child. Yesterday [when the jury returned its guilty verdict] was the first time the heavily pregnant mum had set eyes on her tiny son's murderers. [Her solicitor] said: . . . Denise and her family were delighted about the new baby though it could never replace their dead son. (25 November 1993)[9]

At the moment of sentencing, Lord Justice Morland's speech referred to Denise Bulger's pregnancy. He stated: 'Everyone in the court will especially wish Mrs Bulger well in the months ahead and hope the new baby will bring her peace and happiness' (*The Times*, 25 November 1993). Finally, the press reported on the birth of a baby boy to Denise Bulger, more than two weeks prematurely: 'Mrs Bulger, aged 26, and her 4lb 14oz son, who was on an incubator in a Liverpool hospital, are well after a Caesarian section. . . . Last month, she said she would name a baby boy Michael James' (*The Guardian*, 10 December 1993). Here, the anaesthetic balm offered by Mrs Bulger's pregnancy and new baby son can be seen at work. He is to be given the same name as the dead child. He and his mother are being cared for in a Liverpool

8. What Kristeva (1982) would call the 'abject'.
9. The impossibility of 'seeing' the crime gives rise to a projected 'ordeal of hearing'.

hospital, allowing the city, whose social services received so much criticism during the case,[10] to atone for their perceived inadequacies. And for all those who had identified with Denise Bulger as representative of all mothers, her missing child had been replaced by a new one. This, despite all the comments about how a new baby could never be the same as the one that was lost, is desired intensely in the media discourse. It restores Denise Bulger to the position of Mother that she has occupied symbolically throughout the 10 months since the murder. Now, in addition to functioning as an image of the maternal, Denise Bulger can experience its reality, through the restoration of *a* son (not the one that was lost, but a surrogate, one which encrypts the loss in his name).

While Denise Bulger is constructed in the press discourse as archetypal of the mother figure and her relation to her son as an archetypal maternal one, the mothers of the two convicted children appear as irrecoverably alien. Indeed, the crisis in the representation of the maternal relation, which Denise Bulger's *imago* is required to hold together, is located in the very beings of these two women. While the trial judge refers positively to Denise Bulger's pregnancy, he also demands a public debate on the family backgrounds of the two convicted boys. The press enthusiastically began to investigate the boys and their parents.[11] Ann Thompson is described as a 'troublemaker', and her parents are said not to have spoken to her for years, because of 'her drinking' (*Observer*, 28 November 1993). She was interviewed by the *Daily Star*:

> The mother of Bobby Thompson . . . maintained her son was innocent to the end – and blamed everyone around her for the James Bulger tragedy. Her son, she admitted, was a liar, a truant and a thief – but not a murderer. . . . Ann Thompson claimed she had nothing to be sorry about. 'He's told some lies, but he's also told the truth about what happened', she said . . . 'There isn't a family in the area who will say a good word for us. If things went missing from washing lines people would say it was my kids. I'm not saying they were innocent but they got blamed for things they did not do. They are scallies, little scallies, but they are not f*****g murderers.' About Robert Thompson, she says: 'I'm not proud of Bobby sagging off [playing truant] and thieving. But you name one kid of 10 who doesn't tell lies, does not swear, does not smoke even, who does not go in shops robbing. . . . But what could I do apart from putting padlocks on my back door and screwing down every window so he couldn't run off. I couldn't do more than bring in the social services, the police and his teacher.'

She is compared unfavourably in this report to the parents of Jon Venables ('who wept and spoke of their shame and sorrow'): 'Mrs Thompson remained

10. See comments in the *Independent on Sunday*, 6 and 13 February 1994; also 'Heysel, Hillsborough and now this' (*The Guardian*, 20 February 1993). In this article, the estate in which the Bulger family lived is described as 'a place where the taxi drivers like to get their money first'. In 'Consumed in the bonfire of misery': 'Merseyside [tries] to live with a guilt that will not go away' (*Observer*, 28 November 1993). Liverpool, over the last 10 years, had been represented in contemporary media discourse as one of 'Britain's dangerous places': I am borrowing this phrase from Bea Campbell's (1993) analysis of Newcastle and Liverpool.

11. Note that the police and the *Daily Mirror* tracked down Robert Thompson's father, who had some years before walked out on his family; once his whereabouts were made known, the Child Support Agency required him to pay maintenance to Ann Thompson for one of his children, Christopher.

dry-eyed and defiant, emphasizing points with obscenities.' She resists the position she has been allocated in the narrative: 'they always blame the parents. . . . If I knew the answer [to why Robert had killed James Bulger] I would be a bloody psychologist, I'm just a mum and I'm getting victimized.' Asked about the rest of her children (she has seven sons), she says: 'I've got three left out of seven – not bad going is it? Two are in voluntary care' (25 November 1993).

In this, Ann Thompson can be seen attempting to construct an alternate narrative to that which dominated the press discourse and which characterized her as a cause of James Bulger's death. She acknowledges certain forms of delinquent behaviour by her son, but balks at accepting that he has committed murder. She adverts to the relationship of loss that characterizes every maternal relation ('what could I do . . . so he wouldn't run off') and which has been made to belong to Denise Bulger's reality (but, crucially, her son's 'absence' is achieved through his 'running off' rather than abduction). She attempts to reverse the dynamic pointed out above, whereby James Bulger is perceived as the quintessential child and her son as a non-child, by asking where one might find a child of 10 who does not behave in a delinquent manner. If successful, this would establish her son as representing the norm, while the innocent child would be revealed as a fantasy. She also attempts to disperse the blame that is settling upon her by asking what more she could have done (short of imprisoning her child at home) and insisting that other social agencies should bear responsibility (the social services, the police, teachers). These attempts to deflect the force of the narrative that is being constructed are futile. Even in a report that allows her many paragraphs of verbatim monologue, Ann Thompson's position is confirmed: she speaks with 'obscenities', she is 'defiant' and 'dry-eyed'; several of her children are lost in some way to her (in care or in unspecified locations). This technique, allowing the parents of Robert Thompson and Jon Venables to condemn themselves even as they speak in their own defence, appears in its most extensive form in a two-part article by Gitta Sereny, a writer and psychologist with 'experience of damaged children', in the *Independent on Sunday* (6 February and 13 February 1994, timed to coincide with the anniversary of the murder).

Sereny's lengthy article, based mainly on interviews with Susan and Neil Venables and with Ann Thompson, gave credence to the notion that the rational explanation for what happened (that is, the answer to the question, why did they do it?) involved some familial abuse or trauma, or bad general upbringing.[12] Using the language and tactics of the expert psychologist,

12. Bad parental upbringing was cited in countless articles. Detailed exposition of this view is found in 'How we make demons of our children': '[child care experts] could have predicted many of the background factors [of Thompson and Venables]: disordered and emotionally inadequate families, educational problems, truanting, petty crime, video nasties. Although this murder was an extraordinary act, the context in which it occurred was all-too familiar' (*Observer*, 28 November 1993). A doctor is quoted in *The Daily Telegraph*: 'no words can adequately describe the degraded rootlessness and desolate isolation that I see about me everyday in my practice. When mothers come to consult me with their children, it is clear that they have little control over them' (20 February 1993).

Sereny repeatedly undermines the statements of the parents with her own diagnoses of their lives. In relation to the Venables, Sereny immediately reveals the fact of their separation: 'we knew that the couple had lived apart for years.' She allows Sue Venables to recount the history of their separation and their 10 years spent living in separate flats while remaining sexually involved and seeing the children frequently together. Sereny then comments: '[This] seems at first mature and even sophisticated. But what it sounded like . . . was two people very desperately role-playing a kind of fantasy life. How would this confusion . . . have affected Jon, especially once he started school and saw how other children lived?' It could have been suggested that at a time when divorce rates are estimated at 1 in 3 or 4, and when divorced fathers tend to lose all contact with their children, that a child in this situation might find himself to be better off in these terms than many of his fellow pupils. But Sereny's conclusion is that this living arrangement incontrovertibly affected Jon for the worse, laying a degree of blame at the feet of the separated parents. More than this, Sereny is condemning the couple for a confusion between the semblance of their life together (sophisticated, mature, good for the children) and its substance (desperate, role-playing, confused, bad for the children). The Venables' family life *seemed* harmless; but Sereny diagnoses it as *being* harmful. Just as the confusion between the two boys' appearances (as children) and their real selves ('monsters' or 'freaks') contained the kernel of what the press saw as their evilness, so the confusion between semblance and substance in the Venables' way of life contains the root cause of 'harm' to their son.

She finds Neil Venables to look 'gentle, soft and devastated' while 'Sue seemed angry; she had what I was certain was a nervous habit – but irritating to many people under the circumstances – of fixing her makeup time and time again.' Later, Sereny comments on Sue's clothes: 'she would not have been out of place having tea at the Savoy.' This presumably means that she is out of place being interviewed about her child having murdered another. Her appearance confuses the reality of the event. This, together with her 'inappropriate' and 'irritating' habit of doing her make-up, emphasizes the masque that is her femininity. It is a masque which serves to camouflage her dominance: 'she appeared to lead; Neil followed. . . . When Jon turned around to look at or for his parents, his father often met and held his glance; his mother looked away or through him.' Neil Venables, 'gentle, soft and devastated', is represented as the feminine part of the couple, looking kindly at his child while the mother, who should be behaving thus, looks away, in an imitation of paternal severity. The article states that, in court, 'when Neil cried . . . she whispered to console him', reversing the conventional roles. Sereny also reports how, when the police were trying to get Jon Venables to confess, they took his father aside and told him 'it's time for you *to be* a man' (my emphasis), commenting upon his mere semblance of masculinity. Here, Sereny, and the police, also reveal the desire to keep separate the oppositional categories of masculine/feminine, father/mother.

Sereny goes on to investigate the history of Jon Venables' upbringing and familial environment. He had an elder brother (who was a difficult, crying baby, requiring many hospital trips to correct a cleft lip) and a younger sister (who, like the eldest boy, turned out to be educationally backward and in need of special schooling). While his mother states: 'we don't think Jon suffered from all that [the attention spent on his siblings]', Sereny disagrees, saying:

> Sue's early handling of her screaming baby was not necessarily wrong. . . . But it was obvious that Jon must have spent his first years in an atmosphere of tremendous maternal tension. However loved these children were – and one doesn't for a minute doubt Sue's love – forcing this middle child, Jon, for a long time, perhaps unconsciously, to compensate his mother for her two problem children, put an enormous weight of responsibility on this child from the time he was born.

Sue's professed love for Jon ('he was the best, the sweetest baby . . . I loved him to death') in Sereny's diagnosis takes on a sinister, suffocating dimension. Her maternal love forces him 'to compensate' her for her other two children; her upbringing of him creates 'tension' and an 'enormous weight' on him. Maternal love here becomes the mechanism of Jon's downfall. Instead of loving her child unselfishly, as mothers are called upon to do, Sue Venables is guilty of an excess of love, a heavy, selfish love, which is impure and thus nonmaternal.[13] Here, Sereny claims, is the root cause of the later truancy and behavioural problems which would culminate in murder.[14]

Sereny's diagnosis of Robert Thompson's familial origins operates along a different axis of blame. At first, Sereny tells us, she had heard nothing good about Ann Thompson, described to her as a 'slut', a 'shrew' and a 'slag'. With this litany of abuse reiterated, Sereny confesses to finding Ann 'unexpectedly attractive'. The police have told Sereny of their low opinion of Ann Thompson, based mainly on her being absent from most of Robert's interrogations and from one and a half weeks of the trial: '"Can you imagine", said [a police officer], "a mother who lets her child go through this without her?"'[15] Denise Bulger's absence from most of the trial is deemed appropriate: it is constructed as an unnecessary 'ordeal' for her. For the Venables and Thompson parents, such an ordeal is intended as part of the event: their presence in court is necessary to ensure their suffering. Ann Thompson's absence is constructed as a suspicion that she is evading her required suffering and as an abandonment of her child. The question remains and structures Sereny's investigation of the Thompson family: what kind of mother is Ann Thompson?

Ann Thompson had seven children (all sons, although she wanted a daughter and continually became pregnant in the hope of having one). All but one of the children are described as inadequate or deviant in some way. The eldest

13. Note the role that excessive love is deemed to play in investigations of the causes of incest. This argument is discussed in Rush (forthcoming).

14. All quotations are taken from Sereny's article 'Re-examining the evidence', part one of two parts, in the *Independent on Sunday*, 6 February 1994.

15. This, and all subsequent quotations, is taken from part two of Sereny's article, entitled 'Approaching the truth' in the *Independent on Sunday*, 13 February 1994.

is Michael, 20, a 'pale, thin, desperately diffident young man who has not yet held a job. . . . He is manifestly in charge of the children' (in the absence of a father). Ann Thompson says: 'He took on the father's role years ago.' Two younger sons, Brian and Malcolm, went into voluntary care in 1992, after years of behavioural problems. Even in care, they are still said to be beset with difficulties: both took overdoses of paracetamol. Christopher, 9 years old, has been unable to return to school since the trial of his brother, and 'hardly leaves the house'. The youngest, 18-month-old Tom, ('her only child born outside marriage'), Sereny describes as a 'cheerful, smiling baby', but then notes that he 'hardly ever slept'. Ann's second eldest son, Richard, ran away from home at an early age, 'very sensibly', comments Sereny. He 'went on to become the so far only well-organized boy in the family'. If an act such as running away from home is represented as 'sensible', an image of the Thompson household as pernicious and harmful is conveyed.

After 17 years of marriage, Ann's husband left her for another woman. He is reported as telling the police that he walked out on his children because he had a choice between saving himself 'or letting Ann destroy me'. He was tracked down by the police through an advertisement in the *Daily Mirror*, Sereny notes, and found to be living in domestic bliss in a little cottage filled with pictures of his new children, and none of his children with Ann. Again, the implication is clear: the father may have walked out on them, but he was not incapable of providing a proper and stable family environment; that fault resides with their mother, with whom they were left. Sereny goes on to underline this by relating how Ann Thompson turned to drink when her husband left. 'Within two weeks', says Sereny, 'the children were in trouble.' The separation of the parents has a cataclysmic effect on the children's behaviour, but it is Ann's subsequent drinking and 'many men' which bear the brunt of Sereny's blame. She asks Ann Thompson: 'had it not occurred to [you] that [you yourself] did not do enough for the boys, and, as we see, especially for Robert?' This occurs after Ann Thompson had attempted once more to deflect some of the blame she feels has been directed at her, by again asking why the social services, teachers and police did not provide her with assistance after she asked them for it. Sereny thus blocks up that route of investigation, firmly returning responsibility to Ann's door.

The answer to the question asked by the police is clear: only an improper mother could be absent when her child needs her. Sereny's investigation extends this: Ann Thompson was absent as a mother throughout the childhood of her children. If Robert Thompson can be represented as a non-child by the press, Ann Thompson is a non-mother, absent, ineffective, destructive. Ann Thompson's image operates as an allegory of absence and indifference. Sue Venables' image works as an allegory of suffocation and excessive, limitless presence. Where Sue Venables is found guilty of an excess of love, a selfish love, Ann Thompson is convicted of an absence of it, a lack of maternal feeling. The excessive selfishness of Sue Venables' love means that she does not love *as a mother*; she and Ann Thompson are alike in their abrogation of maternal duty. It is here that the press discourse locates the crisis in the maternal relation that is embedded in the case. Ann Thompson and Susan Venables are made to represent the breach in the maternal relation that *must* have occurred for such an event to be possible.

These two women embody maternity as Other (as a dialectic of excess and absence), based in the confusion between their appearance as mothers and their identities (diagnosed in articles such as Sereny's) as non-maternal. Denise Bulger, on the other hand, is taken as embodying an exact correspondence between the image of motherhood and its actuality. The details of the discourse surrounding Denise Bulger, discussed above, conform to the historical and cultural weighting of motherhood as one of sacrifice, solitary care and familial devotion that has been traced by Warner (1976) and Kristeva (1986). The image of her as archetypal mother is one of the ways in which attempts are made to sew up the wound that has appeared in the cultural understanding of the maternal relation. Other attempts can be discerned in the media's call for a strengthening of maternal values and in the encouragement of a series of paternal surrogates surrounding the boys. The former of these devices can be found mainly in readers' letters to the press in the aftermath of the crime and the trial. For example, one letter to *The Guardian* affirmed that 'we do need to be kinder to each other'; while another wrote that 'we need to teach that fragile virtue, love, to the children of all classes and conditions of mankind' (both 1 December 1993). In Sereny's long article on the case, she claims that there is 'an instinct for good all children are born with', but 'many if not most of today's children . . . get their secondary moral grounding from the TV screen, with its confusing sense of values and its constant emphasis on violence'. Television confuses children, the argument goes, because its images are taken by the child as real. The child's universal acceptance of 'right' is perverted into a general acceptance of 'wrong' (*Independent on Sunday*, 6 February 1994).[16] A common theme connects the excerpts above. While differing in their opinion as to whether children are born 'good' or learn to become 'good', it is generally agreed that 'we' must pass on to children an ethical awareness, a respect for the other, a love for others. This has traditionally been seen as part of the maternal role. Here, there is more going on than a call to mothers to continue performing their conventional duty; rather, this represents a demand that everyone assume the maternal position in relation to the child. As such, the power and purpose of the maternal is shored up, protected from the threatening schism that was ripped in it by the Bulger case. What is at stake in the event is less 'real' mothers (like Ann Thompson, Sue Venables and Denise Bulger) than the need to ensure that the values of the maternal continue to be imagined and performed.

16. The theme of knowing 'right' from 'wrong' appears in 'Should we throw away the key?' (an article about the sentencing of the children). The author writes: 'Robert acted in a moral void . . . [W]rong to him meant little more to him than "punishable if caught". Jon, on the other hand, felt the pain of baby James and is tormented by it. "Wrong" for him means "wicked and awful"'(*Mail on Sunday*, 13 February 1994).

The paternal surrogate

Another device which is used to suture the breach in the maternal relation is the generation of paternal surrogates surrounding the boys. This takes various forms. One of these condenses into the calls for severe punishment of the two boys. Lord Justice Morland, at the end of their trial, had recommended that they be detained at Her Majesty's pleasure, the equivalent of a life sentence. In January 1994, it was discovered that the judge then recommended a minimum detention period of eight years, with Lord Chief Justice Taylor recommending that the boys serve at least 10 years. This was followed in the press by an outcry, through the voices of members of the Bulger family, at the perceived leniency of such a sentence: 'Denise and Ralph Bulger [are] shocked and upset. . . . They believe these two boys should never be released.' James Bulger's uncle, Ray Matthews, is quoted: 'We hope that there is a big public backlash. We are all hoping Mr Howard [the Home Secretary] gives them a very long sentence that deters the same thing from happening again' (*The Guardian*, 27 January 1994). A petition calling for 'life sentences' to mean 'the rest of their lives' had been signed by 270,000 people and was presented to Howard by the Bulgers. George Howarth MP handed over a petition with nearly 6,000 signatures, calling for 25-year sentences. The Home Office received 22,638 items of correspondence on the subject, including 21,281 coupons from readers of *The Sun* calling for a 'whole life tariff' (reported in *The Guardian*, 26 July 1994). A similar reaction was displayed when the media reported on plans by American human rights lawyers to appeal against the sentences given to Thompson and Venables in the European Court of Human Rights. American lawyer Tom Loflin's work towards an appeal in Strasbourg was said to have 'left parents Denise and Ralph Bulger shocked and angered' and was described as 'interference' (*Daily Mail*, 25 May 1994). Howard's handling of the sentencing tariff, and his pronouncements on the case (including his comment that he would take public disapproval into account when fixing the final tariff) were deemed to have been making political capital out of the event.[17] Howard eventually ordered that Venables and Thompson serve a minimum of 15 years (almost one and a half times their short lives). The Bulger case was, of course, used by the government as a pretext for a number of criminal justice initiatives, including the building of 170 further places in secure units for 12- to 16-year-old offenders.[18]

Alongside these generalized demands for the severe punishment of Thompson and Venables, individual voices were made audible. On the front page of the *Daily Star*, the headline shouted: 'How do you feel now you little bastards – James's uncle in court as the boys were led away' (25 November

17. The sentences were initially set at 10 years for Thompson and eight for Venables. Articles criticizing Howard's actions appear in the *Independent on Sunday*, 30 January 1994; *The Guardian*, 3 November 1993; and numerous letters to the press (for example, in *The Guardian*, on 29 January and 1 February 1994).

18. For a comparable development in the United States, see the introduction, in the 1994 Crime Bill, of boot camps for both adults and juveniles, discussed in Cronin (1994).

1993). This was shouted by Ray Matthews after the jury's verdict was announced. Ray Matthews also appeared on a morning television show (*Good Morning . . . with Anne and Nick*, BBC1) to be interviewed about the trial and the verdict. During the phone-in, Ray Matthews said that when the two boys came out of jail 'we'll be fucking waiting'.[19] As the presenters hastily returned to the pre-scripted comments, the ferocity of the response hung in the electronic air. Despite televisual etiquette which does not permit the voicing of such language or emotions, the press representation of such a response was on the whole uncritical of the impulses behind them. The *Observer* characterized these two occasions as moments when 'inevitably, [the Bulger family's] mask of decorum has slipped' (28 November 1993). Such moments fulfilled a desire for harshness, for discipline, for the public witnessing of – and indeed participation in – the suffering of the criminal more associated with the days of spectacle on the scaffold. Such a desire for violence can be seen also in the 'baiting-crowd' (Canetti, 1960: 55–60) that surrounded the police van containing the two boys, as they arrived at court; these are the 'angry crowds' (*The Guardian*, 27 January 1994) and the 'enraged protesters' (*Independent on Sunday*, 28 November 1993) who wish, at the very least symbolically, for the deaths of Venables and Thompson (a result metaphorically achieved by Howard's near-doubling of the trial judge's sentence).

Such a desire is present as an attempt to suture the breach in the cultural unconscious. As the broken marriages of the boys' parents tore out the roots of the Law of the Father, a surrogate for the father is required. The paternal function must be performed and observed. The call to watch the mortification and near-erasure through lifetime imprisonment of the two boys speaks of the will for the father to return. The absent father would be made present; his presence as stern lawgiver would be coupled with his opposite term: the loving mother. A harsh sentence, a threat of lethal vengeance, are coupled with the naming of the children as 'bastards'. In that cry from the courtroom, the breach is acknowledged. Genealogy has been shattered, the children's legitimacy made illegitimate, their lack of filiation (to the Father, to the Law) made obvious. In the Thompson household, the father is absent, the mother as good as absent through her indifference. In the Venables household, the father is a mere image of masculinity, the mother a suffocating excess. In the absence of a 'real' father to fit its image, the press discourse grafts a surrogate father onto the wound. This surrogate will punish severely, permitting no calls for mercy or understanding. The surrogate will not forget the sin that has been committed, awaiting retribution. And while the maternal relation can be reasserted through the pregnant body of Denise Bulger and through the calls for a genealogy of love that can be passed on to children, the paternal surrogate offers a menacing reminder of what happens when the maternal relation is breached.

19. The *Observer* reported the threat as 'we'll be waiting for them – and we'll fucking kill them'. It took the view that this comment 'enlivened' a television phone-in (28 November 1993). See also the *Independent on Sunday*, 28 November 1993.

The technology of the image

Figure 5.1   *Still from a security camera, Strand shopping centre*

The abduction of James Bulger was filmed by 16 security cameras in the
Strand shopping centre. Still photographs from these cameras were shown on
television news programmes and in newspapers; most commonly, one which
had James Bulger hand in hand with Jon Venables, walking a few steps
behind Robert Thompson, with the shop front of 'MOTHERCARE' in large,
ironic capital letters in the background (Figure 5.1). Thirty-eight individuals
witnessed sections of the abduction as the child was led, dragged or carried
more than two miles. Sixty photographs of James Bulger's body were shown
to the jury at the trial of Robert Thompson and Jon Venables. Drawings by
court artists of 'Child A' and 'Child B' appeared in the press and on television
on a daily basis during the trial. Newspapers published maps detailing the
route taken by the boys and marking out the places where James Bulger was
attacked. Portrait photographs of James Bulger, and, after the trial, of Robert
Thompson and Jon Venables were displayed prominently in the media. BBC1
and ITV broadcast reconstructions of the abduction and murder, combining
excerpts from the taped police interrogations with actors playing the children
and their parents.

The security video, which had been played over and over by the media in
the days following James Bulger's abduction and murder, reappeared at the
trial. Newspapers covered its use: 'the jury in a packed courtroom in Preston
Crown Court watched in silence as the drama of the last seconds leading up

to James Bulger's alleged abduction by two 11-year-old boys flickered in front of them on video screens'. (The boys were 10 years old at the time of the abduction and murder; both were aged 11 when the case came to trial.) The prosecution had made what was described, in the language of MTV, as a 'compilation video' of frames from the 16 different cameras. The result 'made the images jump like an early silent movie', 'blurred and of poor definition' (*The Guardian*, 4 November 1993). Stills showing the two boys from the film had been enlarged, originally by the police in an attempt to identify them. They were also used by the press to illustrate articles about the event. Enlargement succeeded mainly in representing the boys as anonymous any-boys: as Mitchell writes, 'once a digital image is enlarged to the point where its gridded microstructure becomes visible, further enlargement will reveal nothing new' (1992: 6). Despite these problems, the film was treated as having the quality of truth. As Godard has said: 'film is the truth 24 times per second' (quoted in Virilio, 1991: 145, n. 4). The presence of 'Child A' and 'Child B' in court superimposed their identities over the unidentifiable faces on screen. The figures are read *as if* they *are* the figures sitting in the dock. In the film, two boys are seen 'jostling or playfully kicking each other' in an uncomfortable precursor of what they would later do to the child. The abduction is shown occurring in a matter of minutes:

> At 3.37pm James Bulger and his mother, Denise, came into view walking towards the camera positioned outside [the] butchers. . . . At 3.38pm, while his mother was paying for some sausages, he was captured on the bottom right-hand corner of the screen standing on his own. He appeared to glance around him, then walked out of the field of vision. A minute and a half later, Denise rushed out of the shop. She was seen hurrying in several directions searching for her son. By 3.41pm the first shots were taken of James walking across the precinct square in close proximity to the two boys. In one frame he was holding the hand of the one said to be child B [Jon Venables]. The three boys were filmed moving away out of the main exit of the precinct's upper level. The final frame, taken at 3.43pm, showed them fading into the distance. (*The Guardian*, 4 November 1993)

Such a fading out is not, however, the end of the representation of the crime. The Crown brought 38 eye-witnesses into court to tell what they saw. In sum, this amounted to a 'compilation memory' beginning in the Strand shopping centre and ending close to the railway embankment beyond which the murder was committed. One woman described how, in a pedestrian subway, she came across James Bulger with the two older boys, who both had hold of his hands. She tried to make them let go, but 'the taller one [Jon Venables] said in a calm manner, as if he was in control, and to the senior of the two, "get hold of his hand". The chubbier one [Robert Thompson] did this without hesitation.' She described asking the little boy if he was all right: 'His little eyes were wide open. I could only see his little eyes. He didn't say anything' (*The Guardian*, 9 November 1993). Another woman, on a bus travelling home, saw two boys with a little child between them: 'The boys were holding the child's hands. One let go as the other swung the child high above his shoulder. I saw the child's white shoes as he came up. I shouted out in the bus: "What the hell are those kids doing to that poor child!" . . . They were being rough with him.

That's what made me shout out. It will never leave me because it upset me so much' (*The Guardian*, 5 November 1993).

Other witnesses described seeing a small child in distress. One man saw a child, later identified as James Bulger, 'crying his eyes out'. A woman saw a child try to run away from an older boy 'but [he] was brought back by a second boy in a dark coat'. A woman cried in the witness box as she recounted seeing a little boy with a fresh bruise on his forehead (*The Guardian*, 5 November 1993). Much of the press coverage focused on these witnesses in a derogatory manner, implying that they bore some of the responsibility for the child's death. 'One woman witness said. . . : "I feel terrible. I have nightmares all the time. My guilt will just not go away"' (*Observer*, 28 November 1993). An editorial in *The Guardian* wrote of 'the dozens who passed by on the other side' (27 November 1993), employing the biblical story of the Good Samaritan to castigate these eye-witnesses. Other articles commented on 'the thirty eight witnesses who did nothing' (*The Guardian*, 26 November 1993); the 'thirty eight witnesses [who] have been vilified' (*Observer*, 28 November 1993); and the '38 adult witnesses who passed on by and who allowed it to pass' (letter to *The Guardian*, 26 November 1993).

Some widened this sense of guilt to include 'the security men who did nothing' (*The Guardian*, 26 November 1993); others wrote of 'James Bulger, the toddler whom none of us saved' and 'our national guilt that we could be the kind of people who let this sort of thing happen' (*Independent on Sunday*, 7 November 1993); and 'the adult world who allowed James Bulger to be led to a pointless, terrifying and wretched death' (letter to *The Guardian*, 26 November 1993).[20] At the trial, the criticism of the witnesses was referred to by the prosecution:

> Many of the witnesses had been shaken to the core when they realized the infant they had seen was dead. Veiled criticism had been levelled at the witnesses in the form of the question: why did they not intervene? Each of those witnesses will have asked themselves that question a thousand times, and they will continue to ask it. I trust they will find some comfort. They made the reasonable assumption that this was a family group. No-one associated murder with 10-year-olds. (*The Guardian*, 20 November 1993)

While some of the witnesses had been concerned at seeing an injury on the child's forehead, or his rough treatment at the hands of the two older boys, none had sought police help or reported what they had seen. All gave the reason for this as being that they thought they had witnessed a group of brothers. As the prosecution stated above: 'They made the reasonable assumption that this was a family group.' A witness who saw James Bulger, attempting to run away and being brought back by an older boy, said: 'I thought they were just relatives.' The woman on the bus who had cried out at the rough treatment of the child, said: 'What kind of parents have they all got to let them out with a child like that?' (*The Guardian*, 5 November 1993). Later, she is reported as

---

20. On the interpellatory strategies employed in the press coverage of this case, see Hay (1995).

saying: 'I feel guilty even though I know I shouldn't. Those boys were cunning. They conned people into believing they were James's brothers' (*Observer*, 28 November 1993). Most of the witnesses, on reaching their homes, saw television reports concerning James Bulger's disappearance; they then realized that they had seen a child being abducted; one, for example, recognized a boy in a black jacket whom she had seen chasing a little boy up a hill from the clips from the security video film that were shown on the television news that night (*The Guardian*, 6 November 1993).

The behaviour of small children – running away from their caretakers, not speaking when asked a question by a stranger, running heedlessly into the road – which was here identified as normal by the witnesses, was in fact the obverse of normality. And yet, the scene that was presented to the witnesses was not able to be decoded by them as its obverse. When James Bulger 'in high spirits', had 'broken free from his mother and run off' in the Strand shopping centre (*The Guardian*, 2 November 1993), that scene was not interpreted as involving a woman abducting a child who was attempting to escape. The presence of a child invites a response in the spectator that they are seeing a family scene. Thus, a toddler with two older boys – one taller than the other and thus perhaps the eldest brother – presents a sibling tableau. As the afternoon got later, and school hours were over, it became less strange to see two 10-year-olds on the street. Those witnesses who spoke directly to the boys, asking if the little boy was all right, or what they were doing with him, received answers which fitted with the projection of a normal family scene: that they were taking him home, or to get his injuries attended to. Despite increasing knowledge of the extent of familial abuse of children, intervention by strangers upon seeing suspected abuse is very rare. There is a cultural lag which prevents or slows awareness that the scene witnessed may not be one of happy innocence, but rather one of pain and fear; that the later scenes were parodies of the child's earlier behaviour with his mother. Thus, when each witness discovered what they had seen, they experienced trauma and guilt. The moment is less one of *realization*; it is rather one of reinterpretation, as the memory of the scene is recoded and a new version of events grafted onto the original one. Realization comes as a moment of self-knowledge: the witnesses realize that they already know what they learn later. With this prosthetic memory in place, the witnesses then made their way to the police stations to give statements as to what they had 'seen'.[21] In court, nine months later, their reiterated accounts – memories of a prosthetic memory – were often criticized by the defence lawyer as inaccurate, embellishing detail and emphasizing the abnormality of the older boys' treatment of the child (*The Guardian*, 6 November 1993). One writer comments: 'motivated by a desire to improve and colour the narrative, the witnesses only blurred it'.[22] Where did this desire to 'colour' the narrative come from? To 'colour' something is to give hue and

21. I am borrowing the term 'prosthetic memory' from Celia Lury (forthcoming). Her recent work on memory and image stimulated many of the ideas in this chapter.

22. This comment is made by Dyer (1994) in a review of Smith (1994) *The Sleep of Reason: The James Bulger Case*.

tint where none existed; or to give something monochrome many pigments and shades. To be 'black-and-white' is to be unambiguous; the witnesses' first interpretation had all the certainty of its acculturation. Their subsequent, grafted memory required colour, nuance, variation. In their struggle to respond to the trauma of reinterpretation, their stories were variously represented as 'inaccurate' and 'understandably slanted towards helping the prosecution' (*The Times*, 6 November 1993).

Through this combination of video film and eye-witness testimony, the court followed the two boys and James Bulger on a journey from the shopping centre along a canal towpath, through a cemetery, past a reservoir, through a subway, along a flyover and, finally, down an embankment to the railway track. At this point, Dyer writes, 'the verifiable narrative petered out, altogether, the boys disappeared from sight and camera and we were left with the mutually incriminating tapes . . . . of the police interviews with the murderers themselves' (1994). However, to these tapes in court were added the 60 photographs that were shown to the jury. They depicted scenes from the two-and-a-half mile route taken by the boys, and also James Bulger's body. The prosecution claimed that 60 was 'as few as [the jury] can properly be shown consistent with our duty to present the case'. The grim nature of these photographs was heralded for the jury when the prosecution 'invited them to steel themselves' before looking at them and, indeed, 'one middle-aged juror recoiled momentarily from a photograph of [James Bulger's] bloodstained, paint-spattered head' (*The Guardian*, 3 November 1993). Some press articles dealt with the difficulties faced by the jury in dealing with the distress of the trial ('Jurors exposed to trial trauma have nowhere to turn', *The Guardian*, 25 November 1993; see also letter on 26 November 1993) and, indeed, some of the jurors sought counselling after the trial.

Of all the images which circulated around the case, the one which seemed most representative was the still from the security video, in which James Bulger, hand in hand with Jon Venables, walks behind Robert Thompson, leaving the shopping centre (Figure 5). One article stated:

> The baby whose image haunted us put his hand in the big boy's hand, a gesture we understand, yet viewed through the distance of the video camera, it became the ghostliest vision because we knew by then what had happened to James. The image lied to us because it made James present, it made us feel intervention was possible. So we saw the image and could do nothing. (*The Guardian*, 26 November 1993)

The failure admitted here (which results in the haunting nature of the image) is the failure of any link between knowledge and action. Simply seeing an image does not lead to action. The sight of violence cannot determine any intervention against violence. The replaying of the image promises the possibility of intervention; trauma is experienced due to the gap between the image's promise and the substance of its referent. Another article comments: 'the camera's last glimpse of James Bulger shows a toddler hand in hand with an older boy – an image of trust resembling the ad for Start-Rite shoes – passing under a sign that says MOTHERCARE' (*Evening Standard*, 25 October

1993).[23] Photography pretends a present tense; the subject of the photograph smiles into the lens and the moment appears frozen; James Bulger's face stared out from newspapers and television screens. Warner writes: 'the phantom face of James Bulger has become the most haunting image of present horrors and social failure – his innocence an appeal and an accusation' (1994: 36). Douzinas and Warrington write: 'The sign of another is the face. . . . The other is her face' (1994a: 414). Levinas states: 'Absolutely present, in his face, the Other – without any metaphor – faces me' (quoted in Derrida, 1978: 100). The photographs of Robert Thompson and Jon Venables, taken on some occasion before they committed murder, and the security video which 'registers the walk of young killers on their way to commit acts of unimaginable violence' (Warner, 1994: 44) hold out the subject, their eyes towards the camera, their actions replayable on the video. Part of the horror of the case lies in the disjunction between the very presence of the image and a memory of what the image is about. Just as Barthes shuddered over a catastrophe which has already occurred when he looked at the photograph of a now-dead young boy, so the security video was castigated as 'heartless', showing a now-dead child walking hand-in-hand with his killer (*The Guardian*, 16 February 1993). If the image offers reality, truth, presence, immediacy, then it can cheat death; yet, in an event filled with death, the spectator is forced to deny the presence of life in the image, acknowledge its demise, consign the event to history and to memory.

After the jury's verdict had been returned, the trial judge's speech made reference to a need for a public debate on parenting, as discussed above, and on the exposure of children to violent films and videos. He said:

> In my judgment the home background, upbringing, family circumstances, parental behaviour and relationships were needed in the public domain so that informed and worthwhile debate can take place for the public good in the case of grave crimes by young children. This could include exposure to violent video films, including possibly *Child's Play 3*, which has some striking similarities to the manner of the attack on James Bulger. (*The Guardian*, 27 November 1993)

From the horror of the security videos, attention is shifted to the horror of the horror film. In addition to the comforting possibility that exposure to violent films might provide the answer to the question that the media had been asking for months (why did these boys do it? – the causal question of the crimino-legal complex), the focus on violent films is linked to the issue of parental care and the breach in the maternal relation.

Sereny describes how police officers told her that they were looking for evidence of 'perversity' when they searched the Thompson and Venables households. She asks whether they found pornographic films and receives the answer: 'nothing . . . and believe me, we were looking for it. But the films Neil had there were quite innocuous' (*Independent on Sunday*, 13 February 1994).

23. Another article commented: 'Not for nothing did Start-Rite shoes use that very same image to persuade parents to trust the beneficial effects of its footwear on their children's growing feet' (*The Guardian*, 16 February 1993).

The *image* of the Venables appeared at home with perversity; the police faced disappointment in their search for its substance. Sereny, however, believes that Jon Venables must have watched *Child's Play 3* and other violent films on satellite television, in the mornings while his father was asleep. Sereny is of the opinion that watching such films would do harm to these children: 'Stable children exposed to violent videos – and adults too – though they may become emotionally desensitized by a surfeit of such films, are unlikely to be particularly harmed by them. Unstable children, from chaotic homes, however, are extremely susceptible to their mesmerizing effect' (*Independent on Sunday*, 13 February 1994). Another psychologist, Elizabeth Newsom, is quoted: 'There is simply no way [children] can [repeatedly watch] such videos without having been desensitized . . . I think children are being abused by having these images so easily accessible' (*Observer*, 28 November 1993). The Thompson and Venables homes are represented as chaotic and unstable, with violent videos easily available to the children, who, in turn, are traumatized by either an excess of love or an absence of it. To these inappropriate manifestations of maternal care, she adds a further element of parental blame: *exposing* the children to violent films. Here, exposure connotes a rendering vulnerable, a laying bare, a stripping of defences, a moral hypothermia. The child is at risk, thanks to adult culpability which can violate the child's essential child-like identity.

The judge in Thompson and Venables' trial claimed definite similarities between the manner of their attack on James Bulger and the narrative of *Child's Play 3*. In the substance of the killing of James Bulger, the judge saw an image that had been marketed as entertainment. For those who had not watched the film, *The Guardian* summarized the plot. A doll named Chucky is possessed by evil and, in *Child's Play 1* and *2*, has been vanquished by a small American boy named Andy. In the third film, the doll rises from the dead to mete out violence and mayhem to those it encounters. Several people die violently and explicitly in the film before the doll is finally destroyed. According to *The Guardian*,

> if one looks to find them, there are echoes in the film of elements of the James Bulger story. . . . Among the more obvious details, there's the stolen blue paint which Jon Venables and Robbie Thompson threw at two-year-old James. In the film, Chucky and others are sprayed with blue paint used in a war game. There's the railway track, where James finally met his death. The movie climax is a scene in a ghost train where a boy narrowly misses being run over on the tracks. (26 November 1993)[24]

The irony of the film's title will not have been missed. Warner writes of a crisis in our expectations of childhood, where 'the most notorious of video nasties is called *Child's Play*' (1994: 44). The puzzle of children's play has long

24. The film was also blamed in another murder trial, in which a 16-year-old woman, Suzanne Capper, was tortured and set on fire by a group of six individuals. One of these, Bernadette McNeilly, was alleged to have taken amphetamines, called herself Chucky, laughed at the injuries she inflicted on her victim and said, while carrying out the torture, 'Chucky wants to play' (*The Guardian*, 19 November 1993).

been an enigma to fascinate writers, parents, psychologists. Children are seen as having a 'proximity to the imaginary' which adults do not; their 'fluid make-believe play' part of an 'observable fantasy life' (Warner, 1994: 37). Bettelheim (1976) argued that it was healthy for children to read stories of violence, and to play at violent games. Fairy tales and nursery rhymes involve acts of extreme violence done to and by children. Today, children play at being dinosaurs, or relish the stories of how the tyrannosaur rips the heart from the little dinosaur: in the midst of consecrating childhood our modern mythology of childhood ascribes to children a rampant appetite for the transgressive pleasures of violence (although not of sex). A novel that was referred to frequently in the press coverage of the Bulger case, *Lord of the Flies*, deals with children's play in its most atavistic form.[25] The press, however, missed the point of Golding's novel, focusing upon the acts of violence which take place, particularly the death of Piggy. The crucial part of the novel involves the arrival, at the very end, of naval officers, to 'rescue' the boys: through adult eyes, the boys are reduced to 'playing games': 'A semicircle of little boys, their bodies streaked with coloured clay, sharp sticks in their hands, were standing on the beach making no noise at all. "Fun and games", said the officer' (1962: 200). Golding's argument, therefore, might well be that children's play is fundamentally incomprehensible to adults. With no authentic memory of childhood, adults are fated to *interpret* what they see children do as play. It is this fate which is obeyed in the interpretations of the eye-witnesses that they saw brothers at play.

In a poetic documentary inspired by the Bulger case and broadcast on Channel 4, Blake Morrison asked: 'what lies behind a child's eyes?' In publishing the portrait photographs of James Bulger, Jon Venables and Robert Thompson, the media encouraged the spectator to project emotions, attitudes and thoughts into those eyes turned towards the lens. Certain emotions are 'preferred' to lie behind the child's eyes. Into the eyes of James Bulger is read innocence; into the eyes of Venables and Thompson is read 'a moral void', 'guileful naivety', 'streetwise defiance' (*Mail on Sunday*, 13 February 1994). When adults interpret a child's behaviour as 'play', it masks a fear that behind the eyes of a child there might lie all that the child is hoped *not* to embody. When a child is called 'carefree', it is used to connote the unfettered luxury of being able to play all day long. However, to be carefree – without care – might equally mean that the child has no care *for anyone,* lacks an ethical sense, is amoral. Thus, in Kundera's novel *The Book of Laughter and Forgetting* (1983a), more apposite to the Bulger case than *Lord of the Flies*, a lone adult upon an island populated entirely by children discovers that their carefree spirit and inquisitive experimenting have no limits, no sense of boundary. Kundera comments on this episode:

A person finds himself in a world of children, from which he cannot escape. And

---

25. *The Guardian* wrote: 'It begins to seem that William Golding's fictional universe of juvenile savagery in *Lord of the Flies* lies all around us in our housing estates and shopping malls' (16 February 1993).

suddenly childhood, which we all lyricize and adore, reveals itself as pure horror. As a trap. . . . The basic event of the book is the story of totalitarianism, which deprives people of memory and thus retools them into a nation of children. . . . And perhaps our entire technical age does this, with its cult of the future, its cult of youth and childhood, its indifference to the past and mistrust of thought. (1983b: 235-6)

Behind the idealization of childhood lies a continuing helpless suspicion 'that children may look like angels and still be devils underneath' (Warner, 1994: 43). Warner here uses the distinction between semblance and substance, visible and invisible, while reiterating the notion that the essential stuff of childhood may be found somewhere between surface and depth. And it seems that 'bad children' are all around: in April 1994, *The Guardian* reported on a 12-year-old accused of rape (9 April 1994); two boys were accused of torturing three younger boys at a railway track, ultimately stabbing one in the arm (*The Guardian*, 7 December 1993); three boys aged between 8 and 10 beat a tramp then threw him to his death down a well in France (*The Guardian*, 27 November 1993), while two 6-year-olds wrecked a house 'for fun' (*The Guardian*, 6 April 1994). Child's play? 'Boys will be boys, people say, when they mean violence, aggression, guns . . . ' (Warner, 1994: 27).

As a result of the judge's comments at the end of Thompson and Venables' trial, a debate was indeed sparked off, taking place between politicians (especially the Liberal Democrat MP, David Alton), film critics and theorists (see, for example, the opinions printed in *The Guardian*, 26 November 1993 on the proposed banning of *Child's Play 3*), and psychologists. In this latter group, two sides were prominent. The first involved a group of '25 leading child psychologists' who had signed a report, entitled *Video Violence and the Protection of Children*, by Elizabeth Newsom, professor of development psychology at Nottingham University, which stated:

> it is now clear that many children watch adult-only videos on a regular basis, with or without their parents' knowledge, and that many parents make less than strenuous efforts to restrict their children's viewing. . . . There must be special concern when children . . . are repeatedly exposed to images of vicious cruelty in the context of entertainment and amusement. (*The Guardian*, 1 April 1994)

On the other side was the Policy Studies Institute, which released a report (by Ann Hagell and Tim Newbury), *Young Offenders and the Media*, covering research which found that persistent young offenders do not watch more violent films or television than 'ordinary' schoolchildren and that they prefer soap operas to video nasties (*The Guardian*, 13 April 1994). Published just days after the Newsom report, this latter study received very little media attention.

The Newsom report was taken up with alacrity by all sections of Parliament, and, on 12 April, Home Secretary Michael Howard announced a new clause to be inserted in the Criminal Justice Bill 1994, placing a duty on the British Board of Film Classification in granting licences to take account both of the psychological impact of videos on children, and the possibility that they will show them 'inappropriate models and techniques'. Video store owners who allow adult films to be rented by under-age children will receive severe penalties: a minimum fine of £20,000 and six months' imprisonment, with a maximum of up to two years' imprisonment and an unlimited fine. The government, unable to regulate the behaviour of children, opted instead to regulate the hire of video films to parents and children. As a target, *Child's Play* was always going to be easier to hit than the inscrutable, indecipherable play of children.

Responses to the event of the killing of James Bulger made extensive use of a *technology of the image*. The event was formed by its reproduction on video, in eye-witness testimony and in forensic detail. It always existed as much as an image of itself as it did in itself. It represented to its audience the oppositions between victim and criminal, mother and child, father and mother. In doing this, the opposition between image and reality was always overlooked. Its images were technologized by virtue of their form and function (the security camera, the routine use of eye-witness testimony in court, the conventional reliance on forensic evidence in criminal cases). However, such images reveal also the commonplace acceptance of the *value* of images in contemporary culture. The image has become confused with the self to the extent that the image is the self. If the subject lives as an image, a persona, the visibility of culture becomes crucial. Hence, the responses to the event of James Bulger's death frantically reiterate substance and semblance in a confusion of two orders of being. The event of the killing of James Bulger speaks to us across the distance between semblance and substance, demanding our responses to its images. The event of James Bulger's death, however, forces a confrontation with the limits of the image (and thus with the limits of humanity, if we live but through our images). If there is a limit to vision, there is also the finitude of the human. Thus the anxiety produced by the realization, after the event of James Bulger's death, that we live through and for our images, is accompanied by the fear that beyond the image lies only death, the inhuman.

The technologization of the images of James Bulger's abduction is the product of this anxiety. The images must be technologized to be incorporated into modernity, to be owned as our selves. In the responses to the event of James Bulger's killing, we are attempting to own our sense of horror, to make ourselves into versions of the oppositions that structure the event. We are mothers or fathers, we are victims not criminals. We *are* our *images*. In all the reproduction of these images, however, the event itself is absent. The killing of James Bulger took place beside a railway track, in the dark, seen only by Venables and Thompson. Everything else, before and after, is re-presented. The abduction is filmed by cameras and seen by bystanders. The body is discovered by children playing near the railway. But the visibility of the event ends as the three boys climb the embankment to the railway line. The crime that is then committed is unpresentable, unimaginable, unthinkable. This is so, not simply because no-one else happened to see it take place, or because no camera was filming. The event exceeds the limits of representation and as such represents the border of what can be imagined.

Its ùnthinkability is accepted in many press articles. James Bulger's grandmother is quoted as saying 'It's like a dream . . . I feel as if I am watching something happen to someone else' (*Daily Mail*, 16 February 1993). The crime, says another, involved 'a cruelty so appalling that one cannot long bear to contemplate it' (*The Daily Telegraph*, 20 February 1993). A court attendant is reported as saying: 'They did it *all in the dark* . . . *I can't get over that*' (*Independent on Sunday*, 13 February 1994; my emphasis). Sereny's article on the Thompson family is illustrated with a photograph of the crime scene, covered by a tent to protect the area from disturbance (*Independent on Sunday*, 13 February 1994). The tent blanks out the immediate scene of the crime. Dyer writes: 'many parts of Britain . . . exist only for bodies to be found in their midst' (*The Guardian*, 12 March 1994). The photographing of a tent over the location of the body acknowledges the unpresentability of what it covers. Sereny writes: 'So – nothing here about that two-mile walk; nothing about the 38 witnesses and their . . . guilt; nothing, *above all*, about what was done to James Bulger' (*Independent on Sunday*, 28 November 1993; my emphasis). In our love of the image, there is one image that we do not wish to own: that of the killing of James Bulger. Only Robert Thompson and Jon Venables are to own that event (hence the fascination displayed in the press for the moment when each boy confessed, recorded by the police and replayed in court).[26] And so, it is there that we have constructed the limit of vision. We allow the image to fade as the boys climb the railway bank, we 'realize' that it is dark, and that we cannot 'see' what is happening. And the darkness obliterates the image of the crime and our imagination of the image.

Crime as heritage

'Children have never been so visible as points of identification, as warrants of virtue, as markers of humanity', writes Warner (1994: 46). For her, the consecration of childhood, with its attendant dual idealization of the innocent child and abomination of the bad child, is a symptom of a contemporary cultural malaise. Yet such a duality has long been identified: examples can be found in texts such as Dickens' *Oliver Twist*, itself adverted to as an index of juvenile goodness versus delinquency in Burt's *The Young Delinquent* (1944: 72).[27] In Burt's text, the duality is plain: children are at risk, in trouble, bad, delinquent; or, they are well behaved, normal, well adjusted, good. This text was on my reading list as an undergraduate student of criminology, under the topic of 'juvenile delinquency'. I had not reread it since; to return to it after the Bulger case made me aware of a startling circumlocution which looped the world of Burt, with its 'gin-palaces', 'alleys of Euston' and 'dens of Limehouse docks' (1944: 62–3), with the contemporary discursive practices which had encircled Jon Venables and Robert Thompson. In this section, I

26. On Venables' confession: 'bit by bit, he went over the whole walk and finally the railway yard and the bricks and the metal bar, and the kicks . . . and the taking off of the trainers and socks' (*Independent on Sunday*, 13 February 1994). During his confession, he 'wailed loudly and inconsolably for 33 minutes, while the court listened [to the tape] in shocked silence' (*Mail on Sunday*, 13 February 1994).

27. The text is part of a larger work entitled *The Sub-Normal School Child*.

will show how the image of the child, existing in all its oppositions – criminal/victim, child/mother, child/father – is constituted within a tradition which inscribes responsibility for its interpretation. The image of the child is owned within a tradition which has always already inherited the notion of good/evil, or delinquent/law-abiding. The image of the child, and its interpretation through the confusion of semblance and substance, is inherited with cultural weight. I use the arguments of Burt merely to illustrate a lack of innovation in all such responses to the child-as-image. Further, I would suggest that the image of the child has a performative function, in the same way that the paternal and maternal relations demand a performative response in interpreting the image of father/mother.

The government and the trial judge found it hard to answer the question, 'why did they do it?' without reference to the twin evils of parenting and violent videos. In the same way, Burt states that 'to measure the intangible influences that impinge upon the human soul is always a hard and baffling task', while being certain that 'heredity and environment may each do their sinister share' (1944: 63). Poverty, noted Burt, was a 'spur to dishonesty and wrong' (1944: 70). The press made much of a rumour that Jon Venables' parents lived apart merely as a means to defraud the Department of Social Security, from whom they received income support and housing benefit (*Independent on Sunday*, 6 February 1994), while Ann Thompson had no fixed source of income. Both families were represented as poor. However, Burt is certain that 'poverty can hardly be the sole or the most influential cause' (1944: 70). The most striking factor, for him, is the subtle and 'easily overlooked' influence of 'defective family relationships' (1944: 93). He notes first the problem of the 'thoughtless begetting of children': much attention was paid to Ann Thompson's having seven children. Sereny describes Ann Thompson's repeated pregnancies ('"All these babies" . . . [Ann] repeated dreamily') as 'instinctive', without conscious or rational thought (*Independent on Sunday*, 13 February 1994). Susan Venables' third child was her first daughter; Sereny presents this pregnancy as selfish, possessive: ('"Now I had my daughter", Sue said') (*Independent on Sunday*, 6 February 1994).

A further form of defective relationship is where a parent, separated from the other biological parent, forms a liaison with another adult. For the child, says Burt, 'the sense of such anomalous relationships, even if but half realized by the child, is bound to tinge and distort his developing outlook upon social relations as a whole' (1944: 94). Again, Ann Thompson's relationships with several men, after her husband left, were represented by the press as symptomatic of her disordered family life. Burt also mentions explicitly families where a parent has been 'separated or divorced'. If, as a result of this, a mother had 'to work during the day, and would be absent throughout the very hours when the child needed her vigilance at home', such families 'have helped greatly . . . to swell the ranks of youthful crime' (1944: 94). With the mother absent from home, her panoptic, disciplinary function (her 'vigilance') is diminished; the child is therefore able to run free (carefree?) and commit crimes. According to Burt:

> The ordinary child in an ordinary home is the member of a small and self-contained society, cared for by the united efforts of both father and mother, and possessing at least one other relative of his own age and outlook to play with him, to grow up with him, to keep with him, and so to some extent to regulate his ways, or at least to report on any serious faults. The delinquent child, too often, is devoid of such benefits. He leads an existence warped, onesided, incomplete; and lacks the most natural check against lawless behaviour. (1944: 95)

In the absence of 'the most natural check', Burt has suggestions for substitute control devices; I will come to these shortly. There is, however, one other major influence upon delinquency that he identifies, which resonates with the Thompson and Venables families; that is, the problem of the 'vicious home' (1944: 99). This is particularly relevant to the Thompson household. Burt writes: 'Of all the features of the vicious home, the commonest and the most remarked is drunkenness' (1944: 99). In these households, according to Burt, is found 'indecency of speech and behaviour' and 'irregular unions' (the press emphasized Ann Thompson's 'obscenities', and her 'promiscuity'); also 'sexual molestation of the child by its own relatives' (much speculation went on, from the police through psychologists to the media, as to whether Thompson and Venables had been abused) (1944: 100). The result is as follows:

> all tend to set up, by their progressive effect upon the young and sensitive mind, such a sense of injustice, such feelings of indignity, wretchedness, and apprehension, that, as he grows more critical and independent, he finds himself at length impelled to seek relief or distraction by some vehement deed of his own. He may lose all self-command, and blindly strike an offending or unoffending party. He may hand on the maltreatment to one of his own tiny juniors, hurting as he has been hurt, cursing as he has been cursed. (1944: 100–1)

This passage might well have been written about Robert Thompson, so closely does it correspond to the press discourse surrounding his background and behaviour. Thompson's loss of 'self-command' is adverted to in the witnesses' descriptions of Jon Venables as 'in control' and Thompson as doing immediately what Venables told him. Robert Thompson's bullying of his younger brothers, as he himself was bullied, is described in the press (*Independent on Sunday*, 13 February 1994). The 'vehement deed' could be the attack on James Bulger, a displacement of familial resentments: much was made in the press of Robert Thompson's comment to the police that 'if he had wanted to kill a baby, he would have killed his own brother' (for example, *The Guardian*, 26 November 1993) and his apparent 'dress rehearsal' of the crime with his younger brother Christopher (*Independent on Sunday*, 13 February 1994). In the attack on James Bulger, Thompson did indeed strike at an 'unoffending party'.

In such a home, with its absence of 'natural' constraints on the child, resulting delinquency requires the interpolation of a disciplinary agent or institution, whether that be prison, places of detention, industrial schools or reformatories. Burt states:

> To remove the child from his family does not necessarily mean branding and stigmatizing him straight away as a criminal unfit for ordinary society . . . by

incarcerating him in some grim penitentiary, even less like home than his own undesirable tenement. These fears of the uninstructed layman, natural enough in former times, should now have no justification. The principle is simply this: that a substitute for a good home, and a deputy for a good parent, have both to be found, before the child can be redeemed. (1944: 105)[28]

Under the Children Act 1908, 'no child under fourteen may . . . be sentenced to imprisonment', and no child between 14 and 16 may be sentenced to imprisonment 'unless the court certifies that he is of so unruly a character that he cannot be detained in a place of detention'. Burt would prefer that age to be higher: 'it would be well if, by future legislation, an age yet higher might be fixed' (1944: 106). Unfortunately for Burt, this has not been the case: instead, the current government has undertaken a series of 'reforms' which permit more juveniles to be locked up, for longer, and in more austere settings (known as 'secure units'). Justices of the Peace have been given more powers to detain teenagers, and in March 1994 the High Court abolished the long-standing rule that children between 10 and 14 can only be convicted of a crime if it is proved that they knew what they were doing was 'seriously wrong' and not merely 'naughty'. This rule, a part of the *doli capax* require-ment, was called 'perverse' and 'outdated' by the judges. In this case, *C (A Minor)* v. *DPP*, Lord Justice Mann said that the rule had not benefited chil-dren 'from what used to be called good homes' in the same way as those from poorer backgrounds. Its perversity led those children 'most likely to offend' to go unpunished, 'free [carefree?] to commit further crimes unchecked'. Rather than requiring that only a child who understood the difference between right and wrong be convicted and punished, Lord Justice Mann said 'it is precisely the youngster whose understanding of the difference . . . is frag-ile and non-existent who is most likely to get involved in criminal activity' (reported in *The Guardian*, 30 March 1994).[29]

The *doli capax* rule had been applied in Thompson and Venables' trial; the jury had been directed that, in considering whether the two boys understood that what they were doing had been seriously wrong, they were to take into account the boys' ages, their being of average intelligence (Venables) and good intelligence (Thompson), the fact of their having attended a Church of England school, the impossibility of their not being aware of James Bulger's suffering, and the number of blows inflicted during the attack. Such a direc-tion, of course, makes it unlikely that a jury would not find the rule to be satisfied. And it is to be expected that more young children will be sent into custody, in secure units, satisfying once more, perhaps, the desire to separate what is really child's play from the behaviour depicted by the likes of *Child's Play*. Thus the government attempts to reconstitute the difference – between image and reality – which the event of James Bulger's killing had brought into crisis.

28. On the 'family principle' in the establishment of juvenile institutions, see Rush (1992).

29. The House of Lords restored on appeal in this case the presumption of *doli capax*: it must be shown that the child knew the act was seriously wrong (*The Guardian*, 17 March 1995). The Divisional Court decision is reported at (1994) *Criminal Law Review* 523.

Punitiveness towards children, whatever their wrongdoing, is a response to a breach that has occurred in the relationship between adults and children. Children are the next generation; they have been generated by adults and so are held to be in a state of indebtedness to adults. That debt is masked, however, as a relationship of *giving*: the adult gives to the child its knowledge, ethics, love, education. Upon the adult's demise, the child inherits wealth (or debts). During the adult's lifetime, a process of legacy is present in the relation between child and adult. In such a legacy, the child receives the law and is thus filiated to the father. Genealogy and law are thus secured. Always, however, the process is fraught with fear: that the legatee will refuse the gift, and thus reject his filiation to the father's law. At that point, the inheritor turns his back on his inheritance and embraces bastardy, that which our social order dreads (since it marks those who exist outside of legal relations). Ray Matthews, James Bulger's uncle, yells 'bastards' at Venables and Thompson to mark the severance of their identities from the law, the family, the father. Hewitt and Leach write: 'As a group, children are recognized as "the future" (although now, as in all previous times, many adults look askance at the new generation that will inherit their work)' (1993: 1). But not only do adults fear that a child is not worthy of its inheritance; the pervasive cultural fear that underwrites social and criminal justice policies is that any or every child might reject the valuable gift of filiation. Such a child would not in fact be a child; and, as Warner writes: 'even the most beautiful and shining examples may be counterfeit' (1994: 44); even the child that appears 'good' to the adult might be 'evil'. The adult generation may well be deceived by its children; even those that look like children might be fraudulent, imitations. Behind the public discourse on the James Bulger case lurks a suspicion that even though 'our' children look (to us) like 'James Bulgers' (innocent, ideal), they might be the non-children that Robert Thompson and Jon Venables are taken to embody. *The Sunday Times* stated:

> [W]e will never be able to look at our children in the same way again. . . . All over the country, parents are viewing their sons in a new and disturbing light. When we see them at the ages of 9, 10 or 11, pushing each other, jostling, or showing impatience with their younger brothers and sisters, we can't help wondering in what circumstances they could end up like Robert Thompson or Jon Venables, the killers of little James Bulger. . . . Parents everywhere are asking themselves and their friends if the Mark of the Beast might not also be imprinted on their offspring. (28 November 1993)[30]

Within the discourse about the event, the breach in the process of generation that is so feared has come to the surface. In Dickens, in Burt, in today's popular press, the duality between the child as victim or criminal is all-pervasive.

---

30. Note that parents are said to be looking with trepidation at their sons, not their daughters. Despite the Mary Bell case, it is one of the characteristics of the press representation of the killing of James Bulger that it was a *masculine* act. Discussing the case recently in a seminar, one student commented that her 13-year-old son had felt victimized by the media's linking of masculinity and violence, to the extent that all activities 'normally' engaged in by young boys (hanging around the street, 'rough' play) had been made signifiers of violent predisposition.

The event, however, is so troubling because it presents us with the spectacle of the child as, at once, both victim and criminal, or neither one nor the other. The comforting dichotomy that culture embraced and endlessly rewrote has been interrupted. And as such, the social order suffers a painful wound; its heritage amputated and an anomic sore left to fester. The writing of childhood as innocence and evil seeks to suture the wound: through Denise Bulger's pregnant body, through an affirmation of the maternal relation as one of love and care, through the resurgence of the legitimate paternal relation in the voices that cry 'bastards' at Thompson and Venables. The semblance of heritage is restored, through a process of grafting, whereby a simulation of tradition and inheritance can be created out of draconian punishment and the regulation of technological threats. And in the graft is located the child, scion of the age, as incomprehensible and fearful as before.

Post scriptum: **Memorial images**

Any graft attached to a wound such as this will never be sufficient to its task. The process of suturing the breach in the cultural order is a fragmented but continuous one. In the weeks approaching the anniversary of the trial of Thompson and Venables, the event of James Bulger's death resurfaced in the press. First, an announcement was made that Denise and Ralph Bulger were seeking a divorce. 'Stress separates Bulger parents', stated *The Guardian* (5 November 1994); while the *Independent on Sunday* described 'the mother of murdered toddler James Bulger [who] has consulted her solicitor in Liverpool about the split from her husband Ralph, who has also talked to lawyers about divorce' (6 November 1994). In an 'exclusive' interview in The *News of the World*, Denise Bulger said: 'What's happened has hurt me deeply after all I have been through. I am very bitter' (6 November 1994). The media interest in the Bulger family as 'news' was cited as one of the reasons for the divorce. Given the secure positioning of the Bulger family on the side of the victim in the victim/criminal opposition, no comment was made in the press about the negative influence their divorce would have on their children.[31]

Two weeks earlier, the delayed release or possible banning of *Natural Born Killers* (an American film by Oliver Stone), was discussed within the context of its having acquired the 'greatest celebrity since *Child's Play 3*' (*The Guardian*, 25 October 1994). *Natural Born Killers* has been linked, somewhat tenuously, to 'copycat' murders in the United States and France, supposedly inspired by the scenes of violence portrayed in the movie, which is an ostensible condemnation of the media's glorification of serial killers. Another American film, *The Good Son*, has also been refused a certificate in Britain: the film, about 'a ruthless cherub without a cause' (ironically starring the

---

31. Some vilification of the Bulger family has begun in the tabloid press, perhaps in response to their break-up. The *Sunday People* wrote of Denise Bulger as a 'drunk' and called Ralph Bulger the 'Merseyside love cheat', revealing his affair with a young woman and their illegitimate children (6 November 1994).

adored child-image Macaulay Culkin of the *Home Alone* films) 'ran into trouble because its release would have come too close to the murder of Jamie Bulger' (*The Guardian*, 28 October 1994). The controversy over *Natural Born Killers* arose one week before the Criminal Justice Bill 1994 became law: this statute contains Howard's requirement that films should not display 'inappropriate' models for children and young adults. Censors now have to apply a formula when awarding a certificate to a film and their decisions can be challenged in court. At the same time as this relived fulmination over the link between representations of violence and violent acts such as the murder of James Bulger, Allison Pearson – a television critic – wrote a polemic against television news, denouncing, in particular, the obscenity of media interest in the death of James Bulger:

> Five years ago, the teddy bears displayed at the funeral of a child killed by other children would not have been the subject of mawkish and macabre comment by newsreaders. Nor would the distress of his parents. The great gulping grief of James Bulger's parents was not news. But it was great television. (*Independent on Sunday*, 30 October 1994)

Images of James Bulger's death continue to circulate: in fears that movies might re-present the motivation that impelled Venables and Thompson, that two more halves of a homicidal pair might 'find each other' and be inspired to wreak havoc.[32] They circulate in guilty admissions that media intrusions into a family's grief might affect relationships between those family members. They circulate, finally, as memorial images. An artist, Jamie Wagg, exhibited a piece of work based on laminated newspaper reproductions from the security video, in Whitechapel Art Gallery. Prints were offered for sale at £2,235 each (including the image reproduced as Figure 5 above).[33] Ray Matthews, James Bulger's uncle, demanded a boycott of the gallery, even after it had removed the prints from sale (while retaining the exhibited original) and the artist had written to the family explaining his intention to create a 'memorial image' and expressing his 'sincere regret' at their distress (*The Times* and *The Guardian*, both 27 May 1994). While the newspaper photographs

32. Venables and Thompson were described as 'two freaks who found each other' (*Independent on Sunday*, 28 November 1993); *Natural Born Killers* depicts 'a demonic couple' (*The Guardian*, 28 October 1994); the *Mail on Sunday* compared Venables and Thompson to 'Leopold and Loeb in Chicago in 1924' and to 'Brady and Hindley on the Lancashire moors in the Sixties' (13 February 1994). Articles on Richard Elsey and Jamie Petrolini, Oxford students who committed murder, represented them as 'cementing a symbiotic relationship' and engaged in a 'waltz of the *folie à deux*' which would lead to murder (*The Guardian*, 9 November 1994). Elsey and Petrolini were also compared to Leopold and Loeb. The latter inspired Patrick Hamilton's play *Rope* (made into a film, *Compulsion*, by Hitchcock).

33. Jamie Wagg published an angry account of the tabloids' campaign against his artwork, commenting in particular on their hypocrisy (having used the same images themselves) (1995: 19–20). For a further critique, see Cousins:

> When the artist Jamie Wagg re-uses [the image], it becomes a scandal. He was attacked for making money out of the image since it was on sale. . . . Why did all this provoke so much fury? One reason is that Jamie Wagg had broken a taboo. He . . . shows that the system of which the image is a part is itself dangerous. (1995: 17)

published around the times of the murder, the trial and the sentencing decision are conceived as part of the process of expressing a national anger or collective guilt, the artwork seems to fit less comfortably into a schema of retributivism and anguish. Its re-representation of the images, detached from their frantic written texts, makes them *more* troubling. It is not that the artist might not be 'condemning' the act of Venables and Thompson. Rather, its status *as memorial* asks questions *of us*: What do we remember? Whose image shall we own? Whose memory shall we enshrine?

6

Criminological Concordats: On the Single Mother and the Criminal Child

Among the responses to the event of the killing of James Bulger, described in the previous chapter, was a frantic drive to *explain* how such a crime came to be committed. Various causes were named: the inherent evil of the two children who carried out the crime; the social problems that beset Liverpool; the impoverishment of our sense of community that would not permit intervention in the child's abduction. In this chapter, I will extend some of the arguments made about what caused the killing of one child by two others to explore the connections between criminology's interest in the family and recent governmental changes in social and criminal justice policy.[1] To that end, three of the dominant causal tropes from the responses to the death of James Bulger have had a wider significance in the recent debates on family background and juvenile crime. The two most prominent causal explanations have involved the effect of the absence of a father from the home of a delinquent child and the perceived inadequacy of maternal care offered in such homes. These two aspects of the familial backgrounds of Venables and Thompson received considerable attention from the media. Their application to the general question of the interrelationship of home circumstances and criminal behaviour will be discussed in detail in this chapter. A third explanation of significance was also found in the representations of Venables and Thompson: this involves the assertion that the crime was emblematic of contemporary society. One article asked: 'Has the age of video nasties, drugs, one-parent families, football hooliganism, yuppiedom, Thatcherism, Kinnockism, lousy education, violent computer games, trainers, the whole rotten lot, finally given us what we so richly deserved?' (*The Sunday Times*, 21 February 1993). Others took the event, along with other by-products such as video games, as a consequence of the liberalizations of the 1960s: 'there are unquestionably many who since the 1960s have promoted an ethos that leads directly to the callous answer given by Robert Thompson to a detective: he

---

1. I am using 'governmental' in the Foucauldian sense; that is, in order both to encompass the notion of government as the policies and laws enacted by the elected body of representatives operating in Parliament and to exceed it. I take as axiomatic the relation asserted by Foucault between government and the family. From the eighteenth century onwards, the family became an instrument of government rather than a model: 'the privileged instrument for the government of the population and not the chimerical model of good government', see Foucault (1991: 100).

killed baby James "because he felt like it'" (*Daily Mail*, 26 November 1993).

The 1960s are made responsible for Venables and Thompson in that their parents, who went through adolescence in that decade, are deemed to be irrevocably marked by the liberalizations and loosening of bonds commonly claimed to have occurred then. Dennis and Erdos write:

> The 1960s saw the beginning of a period of rapid and far-reaching change in the interconnected set of formal and informal social arrangements (a) for controlling who could bring children into the world; (b) for fixing responsibilities for rearing the children, in terms of physique, character and social adjustment; (c) that defined in terms of partners and activities the sources and saliency of sexual pleasure; and (d) that aimed at ensuring so far as possible that each adult had a life-long source of mutual assistance. (1993: 30)

Contraception, feminism, new social movements and the extension of the welfare state: these features characterized the decade's dramatic social changes. Many of those who were adolescent children in the 1960s have become adults with children of their own in the 1990s. With the children of the present decade being viewed as incomparably worse than any other children, their parents were obvious targets in the drive to explain the supposed dreadfulness of their offspring.

As suggested in Chapter 5, children are required to inherit: the parents of contemporary 'delinquents' are now being criticized for having inherited only the bad from the 1960s (lack of respect for authority, moral weakness, predilections for drug-taking, so-called deviant sexualities). Their children can thus only inherit dangerous legacies. The notion of inheritance underlies my interrogation of contemporary governmental and traditional criminological interest in the family and crime, particularly the interpretation of the mother–child relation as instrumental in the generation of delinquency. Chapter 5 concerned the *responses made to the invention of an image of crime*; this chapter will investigate the *invention of images of responsibility for crime*. Governmental and criminological discourses pick out the figure of the single mother as the contemporary embodiment of responsibility for the criminal child. Certain themes in Chapter 2 will be drawn upon; notably, the ambiguity of the figure of the wife-and-mother. Chapter 3's account of the crisis of responsibility that has been located in the domestic sphere will also frame what follows. This chapter reads representations of the 'broken home' and 'marital discord' as the emotional space of criminogenesis, in which the figure of the mother is made a scapegoat for the failure of investment in the link between community and child. As such, my project here is twofold: first, to describe and interpret the *projections* of the family and the single mother in criminological and governmental policy; second, to *restore* the emotional body of the family, in particular the singularity of the single mother as figure of responsibility. My task is therefore both critical and affirmative. The critical aspect will attack the governmental regulation of the family as a site of criminogenesis; a regulation which is based on a projection or *image* of domestic responsibility (containing, internal to it, the identity of mother and child). The affirmative aspect asserts that such regulation is premised on the difference of mother and child *as* difference, as proximate. The singularity of the single mother is not a legal or marital relation (which is based, rather, upon the *appearance* of responsibility) but an emotional relation in which the mother responds to the child as child, rather than as surrogate for the father, the law or the community.

For more than 50 years, there has been an assumption operating in discursive practices, including criminological theory, social policy and criminal justice initiatives, that in a family where there are two heterosexual parents living in harmony, no delinquency should result in their children. Despite the obvious ideality of such an assumption, the discursive practices mentioned above have proceeded to investigate or act upon their concerns as if this assumption represented the real. It is taken as if it described the living situations of the majority of individuals. From that starting-point, the aberrations represented by the 'broken home' or the 'juvenile delinquent' have been examined as the troublesome oddity. In the first section of this chapter, I will consider the position of the family in criminological theory, focusing in particular on the paradigmatic work of Donald West. The second section will uncover the traces of Westian theory in the current governmental practices concerning lone-parent families. My aim is to elucidate the manner in which criminality is taken to reproduce itself through the mechanisms of biological and social reproduction: child-bearing and child-rearing.

The family of criminology

In reading criminology's account of the relationship between familial circumstances and delinquent behaviour, it is almost impossible to discern where criminology ends and psychology begins (or even if such a distinction is feasible). Psychologists from the 1940s onwards have been fascinated with criminality; a strand of criminology has always claimed psychology held the answers to criminology's big questions (who commits crimes? why do they do so? what can be done to stop them doing so?). An excursus through the textual history of the link between family and crime leads through both these disciplines. Whatever the disciplinary affiliations of the researchers, the resulting claims, despite an initial apparent consistency of opinion, fall into two major approaches to the perceived link between familial circumstances and juvenile criminality. On the one hand, there are those who assert a relationship mainly between the notion of a 'broken' home and any observable delinquent or 'anti-social' behaviour in the child. This group comprises, variously and not exclusively, the Gluecks, Burt, Bowlby.[2] The second group tends to emphasize more the nature of the break-up and the nature of stresses within the home, leading them to highlight the differences in *types* of 'broken' home. This group includes Rutter, Biller, the McCords.[3] West's research, as will be seen, tends to oscillate between them.

2. See Glueck and Glueck (1950, 1952, 1959, 1962, 1968); Burt (1944); Bowlby (1951, 1973).
    3. See Rutter (1972, 1974, 1976, 1980); Rutter and Giller (1983); Biller (1971, 1993); McCord and McCord (1959).

To demonstrate some of the differences between these two groups: Burt's assertions about the predominance of separated parents, foster parents or violent parents in the families of the delinquents he studied are found again in the well-known work of the Gluecks in the 1950s, which estimated a delinquency rate in boys whose parents were divorced or separated to be about double that of boys in 'intact' homes. The study by the McCords in 1959, however, found so-called 'broken homes' (where the break occurs through divorce, separation or death of a parent) to lead to considerably less juvenile delinquency than did 'intact' homes marked by quarrels, neglect or abuse. This second body of opinion emphasized that delinquency was associated with breaks which follow from parental discord, or discord without a break of any kind, but not necessarily with a break-up *per se*. Distinctions were thus drawn between families with a lone parent in which the break-up had resulted through the death of the other parent (with the necessary severance of ties between child and deceased parent); families with a lone parent in which the break-up was the result of divorce or separation (and with a potential for continuing intermittent ties between child and absent parent); and families with two parents present (one or both of whom were neglectful, violent, quarrelsome or alcoholic, or any combination of these).

Bowlby's notion of 'maternal deprivation' coined one of the best-known phrases of the century. 'Mother-love' in infancy was held to be as important to the child as the vitamins and proteins that were beginning to be distributed to children at school as free milk, and a functional mysticism of the mother was put in place. However, part of the term's appeal as a (catch)phrase also led to its being frequently misapplied. Bowlby's (1951) original use of the term had emphasized the diversity of experiences covered by 'maternal deprivation'. But the single term implied a single syndrome of unitary causation, leading to a widely held assumption that any blame for delinquent behaviour (which Bowlby had linked to maternal deprivation) could be laid at the feet of the mother. Bowlby certainly posited a uniqueness to the maternal relation: arguing that the child is 'innately monotropic and that the bond with the mother . . . is different in kind from the bonds developed with others' (1951: 124–5). Others reacted against such a focus on the mother. Rutter, for example, responded to Bowlby's arguments thus: 'father, mother, brothers, sisters, friends, school-teachers and others all have an impact on development, but that influence and impact differs for different aspects of development. A less exclusive focus on the mother is required. Children also have fathers!' (1972: 125). With the reduction of his list to 'fathers', Rutter conforms here to a trend that has increasingly stressed the role of the father in the child's upbringing. However, where the influence of the mother is still presented as a constant that should operate to the child's good but which can fester and produce aberrations, the father's influence is seen as a necessary good often ignored by theory and forcibly excluded by divorce. Such a dichotomy has structured much of the discourse on familial backgrounds and will be seen to have exerted an influence on the shape of current policies enacted by the Conservative government.

Delinquency according to Donald West

In the famous longitudinal studies carried out by Donald West (1969, 1973, 1977, 1982), the influence of Bowlby and others can be discerned in this criminological reading of the making of a young delinquent. The aim of the research was to study the personalities, social backgrounds and family histories of young offenders in order to discover differences between them and their non-delinquent social peers that might explain for the criminologist the offenders' deviant conduct. West pre-empted an obvious criticism of this strategy:

> Some radical criminologists would challenge the validity of an enterprise concentrating on the individuals involved instead of upon the social conditions that make individuals behave in the way that they do. . . . In the event, we found our delinquents really were different from their peers in background, life history, in social behaviour and attitude as well as in their propensity for illegal exploits. There is therefore no need to apologize for having carried out the investigation on a false assumption. (1982: 2–3)

West here is articulating the opposition between the individual and the social. He rejects criticism which would allege an exclusive focus on the individual at the expense of the social, for he claims to have found the social conditions that produce individuals as different. West goes on to claim that his study shows that 'delinquency most often arises from an accumulation of different pressures rather than from any single salient cause' (1982: 3). Despite such a multifactorial emphasis, West asserts a primary cause in the form of child–parent interaction, rejecting any criticisms that criminologists have been paying too much attention to this area. He states:

> In the early years of life . . . the social factors that affect children do so through the parents, who are the main transmitters of the expectations and attitudes of their milieu. Early upbringing is probably the most important reason why, even in the most crime-ridden localities, some youngsters successfully resist the pressures to adopt a delinquent lifestyle. In our study, unsatisfactory upbringing . . . was significantly predictive of youthful delinquency, and of recidivism persisting into adulthood. (1982: 52–3)

The articulation of the individual and the social, therefore, is the family. That is, the family mediates the social, either by continuing it or by resisting it. As a result, the project of social policy must be the strengthening of the family against that which threatens society and the eradication of anything that might transmit damaging social conditions. In short, as a conduit between the individual and society, the family becomes a target of governmental strategy.

West's analysis draws upon the theories of Bowlby and others, in a manner which both utilizes their paradigmatic concepts yet which also seeks to distinguish the study from Bowlby's own findings. West comments on how Bowlby suggests that separation from the mother during the early years impairs the child's capacity to form loving, trusting relationships and makes it more likely to pursue an anti-social lifestyle. Contrary to what West (1982: 55) sees as a 'psychoanalytic preoccupation' in Bowlby's work with the events of infancy especially with a need for a close and uninterrupted bond between mother and baby, West's Cambridge study asserted a more complex and variable set of causes and effects. A history of separation from one or both parents for more than one month in the first 10 years, he claims, is indeed significantly associated with later delinquency; however, separations when the child was under the age of 6 were no worse than those experienced by children in the 6 to 10 years age group. Where Bowlby suggested family disruption has worse effects if it occurs early in life, the Cambridge study found no closer association with delinquency when break-ups occurred early.

Where Bowlby would have asserted the greater trauma suffered by a younger child due to its greater dependency, emotional and physical, on its mother, West proposes that if any greater likelihood of future delinquency does result from an early break-up, it is because a 'broken home' stands for a cluster of interacting circumstances. Added to the emotional stress caused by the loss of a parent is the financial stress caused by the consequential loss of income and the 'deterioration in standards of child care' that may come about when a parent is left to cope alone (1982: 55–6). Bowlby (1973: 215) claimed that the 'instabilities of maternal care' resulting after a separation will lead to one of two possible responses in the child – anxious attachment or aggressive detachment – with the latter type the potential delinquent: aggressive, disobedient, neither trusting nor caring for others. West instead returns to multifactorialism in preference to Bowlby's argument:

> The typical criminogenic family is beset by chronic problems. The Cambridge study found no evidence for the predominant importance of the circumstances of early life over those of later years. Delinquents tended to come from families with continuing disturbances that affected children in their schooldays as much as in their infancy and which manifested themselves in many different ways. For instance, parents who let their children spend most of their leisure time away from the family, fathers who never took part in their sons' leisure activities and mothers whose expectations for their sons' future career were low in comparison with his educational achievement, were all more likely than others to have sons becoming delinquent. (1982: 56–7)

Where break-ups do occur, the important issue for West is the reason for the break: 'Temporary or permanent separations occasioned by illness or death bore comparatively little relationship to offending, but separations caused by the breakdown of the parents' marriage were very significant precursors of delinquency' (1982: 55). Here West aligns himself with Rutter and those who draw distinctions between the various natures of break-up that may be experienced within a family. In West's study, the group of delinquents included more than twice as many from homes broken by circumstances other than death; West concludes that 'family discord is the main reason for the link between broken homes and delinquency' (1982: 55). No account is given here of rates of delinquency in families where the parents have remained together but are experiencing 'discord' (violence, arguments, alcoholism and so on). Thus 'discord' is reduced to separation.

However, in the passage quoted above, where West lists the sort of 'chronic problems' that plague the 'typical criminogenic family', a founding paradox becomes clear. Although West is at pains to distinguish his study from Bowlby's theories – by emphasizing that separation trauma in infancy is not the paramount cause of delinquent behaviour and by stressing a variety of 'chronic problems' – West's notions of multifactorialism are dependent upon a version of the parent–child relation as crucial to the child's development. Every example that is cited, from parents lax in their supervisory duties, through fathers who are symbolically absent from their sons, to mothers who care too little about their sons' futures, is a characterization of the parent as having responsibility for moulding the raw material of the child into a law-abiding adult rather than a delinquent adult. West (1982: 56–7) expands on the failures of duty that parents commit: a carelessness or laxity in supervision; a lack of concern over the child's whereabouts or lack of interest in watching over the child's doings; a lack of concern about or interest in the child's companions; a lack of rules about or lack of enforcement of rules about bedtimes, punctuality, manners, television, or tidiness.

The parallels with the press discourse relating to the parents of Venables and Thompson in the Bulger case are striking (discussed in Chapter 5). West is quite specific about his point here: 'However important a "loving" relationship may be in shaping character, it is no insurance against delinquency unless accompanied by adequate social training' (1982: 57). This sentence contains the fundamental aspects of West's theory. First, *love* is important (and, thus, an unloving parent may be criticized first of all), but as a mere emotion, love requires direction and intention. Second, character needs *shaping*; it is amorphous and malleable, plastic, to be given definition and backbone by the directed love of the careful parent. Third, children represent a risk; *insurance* is recommended in risky situations, to manage the risk, to guarantee the outcome and provide surety should 'the worst' happen. Finally, the parent is required to provide *training* for the child, a disciplinary control to teach the child how to act, speak and live. Parental love has been converted into a mode of correction (punishment, albeit represented as just in this model) and a *bond*: a fetter to tie parent to child and a deposit or guarantee that the parent will come up with the necessary goods (a responsible, non-delinquent child).

Criminological reproduction: on the making of criminals

Westian criminology has seen a recent renaissance in the sense that a return to the family as a site of criminogenesis can be discerned in contemporary analyses of criminality.[4] While conventionally presented as part of a multi-factorial study, the analysis symptomatically betrays the primacy it gives to familial circumstances, in its language, structure and implications. Loeber

---

4. For example see: Farrington (1979, 1987); Gottfredson and Hirschi (1990); Laub and Sampson (1988); Loeber and Stouthamer-Loeber (1986); Sampson and Laub (1993); Wilson (1983). For a policy-oriented longitudinal project, see Earls and Reiss (1994), who are studying 11,000 individuals in Chicago over eight years; by drawing these individuals from different age groups they have constructed a study which begins *in utero* and continues to age 30.

and Stouthamer-Loeber created four dimensions of family functioning: the 'neglect' paradigm (which examines parent–child and child–parent involvement and parental supervision); the 'conflict' paradigm (which analyses disciplinary practices and parent–child/child–parent rejection); the 'deviant behaviors and attitudes' paradigm (which focuses on parental criminality and deviant attitudes among parents); and the 'disruption' paradigm (which looks at marital conflict and parental absence) (Loeber and Stouthamer-Loeber, 1986). Such a perspective is, first of all, structuralist in its adoption of a rigid and limited 'square' of possibilities into which all situations surveyed are fitted. The analysis pretends an isomorphism between the four paradigms and the families it examines. Second, the naming of the paradigms and their intended aims reveals the value structures which always already place the parent (as adult, as progenitor, as trainer) subordinate to the child (as dependent, as heir, as malleable substance). For example, in the 'neglect' paradigm, 'parental supervision' is under inspection, presupposing the naturalness of such supervision in such a relationship; in the 'deviant behaviors' paradigm, the notion at work is that of the bad parent as seductive mirror for the child.

In their conclusions, Loeber and Stouthamer-Loeber found that all four paradigms showed a relationship to child delinquency. This should not be surprising: when a paradigm is constructed to prefigure a duty owed by one to another and blame attributed when the duty is abrogated, all discoverable narratives will incorporate a version of this relationship. And so, 'powerful predictors' are said to be lack of parental supervision, parental rejection and lack of parent–child involvement; 'medium predictors' are influences such as parents' marital relations and parental criminality; while 'weak predictors' are lack of parental discipline, parental health and parental absence. The implications of this demonstrate assumptions about the hierarchy of roles expected of a parent, while embedded in these conclusions are gender divisions which separate the neutral 'parent' into 'father' and 'mother'. The 'powerful' predictors contain, by inversion, the most important functions a parent can perform: supervision, affection and involvement. To avoid delinquency, parents are thus placed under a duty to provide surveillance, to give love as surety and to display involvement in their child's activities and interests. Of 'medium' importance are the expectations made of parents as adults: that they live harmoniously and that they live in a law-abiding manner. Finally, of least significance is their punitiveness, their health and their absence from the child or family. In this group, 'parental absence' as a predictive factor is important. When parents separate or divorce, it is conventional that the mother has custody of the child. This is assumed, as will be examined later, in discussions about single parenthood. If the father's absence is only of 'weak' significance in predicting delinquency, then far greater weight and responsibility is attributed to the maternal role after separation. Such asymmetric weighting should also be read into the predictors as a general group: given that in heterosexual relationships, women perform most childcare duties and spend far more time with the child than does the male partner, the research's 'conclusions' can be read as attributing most responsibility to women for the generation of future law-abiding adults. In this respect, the bonds of maternal love become bonds of disciplinary duty.

The notion of a bond appears in another recent reversion to Westian theory. Sampson and Laub propose: 'the probability of deviance increases when an individual's bond to society is weak or broken. . . . In other words, when the social ties (that is, attachment, commitment) that bind an individual to key societal institutions (such as family and school) are loosened, the risk of crime and delinquency is heightened' (1993: 65). In this version of the social contract, a bond is beneficial to the individual. 'Social ties' are not represented as oppressive, but rather as the mechanisms which sustain civil society. Their 'loosening', 'weakening' or 'breaking' threatens not only society but also the individual within those bonds. Without their *protection*, she is at risk of falling from civil society into the amorphous mass of criminals. She is at risk of becoming an outlaw, excluded by necessity from the community.

For a child, according to Sampson and Laub, four factors will increase the likelihood of delinquent behaviour: '(1) erratic, threatening and harsh or punitive discipline by both mothers and fathers, (2) low parental supervision, (3) parental rejection of the child and (4) weak emotional attachment of the boy to his parents' (1993: 65). In the slippage from 'child' to 'boy', the daughter is casually erased from the family romance. The four factors listed are given primary importance in the causing of delinquency. Social factors – such as poverty, poor housing, language difficulties through immigration – are seen as affecting children only indirectly, through their impact on parents and thence on the tight bonds of familial social control. And while some have argued for particular relationships between parental criminality and a child's delinquency – whether that be as a developmental mirror (Loeber and Stouthamer-Loeber, 1986) or genetic (Rutter and Giller, 1983) – for Sampson and Laub, parental deviance influences a child's delinquency only through the disruption of social control: 'Parents who commit crimes and drink excessively are likely to use harsh discipline in an inconsistent manner or to be lax in disciplining their children' (1993: 69). In a statement which demonstrates the causal assumptions at work, Sampson and Laub sum up as follows:

> Family disruption, residential mobility, poverty, foreign-born or immigrant status and both father's and mother's deviance have significant effects on parental rejection of the child. These results suggest that in families with only one parent, frequent moves, disadvantaged financial/ethnic position, and a pattern of deviant parental conduct, parents are more likely to exhibit indifference or hostility toward their children. (1993: 80–1)

After the list of influential or causative factors, the result is stated plainly: parental rejection of the child; that is, 'indifference or hostility toward their children'. At this point, it should be questioned who is imagined as the real deviant here: the child who develops anti-social impulses, or the parent who abrogates her duty, turns her back on a child and, necessarily, behaves selfishly?

Parenting is an activity which, for Sampson and Laub, can be carried out in a skilled or less skilled manner: 'less skilled parents inadvertently reinforce their children's antisocial behaviour and fail to provide effective punishment for transgressions' (1993: 67).[5] A skilled parent is therefore one who reacts to anti-social or transgressive behaviour by punishing 'effectively' (a tautologous argument in this schema, since one can only know *retrospectively* whether punishment has been effective, when a child develops, or not, into a 'delinquent') and by communicating properly 'social' values to the child. Here Sampson and Laub draw on two sources; one is Patterson, who writes, 'Parents of stealers do not track; they do not punish and they do not care' (1980: 88–9). The second source of inspiration is Braithwaite's theory of 'reintegrative shaming' (1989: 56). Sampson and Laub imagine a situation in which 'parents punish in a consistent manner and within the context of love, respect and acceptance of the child' (1993: 68). Echoing Adorno's (1973) comment on hearing how Heidegger lyricized the bucolic lives of poor farmers, one might well ask the child what she thinks about that. Loving parents, then, punish, track, shame and thus reintegrate the wayward child into the social order from which she has strayed. Familial social control, say Sampson and Laub, is about 'discipline, supervision and attachment' (1993: 68). And, as they advert to 'social control', the edifice that has been constructed is in plain view: the family is a panopticon which operates in the name of love.[6]

Disciplining the family

On 6 October 1993, at the 110th Conservative Party Conference at Blackpool, the Home Secretary, Michael Howard, stated:

> All my life in politics I have been utterly convinced that the first duty of Government is to maintain law and order: to protect people's freedom to walk safely on their streets and sleep safely in their homes. You can argue forever about the causes of crime. My approach is based on some simple principles. That children – at home and at school – must be taught the difference between right and wrong. That criminals – and no-one else – must be held responsible for their actions.

On 5 October, in another speech to a fringe meeting at the Conference, Howard had also commented that when the stigma against illegitimacy had been stronger, 'girls' frequently put their babies up for adoption and 'that may have been the best outcome'. Nowadays, housing estates, with their higher incidence of young single mothers, meant that such women were less isolated. This could encourage them, once they had had one child outside marriage, to have 'a second and a third' on their own. He cited the claim of Peter Lilley, Government Minister for Social Security, that '"getting married to the State" may appear a more attractive prospect'. A child 'born into these circumstances' learned to get their own way, emulated the most aggressive

5. See also Gottfredson and Hirschi (1990: 99).
6. Cohen describes the 'indefinite discipline' of a contract between parents and their 16-year-old son (1979: 352). Elsewhere, Cohen comments on the rethinking of the 'biological lifespan' as a 'series of risk periods, each calling for professional observation, check-ups, tutelage and supervision', ending the 'casualness' of child-rearing (1985: 232). Donzelot (1979) most memorably described the encircling of the family in the 'tutelary complex'.

and rebellious boys in the neighbourhood and 'when they get caught learn that the consequences are far from intolerable'.[7]

Howard's comments draw, in a common-sense manner, upon notions conventional in criminology linking criminal behaviour to familial background. However, his comments are significant for distilling a general concern about upbringing and family circumstances into a unitary figure which comes to represent the putative link between parenting and delinquency. The woman bringing up a child or children without a male partner has been subjected to intense governmental interest since late 1993. In this section, I will elaborate the forms in which that interest has appeared and also suggest some explanations for and consequences of such an interest. This is not to suggest that single mothers have never been scrutinized or criticized in the past; on the contrary, the lone mother is a figure who has been called upon at many junctures to represent a social crisis.[8] My aim here is to consider why the figure of the mother is commonly translated into a scapegoat who can represent all manner of social malignancies. As such a scapegoat, she can be sacrificed symbolically, remaining within the social contract while represented as excluded from it. My interest is therefore in uncovering the cultural associations which permit a linking of maternal practices and criminal children.

The single mother as governmental target

Fewer than one in four British households now conforms to the traditional model of a married or cohabiting heterosexual couple with children, according to the most recent General Household Survey.[9] Lone parents head 21 per cent of families (up from 12 per cent in 1979). The survey found that lone mothers typically have to manage on very little money: 42 per cent had gross incomes of less than one hundred pounds per week.[10] Employment rates among lone mothers were found to be low: only 22 per cent with children under 5 years old were in any kind of employment.[11] Home ownership was also less commonly found among lone mothers: less than 30 per cent had bought or had a mortgage on a house, while 77 per cent of married or cohabiting couples had managed this. Among lone parents, 57 per cent were in council housing. Within this dull list of figures can be discerned kernels of the issues which have come to preoccupy government policy. These are the lower employment rates, the higher rate of council housing and the lower income levels among single mothers. While the figures in themselves do not dictate

7. See the discussion of Howard's comments in *The Guardian*, 2 February 1994.

8. See, for example, Smart (1992a, 1992b).

9. General Household Survey 1992, published by the Office of Population Censuses and Surveys. The data result from interviews conducted in 10,034 households throughout Britain between April 1992 and March 1993.

10. In comparison, the survey found that only 4 per cent of married couples had an income of less than £100 per week; while 67 per cent had an income of over £300 per week (an amount achieved by only 14 per cent of lone mothers).

11. Married or cohabiting women achieved an 'economic activity rate' of 67 per cent, compared with only 46 per cent of lone mothers.

the direction policy-makers were to take, they are capable of being used, as I will go on to show, in a manner which underlined government claims about single mothers and crime.

By the phrase 'single mothers and crime', the government is not implying that lone mothers were being driven to commit criminal acts in order to survive (as a result of their poor housing situation, lower income levels and impeded employment opportunities and so on). Such an economic link has been made by a number of different commentators in describing criminal behaviour in a wide variety of circumstances, and by individuals ranging from poor women to unemployed teenagers.[12] Here, for the government, 'single mothers and crime' means that the woman who becomes a single mother shrugs aside responsibility for raising her child to become a moral citizen and instead permits him or her to develop criminal values. For all the sensibly incredulous questions that can be begged of such an equation, this is the basic governmental perspective on single motherhood. I will show how this position emerged.

It was John Redwood, then the Conservative Secretary of State for Wales, who first revealed the government's views. In July 1993, Redwood visited a housing estate in Cardiff and met a number of lone parents (male and female). After this visit, he proposed that government policy should be to withhold state benefits from single mothers until the absent father could be found and returned to the household 'to give the normal love and support that fathers have offered down the ages'.[13] While Peter Lilley, the Minister for Social Security, later denied that benefits would be withheld, other MPs and Ministers reinforced the message that single motherhood was to be viewed not only as a social problem, but perhaps as *the* problem which underlay all social ills. Sackville, a junior Health Minister, blamed single motherhood on feminism, political correctness and the liberalization of the Church (*The Guardian*, 6 July 1993). Graham Riddick MP blamed the welfare system for encouraging 'young women to have babies out of wedlock' (*The Guardian*, 6 July 1993).

The government's assault on single mothers did not remain at the level of political rhetoric. New policies were quickly introduced which were to worsen the economic position of single mothers, diminish their chances of finding employment and restrict their access to low-cost housing. At the 1993 Conservative Party conference, Peter Lilley outlined the government's view of family breakdown:

> The third main area of rising [government] spending is on lone parents. But I am less concerned about the cost than the breakdown of families. There are now 1.3 million lone parents. Many find themselves lone parents against their will. Widows, divorced and separated people struggle alone, but often successfully, to bring their children up well. They deserve not blame but support. However, the fastest growing group are those who never married. Since the sixties their numbers have risen seven-fold. Partly because throughout that period it has been 'politically incorrect'

12. See especially Carlen (1988).
13. Reported in *The Guardian*, 6 July 1993, and discussed in 'Who's left holding the baby?', *The Independent*, 6 July 1993.

to uphold the traditional family as an ideal. Anyone who did so was sneered into silence. Earlier this year I decided it was time to break that taboo. To reaffirm that ideally children need two loving parents; that parents' first duty is to their children; that that duty is for life; that even where parents split up they remain responsible for supporting their children. Yet three out of four lone mothers depend on income support and don't receive a penny of regular maintenance from the absent father. That's why we set up the Child Support Agency this April. To secure more maintenance from more parents for more children. Many married couples on modest incomes have to struggle to support their own families. Why should they pay taxes to support the children of absent parents earning more than they do? While making it harder to abuse the system, I want to make it easier for the millions of genuine claimants to get the help they need.

Around the same time, Redwood was making statements that underlined the view that some single parents should not be criticized:

[In Cardiff in July] I wanted to concentrate on the problems of teenage – particularly schoolgirl – pregnancies. It was others who decided to caricature my remarks as an implied attack on all single parents. I was very careful to distinguish between different types of single parenthood. I've always been sympathetic to those who are widowed, to mothers who are beaten up or abused, or to fathers and mothers who are on the wrong side of a losing relationship, often through no fault of their own. But I do believe that society has a role to play in encouraging young girls to knuckle down at school, to think about a stable relationship before having babies. (*The Guardian*, 13 November 1993)

A number of elisions occur in this statement. First, 'parent' becomes 'mother' in a substitution which is repeated throughout government discourse. This exemplifies the dynamic by which the mother is made a scapegoat: the entire institution of parenthood, all the practices and emotions that make up parenting, are condensed into the figure of the mother. Second, 'teenage' becomes 'schoolgirl', making pregnancy the sole responsibility of the young woman. Third, 'pregnancy' is carefully separated from 'parents', as Redwood begins to enumerate the types of single parent that are not to be criticized. In this, he effects a third elision: the pregnant schoolgirl remains as an implicit figure of contrast to the parents who become single 'often through no fault of their own'. It is the will to become pregnant as a single person that appals Redwood, or, worse, pregnancy as a casual event without planning and commitment. The most terrible single parent is thus the one who either chose single parenthood as a way of life or drifted into it thoughtlessly.[14] Lilley's

---

14. In similar vein, see the comments made by Dan Quayle, then Vice-President of the United States, in the 1992 election campaign: Quayle criticized a television programme, *Murphy Brown*, for showing a single woman's decision to continue her pregnancy while not wanting involvement with a man. Quayle said it was irresponsible to show this as 'just another lifestyle choice'. His comments attracted much criticism: see 'Quayle shoots from the lip as Bush flounders', *The Sunday Times*, 24 May 1992. Quayle later reversed his statement: single mothers were modern 'heroines'. Quayle's original statement, however, is discussed in *The Atlantic Monthly* as 'Dan Quayle was right. After decades of public dispute about so-called family diversity, the evidence from social science is coming in: the dissolution of two-parent families, though it may benefit the adults involved, is harmful to many children, and dramatically undermines our society.' See 'Dan Quayle was right', *The Atlantic Monthly*, April, 1993 p. 47.

conference speech emphasized the 'first duty' of parents: to their children, in a lifelong relationship of obligation. Marriage may no longer be for life, but parenthood is forever ('even when parents split up they remain responsible for supporting their children'). The duty owed to children is also the duty of obedience to a law. Those who choose single parenthood as a way of life, or who drift into it, have shirked their duty to the external law in preference to following an internal urge or impulse. This type of single parent therefore represents a breakdown in the translation of external law into the internal realm of the family. Since the mother has traditionally represented the route by which governmental officials entered the family sphere (Donzelot, 1979), 'parenthood' as a general institution must be translated into the body of the mother. Distinctions between *types* of single mother are therefore necessary in order to discover which women have attempted to obey the external law and which have disregarded it in favour of their own desires.

Distinctions between types of single parent can be found in other governmental statements. In Lilley's speech, quoted above, he mentions with approval 'widows, divorced and separated people' who 'struggle alone, but often successfully, to bring their children up well' and those who 'find themselves lone parents against their will'. The devices which feature in Redwood's comments – that lone parenthood should not be chosen and that parenthood is about committing oneself to the rearing of children – reappear as a preamble to an announcement about restricting the availability of welfare benefits to single parents (only 'genuine claimants' are to receive them). A report from the Royal Society of Arts (the *Start Right* Report), being considered by the government for its proposals to link child benefit to quality of parental care, argued that parents should make a contract to stay together, come what may, until the child is 3 years old. The author of the report, Sir Christopher Ball, is reported as saying that 'it has become a social norm not to honour that contract' (*The Guardian*, 5 March 1994). Here again is the distinction between the parent who puts the child first and the parent who acts selfishly (by separating or divorcing). It also appears in a statement made by Kenneth Clarke, the Chancellor of the Exchequer: 'I think the number of single parents is very sad – most of it a reflection of a personal tragedy in the light of a mother who has been abandoned' (*The Guardian*, 16 November 1993).

The slippage from 'parent' to 'mother' resurfaces, as does the dichotomy which filters out those who have suffered 'a personal tragedy' from those who have, by implication, chosen single parenthood. The statement concludes with a nostalgic reference to Victorian concerns with the 'abandonment' of women by men. Finally, and obviously, the entire debate around the workings of the Child Support Agency and the Child Support Act 1991 was structured upon a division between responsibility and choice: fathers may choose to leave one woman and child but the Act/Agency would not permit them to ignore their financial *responsibilities* to the child; women may choose to live as single parents but the Act/Agency would not permit them to withhold the name of the man who was their child's biological father.

The parent who puts the child first (by not divorcing) is deemed to put society, the future and the government first. In other words, subjection to the
child makes the mother a subject of society. Putting the child first is taken as
evidence that the mother chooses to belong to society; divorcing is taken to
represent a rejection of society. Hence, the selfish single parent can be made
a symbolic outlaw, outside society. The process of subjection is reduced to an
act of will; responsibility becomes a matter of calculation and choice. In turn,
the government demands accountability to society. The Child Support Act
makes that literal (by making parents pay for a child's maintenance, by making finance a manifestation of parental attachment) and metaphorical (by
enforcing the notion that parenthood is a matter of accountability to the law,
the child and the government).

Outside of government pronouncements, a manifest concern about single
parenthood took a similar form. A flurry of articles in all forms of media
appeared in late 1993 and early 1994. One wrote of the problem of children
sexualized, not so much by abuse, but by the 'casualization of their mother's
sex life', children who have a 'childhood without innocence' (*Observer*, 17
October 1993). The distinction between inadvertent single parents and those
seeking it as a lifestyle choice is also found:

> Most single parents are not young unmarrieds but divorced women. Most are
> decent, caring parents struggling against the odds to do the best for their children.
> But the young never-marrieds are the fastest growing group on welfare. The accel-
> erating trend is frightening a number of people who want to support and educate
> rather than punish.

The children from such relationships are described as 'having no stability in
their lives', 'indulged by their parents', 'neglected', 'roaming the streets', 'ter-
rorizing their parents'; their parents 'often little more than children
themselves' and in a cycle of 'neglect, self-loathing and despair'. Elsewhere,
other problematic dimensions of single parenthood are represented. In a feature on 'the family', *Cosmopolitan* magazine described how those women
who decide to have a child without a male partner can look forward only to
'emptiness':

> It is more than just maternal love [between single mother and child], that easy and
> unconditional affection which will let go as simply as it will take back. They are in
> love with their children; the child is what makes it all worthwhile, the child is what
> it is all for. There is no man there to cloud things, to spoil things and dilute them,
> to thump and shout around the place, selfishly demanding sympathy, sex and food.
> But children are born to leave. And the bitter kernel of such sweet fruit is this: your
> child will never love you as much as you love her. Love without hope. How will they
> let go? What emptiness awaits them? . . . It is a huge and passionate love, but one
> with no consummation. A man and a woman at least have some hope of growing
> together; a parent and child can only, in the natural order of things, grow apart.
> (Bywater, 1993: 30)

A single mother's love for her child is portrayed as unnatural: it is 'more
than just maternal love'; it is outwith the 'natural order of things' represented by the heterosexual couple. The single mother's love is represented here

in a manner reminiscent of the descriptions of Susan Venables' love for her son, Jon (see Chapter 5). Her love was also characterized as possessive, selfish and non-maternal. Here, the implication is that the single mother desires her child as a surrogate for heterosexual love. As a surrogate, the child is fated to fail her and to leave her with 'emptiness'. For the child, there will also be a price, as Robert Thompson and Jon Venables remind us: their act of murder was viewed as the culmination of a short history of delinquency and truancy inspired by the inadequacies of their solitary mothers.

Academic interest in single parents takes the form mainly of a curiosity as to how well their children 'perform': as school pupils, as future citizens and as family members. Olson and Haynes (1993) studied 'successful single parents' (by 'parent', they mean 'mother') and concluded that, with the right social and familial support networks, their children might well not suffer problems as they grew up.[15] These supposedly encouraging findings are embedded in a discussion of large-scale surveys on 'family disruption' and 'single motherhood' which indicate that 'children growing up in mother-only families are less likely to complete high school and more likely to be poor as adults than are children who are raised by two natural parents' (1993: 259). Olson and Haynes also emphasize the distinction between voluntary and involuntary single parenthood: 'the offspring of widowed mothers do better than do offspring of divorced or separated mothers in some surveys and on some indicators' (1993: 260). Divorce or separation can include the woman who left her partner, choosing single parenthood, whereas widowhood is redolent with inadvertent tragedy. The distinction is also found in Dennis and Erdos' virulent polemic against 'families without fatherhood': 'The widow was the victim of bereavement. No government policy or public stigma could control that phenomenon. But the unmarried mother was paying the price for her own pleasure and folly' (1993: 18). Etzioni, an academic sociologist, published a report on parenting for Demos, 'an independent think-tank'. He claims: 'Personally I do not know of a single instance in which the children were not harmed by divorce' (1993: 34). His recommendation is that *'divorce should not be banned or condemned, but that it should be discouraged. Easy divorces for parents are not in the interest of children, the community, or . . . the adults involved'* (1993: 38; emphasis in original). The community has a stake in children, argues Etzioni, since 'making a child is a moral act. It obligates the community to the parents. But it also obligates the parents to the community. For we all live with the consequences of children who are not brought up properly' (1993: 6).

A report which received media attention was produced by the Family Policy Studies Centre (Burghes, 1994). It appeared to be critical of government claims that children are worse off in one-parent families and to

---

15. Olson and Haynes agree with findings such as those of Atlas (1981), who claimed that out of 768 parents and 483 children that 75 per cent of parents were 'doing well' and their children 'well-adjusted'. Crucial to this were the continuing involvement of the non-custodial parent and the continuing employment of the custodial parent: see Atlas (1981: 260).

emphasize that no such child is inevitably destined to do less well than a child raised by two parents simultaneously. However, it transpires that the report is underwriting the distinction between voluntary and involuntary single parenthood, for it states that children of widowed lone parents tend to do 'almost' as well as those raised by two parents, implying that the nature of the 'disruption' is more important than the fact of disruption itself (thus recalling the type of argument put forward by criminologists like the McCords in 1959) . An academic study of 152 children in Exeter was also given press attention when its findings emphasized similar issues: children of parents whose relationship was in difficulties, but who were still together, fared far worse in the study than children whose parents had a good relationship, but better than children whose parents had separated or divorced. 'Better' was assessed in terms of school performance, health and social difficulties, varying from bed-wetting and nausea to low self-esteem (Cockett and Tripp, 1994).[16]

The notion of responsibility has been a key trope in current governmental policy on the family. So far in this chapter, I have addressed two issues: first, the meaning of responsibility within this discourse; and second, the ways in which that meaning is made to work. The figure of the mother is made a scapegoat, to be sacrificed in the interests of social government. She is a substitute for the parent, for the law, for society. She is sacrificed to the child through these substitutions, since in all of them she stands in for the figure of the child. In the process of substitution is located the moment of sacrifice, in which the mother becomes a scapegoat, simultaneously internal and external to the community. She is internal to it since she is the necessary term to fix the child in relation to the family, the society and the law. However, she is external to the community since she is always already prepared for sacrifice, the necessary cause of the child's failure to embody all that is desired of it. Hence, the responsibility of the mother in governmental discourse operates always through a law of the child, in which the mother is responsible for the child as the promise – with all its contractual overtones – of social order, of the future. The next section investigates the ways in which the two dominant types of single mothers in governmental discourse, identified above as the inadvertent single mother and the woman who chose single parenthood, are understood to reproduce children as criminals.

The single mother and the reproduction of crime

With the single mother firmly established in public discourse as a general social problem, the specificity of the link between single motherhood and a child's criminality was then elaborated. A spate of articles in the media asked such questions as 'are the children [of single mothers] likelier to go astray?' (*Independent on Sunday*, 14 November 1993). The findings of studies investigating this question are quoted: 'Professor Israel Kolvin of Newcastle

16. See also the study which claimed that children whose parents divorce are almost twice as likely to be bedwetters: Douglas (1973).

University showed that more than half the children rated as "severely deprived of parental care" had criminal records by the age of 33.' The article does not bother to explain what it means to be 'severely deprived of parental care', allowing the reader to connect this with any single mother and her child. In its conclusions, the article states that 'the case against the single mother as such must be judged "not proven". But, if poverty in childhood is indeed the root of later criminality, it must be conceded that lone parenthood is the quickest route to poverty.' The single mother is here acknowledged to be on trial and, at best, is awarded a verdict of 'not proven' (a verdict not available in English law and in Scotland always understood to mean 'she did it but the prosecution haven't done their job'). Recourse to wider social factors such as poverty only extenuates the process of blaming: a single mother's children may turn out to be criminals because of living in poverty as children, but if *she* chose to bring them up in poverty (by rejecting the possibility of bringing them up with two parents) then she can be blamed (for a child has no choice in its childhood) for their later criminality.

Kolvin's team of researchers had studied 264 men and women as a random sample of the babies born in Newcastle upon Tyne in May and June 1947 (aged 32 and 33, at the time of the research). Kolvin sought to investigate the links between the absence of fathers from the family backgrounds of these individuals and their later life experiences. He asked: were there 'deficiencies in wellbeing' associated with the absence of a father? His criteria included parental illness, marital instability, poor physical and emotional care of the child, debt, unemployment, overcrowding and 'general maternal incompetence' (Kolvin et al., 1990: 18). He did not examine families in which the father was absent through death. He concluded: 'In brief, the deprived groups were characterized by the . . . absence of fathers and, even when present, these tended to be inadequate providers who made little contribution to domestic activity and were seldom thought to be competent and caring' (1990: 41). By 1980, of the men in the study who had come from families labelled by Kolvin as multiply deprived, half had criminal records. Commenting on Kolvin's study, Dennis and Erdos write: 'it is pure obscurantism to deny that the *statistical chances* of children being physically smaller, stammering, being poor scorers in intelligence tests, or having a criminal record, depended greatly on their home background' (1993: 54; emphasis in original).

Single parenting was also linked to criminal children through the notion of learned dependency on the welfare state. An independent right-wing think-tank, the Adam Smith Institute (1994) proposed the dismantling of the welfare state on the grounds that this would 'save' the family. One of the authors of the proposal stated: '[The welfare state] is rapidly destroying the family – the main arena of genuine welfare in a free society – and thereby crippling children for life more reliably than "dark satanic mills" ever did. . . . It is turning estates and neighbourhoods right across Britain into factories of crime and arbitrary violence, fuelled by an increasing flow of drugs and alcohol' (quoted in *The Guardian*, 28 February 1994). The nostalgic fear of what social conditions may once have been flows through the language of this passage ('satanic mills', 'factories') and is used to compel the conclusion that single mothers' welfare dependency is a similar problem which must be combated. The Prime Minister, John Major, suggested that crime rates were not falling because parents, especially single parents, were not teaching their children the 'proper' values and lessons, particularly that 'if you do wrong you are likely to get caught, and when you are caught you will be punished' (quoted in *The Guardian*, 13 November 1993).[17] The single mother, identified as a possible breach in the line that links law to the child, is required to guarantee the continuity of the law's relation to the child.

This link was made explicit in an article commenting on a conference paper, presented at the American Association for the Advancement of Science Conference in San Francisco, which claimed that as much as 20 per cent of violent crime was committed by a small proportion of individuals who had suffered birth complications (such as breech birth or forceps delivery) and parental rejection in the first year of life. What is especially significant is that both of these factors were explicitly linked to single mothers; that is, it was claimed that the criminals of the future are the present children of single mothers who had birth complications and who rejected or neglected their children in the first year of life.[18] The article was accompanied by a photograph of a black man, in a car, wearing a hat and sunglasses and a handkerchief tied, bandit-style, over his face. The caption read: 'LA lawlessness. . . . The key may lie in birth complications combined with parental rejection.' The reader is invited to view the man in the photograph as an archetypal criminal whose criminality stems from having a lone mother rather than two parents.

Rejection of a child or neglect of a child are here blamed for the child's later activities as an adult. Rejection or neglect are represented as wilful acts by the mother which produce, many years later, a concomitant act of rejection or neglect by the child against society. The mother's wilful refusal of her responsibilities generates a surrogate refusal in the child. The mother therefore is constituted as the originary point in the breach between the delinquent and society or law. The breach originates with the mother; the community suffers the effect of it. Chapter 5 demonstrated how, in the context of the event of James Bulger's death, extremely punitive responses were advocated for two children who committed murder. The vilification of their parents – particularly their mothers – continued the process of punishment for the children's crime. The constitution of neglectful single mothers as the original cause of a child's later act of criminality demands a punitive response not only against the child but also – or perhaps even more so – against the mother who refused her duty as a mother. The next section elaborates the ways in which the

17. This was part of the Conservative government's 'Back to Basics' campaign which emphasized (Victorian) family values and which came unstuck in December 1993 and January 1994 when a number of Conservative Ministers and MPs were found to have fathered children who were now living with their mothers in single-parent families. For a feminist critique of this campaign and the government's attitude to single mothers, see Laws (1994).
18. Discussed in *The Guardian*, 24 February 1994.

government punished single mothers, as surrogates for the potential criminality of their children and as surrogates for the breach in the law represented by their existence as single mothers.

The single mother as criminal

A variety of punitive responses were utilized by the government. The Child Support Act is one of the most obvious. Another derived from the government's desire to create two-parent family units everywhere. As set out above, greatest opprobrium was reserved in government discourse for those who had become single mothers by choice and who were thus seen as denying their primary responsibility to bring up a child in a two-parent family. On 9 November 1993, a document headed 'Policy in confidence: lone parents' was leaked to a Labour MP, who passed it to *The Guardian* newspaper: the government was considering making the parents of single mothers financially liable for them (in place of giving them housing benefit) and making single mothers work. Responsibility is thus, in governmental terms, something which can be passed around until some family member is made to accede to it. Forcing a single mother's parents to pay her money in lieu of housing benefit rewrites the bonds of family and reduces the single mother to a sort of wayward child. The government's concern is to ensure that the bonds of responsibility within the family flow from parent to child. If the single mother rejects the governmental demand for her to obey her obligations to the law, then she will be infantilized and transformed into a child who requires parents. Generation, whether understood as the process of reproduction or as the divide between one age group and another within a family, is marked as a system of responsibility and duty.

Another governmental response related to the redefinition of priority access to local authority housing. Single parents would be entitled only to temporary, rather than permanent, housing. Local authorities would no longer be under a duty to house anyone made homeless by eviction from the family home (for example, by a violent husband) or by leaving a violent home with no alternative private accommodation available. The government claimed that this would produce a fairer system, with no groups getting special treatment. Criticisms of this abolition of 'homelessness' as a formal category and its predicted consequences, were numerous. Labour politicians criticized the changes as 'forcing irretrievably broken homes to stay together in acrimony' (*The Guardian*, 21 January 1994). As a rebuttal of the general perspective behind the proposals, this did not go very far, since the Conservative government had already stated its preference that parents should indeed stay together rather than divorce.

Occasionally, the opportunity arose for punishment to be meted out to individual single mothers, in a spate of cases involving what became known as 'home alone' children. The most famous single mother in these cases was Heidi Colwell, who received a sentence of six months' imprisonment after she was discovered to have been leaving her child alone at home while she went out to work. She could not afford to pay for child care, and had said that she felt it was better to have a job rather than be on state benefits. At her trial, the judge said: 'economics did not enter into her duty to her child. Leaving her alone for 8 hours a day amounted to psychological ill-treatment. Looking after a child must be an absolute priority. Leaving a child alone was a thing you would not even do to a dog.'[19] After her serving one month of the sentence, the Court of Appeal substituted that for the original sentence. A custodial sentence was still justified, said the Court, since 'a non-custodial sentence would have risked sending the wrong signals to parents tempted to leave very young children alone for long periods of time' (quoted in *The Guardian*, 20 August 1993). Around the same time, the press covered the case of two lesbian single parents who went on holiday, leaving their children in the care of three teenage baby-sitters. Whereas Colwell had been represented as 'misguided', mistaking exhortations to get a job for her primary responsibility, these two women were portrayed as hedonists indulging a whim at the expense of their children.[20]

Children were described as 'left alone' in a variety of circumstances, including a baby who starved to death alongside the body of its mother, a single parent who had fallen into a diabetic coma and died (*The Guardian*, 25 January 1994); and children who were alone at home when their mother was killed in a car crash. In the latter case, the headline read: 'Children found alone at home after mother dies in road crash' (*The Guardian*, 21 August 1993). The article described how the children were found locked in a bedroom after both parents had gone out. The children were taken into temporary care and later sent to live with their grandparents. Neighbours, invited to comment on the situation, said 'it was the first time the couple had left the girls alone' and 'described Mrs Carson as a good mother'. Here, the article manages to imply that the car crash is both a means by which the children have been left alone and simultaneously a punishment visited on the mother for leaving the children alone. Note that culpability is not attributed to the father (who suffered minor injuries in the crash): the neighbours' comment slips from 'the couple' to an evaluation of 'Mrs Carson' as a 'good parent'.

Another widely reported case concerned the child-minder who 'left five youngsters in the care of God' (*The Guardian*, 11 September 1993). This woman left the children alone for 40 minutes while she went to visit a sick friend. She was prosecuted for 'causing unnecessary suffering' on five counts and was sentenced to 100 hours of community service. The trial judge stated that her reason for leaving the children alone (to visit her friend) did not justify her actions and that the only reason that a custodial sentence had not been passed was to avoid causing the child-minder's own children any suffering. In this case, the child-minder was treated as a surrogate for all single

19. Reported and discussed in numerous papers, including *The Guardian*, 3, 6 and 20 August 1993. According to the RSPCA, leaving them alone is far from the worst thing British dog-owners frequently do to their pets.

20. See *The Guardian*, *Daily Mirror* and *Daily Mail*, all 26 August 1993; *Independent on Sunday*, 29 August 1993.

mothers or working mothers who employ child-minders. As a lone woman engaged in the practices of child care (and particularly so in that she earns a living in this way), she constituted a metaphor for all mothers, condensing and displacing cultural anxieties about the remuneration of domestic work, the regulation of maternal behaviour and the risks supposedly posed to children. However, of all the so-called 'home alone' cases reported in the latter half of 1993, the one which encapsulates many of the elements at work in the contemporary idealization of childhood (which is the inverse of the *realization* of motherhood) involved a group of children found alone at home at Christmas by a group of carol singers. For the carol singers and the press, the greatest trauma presented by the case lay in the fact that the children 'apparently did not know it was Christmas'.[21] In the bathetic sentimentality that surrounds contemporary celebrations of Christmas, the story provided a potent image: of children alone at home oblivious to the season which is believed to be truly enjoyed only by the young. Here the 'crime' of leaving children alone at home is subsumed by an apparently greater 'crime': denying a child the pleasures of Christmas.[22]

The carol singers' case led to accusations against the government that inadequate resources existed for dealing with the problem of 'home alone' children. It also permitted some articles to elaborate precisely the legal nature of this problem. In one, the National Society for Prevention of Cruelty to Children (NSPCC) were quoted: 'Legally there is nothing to stop a child being left on their own but if a child under 16 is left alone or in the care of someone under 16 and something happens to that child, then the parents or guardians are responsible' (*The Guardian*, 27 December 1993). However, in all the cases discussed above, prosecutions resulted and children were taken into care, despite the fact that no actual harm had resulted to the children. Whereas the NSPCC statement emphasizes risk – in that *if something happens to the child* then the parent is responsible – the practice of social services and criminal justice agencies has been rather different: it is as if the *creation* of risk is sufficient to merit a custodial or severe non-custodial sentence.[23] Law is usually represented as having to wait until something happens before it can intervene. In the juridical mode, law works by having certain images of what will happen if the law is broken. Law therefore conventionally waits until the rules are breached before the juridical mode is activated. The criminal justice system here, however, acts to supplement the juridical mode. It does not wait until a rule is broken, since, on the basis of actuarial or risk assessments, it can

21. See *The Guardian*, 27 December and 28 December 1993.

22. Ironically, the hugely successful *Home Alone* films, which feature Macaulay Culkin as an idealized version of a child (cute yet naughty, vulnerable yet resourceful), are set at Christmas and were released in Britain as 'Christmas films'. The films represent a child being left alone as an unfortunate mishap (although the mother is also portrayed as overcome with guilt once she realizes what she has done). Being left alone is not, however, the occasion for trauma, as the child both revels in his solitary enjoyment (of the family home in the first film and of New York City in the second) and repels the burglars who are the threat to his family's security.

23. On the insurantial technologies necessitated by such an approach, see Ewald (1991).

make a pre-emptive strike when a norm is deviated from (rather than when a rule is broken). In the United States, a car bumper sticker reads: 'The most dangerous place in America to live is in a mother's womb' (cited in Karpin, 1994: 10). These cases adopt a similar logic: the most dangerous place for a child is in its mother's care, if she is a working mother, or a lone mother, or a selfish mother. The notion of the child 'left alone' creates a gap in the supposed privacy of the home. It is through the lone child that the lone mother may be reached. Once reached, she can be criminalized and penalized, not for any specific maternal practices, good or bad, but simply for her existence. In her existence, she represents deviation from a norm (the two-parent family); in her deviation from the norm, the possibility of intervention is presupposed.

The singularity of the single mother

Such recent interventions betray the superficial nature of the closed space of the home. Privacy is, of course, a construct which has never existed in any pure form, but which is part of the familial mystique: the notion that lives can be conducted and relationships organized outside of any governmental interest is a fantasy which sustains the pleasures and terrors of family life. In Chapter 5, the event of James Bulger's death reveals to us the limits of representation, forcing a response to the unpresentable. Contrary to the rhetoric of the privacy of the familial environment, my aim here is to argue that the emotional space of the family is not beyond the limits of representation and intervention, but rather is the site of an invention of an image of responsibility. This is not simply to reiterate the old arguments around the public/private distinction. The very continuation of such terms – even as the dichotomous opposites of an untenable relation – permits the persistence of governmental incursions such as those described above. Indeed, the very *notion* of the private sphere is an effect of its government. In order to explain and elaborate this argument, I wish to return to West and the Cambridge surveys of juvenile delinquency.

West's teams of researchers were despatched to dozens of families with instructions as to what they were looking for (differences between the lives of delinquents and non-delinquents). The behaviours they discovered were to be recorded within predetermined categories (for example, mothers' attitudes were categorized, following McCord, as 'loving normal', 'loving anxious', 'overprotective' or 'cruel, passive and neglecting') (1982: 54). West comments:

> Although the definitions of these descriptive categories were made as full as possible, and were thought to be understood and consistently applied by the interviewers, these judgements did involve hypothetical distinctions between behaviour motivated by 'love' and similar behaviour differently motivated. It is arguable that such distinctions, however well made, are meaningless, since only actions count. However that may be, it would probably have been better to direct the interviewers' efforts to the recording of specific items from the parents' accounts of their actual behaviour . . . rather than to permit speculation as to parental feelings or try to force complex mixtures of behaviour into a limited number of pre-determined categories. Of course, it is easy to be wise after the event. (1982: 54)

In Chapter 3, I discussed the mapping of geographic space by realist criminology in the attempt to generate an emotional life of the city. In the fascination with the family lives of young offenders, of which West is exemplary, criminology confuses the family as emotional space with the family as physical space. That is, when West says 'only actions count', he is forced to acknowledge the limits of criminology's ability to understand the familial landscape. Such is the behaviourism of positivism. Behaviours are the observable phenomena that can be registered. Everything that is not observable does not count and thus does not exist. However, as West adds, wisdom arises 'after the event'; that is, behaviourism is supplemented by interpretivism. Both are concerned, though, with observable phenomena: a system of happenings which are created by the participants or by the retrospective descriptions of the criminologist. Wisdom arises out of the interaction of immediate observation and retrospective reinterpretation.

Whereas realist criminology will be surrounded by a mass of data relating to actions and reactions with regard to crime in the city, here West and Westian criminologists face the myriad of emotional connections and interconnections that constitute the familial – and which have puzzled psychoanalysis for decades. Realist criminology resorts to notions of civility and tolerance in its plea for the urban space to regain a lost emotional community. Westian criminology approached its own insurmountable problem by asking the interviewers to divorce action from motivation. That the researchers found this difficult is because such a project is based on a confusion between inside and outside, emotion and physicality. Here, this confusion is taken to reside in the body of the mother. The complexity of her emotional body is rewritten as domestic or social responsibility; that is, as duty and obedience to the law. She embodies responsibility, which originates as the secondary part of a couplet of action and reaction. 'Responsibility' derives from the Latin *respondere*, to promise in return, to answer. To 'respond' is to make a reply. 'Responsibility' is to be responsible, to answer an obligation, to be trustworthy, to take on a burden. Responsibility answers a call that has always already been made. The responsible mother is answering the community's question, 'will you?', with an unequivocal 'yes'. The mother of the delinquent child is deemed to have ignored the question, or to have answered 'no'. In the emotional body of the mother, criminological research is seeking a promise made in response to the community's call. In the search for that promise, 'only actions count'; only observable phenomena combined with the researcher's later interpretation might reveal the mother's response. To that extent, West is concerned with the *appearance* of emotion, rather than emotion itself.

In seeking to efface the difference between 'behaviour motivated by "love" and similar behaviour differently motivated', West claims that the distinctions between motivations is meaningless because motivations do not count. Only actions count; only observable phenomena are to be included. Emotions, or 'motivations', are invisible and, although they might inform actions, are not to be included. What is visible (action) is not to be systematized by reference to what is invisible (emotion). Thus, the outside cannot be categorized and typified by reference to the inside. That such a project is impossible can be understood as follows: if the inside is abolished, then the outside no longer exists. If emotion is banished, behaviour no longer exists. If you drive out (expel, banish, *outlaw*) that which is inside, then it will no longer exist. If the invisible is made an outlaw, the visible disappears. These are the inevitable consequences of West's project which has reduced the emotional space of the family to an area of physical relations between family members that can be mapped by researchers. Here, criminology, like law, shows itself to be unable to imagine the emotional body of the family. In striving to imagine it, criminology is limited to a reading taken from the outside (physical behaviour) as a map of the inside (emotion, motivation). Here I am not advocating a rigid separation between thought and action, behaviour and motive. On the contrary, it is my contention that sustaining such a separation will forever limit criminological – or legal, or social – thought to an impoverished schema of predetermined categories, forever causing anxiety to those researchers who seek to describe the fuzziness of emotional relations within its narrow parameters.

In making the assertion that 'only actions count', West is doing more than simply effacing the distinction between action and motivation. With this assertion, a gendered asymmetry is introduced. 'Action' is culturally aligned with masculinity. Their relationship can be seen through a comparison with the tactics of criminal law. Its very structure is concerned with action; hence its preoccupation with the distinctions between acts and omissions, with *mens rea* as agency and activity. The man of law is a man of action. The woman of law, on the contrary, is beyond action, restricted to the sphere of mental (in)stability.[24] To shore up the distinction between active men and emotional women, criminal law engages in an uneasy relationship with psychiatry. In Westian criminology, it is no accident that familial bonds have been interpreted through the prism of psychological theories of deprivation.

In the sexual contract that underlies the marital couple, action is associated with masculine sexuality, in which the sexual drive is represented not as an emotion but as a cause-and-effect process. The sexual drive produces erection which demands sexual action. In contrast, the sexual contract constructs feminine sexuality as endlessly causal, with no effects, no beginnings or ends, requiring a masculine drive to action. Much of the contract that is the inheritance of the legal subject – and indeed much of the social contract itself – reproduces this sexual asymmetry.[25] The enduring appeal of this asymmetric

24. On Woman in various aspects of criminal law, see Young (1993b) on ordinary femininity in a case of shoplifting; Young (forthcoming) on trial by femininity in a case of conjugal homicide. Allen (1987) has analysed the practices of criminal law with regard to defences; the association of man with action makes it more common for a male defendant to succeed in a plea of provocation. Female defendants are more likely to succeed with diminished responsibility pleas.

25. On the sexual asymmetry of contract law, see Pateman (1988); for a parallel argument about rape law, see Naffine (1994).

contract lies in its claim to unify the opposites of masculine and feminine. Just as the polar terms of a binary opposition pretend that each can only be understood through the other, so the sexual contract claims that harmony (whether social, marital or legal) can be achieved through its apparent asymmetry. Its story claims that the 'fit' between the two justifies the strangeness of each when examined in isolation.

Marital discord, then, produces great cultural anxiety. Marital discord literalizes the impossibility of the marriage contract, and, hence, the legal and social contract. In a case where a wife killed her husband in the course of a lengthy 'altercation' (in which, at one point the husband attempted to strangle his wife), the Court of Appeal commented: 'The case arises out of matrimonial discord. . . . Matrimonial disharmony does not in itself and cannot entirely excuse, let alone justify, extreme violence.'[26] Westian criminology responded to concerns about the break-up of families as a result of discord. Recent governmental policy represents an attempt to slow the rate of divorce and to reassert the primacy of the marital contract as the founding model of social relations. Concern about juvenile delinquents being produced and reproduced in discordant households makes a scapegoat of the child and a criminal of the mother. The centrality of the mother as parent can be explained here. Marital discord leads to so-called broken homes. Discord is thus being opposed to concord, or harmony. Concord is also associated with treaties, conventions and agreements. To this extent, it encapsulates the marriage as union or treaty between the two individuals. 'Responsibility', that which obliges the mother, shares the same root as 'spouse', that which compels obligation to the husband (see Chapter 3). Concord, however, derives from *coeur*, the heart, the central emotional space of culture and the one associated with femininity (and perhaps the space of ethics, where justice, and not simply the appearance of justice, is found). Apotheotic representations of Woman,[27] favour images of Woman as harmony, union, concordance. When the marital union breaks down, a degree of blame is always already laid at the feet of Woman. When a marriage breaks down or ends, not from the husband's death or abandonment of the woman, but from her (or her partner's mutual) desire to separate, then her antagonism towards the required feminine role is made plain. With that renegade desire, she can be blamed for raising criminals rather than citizens and penalized accordingly, through reduced access to housing, employment, state benefits.

In the government's draconian policy proposals and interventions, we can see the same elision between action and motivation that animates Westian criminology. For the court, and for the press, it ultimately made no difference whether Heidi Colwell left her child alone all day because she wished to work for her living rather than receive state benefits, or whether she was, as in another 'home alone' case, taking drugs. In the latter situation, three children were found alone at home, again at Christmas, with dirty nappies, soiled

26. The case is *R* v. *Rossiter* [1994] 2 All England Reports. 752 at pp. 752, 753.
27. For example, see Warner's (1985) study of 'monuments and maidens'.

bedding and no food (*The Guardian*, 28 December 1993). While differences in sentencing might result, there is no difference as far as governmental agencies are concerned: the act of leaving a child alone is always to be construed as criminal. Motivations, whether loving or cruel, are irrelevant. Similarly, the gendered association of men with actions and women with emotions enables governmental policy to effect the distinction, pointed out above, between those women who are single parents through choice – whether, for example, through lesbianism or through a desire to live alone – and those who are widowed or who are divorced against their will. The latter group are perceived as reactive, rather than active. Their situation has been forced on them, their emotional state still conforms to the desire for concord and union that is part of femininity. They are single mothers only inadvertently. The former group, on the other hand, are active, they are represented as having chosen their situation and as such as having rejected femininity in favour of a masculine set of values.

In this chapter, my aim has been to criticize the governmental interest in single motherhood as a site for repressive intervention, and to show how that interest shares its discursive authority with the criminological literature on the familial backgrounds of young offenders. Denunciation, however, has not been my sole aim. Underlying the denunciation of government policy and Westian criminological theory has been a desire to restore for consideration the *singularity* of the single mother. Restoration of the mother–child relation does not depend on the appearance or disappearance of the heterosexual couple, upon its presence or absence. Rather, it is to be restored *in itself*, independent of the heterosexual couple (Irigaray, 1981). In the marital couple, the mother–child relation is always subordinated to the relation between the man and woman as parents and as heterosexual intimates. The singular relation between man and woman is given precedence over any relation between parent and child. The identity of the single mother asserts that the mother–child relation is a singular relation that can be lived as such, rather than as a relation secondary to that which structures the heterosexual couple. This is not to say that the single mother effects a denial of the couple, as such – for the mother–child relation is a couplet in itself – but rather a proclamation of a refusal to live that relationship secondarily, in subordination. In the phrase 'single mother', 'single' connotes her deviation from the matrimonial couple and thus embeds secondariness in the mother–child relation. The singularity which must be restored lies in the emotional bond of mother-and-child. It is this emotional relation which has been the object of governmental regulation.

Hence, the single mother lives as a symbolic reminder of difference, of deviation from the marital couplet, as an event which shows the play and possibilities of difference. The mother–child relation is no longer secondary to the marital relation, because she responds to the child as child, rather than as surrogate for the husband, or the law, or the community. This is the key to the single mother's assertion of difference and also to the way in which she has been condemned. The reinstitution of the mother–child relation as primary is viewed as a rejection of the marital; hence, the single mother is represented as unfaithful to the idea of marital love. The inadvertent single mother – who may experience guilt anyway when the generic term 'single mother' is used by the media or the government – is not singled out for criticism and condemnation because she can still be represented as adhering to the notion of marriage, as still in love with the image of marital love. To that extent, the woman who is a single mother through choice and desire embodies a strategy of resistance. The style of life that she embraces is constructed by the governmental culture as transgressive, and thus to be condemned. While acknowledging the transgression present in the single mother, it should be noted that her life is not totally captured by transgression: some part always *exceeds*. That is, it is the government which projects an image of the single mother as someone thoroughly defined by transgression. The *telos* of the single mother's art of life, however, goes beyond that to which it is opposed and thus must be more than merely oppositional. For example, lesbian single mothers are not lesbian single mothers merely because they hate heterosexual marriage and parenthood. Lesbian desire exists in itself and for itself, outside and independent of any relation to heterosexuality. While the lesbian art of life might entail an anti-heterosexual perspective, it is not required by, limited to or defined by such a perspective. The government's construction of the mother who is single by choice as merely anti-marriage denies her desires and emotions, by projecting them as negative, as an inversion of and deviation from dominant norms.

Conclusions

The legislation of marital discord lies at the heart both of criminological theories of the familial production of delinquency and of governmental policies relating to single mothers. Marital discord is one of the preconditions for divorce ('irretrievable breakdown' can be evidenced by 'behaviour such that neither party can reasonably be expected to live with the other') and one of the alleged preconditions for the generation of delinquents in the home. Divorce is itself, of course, regarded as one of the predisposing factors in the production of the delinquent child. Marital discord is thus an originating condition for a downward spiral with moral, fiscal and social consequences: damage done to the status of marriage in society, damage to the psyche of the child resulting in anti-social behaviour, damage to the community through the perpetration of offences, damage to the nation through the cost of responding to delinquent children. The fabled 'broken home' of early criminological theorizing need not actually involve a divorce; discord itself is sufficient to cause harm. The break, or rupture, exists as much at the level of the symbolic, rending the veil of matrimony. Without the veil, goes the logic, the child will grow up *anti*-social, *anti*-marriage.

Just as the dreaded results of marital discord are posed as negatives (*anti*-social), so 'discord' itself is structured in opposition to an idealized state. 'Discord' is a *lack* of agreement or harmony, it is dissonance rather than consonance. It is opposed to 'concord'. 'Concord' refers to a state of agreement, or harmony. In musical terms, it is a harmonious combination of simultaneously heard notes. In more legal terminology, it is a treaty, or covenant. Its origins are in the Old French, *concorde*, and the Latin *concordia*. At its root is the Old French, *cor*, meaning 'heart'. From the Latin, *concordare* (to agree), we derive the concordat, a compact or covenant (often specifically used to denote an agreement with a pope, government or sovereign). Within the concordat is embedded the notion of the *chord*, in its many and various senses. First, there is the musical chord, a combination of notes struck together, from the Middle English *cord*, short for *accord*, which also gives us 'assent', or 'consent', linked to the Old French *acorder*. Further, 'chord' appears in mathematical terms as a line which joins two points on a circle without passing through the circle's centre. 'Cord', of course, also connotes long strands of material twisted together to form a rope or thread, and appears in metaphorical form as a moral, spiritual or emotional bond. Finally, 'cord' is an anatomical structure resembling a rope, most often associated with the umbilical cord that joins mother and foetus.

Each of these derivations is based upon a relationship, whether that be between musical notes, between strands of material, between points on a circle, or between mother and foetus. And each of these relationships is configured so that one element cannot signify without the other. The 'concord' in each relation is precisely the relationship; thus, as a desired state, it cannot exist on its own, but requires co-operation and collaboration. 'Discord' is also a relational phenomenon. Musical discord refers to the sound when notes do not combine well; when a line does not meet both points on a circle's circumference, they remain atomized, separate points. When an emotional or ethical bond is replaced by its lack, or opposite, the result is anomie or alienation. And if no cord links mother and foetus, or mother and child, the maternal relation is thwarted. The notion of discord represents that which is currently feared: anomic, sociopathic rootlessness and disrespectful, selfish hedonism. This fear has been located within the boundaries of the family, as the paradigmatic site of relationality where every member is caught in a network of relationships. And, since the family is, as Foucault and Donzelot have pointed out, the instrument through which the general population can be governed, it represents both the possibility of germinating either a dreaded reality or a desired one. Governmental intervention thus emphasizes the emotional relationships of the family, in an effort to legislate against discord and produce instead eternal concord. Its recent social and criminal justice policies, then, along with the Westian criminology since the post-war period and after, aim to create a monologic, monolithic family form. The difficult languages and infinitely varied practices of the emotions – love, anger, hate, disappointment, fear, hope – are replaced by the simplistic pedagogies and homogeneity of the tutelary family. To that end, government policy and criminological theory together have issued a grim concordat, and await the population's signature.

7

Fatal Frames: HIV/AIDS as Spectacle in Criminal Justice

Another scene

A young man is lying on a bed. His gaze is unfocused, his face sunken and wasted, his arm, which is outside the bedclothes covering him, is thin. He is bearded and has dark hair. His head is cradled in the arm of an older man, who is crying, leaning over the recumbent figure. One hand is held by a person in black. To the left of the weeping man sit a woman and girl, embracing each other. The scene is steeped in intense emotion. The grief felt by those who sit around the bedside is palpable. The weakness and illness of the young man is plain. The arms and hands of the individuals criss-cross and intersect; the effect is to show a strength of bonding and a shared emotion. That emotion, however, is unequivocally anguish. The scene is contained within a photograph, which tells of death, of agony. The grouping of the figures is reminiscent of a *Pietà*; however, a small printed phrase, 'UNITED COLOURS OF BENETTON', in the bottom right-hand corner of the scene informs that it is choreographed by an Italian company which manufactures clothes. It is an advertisement (see Figure 7.1).[1]

This photograph of a man who appears to be dying, surrounded by his grieving family, attracted a great deal of media attention and criticism.[2] It was taken as representing a moment of *extremis*. The emotions manifested by the

1. This is not the only advertisement used by Benetton that depicts HIV or AIDS. One shows a muscled bicep flexed in close-up next to a bare (masculine) torso. The bicep is tattooed 'HIV positive'. Amongst a group of students shown this image, responses included comments on the 'healthiness' of the muscled arm, on the link to Nazism or anti-Semitism in tattooing the arm, on how the shadowy nipple in the foreground looked also like a Kaposi's sarcoma lesion. Another Benetton photograph resembles a mosaic made of dozens of head-and-shoulders shots of people of varying colours, genders and so on. The tiny pictures combine to spell out 'AIDS' in giant capitals. The students commented that it promoted anonymity as a positive value, that it showed predominantly young people, that everyone looked like fashion models, that it showed AIDS as a monolithic problem which overwhelmed the individuality of the people in the pictures.

2. For example, see *The Sunday Times*, 4 December 1994, which describes the dying man as 'Christlike'. The image is one of a series used by Benetton in its advertising campaigns. Others have included a newborn baby, the bloodstained jacket of a dead Croatian soldier, a ship filled with refugees. The image of the dying man was parodied in ACT UP's poster response, which matched the photograph with that of a condom, and a caption stating: 'There's only one pullover this photograph should be used to sell.' The Benetton photograph was used as an index of (post)modern changes in advertising strategies: for example, it was reproduced to advertise a conference on 'Changes in Advertising and Consumption since the 1950s' in London in 1994.

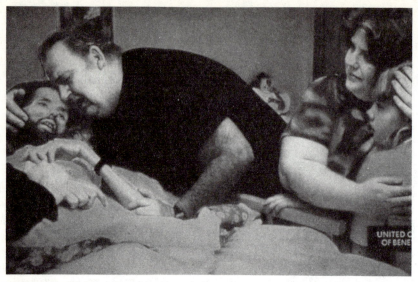

Figure 7.1   *The Benetton advertisement 'David Kirby dying of AIDS'*

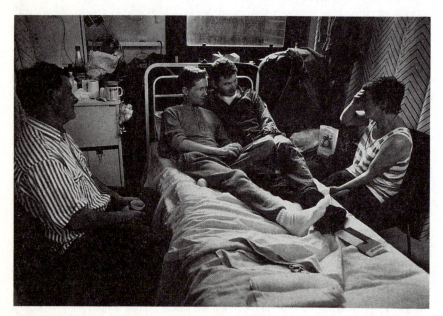

Figure 7.2   *'John', photographed by Gideon Mendel for the Positive Lives · photodocumentary project*

individuals sitting around the bed, the unfocused gaze of the young man: all speak of imminent death. Death has not yet occurred. Although the photograph constitutes a kind of counter-memory (death-defying, the scene of another death), the intensity of the moment implies that no resolution other than death can occur. Death, indeed, is already present in the image. Nothing in the image tells us precisely what the man is dying *of*. More than this, there is nothing in the photograph which says that the man is dying as a result of AIDS.[3] And yet, that is how it has been received. Benetton released this advertisement with the title 'David Kirby dying of AIDS'. Photographing a disease is a difficult task, and one that bears a heavy responsibility, since the photograph will tend to make real its image, saying 'this is how it is' to its audience. The image is the appearance of death (not death itself); the risk is that appearance becomes the total sum of the image. The Benetton image conveys a powerful impression of unmitigated anguish, awful pain and certain death. Its pessimism is unrelenting. While the bedside tableau could have represented the scene as any individual lying in the last moments of any terminal disease, to name the image as representing a man 'dying of AIDS' fixes certain associations with regard to AIDS and the sufferer.

Photographs (light-writing) promise enlightenment (the appearance of light and the disappearance of the dark). The Benetton image makes an aesthetic of the suffering body and says 'this is how it is'. Its story of AIDS is one in which the sufferer dies with eyes unfocused on his family or surroundings, in which the relatives of the person with AIDS experience only pain and tears. Mayes comments: 'It is difficult to photograph illness in any meaningful way: pictures of people who are ill reveal very little beyond the physical symptoms of an invisible microbe's presence. But photography is extremely good at recording social conditions and offering interpretations of human experience' (1993: 14). Invisibility cannot be made visible; instead, the symptoms (gaunt face, unfocused eyes, slack mouth) stand in for the cause (a virus, a collection of illnesses that might together form a syndrome). The visible is reduced to an effect of the invisible. The problem is thus one of the appearance and disappearance of death, of others.

This chapter provides a reading of two domains in which HIV/AIDS appears and aims to think through the appearance of HIV/AIDS in these domains. The domains – or fields of action – under examination are taken, first, from photography and, second, from the discourse of the crimino-legal complex. The former includes two photographs: one, as described above, produced and circulated by Benetton; the other included as part of a photo-documentary project – *Positive Lives* – on HIV/AIDS. The latter ranges from the police, prison, government policy and criminal legal doctrine to their reiteration in the academic and media texts. The first strategy of the chapter is a *juxtaposition* of two domains conventionally treated as very distinct fields. Against the traditional assumption of their separability, my aim is to reveal the *continuity* between the two. This continuity is not simply, or not even, that

3. 'AIDS' and 'HIV' are terms that are often, erroneously, used interchangeably. AIDS is often represented, especially, in the press, as if it were a single disease, rather than a syndrome comprising a large number of distinct diseases, cancers, conditions, and so on, which may arise as a result of the damage done by HIV to the body's immune system. To that extent, no-one dies 'of AIDS', but rather of any of a wide range of consequences of HIV, which can be included in the syndrome AIDS. See, for a more detailed discussion of this, Watney (1989d: 14–7).

both respond to the culture of HIV/AIDS. Rather, in both domains – photographs and criminal justice discourse alike – HIV/AIDS is produced and reproduced as an event, scene or spectacle.[4] In other words, the spectacle of HIV/AIDS exists precisely as a spectacle.

My aim, then, is to read the spectacle of HIV/AIDS *as spectacle* in the photographic projects of activism and advertising, and in the discursive practices of criminal justice. The chapter will also retell the story of the appearance of HIV/AIDS as a problem of and for criminal justice in the arenas of imprisonment, policing and criminal law. In retelling the problematization of HIV/AIDS, the fears, anxieties and desires of criminal justice as it responds to HIV/AIDS are put on display. To that extent, in the narrative of HIV, the end-point or resolution of the narrative is always figured as AIDS, or death. AIDS has become conceptualized as the *telos* of HIV infection, posing death as the certain outcome to the advent of HIV infection. All the earlier stages of HIV infection, or indeed of the risk of HIV infection, are defined by reference to the end-point of AIDS. The Benetton photograph shows the end-point as it occurs, and thus refigures whatever has gone before in this man's life as a series of moments leading up to this death. Criminal justice policy, as I will show, is deployed solely as a response to the predicated certainty of AIDS as the resolution of narratives of HIV. All distinctions between AIDS and HIV infection are effaced. The HIV positive individual is dealt with *as if* she has AIDS, or is about to develop AIDS. The person deemed to be at risk of HIV infection or transmission is dealt with *as if* she has AIDS. As Foucault writes, this 'project[s] upon the living body a whole network of anatomo-pathological markings: to draw the line of the future autopsy' (1973: 162). Such a fearful certainty of approach issues in a strategy of *quarantine*. This strategy necessarily fails; however, the production of HIV/AIDS as a spectacle is a response to the strategy's failure. In short, then, the condition of HIV/AIDS as spectacle is the failure of a (literal and symbolic) quarantine. It is within the space of this failure, this ruin, that the activist project *Positive Lives* effects a restoration, through 'living with HIV' (as opposed to 'dying of AIDS'), of the emotional body of the suffering Other.

Fatal justice: HIV/AIDS and the criminal justice system

HIV/AIDS has always been constituted as a problem to be solved. This was so for scientific research, for medical technology, for governments attempting to draft public health information.[5] It has also been the dominant paradigm

4. For an account of the construction of homosexuality as a spectacle of AIDS, see Watney, who attributes the spectacular linking of AIDS and homosexuality to a desire to see all gay men die: 'an indifference that casually dehumanizes whole categories of persons' (1989a: 85–6). Bersani (1989) also argues that the blaming for AIDS of those most at risk from AIDS is inspired by a homicidal loathing of homosexuality.

5. Garfield (1994) recounts the bafflement of doctors when confronting the first cognizable 'cases' of AIDS. He also describes Conservative government ministers bracing themselves to say 'condom' on television.

for criminal justice. In Britain the Home Office has approached the question of the incarceration of HIV positive prisoners as one of management and accommodation (literally, in the sense of whether a seropositive prisoner should share accommodation with a seronegative one). The police have confronted HIV/AIDS as one more threat to be dealt with, necessitating a defensive and aggressive stance. Health care workers have been viewed as at risk and as a source of risk. Legislation has been extended; new criminal offences have been suggested. Academic commentary and media discourse together reiterate these concerns. In short, HIV/AIDS appears and reappears throughout the crimino-legal complex. The next section of this chapter will elaborate the responses made by three particular spheres of criminal justice discourse to HIV/AIDS. In the final section of the chapter, I will demonstrate how these responses perpetuate HIV/AIDS as spectacle through the strategy of symbolic and literal forms of quarantine.

HIV infection is still often portrayed as if it were a *direct* result of being gay, black, poor or an injecting drug user. Many still fail to distinguish between 'high-risk activities' (such as unprotected anal or vaginal intercourse or the sharing of unsterilized needles) and 'high-risk groups' (the inaccurate and unwarranted label applied to groups who currently appear to show a high incidence of HIV infection).[6] I have argued this elsewhere (McHale and Young, 1992a: 90). During the writing of that article, a friend disputed this criticism, claiming that the distinction had a purchase on reality. His argument was that I stood far greater chance of dying in a car crash or from heart disease than from HIV infection, whereas a gay, black intravenous drug user in New York stood a very good chance of dying from AIDS. My point, however, relates to the conflation of practices and identities: if I began using drugs intravenously while sharing them with others, my risk of being HIV positive increases, despite all the *appearances* of my identity (female, white, middle-class, heterosexual and so on) currently associated as low risk in relation to HIV.[7] Similarly, the gay, black drug user in New York is able to decrease his risks of infection if he practises safe sex and sterilizes his needles.

6. Articles about Roy Cornes, a haemophiliac who was said to have infected four women through heterosexual intercourse, could have been used to emphasize heterosexual risk (see *The Sun*, 24 June 1992: 'AIDS maniac on killer sex spree'; *Daily Mirror*, 24 June 1992: 'Sex bomb: Aids man infects four women in revenge rampage'). Instead, press articles made much of his 'confessed' liking for anal sex. According to a doctor quoted in the *Daily Express*: 'Generally a man who wants anal sex will be bisexual' (2 July 1992). On heterosexual risk in general, see 'AIDS: from them to us' (*Independent on Sunday*, 28 June 1992) (in which 'them' signifies 'homosexuals'); and 'When a man loves a woman, does he always use a condom?' (*The Guardian*, 17 October 1994), in which women are quoted as claiming that condoms are necessary only for a few weeks.

7. A 1994 survey carried out for Durex on 12,603 people between the ages of 16 and 55 reported that 34 per cent felt 'confident' that, as heterosexuals, they would not 'catch' HIV, compared to 15 per cent in 1991. Twenty-two per cent thought that homosexuals and drug addicts are the groups at risk of 'catching' HIV, compared to 7 per cent in 1991. This contrasts with government figures showing that 30 per cent of AIDS cases and 38 per cent of cases of HIV infection reported in 1993 involved men and women who became infected through heterosexual activity rather than through other activities such as intravenous drug use.

In my friend's view, I represented a (low risk) 'type', while the gay, black drug-user represents another 'type'. Typification is the dominant logic of law, with its legislation of activities into identities. My counter-argument was to propose risk as an attribute of activities, not of identities.

The inability to distinguish between high-risk activities and high-risk groups is deeply entrenched within the criminal justice system and produces discriminatory and oppressive policies. A corpus of material has developed which is dedicated to criticizing this perspective and advocating different ways of responding to HIV infection.[8] These tend to follow on from critiques of responses to HIV within the general social sphere.[9] However, the imperative to follow this critical lead is even greater when considering the situation of the HIV positive individual who enters the criminal justice system. The marginal and disadvantaged of society tend to accumulate within the criminal justice system and here HIV is not just 'another problem'. Of all the life-threatening medical conditions which exist today, HIV infection whispers most chillingly of our mor(t)ality, our fragile categories of sexuality, our class-oriented social structures. Nelkin and Gilman write:

> We still use disease to protect our social boundaries or to maintain our political ideals. And, at a time when control over disease is limited, we still blame others as a way to protect ourselves. By drawing firm boundaries – that is, by placing blame on 'other groups' or on 'deviant behavior' – we try to avoid the randomness of disease and dying, to escape from our inherent sense of vulnerability, to exorcize the mortality inherent in the human condition. (1988: 378)

Within the criminal justice system, HIV infection makes visible and explicit the hidden and implicit links between conceptions of criminality and fears of disease. Both are seen as (symbolically or literally) life-threatening. The HIV positive individual is a deadly icon of a psycho-social malaise, a surrogate for the desire to sacrifice the criminal and expel her from the community. Such an ideological agenda, inflected with homophobia, racism, censures based on gender and class, produces a criminal justice policy deriving from the desire to exclude, to outlaw. Offenders are made to represent, and are sometimes called, the 'undeserving' of society (Conrad, 1982). Attempts to produce guidelines for standards of care in prisons or to safeguard the rights of those arrested or awaiting trial are often met with howls of outrage from the penologically repressive, who confuse sending an individual to prison as punishment with sending an individual to prison for further punishment once inside, who confuse arrest with guilt or bail with a 'soft option'. HIV positive individuals therefore constitute a specific outlaw group within the general outlaw class of (suspected) offenders. The following subsections show how typical responses to HIV infection manifest a desire to exclude, to expel and to outlaw: within the prison system, by the police and as a crime in itself.

8. See, among others, Brandt (1987); Dalton and Burris (1987); Dalton, Burris and the Yale AIDS project (1993); Dolgin (1985–6); Fee and Fox (1992); Montgomery (1990); Moran (1988, 1990); Nelkin et al. (1991).

9. For example: Carter and Watney (1989); Patton (1985, 1990b); Shilts (1987); Watney (1989c).

The imprisonment of AIDS

Many of the responses to HIV infection from prison authorities are the product of the widespread image of the HIV positive prisoner as the least worthwhile of the undeserving. In England and Wales, HIV positive prisoners have been segregated in solitary confinement with denial of exercise and work.[10] In the state of New Jersey, in the United States, prisoners with AIDS were shackled to their beds for six months and denied visits from their families. In Texas, four prisoners with AIDS were hospitalized with prisoners who had infectious diseases; this could kill a person with AIDS, whose immune system can easily succumb to opportunistic infections (Vaid, 1987). The existence of such brutal regimes should be understood and condemned as part of an ideological nexus which conjoins a fear of fatal disease, a widespread homophobia, a horror of drug users and their supposed lack of control, and a disdain for the lived experiences and wishes of prisoners.

Several issues are particularly significant with regard to the position of the HIV positive prisoner. These include HIV testing in prisons and the types of prison regime which are deemed appropriate to the situation of the HIV positive prisoner. These issues are clearly linked and will vary according to the institutional ideology which supports them. With regard to testing, given that the standard medical procedure is for testing to be carried out only after counselling, with the specific consent of the patient and on clinical grounds only,[11] there would seem to be no reason why the same standard should not be relevant to prisoners considering taking the test. (Note that mass anonymous screening has been instituted for pregnant women; a positive result obtained this way does not lead to loaded insurance premiums and so on.)[12] However, prison authorities do not always live up to this expectation. Prison officials have expressed enthusiasm for compulsory testing in terms of the improved management decisions that might result.[13] In April 1993, the

10. As described in the Advisory Council on the Misuse of Drugs (1989).

11. This follows the resolution of the British Medical Association, made at its 1989 conference: 'HIV testing should be performed only on clinical grounds and with the specific consent of the patient. . . . As a positive HIV test has serious implications, counselling of patients prior to carrying out the test is essential and further counselling must be offered if the test proves positive' (quoted in d'Eca, 1987: 9).

12. Many doctors have argued for HIV testing (non-anonymous) to be a routine aspect of antenatal care. A study by the Institute of Child Health in London found that less than 20 per cent of HIV positive women were successfully identified before delivery. It is argued that administration of AZT would reduce transmission rates from woman to foetus by up to 66 per cent (see reports in the *Independent on Sunday*, 16 October 1994). There is no doubt expressed as to the wisdom of this ('without question it would improve the quality of their lives'), despite the recent poor showings of AZT in the massive Anglo-French Concorde trial (AZT is now thought to carry considerable risks of toxicity).

13. See, for example, the comments of the then head of the Prison Medical Service, Dr Kilgour, in *Prison Service News*, February 1989: 'we shall have for the first time a solid indication of how many HIV antibody positives there really are, as opposed to those that are reported to me. . . . I look forward to having better information on which to base management decisions.' Dr Kilgour translates 'HIV positive prisoners' into 'HIV antibody positives', allowing the disease to stand in for the individual.

Department of Health announced that inmates in three London prisons would be anonymously tested, by means of blood or saliva, for HIV antibodies (*The Independent*, 31 April 1993). And in January 1995, the Prison Service announced plans to test all prisoners in England and Wales to 'discover the true prevalence of HIV' (reported in the *Independent on Sunday*, 29 January 1995). Their emphasis on 'management' derived from an apparent lack of interest in tackling the health care issues relating to seropositive individuals. The majority of British prisons have approached the 'management' of HIV/AIDS by means of the segregation of HIV positive prisoners and prisoners with AIDS, believing that their isolation would prevent the transmission of the virus within prison. As such, HIV positive prisoners are literally made outlaws.

If segregation for these individuals is the only outcome of testing or declaring antibody status – as opposed to counselling, support or medical advice on treatment, stress management and diet – then no effort is being made to respond to the question of the emotional and physical well-being of the HIV positive individual (and hence their prognosis, since isolation may well increase the likelihood of illness due to the stress and depression it can engender). Casual contact does not spread infection; indeed there are few day-to-day situations that could constitute a health risk for prison officers and for other prisoners.[14] Arguments that screening followed by segregation would halt transmission are also unfounded, given that individuals do not produce antibodies immediately after infection and screening would need to be repeated continuously on all those who test negative. Those who propose segregation would also need to justify the isolation of individuals who falsely test positive (it is recommended by the medical profession that follow-up tests be done on all initial positive results and even then there still exists the statistical risk of a false positive). Many other jurisdictions do not favour compulsory testing. The United States National Institute of Justice (NIJ) sees mass testing no longer as a tool in the control of infection but rather as a means of enabling earlier treatment. Many correctional facilities also offer voluntary or on-request testing.[15] Only two state penitentiary systems currently segregate HIV positive inmates.[16] In the Netherlands, mass testing is considered of little worth. One Dutch governor stated: 'Not knowing and not wanting to know which inmates are seropositive is one of the cornerstones of Dutch policy. Our preventative measures have one starting-point: everyone might be seropositive.' The French Ministries of Justice and Health have forbidden HIV testing except on the prisoner's request. Yet, in Britain, the inclination towards compulsory testing remains. Dr John Kilgour expressed the opinion of the prison authorities thus: 'We have a duty to care for [HIV positive prisoners] and that's sometimes going to drive us into situations which look like segregation but they are not – they are care and support . . .

14. See Grady (1989); National Institute of Justice (NIJ) (1987).
15. See NIJ (1989).
16. See NIJ (1992: xi–xii, 140).

for their own safety.'[17] Mass testing and segregation are tools of a perspective that sees HIV/AIDS as an epidemic which threatens the population. English penal policy thus aims to protect the uninfected at the expense of the interests of the infected. The security of the uninfected population takes precedence over the lives of the infected. In Dutch policy, the population is viewed as an undifferentiated mass which shares equally the same potential (seropositivity). English policy sees the potential for seropositivity as located in typical groups which make up the heteronomous population.[18]

Antibody testing has been an issue of concern due to the consequences which flow from it in current penal practice. In the immediate sense, this includes the manner of diagnosis and the means of communicating the result. Testing ideally should only occur as a result of the prisoner's voluntary consent to and understanding of the process. Counselling should be provided before and after testing; this has not often been available. One prisoner told how his test result was communicated to him in the most blunt fashion possible: 'you're positive' (Bennett, C., 1990). Segregation also constitutes a systemic disincentive to be tested. Although some assert that prison policy is moving away from routine segregation (Casale, 1993), evidence for this comes from a few prisons only. Segregation policies, still prevalent in the majority of prisons, can lead to HIV positive prisoners being forced to live in appalling conditions. Twenty-four hour lock-up is not unknown. Denial of work and sport also occurs. The prisoner is also permanently identified and stigmatized as HIV positive: a generalized lack of compassion and understanding can mean that prison life becomes intolerable. In addition to the burden of the knowledge of seropositivity, a prisoner may be subjected to physical and verbal abuse: for example, at one time in Saughton Prison, Edinburgh, HIV positive prisoners were known as 'riddlers' because they were said to be 'riddled' with disease (Bennett, C., 1990). 'Riddler' also speaks of HIV as an enigma, a problem to be solved. Here its problematic nature inspires solution through derogatory naming.

Much attention has focused on the perceived need to control the transmission of HIV within prisons. For a long time, the Prison Service in England and Wales was opposed to the distribution of needles or condoms in prisons because of the Home Office assertion that such action would be viewed as condoning criminal activity (since, it argued, all drug abuse is illegal and no homosexual act within prison could be said to take place 'in private' – thanks to the existence of the 'judas hole' in cell doors – and thus would not fall within the decriminalizing ambit of the Sexual Offences Amendment Act 1976). The Scottish Prison Service, however, has a rather more radical record in this respect. Saughton Prison in Edinburgh has, for several years, operated no policy of segregation, encouraged voluntary testing and provided educational programmes for all inmates, promoting awareness as to how HIV can

17. In *Prison Service News*, February 1989.
18. For a further comparative perspective (on Australian prison regimes), see Hatty and Burke (1992).

be transmitted (through blood, or semen, but not on cups or toilet seats, for example) (Bennett, C., 1990).[19] In October 1993, Alan Walker, Director of Scottish Prisons, announced that sterilization tablets would be made available to all prisoners (*The Guardian*, 17 November 1993). This move followed the discovery in July 1993 that 10 prisoners at Glenochil Prison were found (in a screening programme carried out by the Forth Valley Health Board and the Communicable Diseases [Scotland] Unit) to have become HIV positive through sharing needles. Drug users had also been trying to clean their 'works' in tea urns, much to the disgruntlement of other prisoners (*The Guardian*, 30 October 1993).

As far as the provision of condoms is concerned, in February 1993 the Home Office dropped its long-standing assertion that all homosexual acts in prison were illegal (*Independent on Sunday*, 28 February 1993). And in March 1994, the AIDS Advisory Committee, made up of prison staff and Home Office workers, agreed to recommend the provision of condoms in prisons, although fears were expressed that Home Secretary Michael Howard might refuse to back this policy.[20] The Committee has also been examining the question of the provision of hypodermic needles. Brixton Prison is regarded as a pioneer in the English system, through its programme of AIDS awareness education. Staff explain the risks of unsafe sex and needle-sharing to all inmates, not simply those identified as HIV positive or members of 'high-risk groups'. Confidentiality is promised to anyone seeking an HIV test; anyone handing in a needle or drugs is not disciplined, although anyone found with a syringe continues to be punished. Ironically, at the same time as the success of this programme was being acknowledged, its chief officer was sacked (*The Guardian*, 10 March 1994). So far, the governmental compromise in the issue is to provide all inmates with a Terence Higgins Trust booklet describing how to clean syringes with soapy water (not as effective as bleach or sterilization tablets, which would have to be dispensed by the authorities and look more like active condonation than 'soapy water').

Concerns about transmission and prevention are couched in terms which betray the underlying ideological agenda. Jan Keene, researching the extent of drug use and HIV transmission in prison and between prison and the community, 'fears the main route for the transmission of HIV in rural areas of Wales may already be through drug-using prisoners returning home' (*The Guardian*, 17 November 1993). In the announcement that sterilization tablets would be made available to all inmates, Alan Walker stated: 'We cannot just stand by and watch people become infected in prison because that source of infection returns to society.' In this latter statement, an individual (part of the group classified as 'people') is translated into a 'source of infection' which will

19. A more detailed description of the variations between regimes in Scotland and in England and Wales can be found in McHale and Young (1992b).

20. Six correctional systems in the United States make condoms available to inmates: see Crawford (1994: 31).

return to society, and, it is implied, infect others.[21] What is chilling about the implications of this statement is its underlying notion that infection within prison would be less of a problem in itself if the prisoner were not released. It therefore subscribes, at base, to the conception of the person in prison as undeserving and to an administrative suspicion that quarantine offers solutions to this problem. The initial problem, that of the prisoner who becomes HIV positive, is brushed aside as being less important than its implications for those outside prison, who 'deserve better'.

In sum, then, the agenda of management of HIV in prisons is one of segregation. Segregation has two purposes. It addresses the relation between inmates in prison (which may be one of needle-sharing, or of sexuality); but it also addresses the relation between the prison and the community. Hence the double victimage of the HIV positive prisoner: segregated inside the prison as HIV positive and segregated from the community as a prisoner. When these two relations become conjoined, the figure of the HIV positive prisoner appears as breaching both relations. In the theme of the prisoner's return to society, there is conjured up the idea of the prison as criminogenic and as infectious: imprisonment therefore fails to segregate the prisoner from the community since the prisoner will always return to the community. And the fear of HIV infection marks the anxiety that a returning prisoner may embody the infectiousness of prison culture, in the form of the virus.

The policing of AIDS

In June 1993, a tabloid headline proclaimed the 'Horror of AIDS cops on the beat' (*Sunday Mirror*, 6 June 1993). The story concerned the 58 officers who were HIV positive and the 3 officers who had died from AIDS, out of the 28,000 officers in the Metropolitan police force. The nice ambiguity of the headline means that it is impossible to tell the source of the eponymous 'horror': is it that police officers who are HIV positive or have AIDS are compelled to continue their stressful workaday lives ('on the beat') or is it that such officers are on the beat at all (and thus in potential contact with members of the public and other police officers)? The preferred reading that is achieved by the headline is the latter interpretation. Here AIDS is represented as a threat to the general public (a conventional representation: see Gilman, 1988; Watney, 1989c). This echoes the view of the threat embodied by HIV positive prisoners returning to the community and bringing disease and danger with them. The 'public' is conceived as a heteronomous mass of groups, some of whom are dangerous and infected (HIV positive prisoners, 'AIDS cops'), the rest of whom are assumed to be HIV negative. The twist to this particular tale lies in the embodiment of the threat as police officers, more usually represented as a bulwark against such popular menaces. The news

21. See Abelove's (1994) analysis of how public health documents – such as a pamphlet on safe sex produced by the Yale-New Haven Hospital and a report from the Surgeon-General on drugs and AIDS – often say very little about the problem they ostensibly confront, teaching instead messages about monogamy, marriage, the association of blacks with drug use.

report's desired outcome can also be read in the headline: if HIV positive police officers represent a 'horror', they should be removed from situations in which they might come into infective contact with the public. Once more segregation (or quarantine) is allowed to figure as a rational and desirable response to HIV/AIDS.

More conventional representations of the police vis-à-vis HIV/AIDS can be found in reports such as that describing the 'lucrative market' for firms supplying the police with 'blood-resistant vests for officers worried about HIV or hepatitis infection' (*The Guardian*, 15 February 1994). The police are seen as being in the 'front line', vulnerable to attack (but taking action to defend themselves).[22] More than this, they act as a synecdoche for the rest of society, poignantly able to protect themselves with a blood-resistant vest, while those in 'high-risk groups', through their dangerous behaviours, are unable to do so and indeed constitute the threat to be repelled.[23] At a protest outside the White House, organized to mark the occasion of the Third International Conference on AIDS and to publicize the Reagan administration's failure to respond adequately to HIV/AIDS, police officers wore thick yellow latex gloves, to 'protect' themselves when arresting protesters. In Scotland, after a thief suspected of being HIV positive crashed a stolen car and bled inside it, police officers had the car compressed rather than have to 'handle' it.[24] The lesbian and gay newspaper *The Pink Paper* told in 1993 how the Metropolitan police, despite Home Office guidelines to the contrary issued in 1992, were persisting in recording the HIV status of suspects and offenders (2 May 1993). In July 1994, the Scottish Office ordered police forces to abandon their practice of marking computer files of individuals suspected of being HIV positive. The computer markers are known as 'contagious warning markers' and are supposed to alert police officers to the risks of infection in making arrests and so on. The Home Office had recommended that 'training and proper hygiene procedures' would constitute a better protection for officers, but admitted that there had been reluctance to abandon the practice of using contagion markers on computer files, in England and in Scotland.[25] Here the police are represented as a threat to the civil liberties of the seropositive, in much the same way as insurance companies have been, through their intrusive questions as to sexual practice and HIV testing.

To that end, insurance companies have been policing the extent of seropositivity, and, in so doing, subscribing to and perpetuating notions about 'high-risk groups'. According to the Association of British Insurers, taking an HIV test does not in itself prevent an individual from obtaining life insurance

22. See also the risk of infection with HIV cited in the context of the routine gagging of deportees, discussed in Chapter 3.

23. See further on this Porter (1986).

24. These two incidents are reported and illustrated in the Benetton magazine, *Colours* (1994) no. 7, pp. 40, 41 in an article on myths about AIDS: 'you don't get AIDS from AIDS demonstrators'; 'you don't get AIDS from a car'.

25. See the report in *Gay Scotland*, no. 83, August 1994, p. 3: 'Police ordered to drop HIV markings.'

(for example, as an endowment mortgage), but if the company decides that an individual is at 'high risk', it is permitted to turn down the application or 'load' any premium.[26] Needless to say, an HIV positive individual is not allowed life insurance by these companies. What is significant is that 'risk' is being determined by factors such as marital status, whether or not an individual over 30 years of age (particularly a man) lives alone, and whether or not an individual admits ever having been advised on any sexually transmitted disease. The underlying assumptions are plain: a married man cannot be homosexual; a man who lives alone probably is homosexual; anyone who has feared having a sexually transmitted disease is at risk of HIV infection. Thus HIV/AIDS is associated with homosexuality and with the general category of STDs, ignoring its ability to affect individuals regardless of sexual orientation, marital status, solitary habits and so on. It was recently reported in the press that scientists had identified a protein mutation which they claimed predisposed individuals to the development of Alzheimer's disease in later life. Researchers were calling for legislation to protect the position of those deemed to be at risk of a condition about which nothing could be done, with regard to life insurance, mortgages and employment prospects. One medical professor was quoted thus: 'The implications . . . are staggering. . . . Politicians will have to take action' (*The Guardian*, 17 September 1993). This makes for an interesting comparison with HIV/AIDS testing and research. No parallels were noted between the position of those testing HIV positive – who at present cannot get life insurance, who are at risk of losing their jobs, of suffering social discrimination and harassment – and the position of those not yet discovered to be at risk of Alzheimer's by a test not yet implemented in the community. Thus is discrimination made routine in the policing of those with AIDS or those who are (at risk of being) HIV positive.[27]

In an article focusing on the trauma suffered by two men wrongly diagnosed as HIV positive by the private laboratories employed by a life assurance company, some of the ways in which life assurance companies decide who should be compelled to take an HIV test are revealed. For example, Midland Life requires a test if a man is seeking more than £150,000 cover and a woman is seeking more than £250,000 in cover. People who have lived abroad, intravenous drug users and homosexual men are also required to take the test (*Independent on Sunday*, 19 September 1993). In addition to the all-too-familiar inclusion of homosexual men and drug users in the 'at risk' category,

---

26. The position of the insurance company is summarized in 'Should you have an AIDS test?', *Cosmopolitan*, October 1993. For an American view, see Berman (1989).

27. The insurance industry is claimed to have toned down its approach; however, the anecdotal evidence provided by individual single men or gay men seeking endowment mortgages and so on seems to contradict this. As personal anecdotal evidence, while being compulsorily tested for HIV as part of an application to emigrate to Australia, I was told that a positive result would preclude my getting life insurance or an endowment mortgage. The doctor then stated that as a Western woman my chances of being HIV positive were extremely low, unless, he said, I had had sex with an injecting drug user, a bisexual man or a man who had recently been in Africa. Thus medical practice routinely incorporates and perpetuates stereotyped 'knowledge'.

people who have lived abroad are included due to the assumption that HIV/AIDS is a 'foreign' affair, 'caught' by the careless, like cholera.[28] In an ironic inversion of the policing of AIDS undertaken by insurance companies, which identify certain groups and individuals as financial risks to be avoided, a sub-group of financial companies has evolved which specializes in buying the life assurance policies, for cash, of individuals who became HIV positive or ill from AIDS *after* taking out the policy. These companies will offer cash in return for the policy: this may seem attractive to individuals who are faced with a void or much reduced policy owing to the advent of HIV/AIDS.[29] Where some financial companies have targeted HIV as risking the loss of revenue, others have identified it as a source of profit. Thus do insurance companies police the financial movements of HIV positive individuals (and those deemed at risk of HIV infection).

The crime of AIDS

HIV/AIDS is often represented as a consequence of illegal behaviours (such as intravenous drug use) but an additional constellation of images has developed around the notion that certain activities or items, which would otherwise be quite legitimate, are or should be seen as criminal once they are associated with or deployed by the HIV positive individual. This includes certain types of sexual activities, for example. In relation to *HIV infection as a consequence of illegal behaviour*, HIV infection has always been associated with behaviours deemed to be deviant. Such associations have structured the representation of and response to AIDS since the syndrome and virus were recognized. Gilman notes that the original term for HIV/AIDS was 'GRID', an acronym standing for 'gay-related immune deficiency':

> This label structured the idea of the patient suffering from AIDS in such a manner that the patient was not only stigmatized as a carrier of an infectious disease but also placed within a very specific historical category. For AIDS . . . was understood as a specific subset of the greater category of sexually transmitted diseases, a disease that homosexuals suffered as a direct result of their sexual practices or related group-specific activities. . . . Even though the MMWR [Morbidity and Mortality Weekly Report, issued by the Centers for Disease Control in Atlanta] began, in late 1982, to record the appearance of the disease among such groups as hemophiliacs and IV drug users, groups that could be defined by qualities other than sexual

---

28. While I was writing this chapter, a friend told me that the building society arranging a mortgage for her wanted her to be tested for HIV because she had been born in Uganda. On the ethnicity of the spectacle of HIV, see, for example: Patton (1990a, 1990b); Watney (1989b). In a recent article on heterosexual risk, one man is quoted: 'One tends to check on the antecedents [of a sexual partner]. . . . If someone's been to Africa, then I'll take double care' (*The Guardian*, 17 October 1994). Another article states that most infected heterosexuals will have become seropositive 'while travelling abroad' (*Independent on Sunday*, 28 June 1992).

29. Companies such as these advertise in the burgeoning press for HIV positive individuals: in the United States these publications include *Plus Voice* and *POZ*. Other advertisers include pharmaceutical companies offering the hope of a cure; sunshine cruises and holidays abroad for ailing individuals; and silver bracelets engraved with the names of those who have died from AIDS.

orientation, sexual orientation remained the salient characteristic used to exemplify the person living with AIDS. (1988: 247)[30]

Nelkin reports on the American news media's description of Ryan White, a haemophiliac child with AIDS, as a 'homophiliac' (cited in Nelkin, 1991: 305). And the linking of HIV with a sexual orientation that was frequently represented as both morally reprehensible and criminal has proved unshakeable. Homosexuality and HIV have been repetitively referenced through each other. It is as if the invisibility of the disease invited associative images to be generated around it, in order to give it meaning, direction and intention. Although there might be nothing with less *motive* than a virus, a persistent denial of HIV's lack of motivation characterized it, variously, as divine punishment, a backlash from the natural order against unnatural acts, and as a minority problem. These associations continue to influence both policy-making and the assumptions of the general public.[31] Here the formal decriminalization of homosexual acts that occurred in 1967 in England and Wales is not a relevant issue (nor the recent lowering of the age of consent to homosexual acts to 18 years): I am using 'illegal' in the sense that heterosexuality has always been attributed the status of norm or 'law'; hence homosexuality acquires a deviant status whatever formal legal category it occupies. Thus, in *R* v. *Brown and others*, a case involving a group of sado-masochistic homosexual men, Lord Lowry stated: 'When considering the danger of infection, with its inevitable threat of AIDS, I am not impressed by the argument that this threat can be discounted on the ground that, as long ago as 1967, Parliament, subject to conditions, legalized buggery, now a well-known vehicle for the transmission of AIDS.'[32]

The first public acknowledgement of HIV, published in medical journals, bears some of the responsibility for this repetitive reading of HIV through homosexuality (and vice versa): the article's title is 'Kaposi's sarcoma and *pneumocystis* pneumonia among homosexual men – New York City and California' (Friedman-Kien et al., 1981). Researchers were unable to resist the temptation that the baffling symptoms they saw were linked to the sufferer's *sexuality* (rather than, as it turned out, to a specific form of sexual activity, practised by both heterosexuals and homosexuals – anal intercourse – as one of a variety of methods through which bodily fluids might be exchanged). Thus, rather than being classified as a viral disease – like hepatitis – HIV was seen from the outset as a sexually transmitted disease, with all the stigma and censorious connotations that inevitably attend. Gilman (1988: 247) posits that the irresistible impulse to link a disease with a form of sexuality sprang from social anxieties about the spread of sexually transmitted diseases in general and the growth in public awareness of the Gay Liberation Movement in America, following events such as the 'riot' at the Stonewall Inn in New

---

30. See also Leibowitch (1985: 3–9).

31. See again the study by Durex in 1994: 22 per cent of respondents cited 'homosexuals' as the group at risk of 'catching' HIV. See also the arguments of writers such as Fumento (1989).

32. [1993] 2 All England Reports 75 (HL) at p. 100.

York City. Associating HIV with a 'deviant' form of sexual activity permitted both an institutional apathy as to its cause and cure, and a stigmatizing of the group deemed to be practising that sexual behaviour as the source of a wide-spread threat to public life and individual health.[33]

The so-called '4-Hs' – homosexuals, heroin addicts, haemophiliacs and Haitians – attest to the associative powers of HIV. Homosexuals are linked to HIV through sexual activity; heroin addicts through their intravenous drug use. Haemophiliacs, who were given HIV-infected blood products in transfusion, are linked to HIV through their perceived utter vulnerability. Haitians represent the racial dimensions of HIV, tracing both a popular holiday route and a frequent jumping-off point for refugees coming to the United States (and thus bringing a 'foreign' disease with them). Haitians are thus regarded as similar to the prisoner who returns to the community with HIV infection. The inevitable response from this perspective is a desire to prevent the Haitian from entering the country, just as fears about HIV infection in prisons invites the desire to keep the HIV positive prisoner in prison. The omission of the heterosexual from the list of 'Hs' has been remarked by others (Gilman, 1988; Patton, 1990b; Treichler, 1989). Its absence attests to the cultural weighting which prevents something considered the norm from being associated with HIV. The heterosexual heroin addict or Haitian is viewed as becoming HIV positive through some flaw (drug use, ethnic origin) which is unrelated to her sexuality.[34]

In relation to *HIV infection as a form of criminal behaviour in itself*, attention has been directed at two issues. First, the transmission of HIV infection has been considered for criminalization (and has been made criminal, in some jurisdictions). Second, certain activities, previously considered unproblematic, have become associated with crime and deviance. A good example of this is the reporting of incidents where robberies are alleged to take place with syringes used as the threatening weapon. Here the act of holding a syringe, which would be unthreatening when done by a medical worker, or merely strange if done by a member of the public before HIV existed, becomes a menace to life and health. In one case in London, an 'AIDS raider used syringe to terrify' (*The Guardian*, 1 March 1994). This story related to a man suffering from AIDS who had allegedly carried out several robberies in

33. See Shilts (1987) for an account of this dual process. Note that Shilts himself gives in to a form of this stigmatizing, in his acceptance of the notion that HIV originated in Africa and that one promiscuous individual – the so-called Patient Zero – was deliberately responsible for infecting hundreds of men in North America.

34. HIV and homosexuality were again conjoined when five gay men were murdered by the same man, who had engaged each one in conversation in a gay pub in London, had gone home with them and killed them. While many newspapers disclosed the HIV status of some of the victims, it was also speculated that the murders 'could be revenge for an HIV infection or a desire to destroy homosexuals' (*The Times*, 17 June 1993). The London Gay Pride March in 1993 was described by the press as being watched by the murderer: '[the marchers] knew it was almost certain that a murderous psychopath was either walking alongside or watching closely' (*The Sunday Times*, 20 June 1993). See also the discussion in Stychin (1994), from where these press excerpts are taken.

London on the same day by 'brandishing a syringe containing what he claimed was his contaminated blood'. The man was sentenced to two-and-a-half years' imprisonment, which if the report was correct in describing him as having AIDS, would be likely to turn into a life sentence. The report claimed, oddly, that in his defence he had stated that he was attempting to raise money for the Terence Higgins Trust.

Further coverage was given to a series of incidents taking place in Paris, under the headline 'Needle of terror on Paris streets' (*Independent on Sunday*, 28 August 1994). The article conjures up a 'nightmarish trend' whereby 'muggers armed with syringes allegedly tainted with the AIDS virus' carry out robberies by frightening people with the threat of infection. Between April and August 1994, the police had received eight reports of such attacks. In late August, the Paris police issued a formal statement warning that hypodermic needles 'had now become an instrument of crime'. The syringe is thus viewed in the same way as a gun or as a penis in rape cases. The syringe is the instrument which makes literal the threat of HIV infection.[35] The police in Paris were said to be torn 'between a responsibility to inform the public and a fear that publicizing the new outrage might lead to it becoming more widespread'. One incident was described in detail: a woman had been stabbed with a supposedly infected syringe as her assailant grew impatient with the speed at which she looked for money. The woman was said to be waiting for three months to pass before she could undergo an HIV test to see if she had indeed become infected. In another incident, a man robbed a pharmacist, forcing him to hand over drugs by threatening him with a syringe. A police officer was quoted: the attacks are 'probably a sign of the times'. Here HIV infection is linked to drug use; the individuals carrying out the attacks are implied to be drug users desperate for money. The activity which led to their infection (injecting drugs) provides the means by which they can frighten individuals into giving up money or drugs: the syringe.[36]

Blood also featured as a source of danger in reports of an HIV positive remand prisoner who, while in prison hospital, had allegedly ripped an IV drip from his arm and run from the hospital (see, for example, *The Sun*, 12 March 1993). The potency of this report relates to the notion of the puncture wound in the vein, created by the drip, safe while the drip is in place. If the drip needle is removed, the puncture wound is open, allowing blood to flow out of it, rather than fluid into it. The notion of the dangers of infected blood flow features as a trope in the case of *R. v. Brown and others*, in which the House of Lords turned down the appeal of a group of sado-masochistic homosexuals against their myriad convictions for assault, keeping a disorderly house, and so on.[37] With regard to the possibility of blood being allowed

35. The film *Les Nuits Fauves* (*Savage Nights*) shows a seropositive man use his blood as a threat to frighten off racists beating up an Arab: he cuts his hand and holds it over the face of the ringleader, threatening to rub his blood into the man's mouth.

36. See further Stansbury (1989), relating to the decision *US v. Moore* 846 F 2d 1163 (8th Cir 1988).

37. See n. 32 above. See also its discussion in Rush (forthcoming).

to flow as a consequence of the activities carried out by the men, Lord Jauncey said: 'the free flow of blood from a person who is HIV positive or who has AIDS can infect another' (at p. 91). Lord Templeman stated: 'blood-letting and the smearing of human blood produced excitement. There were obvious dangers of serious personal injury and blood infection' (at p. 83). Blood has been converted, in this judgement and in the press reports cited above, from the medium of life, carrying oxygen around the body, to a trans-porter of death, allowing a virus to escape the confines of the body it has infected and to have access to others.

In other cases, blood transfusion was a means of infection. Here, the sim-ple medical procedure which had come to be regarded as straightforward and life-giving, an act of socio-medical responsibility, became a means of transmitting the virus. In the mid-1980s, before screening had been intro-duced, those individuals who donated blood while infected with HIV were seen as socially irresponsible and dangerous. Before the advent of the HIV test, proposals were debated to exclude gay men from blood donation, on the grounds of the prevalence of HIV among that community (Shilts, 1987). Once screening was implemented, a new kind of crime was discovered: that of doctors who knowingly gave infected blood products to patients. In 1993, French doctors were sentenced to imprisonment after distributing HIV-infected blood products. The doctor described as the 'main villain' was Dr Michel Garretta, sentenced to four years' imprisonment; another, Dr Jean-Pierre Allain, received a sentence of four years' imprisonment with two of the years suspended (*The Sunday Times*, 13 June 1993). Another doctor who was found by a French court to have deceived haemophiliacs by supplying them with HIV-contaminated blood products was later judged by a British court to be 'ethically fit' to resume his hospital post. He has since been awarded a professorship (*The Daily Telegraph*, 17 June 1993).

The position of health care workers is an ambiguous one. On the one hand, they are represented as at risk of infection themselves from patients who do not declare their antibody status, through needlestick injury and so on. (This is similar to the position of prison officers, who are overwhelmingly repre-sented as being at risk of infection from inmates during scuffles or disturbances or attacks; little consideration is given to the possible risk posed to inmates by any seropositive officers, during any such scuffles, disturbances or attacks.)[38] On the other hand, health care workers are also viewed as a pos-sible source of infection, due to their often intimate contact with patients. In 1994, newspapers reported on the three dozen women being contacted and offered counselling and the opportunity of an HIV test after a midwife at

---

38. See also the actions of the police during a raid on a gay club in Melbourne in 1994. On the supposed justification that they were conducting searches for drugs, police officers carried out full body searches on the 463 men and women who were in the club, without changing the latex gloves worn for rectal and vaginal searches. Fifty lesbians and gay men joined together to form COPIT, a group attempting a class action suit against the Victoria police. The police seem in this situation to have used the possibility of HIV infection in any of the clubgoers as a weapon against all the individuals present.

University College Hospital in London was found to be HIV positive (*The Guardian*, 23 March 1994). And more than 120 women who had been treated by an HIV positive doctor were given leave to bring a joint claim for negligence against Tameside and Trafford hospitals in Greater Manchester (*The Guardian*, 30 March 1994). In Australia, a search of 8,000 women was carried out after a doctor was found to be HIV positive. He had performed caesarian deliveries or vaginal surgery after delivery on these women 'with maximum risk to the patient of exposure to HIV' (*Sydney Morning Herald*, 4 August 1994). One hundred and forty nine were eventually decided to be at risk, inspiring a debate on regular compulsory testing of health workers and the enforced disclosure of any HIV positive status. Since September 1994, as a result of the furore this incident caused, all health care workers have been required to undergo regular testing for HIV and hepatitis B and C (*Sydney Morning Herald*, 3 August 1994).

Two separate stories were reported concerning how the doctor concerned, a trainee obstetrician, had become HIV positive. In one, he had accidentally pricked himself with a needle after injecting a woman. In another, involving comments made by the New South Wales Chief Medical Officer, the 'personal habits' and implied homosexuality of the doctor were criticized. The narrative surrounding this doctor exemplified the dual position occupied by the health care worker, as a risk and as at risk. An article entitled 'HIV, your doctor and you' (*Sydney Morning Herald*, 3 August 1994) picked up this ambiguity by illustrating its question-and-answer provision of facts with a photograph showing a bare arm being injected with a hypodermic syringe, held in two hands clad in surgical gloves. The recipient of the injection is clasping a hand around the shoulder above the injection site; the arm is muscled but the hand wears two rings, thus combining two gender signifiers in one body. The hands of the doctor are asexual, and are positioned in a more obviously threatening gesture, to which the patient responds (by clasping him- or herself). Vulnerability is indeterminate, however: the needle, which initially appears more threatening, may infect the doctor if a needlestick injury occurs; the rubber gloves may not protect the patient if the doctor is HIV positive. Risk circulates in the image like blood in a vein.

When doctors or health care workers commit acts such as distributing HIV-infected blood to transfusion patients, they step out of this ambiguous sphere of risk tempered by liability, and into a realm much more explicitly criminalized. However, their liability here still seems proportionally lower than that which results when infection of others occurs through sexual intercourse, or when a member of a so-called 'high-risk group' has transmitted the infection. The relatively low sentences imposed on the doctors who knowingly gave infected Factor VIII to haemophiliacs can be compared with the sentence of five years' imprisonment, followed by extradition, given by a Swedish court to a refugee from Zaïre who was found to have knowingly infected two women through sexual intercourse (*Birmingham Post*, 24 April 1993).

In many of the above instances, what was a medical or health problem has been quickly translated into a legal problem. As soon as HIV/AIDS has been posed as a juridical problem, commentators have suggested the creation of a systematic prohibition of the transmission of HIV (for example, Robinson, 1985–6; Smith, 1991). Such prohibition would proceed in two ways: first, the extension of existing juridical categories to novel circumstances (that is, moving from the general legal doctrine to the specific issue); and second, the addition of new juridical categories which attend solely to the details of HIV transmission. Some English commentators have argued that the existing common law could easily be adapted, through judicial reasoning, to cover cases in which a person with HIV or AIDS transmits infection to another, either through sexual intercourse or through needlestick injury. For example, Smith considers the ease with which offences such as assault, rape and the procurement of sexual intercourse, the administration of a destructive or noxious thing and attempted murder, could be used to prosecute 'those who knowingly risk infecting (or actually infect) others with the AIDS virus' (1991: 322). In response to the imagined questioning of the desirability or ethics of the criminal law's extension to cover this area, Smith contends that any such objections are met if HIV poses a clear risk of public or individual harm, if civil liberties can be balanced while giving credence to the threat posed by HIV, and if the criminal law could make a worthwhile contribution to the control of HIV transmission.

In answering these conditions, Smith asserts that the 'details of diagnosed cases of HIV' leave 'no room for doubt as to the chilling extent and nature of the actual and potential harm'; that extension of the law 'will not constitute any noticeable departure from liability already widely accepted in the same or adjacent areas of human activity'; and the criminalization of certain behaviours might 'promote changes in sexual mores and behaviour by most emphatically underscoring the social rejection of highly dangerous practices' (1991: 320–1). Not satisfied with a debate on the extension of existing offences, Smith argues further for the legislation of new offences, relating to 'endangering behaviour', focusing upon the bodily fluids which transmit infection. Although stopping short of proscribing 'social kissing', Smith includes the other forms of sexual activities and the use of contaminated hypodermic needles.[39] Having proposed the not inconsiderable extensions, Smith acknowledges, at the very close of the article, the 'predictable' concern being voiced in America over such extensions of the law, by 'high risk group organizations' and from 'less sectional quarters' (1991: 329), concerns relating to the isolation or alienation of those infected. Such lip service expressed in derogatory and biased terms does nothing to counterbalance the weight of the overall argument, which inclines most definitely towards increased regulation through criminalization of these behaviours. This is an argument generated by fear, which reveals itself in the linguistic solipsisms linking 'venereal disease' with 'AIDS', 'risk' with 'harm', 'chilling' details of AIDS with 'public harm'.

In the United States, the issue has gone beyond the fearful theorizing

---

39. An alternative view is found in Burdt and Caldwell (1987–8).

indulged in by Smith. In *Barlow* v. *Superior Court*, a participant in a Gay Pride march in San Diego, believed to have AIDS – although it is not clear by whom this was believed – bit two police officers during a scuffle. The prosecution tried to charge him with attempted murder; this failed due to the court's refusal to permit a compulsory testing of the defendant's blood. The results from any previous HIV test the defendant had undergone could not be released to the court because of the state of California's provisions protecting the confidentiality of HIV test results.[40] A number of American state legislatures have enacted criminal sanctions specific to the transmission of AIDS and have also resorted to the use of general criminal offences – particularly the 'endangerment' type of offence advocated by Smith for the English situation – to criminalize a range of behaviours not previously dealt with by the criminal law.[41] This development can be seen in other jurisdictions, such as Australia. Laufer argues that threatening another person with an HIV-infected syringe constitutes an assault; while to have sexual intercourse in order knowingly to infect another could be attempted murder or manslaughter. The year-and-a-day rule (that death must occur within a year and a day of the injury for homicide to occur in law) has spurred several states to enact specific legislation in relation to HIV infection: for example, New South Wales introduced the Public Health (Proclaimed Diseases) Amendment Act 1985, which makes it an offence maliciously to cause (or attempt to cause) any person to contract a 'grievous bodily disease'. The maximum sentence is 25 years' imprisonment. Behind this legislative development is the fear of attacks on prison warders.[42] Knowingly having sexual intercourse with another while infected is subject to heavy fines. In Britain in 1985, the Public Health (Control of Diseases) Act – which permits the detention of individuals if they pose a 'health risk' to the public – was extended to cover individuals with AIDS (although not HIV positive individuals).[43] Taken together, these legislative developments, proposed extensions of the criminal law and willingness to criminalize individuals and behaviours, speak of a fearfulness and a panic that seeks to deploy the law as a weapon in a perceived battle. Here, law is imaged as an instrument (of self and social defence) in the same way that HIV has been imaged as a threat which can be literalized in weapons such as syringes.[44] Both are viewed as instruments, techniques,

40. See 236 Cal Rptr 134 (1987).

41. See commentators such as Gostin (1989, 1990); Sullivan and Field (1988).

42. Laufer (1991) cites one instance of a warder who seroconverted after one such attack (although very quickly, provoking doubts that the attack was the actual source of infection).

43. That the Act had not been extended to cover the HIV positive was described as a 'legal anomaly', in the context of health officials' inability to detain Roy Cornes, the HIV positive haemophiliac who claimed to have infected at least four women through sexual intercourse, while knowing his seropositive status (*The Guardian*, 17 August 1992). See also *Today* (24 June 1992): 'Revenge of AIDS Romeo. He's killed one woman, infected three others and there's no law to stop him.'

44. Montgomery (1990: 26–30) poses the question as to whether the HIV positive constitute 'victims or threats', within an analysis which sees legal practice as 'framing' the HIV positive. He does not extend the notion of frame to include its imagistic function.

procedures. The instrumentality of law, however, is presented only as acting in defence to a threat which has already been made. It is likely that such tactics will gather force. As Gostin has remarked, 'The politics of AIDS is moving steadily in the direction of the use of compulsory powers of the state' (1989: 1017). Singer writes that 'the [construction of a disease as an] epidemic provides an occasion and a rationale for multiplying points of intervention into the lives of bodies and populations' (1993: 117).

Quarantine, criminality and HIV

In Derbyshire, there is a ruined village called Eyam. It is famous for an act of self-sacrifice, in which its inhabitants agreed to quarantine themselves in order to halt the transmission of plague to other villages. No-one left or entered the village until the disease had run its course through the village. This story is recounted in tourist guides and on television programmes. It is told admiringly, with the inhabitants of Eyam represented as simultaneously heroic, stoic, brave and fatalistic. Their self-sacrifice is portrayed as a generous, noble gesture by which others were able to survive. As a parable of social ethics, its traces can be detected in the contemporary responses to HIV/AIDS and to those who are HIV positive. It is my argument that the criminal justice system's response to HIV positive individuals betrays a desire to quarantine them. This occurs in all its institutions, not merely in the most obvious forms such as prison policies and regimes. In the examples elaborated above, from segregation in prisons through the recording of seropositivity on police computers to the doctrinal and legislative debates on new offences involving the transmission of HIV, the criminal justice system has shown itself to be susceptible to the urge to separate out the HIV positive individual and to create forms of literal and symbolic quarantine for them. In the concluding part of this chapter, I wish to consider why this is so.

Quarantine has a long history as a socio-medical practice responding to the notion of infection. The inhabitants of Eyam may well have been lauded for their voluntary self-quarantine, since the practice's history is more associated with the compulsory segregation of the sick. During World War I, in the United States, thousands of women believed to be prostitutes were incarcerated in camps as part of a public health move to protect army recruits from the perceived threat of infection with syphilis from these women.[45] Quarantine in the form of restricted movement and enforced medical inspections occurred in Britain in the 1860s when the Contagious Diseases Acts were deployed in order to compel prostitutes to remain within designated areas and be subjected to regular medical inspections, again due to a fear of syphilis. Public responses to HIV have been strikingly similar to the reactions and practices instituted with regard to syphilis. In addition to the impulse to incarcerate suspected carriers (the most explicit mode of quarantine), measures were introduced which derived from a fear of infection and a fantasy of

45. Cited in Sontag (1991: 167).

its control. For example, on United States naval vessels, doorknobs were removed and swing doors introduced, as a result of fears that sailors visiting prostitutes would spread the infection through such casual contact amongst themselves.

Similarly, metal drinking cups were removed from water fountains in American cities and children were, for the first time, instructed to place layers of toilet paper on the seats of public toilets, out of fears of 'catching' syphilis. Thus the disease was thought to be spread by those who had acquired it through their own culpability (lax morals leading to a visit to a prostitute) among those who did not 'deserve' the disease (the more morally upright sailors, children, innocent citizens drinking from public water fountains). Syphilis was thought to bring the 'respectable' classes into contact with a sexually deviant, ethnic, working-class underworld. Infectious diseases to which sexual fault is attached inspire fears of easy contagion and bizarre fantasies of non-sexual transmission. HIV/AIDS has revived similar fantasies among those defined as the general population by medical and governmental institutions (that is, the white, heterosexual, married, middle-class, non-injecting drug user). Thus, as Sedgwick (1992) has shown, the addicted drug user and the homosexual became subjected to the same discourses of will; Watney demonstrates how 'the mere fact of gay sex is held to be dangerous for *other people*' (1989c: 85; my emphasis). A rhetoric of extrapolation inexorably transferred risk from one set of individuals to another: the so-called 'general population', who are envisaged as an undifferentiated mass as against the heteronomous groups who constitute risk. In this way, HIV positive children have been excluded from schools in the United States,[46] in the mid-1980s panics broke out concerning the 'safety' of sharing beer bottles at parties, and airport toilets now routinely offer plastic toilet rim covers for use by passengers.

HIV is represented as akin to syphilis in many ways. It also draws from the iconography and symbolism associated with cancer. To that extent, HIV is founded upon metaphors of invasion and pollution, the notion of invasion deriving from representations of cancer, pollution from the imagery of syphilis. Invasion moves from the outside to the inside (from other to self); while pollution moves from the inside to the outside (from self to other). Both depend on the notion of a boundary marked at the edge of the body; both can inspire the impulse to quarantine in the desire to halt the movement of infection back and forth across the body's borders. In HIV infection, the virus is often said to invade the body, sometimes 'lurking' unnoticed for a time, but eventually making an assault on the immune system, by means of its destruction of the blood's T cells.[47] Similarities with cancer discourse are marked, particularly the spatial metaphors. Cancer is a disease of the body's geography; it spreads, colonizes, travels, migrates (Sontag, 1991; Stacey,

46. See Brandt (1988) and Gilman (1988).

47. For an illustration of this type of discourse, see the varying explications given on how the immune system reacts to HIV infection in Martin (1994: 64–81, 127–42).

forthcoming). However, in HIV infection, the virus is also associated with pollution, through its transmission in blood and semen. Blood is sometimes represented as the body's vital fluid (and thus essential to life); however, it also has a dimension which connotes it as detritus, waste. Waste is matter out of place (Douglas, 1966); blood when circulating in the veins is vital fluid, but waste material when it spurts from a vein, or dries up in a syringe, or stains a tampon (see Martin, 1987). Semen signifies sexuality, ejaculation and orgasm. Its visible presence inevitably connotes masculine sexuality and the culmination of a sexual act. It is thus easily characterized as waste.[48] It is also the bodily fluid most directly associated with HIV, due to the disease's perceived epidemiological origins as a sexually transmitted disease of gay men, and due to a cultural willingness to link HIV with homosexuality. Through these waste products, blood and semen, the pollution of the healthy body takes place and the virus is admitted to a new victim.

HIV thus shares with cancer its invasion metaphors and with syphilis its connotation as pollutant. HIV and syphilis are also alike in their temporal – as opposed to cancer's spatial – imagining of progression. Where cancer 'spreads', HIV and syphilis have 'stages'. Syphilis has three stages, leading up to tertiary syphilis, the most dreaded and fatal stage. HIV similarly has three stages: seropositivity, in which antibodies are produced but no other symptoms may be present; ARC, or AIDS-Related Complex, in which the individual may experience minor health problems such as skin diseases, or night sweats; and AIDS, in which any of a vast array of illnesses and infections may be present, representing the breakdown of the immune system. Although an individual is thought to be most infectious during the earliest stage of HIV (seropositivity) despite perhaps having no symptoms of illness, the latter stage is represented as the most dreadful, as with syphilis. Here, medical science and popular discourse deploy the term 'full-blown' AIDS. This expression has always seemed derogatory, in its harking to 'fly-blown' meat; in its zoological dimension (it is the opposite of fledgeling); in its botanical aspects, implying some floral bloom gone past its best.

Such metaphorical flourishes abound in public discourses (including legal and criminological) on HIV. Sontag comments: 'cancer [was made] synonymous with evil . . . [H]aving cancer has been experienced by many as shameful . . . and also unjust, a betrayal by one's body. Why me? the cancer patient exclaims bitterly. With AIDS, the shame is linked to an imputation of guilt; and the scandal is not at all obscure' (1991: 110). Heart disease is viewed as the price to be paid for an executive lifestyle, the bill that comes after too many business lunches. Lung cancer is seen as the price you pay for smoking, but smoking is displaced from individual choice to addiction to a legal chemical. With HIV, *judgement* of the sick is an integral part of diagnosis and public responses alike. The HIV positive individual is judged to have 'caught AIDS' through more than just the weakness that prevents a cigarette smoker from kicking the habit: 'it is indulgence, delinquency – addiction to

48. See the discussion of semen in Grosz (1994: 198–202).

chemicals that are illegal and dangerous and to sex viewed as deviant' (Sontag, 1991: 111). Diagnosis of seropositivity or AIDS, then, 'provides a new coercive technology of confession' (Patton, 1990b: 128). A homosexual man who wished to remain 'closeted' might dread the diagnosis of HIV for more than just its meaning for his future health; it meant the end to the invisibility of his homosexuality, marking him as a text, to be read as deviant and punished. 'The illness flushes out an identity that might have remained hidden from neighbors, jobmates, family, friends. It also confirms an identity' (Sontag, 1991: 111).[49] And in confirming an identity, HIV permits the governmental rewriting of the closet as the lair in which the HIV positive individual hides from the 'rest' of society (and from which she might strike at the 'rest of society').

'AIDS, like other sexually transmitted diseases, has been viewed as a fateful link between social deviance and the morally correct' (Brandt, 1988: 155). The 'morally correct' in this scenario are positioned as different to and separate from the 'social deviance' deemed to reside in homosexuality. To that extent, the deviance of homosexuality constitutes a sort of Bakhtinian grotesque against which the morally righteous occupy the position of the classical body, asexual, clean, elevated, bourgeois (Bakhtin, 1968). The homosexual grotesque is portrayed as fixating on orifices whose existence the dominant culture might prefer to disavow, such as the anus (Bersani, 1989), multiplying without control (through the well-known popularity of the gay bath-houses, or the imputed promiscuity of homosexual men) and, now, bound up in disease. Patrick Buchannan, the prominent American right-winger, stated: 'The poor homosexuals – they have declared war on Nature, and now Nature is exacting an awful retribution' (quoted in the *New York Post*, 24 May 1983).[50] In the linking of social deviance and moral correctness, HIV/AIDS has conventionally been viewed as the cause of the breakdown in the separation of deviant from law-abiding, homosexual from heterosexual, and so on. However, it is my suggestion here that the spectacle of HIV/AIDS is a symptom of the systemic failure to separate groups and behaviours in this way. Thus, HIV, as image and as symptom, is quarantined because it represents the system's own failure to create successfully a society of quarantine, to keep infection out or absent. Hence, HIV represents the confusion of deviance and correctness, secularity and morality. And so, these categories are revealed to be mutually constitutive of each other. The spectacle of HIV/AIDS operates as the mutually constitutive link between prison and community, police and policed, health and sickness, living and dead.

As part of this process of linking the 'morally correct' and the 'sexually deviant' as mutually constitutive, channels of infection were being mapped in an epidemiological allegory of control. In addition to the fears over cups

49. The film *Philadelphia* makes this the dynamic of its narrative.

50. For an alternative view of 'Nature', see Weeks (1991). Buchannan's views of course echo the sentiments of some British commentators, such as the erstwhile Chief Constable of Greater Manchester, James Anderton, notorious for his anti-gay comments.

and toilet seats, again mirroring reactions to syphilis, the closet was pin-
pointed as one of the means by which the deviant few might infect 'the rest'.
How is this thought to occur? Fears about the closet crystallized around the
Rock Hudson 'scandal'. When Hudson was discovered to be gay and dying
from AIDS, much speculation arose as to how he had managed to be gay
without it becoming generally known.[51] Hudson then became a synecdoche
for all the men who were gay without any general awareness of their sexuality; that is, who were in the closet. 'Passing' as heterosexual was viewed as
being a form of moral deception, which could defraud others: for example, a
heterosexual woman might have sexual intercourse with a man who was
'really' gay (or bisexual) and who was merely pretending his heterosexuality.
In this respect, the closeted homosexual is viewed as a *rat*, deceiving others,
but also travelling from one site of infection to another, linking the world of
the 'morally correct' with the underworld of the 'sexually deviant'. He
embodies a confusion of semblance and substance, appearing to possess a
heterosexual self but owning instead a secret, true self that is homosexual.
This true self exists in the dark, in secret, hidden from the general population
who are deceived by the false image of 'normality'. Here the closeted homosexual is asked to bear the same kind of responsibility that was attributed to
the rats which spread the plague from house to house in the seventeenth century. And in the same way, the individuals who deem themselves 'morally
correct' can absolve themselves of responsibility in relation to HIV/AIDS.

When HIV did touch individuals outside the world of the homosexual (or
the drug user, although that group were always portrayed as incidental to the
main narrative of HIV as a gay disease), this was represented as far more
tragic than when it killed homosexuals. Henig (1983) writes:

> The groups most recently found to be at risk for AIDS present a particularly
> poignant problem. Innocent bystanders caught in the path of a new disease, they
> can make no behavioral decisions to minimize their risk: hemophiliacs cannot stop
> taking bloodclotting medication; surgery patients cannot stop getting transfusions;
> women cannot control the drug habits of their mates; babies cannot choose their
> mothers.[52]

With the assumptions contained in this passage (AIDS is not such a problem
when it affects gay men and drug users; compared to the innocence of these
listed sufferers, gay men and drug users are guilty; AIDS is a problem of
homosexuality), the answer becomes plain to the question asked by public

51. See 'Fear and AIDS in Hollywood', in *People*, 23 September 1985; *New York Times*, 7
November 1985.

52. The passage also implies that a woman is able to control her reproduction; that a woman
can control her economic life, thereby avoiding the route that leads through debt and poverty into
prostitution and that leads clients to offer more money for sex without a condom (see Lawrinson,
1990); and that drug use is not an active choice but a compulsion (whereas research on drug use
seems to show that addiction is less of an overwhelming urge than a pleasurable choice: see
Manning, 1991). Smith (1991) implies the culpability of HIV positive women who choose to have
children and emphasizes the 'high' risk of infection to the foetus; that risk has been estimated as
a 15 to 25 per cent chance of passing on the infection.

health agencies and governmental institutions: what is to be done? Quarantine, in all its actual and symbolic forms, responds to these anxieties. In prisons, the segregation of the HIV positive prisoner makes an outlaw of him, excludes him from the excluded community that is the rest of the prison. In requiring HIV tests by those men who live alone, or individuals born in Africa, the insurance company makes a scapegoat of certain groups which remain introjected within the population, to be feared and marked out. Quarantine promises to remove the HIV positive individual from circulation. It promises to erect a barrier between the world of the HIV positive and the world of the others. It promises control, prevention and an end to infection. That it can do none of these is not the point (indeed, the strategy of quarantine exists as a consequence of the impossibility of its desires). Quarantine is a disciplinary mechanism which marks out a deviant identity and which permits the stigmatizing[53] of the HIV positive body as a site to be repressed, controlled, 'made into the spectacle of AIDS' (Patton, 1990b: 129).

In resistance to the enforced occupation of an identity proclaimed simultaneously deviant and linked to disease, groups have organized themselves into a rewritten spectacle of AIDS. From the Names Project (which commemorates the lives of those who have died of AIDS, by stitching a quilt out of the textile patches – six feet by three feet, the size of a coffin – sewn by family and friends), through ACT UP's demonstrations of anger at under-funding of AIDS research and governmental hypocrisies, to the *Positive Lives* photography project, HIV/AIDS has been established as a site of social contestation rather than a *fait accompli* demanding the symbolic or literal annihilation of gay men, intravenous drug users, African or Haitian immigrants and prostitutes.[54] And, in resistance to the enforced confession that is a diagnosis of HIV, these acts of resistance recuperate speech and assert its vitality, in the statement 'Silence = Death'.

Discourses of quarantine and criminality, however, are deep-rooted and hard to shake. HIV lends itself to an association with criminality through two main routes. First, seropositivity is represented as a state one has brought upon oneself. Syphilis was also viewed as a self-inflicted punishment for sexual activity, but this is more acute in the case of HIV, since a specific practice has been named, one which fixes the infection as a result not just of excess but of perversity. HIV infection connotes a voluntary risk-taking, an indifference to health. Addicts who needle-share are viewed as committing a kind of inadvertent suicide, which merely completes the risks they take as part of drug-taking behaviour. Sexual transmission is therefore much more blameworthy. Traces of this distinction can be found in the Home Office's willingness to countenance drug-taking in prisons (by distributing

53. I am using 'stigma' in Goffman's (1963) sense to connote a 'spoiled' identity.

54. On the spectacular politics of resistance by AIDS pressure groups, see: Crimp (1989); Crimp with Rolston (1990); Dubin (1992: Chapter 8). On the Names Project, see Abelove (1994). On *Positive Lives*, see Mayes and Stein (1993). On social movements concerning AIDS, see Gamson (1989).

sterilization tablets) and reluctance to admit the fact of homosexual anal intercourse in prisons by distributing condoms.[55] Second, the history of medicine demonstrates a link with criminal justice in its choice of discursive metaphors. Medicine has fought the 'war against disease' since well before the sixteenth century.

Latterly (and particularly since the discourses on syphilis and tuberculosis during and after World War I), with the development of more and more sophisticated techniques of seeing viruses and micro-organisms such as bacteria, illness was understood as a consequence of the body's invasion by a foreign entity. In the war against disease, therefore, the body is taken over by an alien organism; to which the body must respond by fighting back with its defence forces in the immune system. The parallels with the 'war against crime' are plain. Society is being taken over by a malignant force, against which defences – such as the police, Neighbourhood Watch, courts and prisons – must be mobilized. The malign force can originate within (as when members of the polity become corrupted by greed or anger and thus turn to crime, in the same way that healthy cells are corrupted by cancer and then turn to aggression against other healthy cells); or, the threat may originate outside society, as *aliens* seek to colonize and settle (in the same way that a virus such as HIV takes over the body). Whichever originary cause is proposed, the dynamic remains the same: the enemy is introjected by the social body, which then struggles to expel the foreign entity. On occasions, expulsion may be literalized (and the foreign or diseased or criminal body made an outlaw); on others, it may be symbolic (and a scapegoat created instead, a surrogate for the desire to expel).

HIV's narrative of pollution and invasion combines elements of corruption and colonization. An analogy is thus created which establishes the HIV virus as immigrant and as the agent of decay. In the same way, immigrants are represented as having a relationship to disease, threatening the life of their host society. Thus do nationalism and racism structure discourses of criminality and disease. Sontag cites many examples of nationalism in response to AIDS: for example, a French public health poster depicting the shape of that country being overshadowed by a dark cloud, with the captions 'Il depend sur chacun de nous d'effacer cette ombre' and 'La France ne veut pas mourir du sida' ('It depends on each of us to erase this shadow' and 'France doesn't want to die of AIDS') (1991: 171). From a country's outline to a country's borders, from public health to the restriction of immigration: the discursive line is short and shortening further. Metaphors of the 'war' against disease

---

55. Sedgwick has described the collapse of the categories of the 'gay man' and the 'addict' into each other: 'any substance, any behavior, even any affect may be pathologized as addictive' (1992: 584); 'while any assertion that one can act freely is always read in the damning light of the "open secret" that the behavior in question is utterly compelled . . . while one's assertion that one was, after all, compelled shrivels in the equally stark light of the "open secret" that one might at any given moment have chosen differently' (1992: 587). Thus are homosexual acts capable of being read simultaneously as addictive or as willed, while acts such as injecting drugs show the user as both seduced and willing. See also the discussion in Stychin (1994).

encourage militaristic postures in which the body is viewed as a citadel or fortress. In the war against crime, the criminal justice system's response to HIV has demonstrated what moves are made when the analogous threats (the invaders and pollutants) are simultaneously the diseased: the HIV positive homosexual, prostitute or drug user.

The war against disease and the war against crime intersect in other ways. In contemporary socio-medical discourses, it is not only the physician who is conjoined to fight disease, but also the patient. Health management by the individual, both actually suffering and at risk of suffering (and thus every one of us), is considered a crucial aspect of modern living. In this way, we are all patients, all sufferers, but by risk management we can act as agents against the force of ill-health. This is represented as an essential aspect of psycho-social welfare (Stacey, forthcoming). In Chapter 3, I demonstrated how discourses of crime prevention and victimization, such as those employed by realist criminology, assert the commonality of criminal victimization as analogous to illness. Taking arms against victimization, through crime prevention strategies such as fixing locks to windows or joining Neighbourhood Watch, become badges of citizenship. Through these actions, the individual enters the social body. To that extent, the divisive discourse of HIV that makes criminals of the sick straddles the twin rhetorics of health management and crime prevention. In this instance, however, the citizen is assumed to be a white, heterosexual, middle-class, married, non-injecting drug user, who can be relied upon to erect a strong door for his house, fix locks upon his windows, and keep out the homosexual, prostitute and drug-using HIV positive individuals. HIV as a criminal justice issue has been framed in terms of its necessary quarantine. The criminal justice system promises to do its bit (by worrying about prisoners becoming HIV positive through dirty needles and then spreading infection in the 'community' upon release); the community of individuals is exhorted to respond in kind, by shunning the HIV positive and those deemed at risk of seropositivity.

Fatal frames: Dying of AIDS, living with HIV

Quarantine is about the creation of impassable boundaries and borders. It means to isolate from normal relations of communication. It is excommunication. It is assignation to the abnormal. In the encounter with HIV, a choice presents itself: to quarantine or not, to make HIV/AIDS appear or not. The photograph used in the Benetton advertisement, known as the 'man dying of AIDS' or 'David Kirby dying of AIDS', deploys a strategy of quarantine in framing AIDS as a moment of agony and inevitable death which re-marks all that has gone before in the man's life. There is a continuity between this photograph and the policies of criminal justice elaborated above. That is, in both, HIV/AIDS appears as a problem-to-be-solved. Its solution, for both, is provided by death: the Benetton photograph shows death as moments away; criminal justice policy treats the HIV positive individual as always already existing in relation to death, as embodying death (not only for herself, but also for the 'rest' of the population). As such, HIV/AIDS appears as spectacle. In stating this, I do not mean to imply that the appearance or spectacle of HIV/AIDS is in some way distinct from the 'reality' of HIV/AIDS (as if its appearance somehow required the disappearance of the real). Rather, this chapter has aimed to respond to the question of how to read the spectacle of HIV/AIDS as *spectacle*, a process that is endlessly occurring in the practices and knowledges of criminal justice as much as in the products of advertising or activism.

In these terms, what becomes important is how HIV/AIDS is spectacular-*ized*. The debate is posed, therefore, not as a question of the gap between how it looks and how it is, but of how it is made to look, how it is made a spectacle. It is this question that marks the continuity between the Benetton photograph and the discourse of criminal justice; yet marks a difference between the Benetton photograph and an image included in a photo-documentary project entitled *Positive Lives* (and between this latter photograph and criminal justice discourse). Within the collection *Positive Lives* (Mayes and Stein, 1993), there is a series of photographs, under the title 'John'. The first shows two young men, lying on a hospital bed. On opposite sides of the bed sit a man and a woman, perhaps the parents of one of the young men. A conversation is taking place. All four participants look engaged, involved, alert. Another photograph, a head-and-shoulders shot, shows the two men lying together under the covers of the hospital bed. One may be asleep or resting, his eyes closed. The other leans up on one elbow, watching. The third image occupies two full pages. It shows the two men, one lying under the sheets, the other on top of them. They are kissing, passionately embracing. Their bodies, albeit separated by sheets, are pressed together from head to toe. There are flowers by the bed. A text accompanies the images:

> Since these pictures were taken, John has died. John showed remarkable fortitude and spirit during his illness, and the ward staff expressed great admiration for his courage. He was in and out of the ward ever since it opened. On a number of occasions he chose to break off his treatment and go on holiday, and in his last year he travelled to Florida, Turkey and Spain, continuing his treatment on his return. For John, his partner, his parents and friends, the ward became almost a home. His mother and lover would often sleep over at the hospital. Such informal images of life in a hospital ward would not have been possible even a few years ago. (Mayes and Stein, 1993: 128–33)

The photograph showing John with his lover and parents all gathered around his hospital bed, was chosen as the cover photograph for the book *Positive Lives* (see Figure 7.2). Audiences are prefigured for and in the photographs. John is being responded to by his parents and lover in the first photograph; in the second and third by his lover alone. The text constitutes medical staff as part of his audience, responding to him in ways that would not have been possible a few years ago. Using the first photograph as the cover for the collection invites those who buy or see the book to respond to John, as a person with AIDS, sitting with his gay lover and his parents, in hospital. In contrast, the audience of the Benetton image is conceived, primarily, as having a consumerist potential (for the image is an advertisement and seeks to sell Benetton's clothes). The photograph's other audience (the family surrounding the man's bedside) is secondary, reactive, responding to the man's imminent death. In contrast, the photograph of John is imbued with optimism, with peacefulness, with participatory family life, despite its location in a hospital ward where a person with AIDS is being treated. Instead of the unremitting anguish that hurtles towards death in Benetton's image, the photograph of John shows AIDS as an event in which fear can be overcome and agony kept at bay. John, a person with AIDS, sits upright, engaging with his family, communicating, active. The pictures as a series emphasize sexuality and passion. They celebrate an ordinary life. The man in Benetton's image lies back, waiting for death, eyes unfocused on his family, mouth open, wordless.[56] The text in *Positive Lives* acknowledges that John does not overcome the illness, and thus the image does not pretend false miracles. But it is remarkable for its *promise* of normality, of life continuing as it was *before AIDS*, as long as possible. In this image, there is no anguish that can only be resolved by death.

In celebrating John's ordinary life, the spectacle of AIDS in these photographs tells a narrative that is quite different to the story of imminent death in the Benetton image and to the story of inevitable risk in criminal justice policy. The *Positive Lives* photograph of John shows him *living with HIV/AIDS*, where the Benetton image shows a man *dying of AIDS*. In the midst of what we know to be the certainty of death, the spectacle of living with HIV/AIDS testifies to life. Life becomes, paradoxically, internal to the externality of death. In the *Positive Lives* photograph, it is impossible to distinguish living from dying; each is bound up in the other. The photograph reveals that the border between the two – so strenuously managed in contemporary culture – is imperceptible. The Benetton image turns upon a popular fear: that the moment at which the border is reached is a recognizable moment, marked by fear and agony. The man in the Benetton photograph is 'dying of AIDS', a tautology within the structure of this fear, since he is then 'dying of death'. Given that there is nothing in the photograph that says, definitively, that this man is dying of AIDS, the received story of its subject-matter is used to push the interpretation that this is how 'dying of AIDS' is. As the scene of HIV/AIDS, the Benetton photograph asserts AIDS as a spectacle in which HIV/AIDS can only appear as pain, agony and abjection. The *Positive Lives* photograph also creates a scene of AIDS as spectacle, but its images insist upon an interpretation of the subject as 'living with HIV/AIDS'. The photographs of John therefore open a paradox: the possibility of *living with death*.

All photographs exist in the shadow of death (Barthes, 1984). Never a memory, the photograph instead de-creates the past, blocks memory and becomes a counter-memory. Pretending immediacy, the photograph always records a

56. To borrow from Phelan's reading of a Mapplethorpe photograph: 'The vanishing point of the photograph is the . . . hollow open mouth . . . [The] open mouth makes viewers shudder when they see the moment when [the] shutter shut' (1993: 40-2).

moment that is past, that is dead.[57] Criminal justice policy relating to
HIV/AIDS exists in the shadow of death, in that it has prefigured HIV/AIDS
as certain death, as dying of death. Living with HIV/AIDS is not permitted to
enter the frame of criminal justice.[58] Like the Benetton photograph, the frame
of criminal justice is constituted to ensure that HIV/AIDS has no shape other
than as a spectacle of death. For criminal justice policy, the person with AIDS
will resemble her 'disease'. Her face will waste, become gaunt. She will experience pain, and will certainly die. Moreover, as the embodiment of death, she
will constitute risk and danger. She will be a threat to the 'rest' of the population, the undifferentiated mass of the 'normal' who struggle to keep at bay the
various risk groups. In the Benetton photograph, the man has no identity
except that of the AIDS patient; the gaunt, wasted face is read as death in its
physiognomic rewriting of body as self. The photograph *confesses* AIDS. The
photograph is framed (in its *mise-en-scène* and also in its reception as an
image of 'a man dying of AIDS') to exclude other possibilities.

Similarly, criminal justice policy frames the person with AIDS. In its image
of her as the embodiment of death, it includes the HIV positive person, who
has begun the downward progression that criminal justice regards as
inevitable. But more than this, it also includes anyone who might fit the frame:
any person who might be gay, or drug-using or of certain 'ethnic origins' or
'promiscuous'. They too are required to embody risk. As such, criminal justice
policy can proceed with its strategy of quarantine, marking out the dangerous
from the safe, policing the border between life and death. The *Positive Lives*
image offers at least the possibility of another narrative. In keeping with its
paradoxical image of 'living with death', its borders have less force. Its spectacle of HIV/AIDS is one of communication, of process, of fluid identities
(son, friend, lover, patient). Outside the image will be found other friends, family, nurses, doctors. The Benetton picture and criminal justice policy both
forget our responsibility to read the man as having an identity before his
embodiment of death; and in so doing absolves us of our responsibility to read
him otherwise. In fixing his identity, his guilt is confirmed. In framing
HIV/AIDS as a spectacle of death, the dying man is also framed for the crime
of HIV/AIDS, for the crime of risk, of danger and death. The man is not only
required to die; he is required to die bearing the responsibility of his risk to
others, the risk that others have written on his body. In such a way, the practices of criminal justice in relation to HIV/AIDS create a system of quarantine
which operates both symbolically and literally to segregate the HIV positive
through the imposition of a fatal frame of identities as rigid and culpable.

57. See Barthes (1984); Sekula (1990); Spence and Holland (1991), especially the essays by
Kuhn and Rosenblum; Tagg (1988).
58. On the frame, see Culler, who writes: 'framing is something we do; it hints of the frame-
up . . . and it eludes the incipient positivism of "context" by alluding to the semiotic function of
framing in art, where the frame is determining, setting off the object or event as art, and yet the
frame itself may be nothing tangible, pure articulation. Although analysis can seldom live up to
the complexities of framing . . . let us at least keep before us the notion of framing – as a frame
for these discussions' (1988: ix).

Afterthoughts: The Imagination of Crime

For the past two weeks, I have been thinking about a fax that was sent to me. The fax digitally reproduces a black-and-white photograph taken by a friend of a black-and-white poster on a notice-board outside a police station in a village in the Lake District, prominent tourist centre of England. The poster was not unique to this location, but had been distributed throughout the villages, suburbs, towns and cities of Britain. My friend had suggested that it might make an appropriate emblem for this book.[1] To the extent that any single image could encapsulate the contemporary ethos of the crimino-legal complex, I think that this faxed photograph does so (Figure A.1).

Figure A.1   *Crime information poster (photographed by Peter Rush)*

1. The photograph was taken, and its use in relation to this book suggested, by Peter Rush. For thinking of it, and for faxing it to New York, in this as in everything I am very grateful.

The poster, as shown in the faxed photograph, incorporates many frames, not least the statement at its very bottom indicating its point of production and reproduction: 'Prepared for the Home Office by the Central Office of Information. Printed in the UK for HMSO. Dd. 8832523 JO155 NJ.' In the faxed photograph, however, I can see also the edges of the poster itself, marked off by the notice-board on which it has been plastered. Although the photograph flattens the surface of reality, it is still possible to make out the tattered remnants of previous posters now overlaid by this one. Moving inside its borders, at the top and bottom of the rectangular image are inscribed formulas, legends, myths. In heavy bold lettering at the top, a single word: **crime**. As if to emphasize that this is a self-contained sentence, a full stop follows the word. At the bottom runs the legend: **Don't let them get away with it.** Again, the full stop is supplied and – like the earlier punctuation – brings with it a self-evidence, a matter-of-factness. Crime. Don't let them get away with it. Thus, its matter-of-factness translates the heavy print into the soft sense of the everyday.

These wordy formulas provide a frame for the central image. Off to one side, however, as a hinge, in the lower right-hand corner, joining two sides, there is an ornithological myth. A magpie sits with a trinket, perhaps a pearl bracelet, clasped in its beak.[2] From this pictorial myth at the border, my eyes are drawn in to the central image it frames.

A pair of eyes stare out from the centre of the poster. They engage the eyes of the viewer, but obliquely. They gaze slightly to my right, as if looking over my right shoulder. Whereas, all I have to look at is a pair of eyes. There is no depth of field, no breadth of subject matter. The eyes are separated from the ponderous words of the border by a rectangle of heavy black lines. These black bands crop the face; they cut out forehead, ears, hair, mouth. Only two eyes, two faint eyebrows and the bridge of the nose remain on view. They stand out against the white, whited-out and smooth surface of the flesh. There is a hesitant boldness to the eyes, stark within the cropped image.

The eyes have it. They fascinate.

These eyes that meet my eyes are wide-eyed. They are no 'windows on the soul'. They do not express: they show no good humour or bad, no impatience, fear or knowledge. Rather, they simply embody *watchfulness*. They make visible the condition of watching. I am transfixed by the experience of looking at someone simply watching. These eyes are not possessed by anyone, they are simply *being watchful*. Wide-eyed and on the look-out, they make vision itself apparent. No mirrors on the soul, but self-referential eyes, pure signifiers of watchfulness.

Who is this wide-eyed watcher who so fascinates me? The poster certainly encourages me to put a name to these eyes. The surrounding words, legends

---

2. The image of the thieving magpie has a certain appeal for illustrators of law and crime. The leading – in the sense of its hegemony – textbook on English criminal law (Smith and Hogan, 1992) took as its cover illustration a drawing of a magpie, wings spread (about to fly?), perched on a bough of a tree, holding a gold ring in its beak.

and myths demarcate the subject who might look out from behind these eyes. It might be that they belong to a person who has committed or who is contemplating a criminal act. These may be *criminal eyes*. Is she looking around to assess the chances of getting away with it, calculating costs and benefits like a rational individual? The eyes would then be less wide-eyed than shifty-eyed – that ocular and phrenological metaphor we use to describe those whom we do not trust, or who appear dishonest. Hence, the disturbing obliqueness of this sideways gaze, looking *not quite at you*. In not meeting the eyes of the spectator, the eyes engage only with the viewer's fears of who the watcher might be. 'Crime', that word suspended at the top of the poster, might thus refer to the eyes below, in nominating their owner as 'criminal' and categorizing her as one of 'them' from the legend at the poster's lower border.[3]

The poster is weighted so that the imperative 'Don't' . . .' is to be read as describing criminals as 'them'. This is to be expected of a police information poster, but it is also an effect of the image of the magpie. These birds are traditionally associated with theft, with the inability to resist glittering objects – the pearl bracelet of the poster. According to folklore, they will fly through open windows to steal bits of jewellery from unsuspecting owners, if precautions are not taken (jewellery should be kept hidden away; windows should not be open wide enough to permit illicit entry). Many dominant cultural narratives of the criminal deploy similar associations. The opportunistic thief will steal your car *if* it is unlocked; she will break into your house *unless* you install an alarm system; she will steal your wallet *unless* you wear it in an inside pocket. He will assault a woman *if* she walks alone at night; or *if* she dresses in a particular way. Criminality is taken for granted to exist in a matrix of relational opportunities offered or thwarted; risk averted or ignored. Just as the magpie will swoop through open windows, stealing the jewellery and getting away with it, so will the criminal, *if she is permitted to do so*.

Permission, according to current crime prevention strategies, must always be denied. The only way we can watch out for ourselves is by being on the look-out for the criminal. Looking out for the criminal means the citizen must lock doors and windows; install alarms; dress soberly and modestly; observe late-night curfews or take taxis. The citizen must be on alert at all times. Being alert involves keeping eyes open for risk, for danger, for crime. The eyes in the photograph are not *criminal eyes*; they are *law-abiding eyes*, possessed by the legitimate against the ever-present danger of crime and

3. Recent statistics show that this might also apply to the government (for failing to prevent crime) or the judiciary (whose sentences do not rehabilitate or deter). A survey carried out by BRMB International for BBC Radio 4's *Law in Action* programme in January 1995 revealed the following. When asked to choose the statement most accurately describing the way criminal courts operate, 47 per cent chose 'wrongly acquit the guilty'; 28 per cent chose 'correctly decide'; 15 per cent chose 'wrongly convict the innocent'; and 10 per cent selected 'don't know'. Furthermore, 75 per cent of the survey believed that judges are out of touch with public opinion and the problems of ordinary people. The survey was reported in *The Guardian*, 27 January 1995.

criminals. In the photograph's continuous present tense, the eyes are forever unblinking. The poster's strategy is to idealize this continuing watchfulness as an integral part of a crime control policy. The citizen is involved (under orders: '*Don't* let them . . .'). Permissiveness is the danger ('Don't *let* them . . .'), ushering in the criminal (one of '*them*'). The result would be '**Crime**.' in bold typeface and heavy tread, complete with full stop as if it were the last word, the first cause, the thing itself and the end of things. There is no gainsaying the matter-of-factness with which crime appears on the scene of these imaginative posters, with their folkloric emblems and urban myths. For they are by order of the sovereign, or in this case, by order of the Home Office and the Central Office of Information.

Throughout this book, I have been suggesting that such imaginative ingre-dients as posters, emblems and narratives embody, in their very materiality, the condition of the crimino-legal complex. That condition is designated by the wide-eyed gaze of the poster and communicated to all as one of ever-pre-sent watchfulness. The crimino-legal complex produces a community as an enclosed enclave of citizen-seers, watching for and dreading their common fate, unseen but always already knocking at the door, the window, the school-yard, the street corner. Thus the unseen death of James Bulger reproduced in a media frenzy of the visible. Thus the Benetton image of a man 'dying of AIDS' and the criminal justice policy of inspecting and quarantining the HIV positive. Thus the current British government heralds – in the strict sense of that word – one new initiative after another: Neighbourhood Watch, Street Watch, Truancy Watch, Vehicle Watch. All seek to mark the time of the criminal by marshalling a citizenry against her as the subject-to-be-looked-at; all mark the face of the citizen as the subject-who-looks, in an ever-present state of watchfulness. In the emblems of the crimino-legal complex, the exis-tence of 'us' and 'them' can be imagined. Without needing to see her, to arrest and try her, we know that the criminal exists (because we can imagine her). And her conviction in the crimino-legal complex is our conviction that she exists. This is not yet to say that we live in a society of surveillance and discipline, although many of the techniques of such a society have figured throughout the book – from the security cameras in shopping malls to the body-belts of the deportation squads.[4] Rather, my argument has been con-cerned with the cultural reception of this presumed *will-to-watch*. Arguments about the society of surveillance are concerned more with the will-to-see of (on the whole) state apparatuses; whereas I have examined the will-to-watch and the effects of cultural participation in it. *Watching* is responsive and par-ticipatory; whereas *seeing* is more an effect of the distanced gaze that is produced by surveillance (*sur-veillance*: watching from above).

Hence, several chapters have revolved around events in which the crimino-legal complex has fractured under the manifold strains of visibility, and in which this crisis has critical effects for our desire to watch. Chapter 2

4. On the society of surveillance, see Cohen (1985); Foucault (1977); Shearing and Stenning (1981).

developed the notion that femininity is constituted as enigma within criminological theory, for it is as simultaneously seen and unseen that the figure of
femininity can be productive for criminology. Chapter 3 described the ways in
which the response to the victim in the crimino-legal tradition has been an
imaginative straining to see its criminals, seeking them in the dark corners of
the city, in the hidden spaces of the home, and in the abrupt contours of the
nation. Where both these chapters described watching as a fearful response to
the (in)visible Other, Chapter 4 emphasized the pleasures of being on the
look-out for crime through a reading of voyeurism and the semiotics of the
gaze in detective fiction. Chapter 5 took this excursion further, speculating on
the limits of the gaze and the trauma of living as an image. Both these concerns returned in Chapter 6, in terms of the ways single mothers have been
identified as criminogenic and thus subjects of and to the inspections of
British social policy. And finally, Chapter 7 was inspired by the virulence of
the crimino-legal imagination into a comparison of criminal justice policy on
HIV/AIDS and photographic techniques in advertising and activism.

The police information poster may be read as an emblem of the will-to-
watch in the crimino-legal complex; a kind of unblinking fascination with all
that can be seen (or imagined), all that is probable and perceptible. But this
will-to-watch cannot be allocated to a fixed subject: just as the crimino-legal
tradition cannot guarantee the difference between the victim and the criminal, so too the poster shifts and slips when it comes to fixing a subject to the
wide-eyed gaze (a slippage from the eyes of a criminal to the eyes of the community). These slippages are required by the fact that the crimino-legal
tradition is nothing if it is not *communicated*, and specifically communicated
through news, scraps of worn-out truths, advertising photographs, media
panics and personal anecdotes, among others. In other words, the crimino-
legal imagination is condemned to communicate and hence to erase much of
what it purports to guarantee: a subject that is in control, a community entire
unto itself, a tradition on the look-out and alert for what it cannot see but
which it imagines as a threat.

Our responses to this imagination are also fated to lose much of what they
set out to retrieve for us. A note in the margins of the fax of the photograph
of the poster informed me that as the photocopier did not have high quality
resolution he would mail the original photograph to me in New York. It
took a long time to arrive (after this conclusion was underway, in draft form).
Now I can stare at the original photograph, and compare it with its photocopied and faxed reproduction. Lost, in that reproduction, were the shadows
and shading around the imaged eyes. What returned with the original photograph was the gender of that wide-eyed look (see front cover). The eyes are,
for me, unmistakably feminized. The eyebrows are plucked into neat arches;
the eyelashes long and darkened. Aside from the fact that much of the criminal justice policy on victimization and fear of crime is addressed to women,
the restoration of gender to the wide-eyed eyes takes me elsewhere. Here is an
emblem of justice: justice with her blindfolds removed, justice as all-seeing.
But she cannot believe what she sees; incredulous or suspicious of what

travesties are done in her name, the eyes are transfixed by injustice. Perhaps in this moment – as justice sees the injustice of it all – there is both time and space for an ethics of difference.

Perhaps the most difficult moment of such an ethics occurs when it encounters violence. Much of this book has repeatedly come up against the most obvious modes of violence. A woman dies during deportation; a woman kills her abusive husband. Two children kill another child. A man is photographed as he dies of AIDS. These events are occasions of extremity, in which the fragility of social structures (such as the legal system, the family) are made apparent. In their extremity, they demand interpretation. In their extremity, they forbid it. As events which take place on the border between that which can be interpreted and that which cannot, they expose the framing devices with which we seek to contain the unruly and to understand the uncanny. Giving rise to interpretation, they remain uninterpretable. To imagine them is to ruin our capacity for imagination; in seeing these events, we construct frames for their interpretation which block out other interpretations, erase other memories, obliterate the nuances. Imagination, as I hope to have shown, is always doubled: in including one vision, it rules out another. All our understandings of crime exist in a tense relation with these *other* stories, sights, voices which are now *beyond* the narrative, the frame, the listening ear.

In addition to these obvious versions of violence, I have hoped to show the more subtle violence that crowds around the frames that we construct. A discipline – an institution of interpretation – such as criminology has secreted femininity in its own folds to such an extent that feminist critics can only hope to resist and critique the persistent translation of women into an instance of interpretation. The woman who has a child without a male partner is required to submit her body, indeed her life, to the governmental gaze which seeks to eradicate the singularity of the single mother's desire. In replaying and relaying the violence of James Bulger's death, public discourse on that event rushed headlong toward the abyss of representation; locating it in a dark railway yard and needing endlessly to repeat its unthinkability, to imagine the unimaginable. In order to achieve a glimpse of the limit of representation, a metaphorical murder had to be carried out upon the bodies of the two children convicted of the crime of looking into the abyss.

Borrowing from Kristeva, Phelan writes: 'Memory. Sight. Love. All require a witness, imagined or real' (1993: 5). To borrow in my turn from Phelan, I would offer this book as an act of witnessing. Each of the events I chose to write about, from feminist criminology to the spectacularization of HIV/AIDS in criminal justice, both requires and constitutes a witnessing. That is, each event can be read as embodying (for each has been about a forgotten body, a body in pain) a *response* to a trauma buried in the crimino-legal condition. The event witnesses the violence that is done and seen to be done in each case. And each event demands that we read it and attempt to witness its meaning. That has been my aim: to constitute these 'issues' as embodiments of crisis, complete in themselves and yet understandable only as partial and discrete increments in a process of repression and representation that is contingent and continuous. In responding to these events, which are themselves responses to a crisis, we might begin to imagine an otherwise, an elsewhere, a scarcely heard whisper in a conversation that has been going on and is ongoing and cannot yet be understood. At that moment of imagination, eyes – such as those photographed for the police information poster – might begin to blink, unfix themselves and look beyond the frame. Until then, our eyes will be frozen in a never-ending gaze, fearfully seeking the criminal, imagining her crimes.

References

Abelove, H. (1994) 'The politics of the "gay plague": AIDS as a US ideology', in M. Ryan and A. Gordon (eds) *Body Politics: Disease, Desire and the Family*. Boulder, CO: Westview Press.

Adam Smith Institute (1994) *The End of the Welfare State*. London: Adam Smith Institute.

Adorno, T.W. (1973) *The Jargon of Authenticity*. Evanston, IL: Northwestern University Press.

Advisory Council on the Misuse of Drugs (1989) *AIDS and Drug Misuse Part 2*. London: HMSO.

Allen, H. (1987) *Justice Unbalanced: Gender, Psychiatry and Judicial Decisions*. Milton Keynes: Open University Press.

Anderson, B. (1983) *Imagined Communities*. London: Verso.

Atkinson, P. (1990) *The Ethnographic Imagination: the Textual Construction of Reality*. London: Routledge.

Atlas, S. (1981) *Single Parenting*. Englewood Cliffs, NJ: Prentice-Hall.

Auden, W.H. (1962) 'The guilty vicarage', in *The Dyer's Hand and Other Essays*. New York: Random House.

Auster, P. (1990) *The New York Trilogy*. New York: Penguin.

Bakhtin, M. (1968) *Rabelais and His World*. Cambridge, MA: MIT Press.

Barnes, L. (1990) *The Snake Tattoo*. Sevenoaks: Coronet.

Barron, A. (1993) 'The illusion of the "I": citizenship and the politics of identity', in A. Norrie (ed.) *Closure or Critique: New Directions in Legal Theory*. Edinburgh: Edinburgh University Press.

Barthes, R. (1984) *Camera Lucida*. London: Fontana.

Barthes, R. (1986) *The Rustle of Language*. Oxford: Blackwell.

Battersby, C. (1989) *Gender and Genius: Towards a Feminist Aesthetics*. London: The Women's Press.

Baudrillard, J. (1987) *The Evil Demon of Images*. Sydney: Power Institute of Fine Arts, University of Sydney.

Baudrillard, J. (1991) *La Guerre du Golfe n'a pas eu lieu*. Paris: Gallilee. (Translated 1995 as *The Gulf War Did Not Take Place*. Sydney: Power Institute.)

Baudrillard, J. (1994) 'The illusion of war', in *The Illusion of the End*. Cambridge: Polity.

Beck, U. (1992) *Risk Society*. London: Sage.

Benhabib, S. (1987) 'The generalized and concrete Other: the Kohlberg–Gilligan controversy and feminist theory', in S. Benhabib and D. Cornell (eds) *Feminism as Critique*. Cambridge: Polity.

Benhabib, S. (1992) *Situating the Self: Gender, Community and Postmodernism in Contemporary Ethics*. London and New York: Routledge.

Benjamin, W. (1968) 'The work of art in the age of mechanical reproduction', in *Illuminations*. New York: Schocken Books.

Benjamin, W. (1973) *Charles Baudelaire*. London: New Left Books.

Bennett, C. (1990) 'A life sentence cut short', *The Correspondent Magazine*, 18 March.

Bennett, T. (1990) *Evaluating Neighbourhood Watch*. Aldershot: Gower.

Berman, J.A. (1989) 'AIDS antibody testing and health insurance underwriting: a paradigmatic inquiry', *Ohio State Law Journal*, 49: 1059–76.

Bersani, L. (1989) 'Is the rectum a grave?', in D. Crimp (ed.) *AIDS: Cultural Analysis, Cultural Activism*. Cambridge, MA: MIT Press.

Bettelheim, B. (1976) *The Uses of Enchantment: the Meaning and Importance of Fairy Tales*. New York: Knopf.

Bhabha, H.K. (1990) 'DissemiNation: time, narrative and the margins of the modern nation', in H.K. Bhabha (ed.) *Nation and Narration*. London: Routledge.

Bhabha, H.K. (1994) *The Location of Culture*. London: Routledge.

Bhabha, J. (1993) 'Legal problems of women refugees', *Women: A Cultural Review*, 4(3): 240–9.

Biller, H.B. (1971) *Father, Child and Sex Role: Paternal Determinants of Personality Development*. Lexington, MA: Heath Lexington Books.

Biller, H.B. (1993) *Fathers and Families: Paternal Factors in Child Development*. Westport, CT: Auburn House.

Birkett, Sir N. (ed.) (1951) *Newgate Calendar*. London: Folio Society.

Blake, A. (1990) 'Deadlier than the male: women as readers and writers of crime fiction', *Law in Context* 8(2): 54–69.

Blake, A. (1991) 'The deadlier of the species', *America*, 29 June.

Bloch, E. (1988) 'A philosophical view of the detective novel', in *The Utopian Function of Art and Literature*. Cambridge, MA: Harvard University Press.

Block, L. (1993) *The Burglar Who Painted Like Mondrian*. Harpenden: No Exit Press.

Blondel, E. (1985) 'Nietzsche: life as metaphor', in D.B. Allison (ed.) *The New Nietzsche: Contemporary Styles of Interpretation*. Cambridge, MA: MIT Press.

Boffin, T. and Gupta, S. (eds) (1990) *Ecstatic Antibodies: Resisting the AIDS Mythology*. London: Rivers Oram Press.

Borges, J.L. (1962) 'Death and the compass', in *Labyrinths*. New York: New Directions Books.

Bornstein, K. (1994) *Gender Outlaw: On Men, Women and the Rest of Us*. London: Routledge.

Bowlby, J. (1951) *Maternal Care and Mental Health*. Geneva: World Health Organization.

Bowlby, J. (1973) *Separation: Anxiety and Anger*. London: Hogarth.

Braidotti, R. (1991) *Patterns of Dissonance*. Cambridge: Polity.

Braidotti, R. (1994) *Nomadic Subjects: Embodiment and Sexual Difference in Contemporary Feminist Theory*. New York: Columbia University Press.

Braithwaite, J.B. (1989) *Crime, Shame and Reintegration*. Cambridge: Cambridge University Press.

Brand, D. (1990) 'From the *flâneur* to the detective: interpreting the city of Poe', in T. Bennett (ed.) *Popular Fiction*. London: Routledge.

Brandt, A.M. (1987) *No Magic Bullet: A Social History of Venereal Disease in the United States since 1880*. New York: Oxford University Press.

Brandt, A.M. (1988) 'AIDS: from social history to social policy', in E. Fee and D. Fox (eds) *AIDS: The Burdens of History*. Berkeley: University of California Press.

Brown, B. (1985) 'Women and crime: the dark figures of criminology', *Economy and Society*, 15(3): 355–402.

Brown, B. (1990) 'Reassessing the critique of biologism', in L. Gelsthorpe and A. Morris (eds) *Feminist Perspectives in Criminology*. Milton Keynes: Open University Press.

Brown, B. (1991) 'Litigating feminisms', *Economy and Society*, 20(4): 411–33.

Burdt, A. and Caldwell, J. (1987–8) 'The real fatal attraction: civil and criminal liability for the sexual transmission of AIDS', *Drake Law Review*, 37: 657–97.

Burghes, L. (1994) *Lone Parenthood and Family Disruption*. London: Family Policy Studies Centre.

Burt, C. (1944) *The Sub-Normal School-Child: Vol.I. The Young Delinquent*. 4th edn. London: University of London Press. (First published, 1925.)

Bywater, M. (1993) 'Date babies', *Cosmopolitan*, December: 26–30.

Cain, J.M. (1934) 'The postman always rings twice', in *The Five Great Novels of James M. Cain*. London: Picador 1985.

Cameron, D. (1985) *Feminism and Linguistic Theory*. New York: St Martin's Press.

Cameron, D. and Frazer, L. (1987) *The Lust to Kill: a Feminist Investigation of Sexual Murder*. Cambridge: Polity.

Campbell, B. (1993) *Goliath: Britain's Dangerous Places*. London: Methuen.

Campbell, D. (1993) 'London jails' belt shame', *Time Out*, 11–18 August.

Canetti, E. (1960) *Crowds and Power*. London: Penguin.

Caputi, J. (1987) *The Age of Sex Crime*. Bowling Green, OH: Bowling Green State University Popular Press.

Carlen, P. (1983) *Women's Imprisonment: a Study in Social Control*. London: Routledge.

Carlen, P. (1987) 'Out of care, into custody: dimensions and deconstructions of the state's regulation of 22 young working-class women', in P. Carlen and A. Worrall (eds) *Gender, Crime and Justice*. Milton Keynes: Open University Press.

Carlen, P. (1988) *Women, Crime and Poverty*. Milton Keynes: Open University Press.

Carlen, P., Hicks, J., O'Dwyer, J., Christina, D. and Tchaikovsky, C. (1985) *Criminal Women*. Cambridge: Polity.

Carlson, A. (1991) 'Is this what feminism is all about?', *Time*, 24 June.

Carter, E. and Watney, S. (eds) (1989) *Taking Liberties*. London: Serpent's Tail.

Casale, S. (1993) 'AIDS in custody', *S.P.A.R.C. Newsletter*, (Summer): 1.

Cawelti, J. (1976) *Adventure, Mystery and Romance*. Chicago: Chicago University Press.

Certeau, M. de (1984) *The Practice of Everyday Life*. Berkeley, CA: University of California Press.

Chandler, R. (1939) *The Big Sleep*. London: Hamish Hamilton.

Chandler, R. (1940) *Farewell, My Lovely*. London: Hamish Hamilton.

Chandler, R. (1943) *The High Window*. London: Hamish Hamilton.

Chandler, R. (1944) *The Lady in the Lake*. London: Hamish Hamilton.

Chandler, R. (1949) *The Little Sister*. London: Hamish Hamilton.

Chandler, R. (1953) *The Long Goodbye*. London: Hamish Hamilton.

Chandler, R. (1958) *Playback*. London: Hamish Hamilton.

Chandler, R. (1964) 'The simple art of murder', in *Pearls are a Nuisance*. London: Penguin.

Cixous, H. and Clément, C. (1986) *The Newly Born Woman*. Minneapolis: University of Minnesota Press.

Cockett, M. and Tripp, J. (1994) *Children Living in Re-ordered Families – Social Policy Findings 45*. York: Joseph Rowntree Foundation.

Cohen, S. (1979) 'The punitive city', *Contemporary Crises*, 3: 339–63.

Cohen, S. (1985) *Visions of Social Control*. Cambridge: Polity.

Conrad, J.P. (1982) 'What do the undeserving deserve?', in R. Johnson and H. Toch (eds) *The Pains of Imprisonment*. London: Sage.

Cooper, D. (1993) 'The Citizen's Charter and radical democracy: empowerment and exclusion within citizenship discourse', *Social and Legal Studies*, 2(2): 141–71.

Cornell, D. (1991) *Beyond Accommodation: Ethical Feminism, Deconstruction and the Law*. London: Routledge.

Cornwell, P. (1990) *Post Mortem*. New York: Avon.

Cornwell, P. (1991) *Body of Evidence*. New York: Avon.

Cornwell, P. (1992) *All That Remains*. New York: Avon.

Cornwell, P. (1993) *Cruel and Unusual*. New York: Avon.

Cornwell, P. (1994) *The Body Farm*. New York: Scribner's Sons.

Cousins, M. (1995) 'Danger and safety', *Coil*, One: 14–18.

Cranny-Francis, A. (1990) *Feminist Fiction*. Cambridge: Polity.

Crawford, A., Jones, T., Woodhouse, T. and Young, J. (1990) *Second Islington Crime Survey*. Middlesex Polytechnic: Centre for Criminology.

Crawford, C.A. (1994) 'Health care needs in correctional facilities: NIJ responds', *National Institute of Justice Journal*, 228: 31–8.

Crimp, D. (ed.) (1989) *AIDS: Cultural Analysis/Cultural Activism*. Cambridge, MA: MIT Press.

Crimp, D. with Rolston, A. (1990) *AIDS/DEMO/GRAPHICS*. Seattle: Bay Press.

Cronin, R.C. (1994) *Boot Camps for Adult and Juvenile Offenders: Overview and Update*. Washington, DC: United States Department of Justice.

Culler, J. (1988) *Framing the Sign*. Oxford: Blackwell.

Dalton, H.L. and Burris, S. (1987) *AIDS and the Law*. New Haven: Yale University Press.

Dalton, H.L., Burris, S. and the Yale AIDS Law Project (eds) (1993) *AIDS Law Today: a New Guide for the Public*. New Haven: Yale University Press.

d'Eca, C. (1987) 'Medico-legal aspects of AIDS' in *AIDS: a Guide to the Law*. London: Routledge.

Dennis, N. and Erdos, G. (1993) *Families Without Fatherhood*. 2nd edn. London: IEA Health and Welfare Unit.

De Quincey, T. (1854) 'Murder considered as one of the fine arts', in *Writings*. Boston: Ticknor and Fields.

Derrida, J. (1973) *Speech and Phenomena*. Evanston, IL: Northwestern University Press.

Derrida, J. (1978) *Writing and Difference*. London: Routledge and Kegan Paul.

Derrida, J. (1979) *Spurs: Nietzsche's Styles/Eperons: Les Styles de Nietzsche*. Chicago: University of Chicago Press.

Derrida, J. (1981) *Dissemination*. Chicago: University of Chicago Press.

Derrida, J. (1982) 'White mythologies', in *Margins of Philosophy*. Chicago: University of Chicago Press.

Dijkstra, B. (1986) *Idols of Perversity: Fantasies of Feminine Evil in the Fin-de-Siècle*. New York: Oxford University Press.

Dobash, R.P., Dobash, R.E. and Gutteridge, S. (1986) *The Imprisonment of Women*. Oxford: Blackwell.

Dolgin, J.L. (1985–6) 'AIDS: social meanings and legal ramifications', *Hofstra Law Review*, 14 (Spring): 193–209.

Donzelot, J. (1979) *The Policing of Families*. New York: Pantheon Books.

Douglas, J.W. (1973) 'Early disturbing events and later enuresis', in I. Kolvin (ed.) *Bladder Control and Enuresis*. London: Spastics International Medical Publishers.

Douglas, M. (1966) *Purity and Danger: an Analysis of Concepts of Pollution and Taboo*. London: Routledge and Kegan Paul.

Douzinas, C. and Warrington, R. (1994a) 'The face of justice: a jurisprudence of alterity', in A. Young and A. Sarat (eds) *Beyond Criticism: Law, Power and Ethics*, Special Issue of *Social and Legal Studies*, 3(3): 405–25.

Douzinas, C. and Warrington, R. (1994b) *Justice Miscarried*. Hemel Hempstead: Harvester Wheatsheaf.

Downes, D. and Rock, P. (1982) *Understanding Deviance*. 1st edn. Oxford: Oxford University Press.

Downes, D. and Rock, P. (1988) *Understanding Deviance*. 2nd edn. Oxford: Oxford Univerwity Press.

Doyle, Sir A. Conan (1890) *The Sign of Four*. London: Pan Books, 1975.

Doyle, Sir A. Conan (1892) *The Adventures of Sherlock Holmes*. London: Penguin, 1982.

Doyle, Sir A. Conan (1894) *The Memoirs of Sherlock Holmes*. London: Penguin, 1978.

Doyle, Sir A. Conan (1902) *The Hound of the Baskervilles*. London: Penguin, 1981.

Drummond, B. (1986) 'Seronegative 18 months after being bitten by a patient with AIDS', *Journal of the American Medical Association*, 256: 2342.

Dubin, S.C. (1992) *Arresting Images: Impolitic Art and Uncivil Actions*. New York and London: Routledge.

Duden, B. (1993) *Disembodying Women: Perspectives on Pregnancy and the Unborn*. Cambridge, MA: Harvard University Press.

Durham, P. (1963) *Down These Mean Streets a Man Must Go: Raymond Chandler's Knight*. Durham, NC: University of North Carolina Press.

Durkheim, E. (1964) *The Rules of Sociological Method*. New York: Free Press.

Dyer, G. (1994) 'Journey to the heart of darkness', *The Guardian*, 12 March.

Earls, F.J. and Reiss, A.J. (1994) *Breaking the Cycle: Predicting and Preventing Crime*. Washington, DC: United States Department of Justice.

Eaton, M. (1986) *Justice For Women? Family, Court and Social Control*. Milton Keynes: Open University Press.

Eaton, M. (1987) 'The question of bail: magistrates' responses to applications for bail on behalf of men and women defendants', in P. Carlen and A. Worrall (eds) *Gender, Crime and Justice*. Milton Keynes: Open University Press.

Elias, R. (1990) *The Politics of Victimization*. New York: Oxford University Press.

Elias, R. (1993) *Victims Still: the Political Manipulation of Crime Victims*. Thousand Oaks, CA: Sage.

Ellis, H. (1904) 'Sexual inversion in women', in *Studies in the Psychology of Sex, vol. 2*. Philadelphia: F.A. Davis Company.

Estrich, S. (1987) *Real Rape*. Cambridge, MA: Harvard University Press.

Etzioni, A. (1993) *The Parenting Deficit*. London: Demos.

Ewald, F. (1991) 'Insurance and risk', in G. Burchell, C. Gordon and P. Miller (eds) *The Foucault Effect: Studies in Governmentality*. Hemel Hempstead: Harvester Wheatsheaf.

Farrington, D.F. (1979) 'Longitudinal research on crime and delinquency', in N. Morris and M. Tonry (eds) *Crime and Justice, vol. 1*. Chicago: Chicago University Press.

Farrington, D.F. (1987) 'Early precursors of frequent offending', in J.Q. Wilson and G.C. Loury (eds) *From Children to Citizens, vol. III: Families, Schools and Delinquency Prevention*. New York: Springer.

Farrington, D.F. and Morris, A. (1983) 'Sex, sentencing and reconviction', *British Journal of Criminology*, 23(3): 229–48.

Fee, E. and Fox, D. (eds) (1992) *AIDS: the Making of a Chronic Disease*. Berkeley, CA: California University Press.

Foucault, M. (1973) *The Birth of the Clinic*. New York: Pantheon Books.

Foucault, M. (1977) *Discipline and Punish*. Harmondsworth: Penguin.

Foucault, M. (1980) 'Prison talk', in C. Gordon (ed.) *Power/Knowledge*. Brighton: Harvester.

Foucault, M. (1991) 'Governmentality', in G. Burchell, C. Gordon and P. Miller (eds) *The Foucault Effect: Studies in Governmentality*. Hemel Hempstead: Harvester Wheatsheaf.

Frazer, E. and Lacey, N. (1993) *The Politics of Community*. Hemel Hempstead: Harvester.

Freud, S. (1914) 'On narcissism', in *The Standard Edition of the Complete Psychological Works of Sigmund Freud, vol. 14*. London: Hogarth Press, 1957.

Freud, S. (1928) 'The uncanny', in *The Standard Edition of the Complete Psychological Works of Sigmund Freud, vol. 18*. London: Hogarth Press, 1955.

Freud, S. (1935) 'Beyond the pleasure principle', in *The Standard Edition of the Complete Psychological Works of Sigmund Freud, vol. 18*. London: Hogarth Press, 1955.

Friedman-Kien, G. et al. (1981) 'Kaposi's sarcoma and *pneumocystis* pneumonia among homosexual men – New York City and California', *Morbidity and Mortality Weekly Report*, 30: 305–8.

Frug, M.J. (1992) *Postmodern Legal Feminism*. New York and London: Routledge.

Fumento, M. (1989) *The Myth of Heterosexual AIDS*. New York: Basic Books.

Gallop, J. (1982) *The Daughter's Seduction: Feminism and Psychoanalysis*. London: Macmillan.

Game, A. (1991) *Undoing the Social*. Milton Keynes: Open University Press.

Gamson, J. (1989) 'Silence, death and the invisible enemy: AIDS activism and social movement "newness"', *Social Problems*, 36(4): 351–75.

Gandelman, C. (1991) *Reading Pictures, Viewing Texts*. Bloomington and Indianapolis: Indiana University Press.

Garfield, S. (1994) *The End of Innocence: Britain in the Time of AIDS*. London: Faber and Faber.

Garland, D. (1994) 'The development of British criminology', in M. Maguire, R. Morgan and R. Reiner (eds) *The Oxford Handbook of Criminology*. Oxford: Clarendon Press.

Gasché, R. (1986) *The Tain of the Mirror: Derrida and the Philosophy of Reflection*. Cambridge, MA: Harvard University Press.

Gatens, M. (1991) *Feminism and Philosophy: Perspectives on Difference and Equality*. Bloomington: Indiana University Press.

Gelsthorpe, L. and Morris, A. (eds) (1990) *Feminist Perspectives in Criminology*. Milton Keynes: Open University Press.

Gilligan, C. (1982) *In a Different Voice: Psychological Theory and Women's Development*. Cambridge, MA: Harvard University Press.

Gilman, S. (1988) *Disease and Representation*. Ithaca, NY: Cornell University Press.

Gilroy, P. (1987) *'There Ain't No Black in the Union Jack': the Cultural Politics of Race and Nation*. London: Hutchinson.

Girard, R. (1986) *The Scapegoat*. Baltimore: Johns Hopkins University Press.

Girard, R. (1987) *Things Hidden Since the Foundation of the World*. Stanford, CA: Stanford University Press.

Glueck, S. and Glueck, E. (1950) *Unraveling Juvenile Delinquency*. New York: Commonwealth Fund.

Glueck, S. and Glueck, E. (1952) *Delinquents in the Making: Paths to Prevention*. New York: Harper.

Glueck, S. and Glueck, E. (1959) *Predicting Delinquency and Crime*. Cambridge, MA: Harvard University Press.

Glueck, S. and Glueck, E. (1962) *Family Environment and Delinquency*. Boston: Houghton Mifflin.

Glueck, S. and Glueck, E. (1968) *Delinquents and Nondelinquents in Perspective*. Cambridge, MA: Harvard University Press.

Goffman, E. (1963) *Stigma: Notes on the Management of Spoiled Identity*. Englewood Cliffs, NJ: Prentice-Hall.

Goldberg, D.T. (1993) *Racist Culture*. Cambridge, MA, and Oxford: Blackwell.

Golding, W. (1962) *Lord of the Flies*. New York: Coward-McCann.

Goodrich, P. (1990) *Languages of Law: From the Logics of Memory to Nomadic Masks*. London: Weidenfeld and Nicolson.

Goodrich, P. (1992) 'Poor illiterate reason: history, nationalism and common law', *Social and Legal Studies*, 1(1): 7–28.

Goodrich, P. (1993) 'Sleeping with the enemy: an essay on the politics of Critical Legal Studies in America', *New York University Law Review*, 68 (April–June): 389–425.

Gostin, L. (1989) 'The politics of AIDS: compulsory state powers, public health and civil liberties', *Ohio State Law Journal*, 49: 1017–58.

Gostin, L. (1990) 'A decade of a maturing epidemic: an assessment and directions for future public policy', *American Journal of Law and Medicine*, 16: 1–7.

Gottfredson, M. (1984) *Victims of Crime: the Dimensions of Risk*. London: HMSO.

Gottfredson, M. and Hirschi, T. (1990) *A General Theory of Crime*. Stanford: Stanford University Press.

Grady, J.C. (1989) 'AIDS challenges the criminal justice system', *New Jersey Lawyer*, 126: 36–9.

Grafton, S. (1986) *A is for Alibi*. London: Macmillan.

Grafton, S. (1991) *G is for Gumshoe*. London: Macmillan.

Grafton, S. (1994) *K is for Killer*. New York: Henry Holt & Co.

Green, E. (1961) *Judicial Attitudes in Sentencing*. London: Macmillan.

Greimas, A.J. (1970) *Du Sens*. Paris: Editions du Seuil.

Grosz, E. (1994) *Volatile Bodies: Towards a Corporeal Feminism*. Bloomington and Indianapolis: Indiana University Press.

Haft, M.G. (1980) 'Women in prison: discriminatory practices and some legal solutions', in S. Datesman and F.R. Scarpitti (eds) *Women, Crime and Justice*. New York: Oxford University Press.

Hagan, J. (1987) *Modern Criminology*. Singapore: McGraw-Hill.

Hagan, J., Simpson, J. and Gillis, A.R. (1979) 'The sexual stratification of social control: a gender-based perspective on crime and delinquency', *British Journal of Sociology*, 30: 25–38.

Hanmer, J. and Saunders, S. (1984) *Well Founded Fear*. London: Hutchinson.

Hart, L. (1994) *Fatal Women: Lesbian Sexuality and the Mark of Aggression*. Princeton, NJ: Princeton University Press.

Hartman, G.H. (1983) 'Literature high and low: the case of the mystery story', in G.W. Most and W.W. Stowe (eds) *The Poetics of Murder*. San Diego, CA: Harcourt Brace Jovanovich.

Hatty, S.E. and Burke, S. (1992) 'The vermin and the virus: AIDS in Australian prisons', *Social and Legal Studies*, 1(1): 85–106.

Hay, C. (1995) 'Mobilisation through interpellation: James Bulger, juvenile crime and the construction of a moral panic', *Social and Legal Studies*, 4(2) 197–223.

Heidensohn, F. (1985) *Women and Crime*. London: Macmillan.

Henig, R.M. (1983) 'AIDS: a new disease's deadly odyssey', *New York Times Magazine*, 6 February.

Henry, S. and Milovanovic, D. (1993) 'Back to basics: a postmodern redefinition of crime', *The Critical Criminologist*, 5(2/3): 1–2, 12.

Henry, S. and Milovanovic, D. (1994) 'The constitution of constitutive criminology: a postmodern approach to criminological theory', in D. Nelken (ed.) *The Futures of Criminology*. London: Sage.

Hewitt, P. and Leach, P. (1993) 'Social justice, children and families', *Commission on Social Justice Discussion Paper 4*. London: Institute for Public Policy Research.

Hilfer, A.C. (1990) *The Crime Novel: a Deviant Genre*. Austin: University of Texas Press.

Hindelang, M. et al. (1978) *Victims of Personal Crime*. Cambridge: Bollinger Publishing Co.

hooks, b. (1995) *Outlaw Culture: Resisting Representations*. London: Routledge.

Ignatieff, M. (1994) *Blood and Belonging: Journeys into the New Nationalism*. New York: Farrar, Straus, and Giroux.

Irigaray, L. (1981) 'And the one doesn't stir without the other', *Signs*, 7(1): 60–7.

Irigaray, L. (1985a) *Speculum of the Other Woman*. Ithaca, NY: Cornell University Press.

Irigaray, L. (1985b) *This Sex Which is Not One*. Ithaca, NY: Cornell University Press.

Jiles, P. (1986) *Sitting in the Club Car Drinking Rum and Karma Cola: A Manual of Etiquette for Ladies Crossing Canada by Train*. Winlaw, BC: Polestar Press.

Jones, A. (1980) *Women Who Kill*. New York: Fawcett Columbine.

Jones, T., MacLean, B. and Young, J. (1986) *The Islington Crime Survey*. Aldershot: Gower.

Kaplan, E.A. (1980) *Women in Film Noir*. London: BFI Publishing.

Karpin, I. (1994) 'Foetalmania', *Polemic*, 5(1): 10–12.

Kerr, P. (1993a) 'March violets', in *Berlin Noir*. Harmondsworth: Penguin.

Kerr, P. (1993b) 'The pale criminal', in *Berlin Noir*. Harmondsworth: Penguin.

Kinsey, R., Lea, J. and Young, J. (1986) *Losing the Fight Against Crime*. Oxford: Blackwell.

Klein, D. and Kress, J. (1976) 'Any woman's blues: a critical overview of women, crime and the criminal justice system', *Crime and Social Justice*, 5: 34–49.

Klein, K.G. (1988) *The Woman Detective: Gender and Genre*. Urbana and Chicago: University of Illinois Press.

Knight, S. (1980) *Form and Ideology in Crime Fiction*. Bloomington: Indiana University Press.

Knuttschnitt, C. (1982) 'Respectable women and the law', *The Sociological Quarterly*, 23: 221–34.

Knuttschnitt, C. (1984) 'Sex and criminal court dispositions: the unresolved controversy', *Journal of Research in Crime and Delinquency*, 21: 213–32.

Kofman, S. (1985) *Freud and the Enigma of Woman: Woman in Freud's Writings*. Ithaca, NY: Cornell University Press.

Kolvin, I., Miller, F.J.W., Scott, D., Gatzanis, S.R.M. and Fleeting, M. (1990) *Continuities in Deprivation? The Newcastle 1000 Family Study*. Aldershot: Avebury.

Kristeva, J. (1982) *Powers of Horror: an Essay on Abjection*. New York: Columbia University Press.

Kristeva, J. (1984) *Revolution in Poetic Language*. New York: Columbia University Press.

Kristeva, J. (1986) 'Stabat mater', in T. Moi (ed.) *The Kristeva Reader*. Oxford: Blackwell.

Kuhn, A. (1991) 'Remembrance', in J. Spence and P. Holland (eds) *Family Snaps: the Meanings of Domestic Photography*. London: Virago.

Kundera, M. (1983a) *The Book of Laughter and Forgetting*. Harmondsworth: Penguin.

Kundera, M. (1983b) 'Afterword: a talk with Philip Roth', in *The Book of Laughter and Forgetting*. Harmondsworth: Penguin.

Lacan, J. (1973) 'Scilicet' 2–3: 120–38.

Lacan, J. (1977a) 'Seminar on "The purloined letter"', in *Ecrits*. New York: W.W. Norton.

Lacan, J. (1977b) 'The subversion of the subject', in *Ecrits*. New York: W.W. Norton.

Lacan, J. (1978) *Four Fundamental Concepts of Psychoanalysis*. New York: W.W. Norton.

LaGrange, R.L. and Ferraro, K.F. (1989) 'Assessing age and gender differences in perceived risk and fear of crime', *Criminology*, 27(5): 697–719.

Laub, J.H. and Sampson, R.J. (1988) 'Unraveling families and delinquency: a reanalysis of the Gluecks' data', *Criminology* 26: 355–80.

Laufer, S. (1991) 'AIDS and the law', paper presented at Osgoode Hall Law School, York University, Ontario, 22 September.

Lawrinson, S. (1990) 'Prostitutes and safe sexual practice', paper presented to the British Sociological Association conference.

Laws, S. (1994) 'Un-valued families', *Trouble and Strife*, 28 (Spring): 5–11.

Layton- Henry, Z. (1992) *The Politics of Immigration: Immigration, 'Race' and 'Race Relations' in Post-War Britain*. Oxford: Blackwell.

Lea, J. and Young, J. (1984) *What Is To Be Done About Law and Order?* Harmondsworth: Penguin.

Leibowitch, J. (1985) *A Strange Virus of Unknown Origin*. New York: Ballantine.

Lloyd, G. (1984) *The Man of Reason: 'Male' and 'Female' in Western Philosophy*. London: Methuen.

Loader, I. (1994) 'Democracy, justice and the limits of policing: rethinking police accountability', *Social and Legal Studies*, 3(4): 521–44.

Loeber, R. and Stouthamer-Loeber, M. (1986) 'Family factors as correlates and predictors of juvenile conduct problems and delinquency', in M. Tonry and N. Morris (eds) *Crime and Justice, vol. 7*. Chicago: University of Chicago Press.

Lombroso, C. and Ferrero, W. (1895) *The Female Offender*. New York: D. Appleton and Co.

Lury, C. (forthcoming) *Possessing the Self*. Manuscript on file with author.

Lyotard, J.-F. (1984) *The Postmodern Condition*. Manchester: Manchester University Press.

MacCannell, J.F. (1986) *Figuring Lacan*. London: Croom Helm.

McConville, M. and Shepherd, D. (1991) *Watching Police, Watching Communities*. London: Routledge.

McCord, W. and McCord, J. (1959) *The Origins of Crime: a New Evaluation of the Cambridge-Somerville Youth Study*. New York: Columbia University Press.

McDermid, V. (1987) *Report for Murder*. London: The Women's Press.

McDermid, V. (1989) *Common Murder*. London: The Women's Press.

McDermid, V. (1991) *Final Edition*. London: The Women's Press.

McDermid, V. (1993) *Union Jack*. London: The Women's Press.

McHale, J. and Young, A. (1992a) 'The dilemmas of the HIV positive prisoner', *Howard Journal of Criminal Justice*, 31 (2): 89–104.

McHale, J. and Young, A. (1992b) 'Rights, policy and regulation: the HIV positive prisoner', in S. McVeigh and S. Wheeler (eds) *Law, Health and Medical Regulation*. Aldershot: Dartmouth.

Mackey, L. (1991) 'Eros into logos: the rhetoric of courtly love', in R.C. Solomon and K.M. Higgins (eds) *The Philosophy of (Erotic) Love*. Lawrence: University Press of Kansas.

Maclean, I. (1980) *The Renaissance Notion of Woman*. Cambridge: Cambridge University Press.

MacNeil, W.P. (1994) 'Enjoy your rights! Fantasy, symptom and identification in the discourse of rights', manuscript on file with author.

Maguire, M. and Pointing, J. (1989) *Victims of Crime: a New Deal?* Milton Keynes: Open University Press.

Maguire, M., Morgan, R. and Reiner, R. (eds) (1994) *The Oxford Handbook of Criminology*. Oxford: Clarendon Press.

Manning, P. (1991) 'Motivations for needle-sharing among intravenous drug users: ethnographic contributions to the prevention of AIDS', manuscript on file with author.

Martin, E. (1987) *The Woman in the Body*. Boston: Beacon Press.

Martin, E. (1994) *Flexible Bodies: Tracking Immunity in American Culture: From the Days of Polio to the Age of AIDS*. Boston: Beacon Press.

Matthews, R. (1992) 'Replacing "broken windows": crime, incivilities and urban change', in R. Matthews and J. Young (eds) *Issues in Realist Criminology*. London: Sage.

Mayes, S. (1993) 'Photographing the invisible – a statement of intent', in S. Mayes and L. Stein (eds) *Positive Lives: Responses to HIV*. London: Cassell.

Mayes, S. and Stein, L. (eds) (1993) *Positive Lives: Responses to HIV*. London: Cassell.

Mayhew, P., Dowds, L. and Elliot, D. (1989) *The 1988 British Crime Survey*. London: HMSO.

Melossi, D. and Pavarini, M. (1981) *The Prison and the Factory: Origins of the Penitentiary System*. Totowa, NJ: Barnes and Noble.

Millman, M. (1975) 'She did it all for love: a feminist view of the sociology of deviance', in M. Millman and R. Moss Kanter (eds) *Another Voice: Feminist Perspectives on Social Life and Social Science*. New York: Anchor Books.

Minh-ha, T.T. (1989) *Woman, Native, Other*. Bloomington: Indiana University Press.

Mitchell, W.J. (1992) *The Reconfigured Eye: Visual Truth in the Post-Photographic Era*. Cambridge, MA: MIT Press.

Modleski, T. (1988) *The Women Who Knew Too Much: Hitchcock and Feminist Theory*. London: Routledge.

Montgomery, J. (1990) 'Victims or threats? The framing of HIV', *Liverpool Law Review*, XII(1): 25–53.

Montrelay, M. (1978) 'Inquiry into femininity', *m/f*, 1: 83–101.

Moran, L.J. (1988) 'Illness: a more onerous citizenship?', *Modern Law Review*, 5: 343–54.

Moran, L.J. (1990) 'HIV, AIDS and human rights', *Liverpool Law Review*, XII(1): 3–23.

Moretti, F. (1990) 'Clues', in T. Bennett (ed.) *Popular Fiction*. London: Routledge.

Morrison, W. (1994) 'Criminology, modernity and the "truth" of the human condition: reflections on the melancholy of postmodernism', in D. Nelken (ed.) *The Futures of Criminology*. London: Sage.

Mukherjee, S.K. and Scutt, J.A. (1981) *Women and Crime*. Sydney: Australian Institute of Criminology with Allen and Unwin.

Naffine, N. (1987) *Female Crime: the Construction of Women in Criminology*. Sydney: Allen and Unwin.

Naffine, N. (1990) *Law and the Sexes*. Sydney: Allen and Unwin.

Naffine, N. (1994) 'Possession: erotic love in the law of rape', *Modern Law Review*, 54: 10–36.

Naffine, N. (forthcoming) *Feminism and Criminology*. Cambridge: Polity Press.

Nagel, S. and Weitzman, L.J. (1972) 'The double standard of American justice', *Society*, 9: 18–25, 62–3.

National Institute of Justice (NIJ) (1987) 'The cause, transmission and incidence of AIDS', *AIDS Bulletin*, June.

National Institute of Justice (NIJ) (1989) *Update: AIDS in Correctional Facilities*. Washington, DC: United States Department of Justice.

National Institute of Justice (NIJ) (1992) *Update: HIV/AIDS in Correctional Facilities*. Washington, DC: United States Department of Justice.

Nelkin, D. (1991) 'AIDS and the news media', *The Millbank Quarterly*, 69(2): 293–307.

Nelkin, D. and Gilman, S. (1988) 'Placing blame for devastating disease', *Social Research*, 55(3): 361–78.

Nelkin, D., Willis, D.P. and Parris, S.V. (eds) (1991) *A Disease of Society: Cultural and Institutional Responses to AIDS*. Cambridge: Cambridge University Press.

Norris C. (1992) *Uncritical Theory: Postmodernism, Intellectuals and the Gulf War*. Amherst: University of Massachusetts Press.

Oakley, A. (1974) *The Sociology of Housework*. Oxford: Martin Robertson.

Oakley, A. (1980) *Woman Confined: Towards a Sociology of Childbirth*. Oxford: Martin Robertson.

O'Donovan, K. (1993) *Family Law Matters*. London: Pluto Press.

O'Dwyer, J., Wilson, J. and Carlen, P. (1987) 'Women's imprisonment in England, Wales and Scotland: recurring issues', in P. Carlen and A. Worrall (eds) *Gender, Crime and Justice*. Milton Keynes: Open University Press.

Olivier, C. (1990) *The Imprint of the Mother*. London: Routledge.

Olson, M.R. and Haynes, J.A. (1993) 'Successful single parents', *Familes in Society*, 74(5): 259–67.

Painter, K. (1989) *Lighting and Crime: the Edmonton Project*. Middlesex Polytechnic: Centre for Criminology.

Painter, K. (1992) 'Different worlds: the spatial, temporal and social dimensions of female victimization', in D. Evans et al. (eds) *Crime, Policing and Place*. London: Routledge.

Painter, K., Lea, J., Woodhouse, T. and Young, J. (1989) *The Hammersmith and Fulham Crime Survey*. Middlesex Polytechnic: Centre for Criminology.

Painter, K., Woodhouse, T. and Young, J. (1990) *The Ladywood Crime and Community Safety Survey*. Middlesex Polytechnic: Centre for Criminology.

Palmer, J. (1993) 'Violence with a clean conscience', *Criminal Justice Matters*, 11 (Spring): 15–16.

Paretsky, S. (1987a) *Indemnity Only*. London: Penguin.

Paretsky, S. (1987b) *Killing Orders*. London: Penguin.

Paretsky, S. (1987c) *Deadlock*. London: Penguin.

Paretsky, S. (1988a) *Bitter Medicine*. London: Penguin.

Paretsky, S. (1988b) *Blood Shot* (also published as *Toxic Shock*). London: Penguin.

Paretsky, S. (1988c) 'Dealer's choice', in B. Preiss (ed.) *Raymond Chandler's Philip Marlowe*. New York: Perigee.

Paretsky, S. (1990) *Burn Marks*. London: Chatto and Windus.

Paretsky, S. (1992) *Guardian Angel*. New York: Delacorte Press.

Paretsky, S. (1994) *Tunnel Vision*. New York: Delacorte Press.

Parker, R.B. (1990) *Poodle Springs* (incorporating the unfinished Raymond Chandler novel *The Poodle Springs Story*). London: Futura.

Pateman, C. (1988) *The Sexual Contract*. Stanford, CA: Stanford University Press.

Patterson, D. (1980) 'Children who steal', in T. Hirschi and M. Gottfredson (eds) *Crime: Current Theory and Research*. Beverly Hills, CA: Sage.

Patton, C. (1985) *Sex and Germs: the Politics of AIDS*. Boston: South End Press.

Patton, C. (1990a) 'Inventing African AIDS', *New Formations*, Summer: 195–216.

Patton, C. (1990b) *Inventing AIDS*. New York and London: Routledge.

Pearce, L. (1991) *Woman, Image, Text: Readings in Pre-Raphaelite Art and Literature*. Toronto: University of Toronto Press.

Pederson-Krag, G. (1983) 'Detective stories and the primal scene', in G.W. Most and W.W. Stowe (eds) *The Poetics of Murder*. San Diego, CA: Harcourt Brace Jovanovich.

Phelan, P. (1993) *Unmarked: the Politics of Performance*. New York: Routledge.

Poe, E.A. (1842) 'The mystery of Marie Rogêt', in *The Works of Edgar Allan Poe*. New York: Avenel Books, 1985.

Pollak, O. (1960) *The Criminality of Women*. New York: A.S. Barnes.

Pollak, O. and Friedman, A.S. (1969) *Family Dynamics and Female Sexual Delinquency*. Palo Alta, CA: Science and Behaviour Books.

Pope, C.E. (1975) *Sentencing of California Felony Offenders*. Washington, DC: Criminal Justice Research Center.

Porter, D. (1981) *The Pursuit of Crime*. New Haven: Yale University Press.

Porter, R. (1986) 'History says "no" to the policeman's response to AIDS', *British Medical Journal*, 293: 1589.

Probyn, E. (1990) 'Travels in the postmodern', in L. Nicholson (ed.) *Feminism/Postmodernism*. London: Routledge.

Propp, V. (1968) *The Morphology of the Folk Tale*. Austin: University of Texas Press.

Radford, J. (1987) 'Women and policing: contradictions old and new', in J. Hanmer, J. Radford and E. Stanko (eds) *Women, Policing and Male Violence*. London: Routledge.

Radzinowicz, L. (1966) *Ideology and Crime*. New York: Columbia Press.

Rafter, N.H. (1985) *Partial Justice: Women in State Prisons, 1800–1935*. Boston: Northeastern University Press.

Robinson, D. (1985–6) 'AIDS and the criminal law: traditional approaches and a new statutory proposal', *Hofstra Law Review*, 14 (Spring): 91–105.

Robson, R.A. (1992) *Lesbian (Out)law: Survival under the Rule of Law*. Ithaca, NY: Firebrand Press.

Rock, P. (1988) 'The present state of criminology in Britain', *British Journal of Criminology*, 28(2): 188–99.

Rodwell, S. (1981) 'Men, women and sexuality: a feminist critique of the sociology of deviance', *Women's Studies International Quarterly*, 4: 145–55.

Ronell, A. (1990) *The Telephone Book: Technology, Schizophrenia and Electric Speech*. Lincoln: University of Nebraska Press.

Rorty, R. (1989) *Contingency, Irony and Solidarity*. Cambridge: Cambridge University Press.

Rosenblum, B. (1991) 'I have begun the process of dying', in J. Spence and P. Holland (eds) *Family Snaps: the Meanings of Domestic Photography*. London: Virago.

Rottman, D.B. and Simon, R.J. (1975) 'Women in the courts', *Chitty's Law Journal*, 23: 52.

Rousseau, J.-J. (1959) 'Essai sur l'origine des langues', in *Oeuvres complètes*. Paris: Gallimard.

Rush, P. (1992) 'The government of a generation', *Liverpool Law Review*, XIV(1): 3–43.

Rush, P. (forthcoming) *Trials of Sex*. London: Routledge.

Rush, P., McVeigh, S. and Young, A. (eds) (forthcoming) *Criminal Legal Practices*. Oxford: Oxford University Press.

Rutter, M. (1972) *Maternal Deprivation Reassessed*. Harmondsworth: Penguin (reprinted 1981).

Rutter, M. (1974) *The Qualities of Mothering: Maternal Deprivation Reassessed*. New York: J. Aronson.

Rutter, M. (1976) *Cycles of Disadvantage*. London: Heinemann.

Rutter, M. (1980) *Changing Youth in a Changing Society*. Cambridge, MA: Harvard University Press.

Rutter, M. and Giller, H. (1983) *Juvenile Delinquency: Trends and Perspectives*. New York: Guilford Press.

Salecl, R. (1993) 'Crime as a mode of subjectivization: Lacan and the law', *Law and Critique*, IV(1): 3–20.

Sampson, R.J. and Laub, J.H. (1993) *Crime in the Making*. Cambridge, MA: Harvard University Press.

Scoppetone, S. (1991) *Everything You Have Is Mine*. New York: Ballantine.

Scoppetone, S. (1993) *I'll Always Be Leaving You*. New York: Ballantine.

Sedgwick, E.K. (1990) *The Epistemology of the Closet*. Berkeley, CA: University of California Press.

Sedgwick, E.K. (1992) 'Epidemics of the will', in J. Crary and S. Kwinter (eds) *Incorporations*. New York: Zone Books.

Sekula, A. (1990) 'On the invention of photographic meaning', in V. Burgin (ed.) *Thinking Photography*. Houndmills, Basingstoke: Macmillan Education.

Sennett, R. (1990) *The Conscience of the Eye*. London: Faber and Faber.

Shapland, J. and Vagg, J. (1988) *Policing by Communities*. London: Routledge.

Shearing, C.D. and Stenning, P.C. (1981) 'Modern private security: its growth and implications', *Crime and Justice: A Review of Research*, 3: 193–246.

Shilts, R. (1987) *And the Band Played on*. New York: St Martin's Press.

Simpson, S. (1989) 'Feminist theory, crime and justice', *Criminology*, 27(4): 605–31.

Singer, L. (1993) *Erotic Welfare*. London: Routledge.

Smart, C. (1976) *Women, Crime and Criminology: a Feminist Critique*. London: Routledge and Kegan Paul.

Smart, C. (1984) *The Ties That Bind: Law, Marriage and the Reproduction of Patriarchy*. London: Routledge and Kegan Paul.

Smart, C. (1989) *Feminism and the Power of Law*. London: Routledge.

Smart, C. (1990) 'Feminist approaches to criminology, or postmodern woman meets atavistic man', in L. Gelsthorpe and A. Morris (eds) *Feminist Perspectives in Criminology*. Milton Keynes: Open University Press.

Smart, C. (1992a) 'Disruptive bodies and unruly sex: the regulation of reproduction and sexuality in the nineteenth century', in C. Smart (ed.) *Regulating Womanhood: Historical Essays on Marriage, Motherhood and Sexuality*. London: Routledge.

Smart, C. (1992b) 'The woman of legal discourse', *Social and Legal Studies*, 1(1): 29–44.

Smith, D.A. and Visher, A.C. (1980) 'Sex and involvement in deviance/crime: a quantitative review of the empirical literature', *American Sociological Review*, 45: 691–701.

Smith, D.J. (1994) *The Sleep of Reason: The James Bulger Case*. London: Century.

Smith, J. and Hogan, B. (1992) *Criminal Law*. 7th edn. London: Butterworths.

Smith, K.J.M. (1991) 'Sexual etiquette, public interest and the criminal law', *Northern Ireland Legal Quarterly*, 42 (4): 309–29.

Smith, S. (1986) *Crime, Space and Society*. Cambridge: Cambridge University Press.

Sontag, S. (1991) *Illness as Metaphor* and *AIDS and Its Metaphors*. Harmondsworth: Penguin.

Sparks, R. (1992) *Television and the Drama of Crime*. Milton Keynes: Open University Press.

Spelman, E.V. and Minow, M. (1992) 'Outlaw women: an essay on *Thelma and Louise*', *New England Law Review* 26(4) (Summer): 1281–96.

Spence, J. and Holland, P. (eds) (1991) *Family Snaps: the Meanings of Domestic Photography*. London: Virago.

Spivak, G.C. (1987) *In Other Worlds: Essays in Cultural Politics*. New York and London: Methuen.

Stacey, J. (forthcoming) *Teratologies*. Manuscript on file with author.

Stanko, E.A. (1990a) *Everyday Violence*. London: Pandora.

Stanko, E.A. (1990b) 'When precaution is normal: a feminist critique of crime prevention', in L. Gelsthorpe and A. Morris (eds) *Feminist Perspectives in Criminology*. Milton Keynes: Open University Press.

Stanko, E.A. (1992) 'The case of fearful women: gender, personal safety and fear of crime', *Women and Criminal Justice*, 4(1): 117–35.

Stanko, E.A. (1994) 'Warnings to women: police advice and women's safety', manuscript on file with author.

Stansbury, L. (1989) 'Deadly and dangerous weapons and AIDS: the *Moore* analysis is likely to be dangerous', *Iowa Law Review*, 74: 951–67.

Stychin, C. (1994) 'Unmanly diversions: the construction of the homosexual body (politic) in law', paper presented at the Law and Society Association Meeting, Phoenix, 15–19 June.

Sullivan, M. and Field, D. (1988) 'Aids and the coercive power of the state', *Harvard Civil Rights–Civil Liberties Law Review*, 23: 139–65.

Sunder Rajan, R. (1993) *Real and Imagined Women: Gender, Culture and Postcolonialism*. London: Routledge.

Tagg, J. (1988) *The Burden of Representation: Essays on Photographies and Histories*. London: Macmillan.

Tate, T. (1993) 'Children who kill', *Woman's Journal*, November.

Taylor, M.C. (1994) *Imagologies: Media Philosophy*. London: Routledge.

Thomas, W.I. (1967) *The Unadjusted Girl*. New York: Harper & Row.

Thompson, J. (1993) *Fiction, Crime and Empire*. Urbana and Chicago: University of Illinois Press.

Toby, J. (1957) 'The differential impact of family disorganization', *American Sociological Review*, 22: 505–12.

Todorov, T. (1971) 'Le typologie du roman policier', in *La Poétique de la prose*. Paris: Editions du Seuil.

Treichler, P. (1989) 'AIDS, homophobia and biomedical discourse: an epidemic of signification', in D. Crimp (ed.) *AIDS: Cultural Analysis, Cultural Activism*. Cambridge, MA: MIT Press.

Umphrey, M. and Shuker-Haines, T. (1991) 'The mystery of gender: the female hard-boiled detective', *Michigan Feminist Studies*, 6 (Fall): 3–16.

Vaid, U. (1987) 'Prison', in H.L. Dalton and S. Burris (eds) *AIDS and the Law*. New Haven: Yale University Press.

Vattimo, G. (1992) *The Transparent Society*. Baltimore: Johns Hopkins University Press.

Vidler, A. (1992) *The Architectural Uncanny*. Cambridge, MA: MIT Press.

Virilio, P. (1991) *The Lost Dimension*. New York: Semiotext(e).

Wagg, J. (1995) 'History painting', *Coil*, One: 19–21.

Walklate, S. (1989) *Victimology: the Victim and the Criminal Justice Process*. London: Unwin Hyman.

Warner, M. (1976) *Alone of All Her Sex: the Myth and Cult of the Virgin Mary*. New York: Knopf.

Warner, M. (1985) *Monuments and Maidens: the Allegory of the Female Form*. New York: Atheneum.

Warner, M. (1994) *Managing Monsters: Six Myths of Our Time*. London: Vantage.

Watney, S. (1989a) 'The spectacle of AIDS', in D. Crimp (ed.) *AIDS: Cultural Analysis/Cultural Activism*. Cambridge, MA: MIT Press.

Watney, S. (1989b) 'African AIDS', *Differences*, 1: 83–100.

Watney, S. (1989c) *Policing Desire*. London: Comedia.

Watney, S. (1989d) 'Taking liberties: an introduction', in E. Carter and S. Watney (eds) *Taking Liberties: AIDS and Cultural Politics*. London: Serpent's Tail.

Weeks, J. (1991) *Against Nature: Essays on History, Sexuality and Identity*. London: Rivers Oram.

Weisman, L. (1992) *Discrimination by Design: a Feminist Critique of the Man-Made Environment*. Urbana: University of Illinois Press.

West, D. (1969) *Present Conduct and Future Delinquency. First Report of the Cambridge Study in Delinquent Development*. London: Heinemann Educational.

West, D. (1973) *Who Becomes Delinquent? Second Report of the Cambridge Study in Delinquent Development*. London: Heinemann.

West, D. (1977) *The Delinquent Way of Life. Third Report of the Cambridge Study in Delinquent Development*. London: Heinemann.

West, D. (1982) *Delinquency: Its Roots, Careers and Prospects*. London: Heinemann Educational.

Williams, P. (1991) *The Alchemy of Race and Rights*. Cambridge, MA: Harvard University Press.

Wilson, J.Q. (1983) 'Raising kids', *The Atlantic*, October: 45–56.

Wings, M. (1992) *Divine Victim*. London: The Women's Press.

Young, A. (1990) *Femininity in Dissent*. London: Routledge.

Young, A. (1991) 'Traces and clues: the semiotics of law and disorder in detective fiction', in R. Kevelson (ed.) *Law and Semiotics, vol. 4*. Boston: Peter Lang.

Young, A. (1993a) 'Decapitation or feticide: the fetal laws of the universal subject', *Women: a Cultural Review*, 4(3): 288–94.

Young, A. (1993b) 'Femininity on trial', *Studies in Law, Politics and Society*, 13: 55–68.

Young, A. (1994) '*Caveat sponsa*: violence and the body in law', in J. Brettle and S. Rice (eds) *Public Bodies, Private States*. Manchester: Manchester University Press.

Young, A. (forthcoming) 'Femininity as marginalia: two cases of conjugal homicide', in P. Rush, S. McVeigh, and A. Young (eds) *Criminal Legal Practices*. Oxford: Oxford University Press.

Young, A. and Rush, P. (1994) 'The law of victimage in urbane realism: thinking through inscriptions of violence', in D. Nelken (ed.) *The Futures of Criminology*. London: Sage.

Young, A. and Sarat, A. (1994) 'Introduction to *Beyond Criticism: Law, Power and Ethics*', *Social and Legal Studies*, 3(3): 323–31.

Young, J. (1987) 'The tasks of a realist criminology', *Contemporary Crises*, 11: 337–56.

Young, J. (1992) 'Ten points of realism', in J. Young and R. Matthews (eds) *Rethinking Criminology: the Realist Debate*. London: Sage.

Young, J. and Matthews, R. (eds) (1992) *Rethinking Criminology: the Realist Debate*. London: Sage.

Zedner, L. (1991) 'Women, crime and penal responses: an historical account', in M. Tonry and N. Morris (eds) *Crime and Justice: a Review of Research, vol. 14*. Chicago: University of Chicago Press.

Žižek, S. (1989) *The Sublime Object of Ideology*. London: Verso.

Žižek, S. (1992) *Enjoy Your Symptom! Jacques Lacan in Hollywood and out*. New York and London: Routledge.

Index